Library Services for Open and Distance Learning

Library Services for Open and Distance Learning

The Third Annotated Bibliography

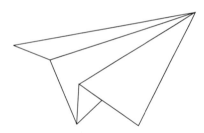

Alexander L. Slade

Head, Document Supply Services
University of Victoria Library
Victoria, British Columbia

and

Marie A. Kascus

Director of Library Services
Newbury College
Brookline, Massachusetts

2000
Libraries Unlimited, Inc.
Englewood, Colorado

Libraries Unlimited, Inc.
P.O. Box 6633
Englewood, CO 80155-6633
1-800-237-6124
www.lu.com

Library of Congress Cataloging-in-Publication Data

Slade, Alexander L.
    Library services for open and distance learning : the third annotated bibliography /
Alexander L. Slade and Marie A. Kascus.
        p. cm.
    Rev. ed. of: Library services of off-campus and distance education. 1996.
    Includes bibliographical references and index.
    ISBN 1-56308-745-6
    1. Academic libraries--Off campus services--Bibliography. 2. University
extension--Bibliography. 3. Distance education--Bibliography. 4. Libraries and
students--Bibliography. I. Kascus, Marie. II. Slade, Alexander L. Library services of
off-campus and distance education. III. Title.

Z675.U5 S56 2000
016.0255'2777--dc21
                                                                                    00-027149

Contents

Acknowledgements

We owe a debt of gratitude to the many people who helped in identifying and acquiring literature to include in this bibliography. Through electronic mail, fax, and regular mail, librarians in several countries assisted us in a spirit of cooperation and collegiality. We would especially like to thank the following colleagues for their extra efforts in obtaining material for us: Tony Cavanagh at Deakin University in Australia, Lorraine Grobler at the University of South Africa, and Neela Jagannathan at Indira Ghandi National Open University in India. We also wish to thank SilverPlatter Information, Inc., for providing trial access to a number of their databases to facilitate our literature search process. A note of gratitude is due as well to the staff of the Interlibrary Loan Office at the University of Victoria for their support and assistance in obtaining numerous items for inclusion in this bibliography.

Listed below, in alphabetical order, are the names of the individuals who provided us with copies of publications or otherwise helped with this project. We offer our sincere thanks to:

- Kate Adams, University of Nebraska-Lincoln, United States
- John Allred, Information for Learning, United Kingdom
- Margaret Appleton, Central Queensland University, Australia
- Toby Bainton, SCONUL, United Kingdom
- Linda Bilby, Leeds Metropolitan University, United Kingdom
- Peter Brophy, CERLIM, Manchester Metropolitan University, United Kingdom
- Anne Marie Casey, Central Michigan University, United States
- Tony Cavanagh, Deakin University, Australia
- Alison Chan Hung Yin, Open University of Hong Kong
- David Clover, The Open Polytechnic of New Zealand
- Louisa Coles, Robert Gordon University, United Kingdom
- Christine Cother, University of South Australia
- Madeleine Coyle, CoFHE, United Kingdom
- Jenny Craven, CERLIM, Manchester Metropolitan University, United Kingdom
- Guy Field, Christchurch Polytechnic, New Zealand
- Sue Fowell, University of New South Wales, Australia
- Gary Gibson, Micromedia Ltd., Canada
- Lorraine Grobler, University of South Africa
- Judy Henning, Technikon SA, South Africa
- Lisa Hinchliffe, Illinois State University, United States
- Nazira Ismail, International Centre for Distance Learning, United Kingdom

- Debbie Jones, Florida Christian College, United States
- Doug Kariel, Athabasca University, Canada
- Roy Kirk, Leicester University, United Kingdom
- Neela Jagannathan, Indira Ghandi National Open University, India
- Gloria Lebowitz, State University of West Georgia, United States
- Peter Macauley, Deakin University, Australia
- Gene Mah, University of Victoria, Canada
- Rob Morrison, Utah State University, United States
- Carol Moulden, National-Louis University, United States
- Russell Nicholson, University of New England, Australia
- Sue Samson, University of Montana, United States
- Steve Schafer, Athabasca University, Canada
- Suzanne Sexty, Memorial University of Newfoundland, Canada
- Kate Stephens, University of Sheffield, United Kingdom
- Mike Tavares, SilverPlatter Information, Inc., United States
- Anette van Vuren, Technikon SA, South Africa
- Peg Walther, City University, United States
- Elizabeth Watson, University of the West Indies
- Vicky Wilson, Edith Cowan University, Australia

Finally, this book is dedicated to the memory of a colleague who assisted with the second bibliography, Sue Cullen, formerly of Southern Cross University, Australia.

Alexander L. Slade
Marie A. Kascus

February 2000

About This Book

Background

Library Services for Off-Campus and Distance Education: An Annotated Bibliography, published in 1991, was the premier attempt to identify and describe the various works dealing with the provision of library services for students and academic programs located away from the main campuses of postsecondary educational institutions. The bibliography listed references to 535 articles, papers, reports, book chapters, theses, and dissertations written between 1930 and early 1990. It was intended to be comprehensive through 1989.

In 1996, *Library Services for Off-Campus and Distance Education: The Second Annotated Bibliography* was published, continuing the work of its precursor by identifying a further 518 references on the topic. Of those references, 108 were dated prior to 1990 and represented items missed in the first bibliography. The remainder of the entries covered works published or released between 1990 and early 1995.

By 1998, a considerable amount of new literature on library services for open and distance learning had been identified. Based on the quantity of items available, a decision was made to publish a third bibliography that would extend coverage of the literature to 1999.

Scope of the Bibliographies

The objective of this project has been to provide a comprehensive record of the literature on library issues pertaining to open and distance learning. The intention was to include references to all types of material, from brief news items to major research reports and dissertations. No attempt has been made to exclude material based on any evaluative criteria other than relevance of content. The authors believe that the inclusiveness of the bibliographies provides a valuable historical and contemporary perspective on the development and issues in this field.

This bibliography continues the pattern established by its two precursors. In addition to listing material published through conventional channels, it includes many unpublished items. Wherever possible, a source of acquisition has been noted for each of these items. A new addition to the third bibliography is the listing of online documents accessible via the World Wide Web. The URLs of these documents were checked several times during the compilation of the bibliography, most recently on April 13, 2000. However, because of the transitory nature of Web documents, the authors cannot guarantee that all URLs listed in this work will remain active after publication. To report a broken line or obtain a paper copy of a missing document, please contact Alexander Slade at his e-mail address: als@uvic.ca

This bibliography lists 764 works identified since its precursor was completed in 1995. Unlike the second bibliography, every work included in this volume dates from the 1990s and most are dated between 1994 and mid-1999. A few items from the early 1990s, missed in the second bibliography, are covered in this volume.

The number of works listed in the new bibliography is significant because it indicates that almost as much has been written about library services for open and distance learning in the past 5 years as in the previous 65 years. The phenomenal growth of the literature reflects to a large degree the changing role of the library at the end of the twentieth century and the convergence of on- and off-campus library services as the electronic era blurs the boundaries between conventional and distance education and between remote and in-person users of libraries.

The topics covered in this bibliography are library issues pertaining to postsecondary education offered at a distance from the main institutional campus, library issues in open learning, library services for part-time students, remote access to electronic library resources, electronic reference services, networked learner support, and library instruction offered via the World Wide Web. For further information about the various terms covered by this bibliography, see the "Terminology" section in the Introduction.

The topics intentionally excluded from this bibliography are library support for on-campus students, library issues in elementary and secondary education, extension activities of public libraries, commercial document delivery services, library science programs offered by distance education (unless the publication concerns library services for the distance students), library issues in the broad field of adult education, library support for self-directed learning that is not associated with postsecondary education, and general discussions of electronic or virtual libraries.

The Literature Search Process

The following online indexes and databases were searched for references pertaining to library services for open and distance learning:

- ArticleFirst (last accessed June 3, 1999)
- Australian Education Index (1978 to July 1999)
- Australian Library and Information Science Abstracts (1982 to May 1999)
- BUBL Journals: Library & Information Science (last accessed June 3, 1999)
- CARL UnCover (last accessed June 3, 1999)
- CINAHL (1993 to March 1999)
- Current Contents (January 1, 1999 to May 28, 1999)
- Dissertation Abstracts (last accessed June 3, 1999)
- EBSCOhost Academic Search FullTEXT Elite (last accessed June 3, 1999)
- ERIC (1992 to March 1999)
- ICDL Distance Education Library (last accessed June 3, 1999)
- Information Science Abstracts (1966 to March 1999)
- Library and Information Science Abstracts (1969 to June 1999)

- Library Literature (1984 to April 1999)
- PapersFirst (last accessed June 3, 1999)

Through electronic and regular mail, contacts were initiated with librarians working in the area of distance learning library services. Colleagues in Australia, New Zealand, India, the West Indies, and the United Kingdom supplied many references that were not easily obtainable in North America. See the Acknowledgements section for a list of the individuals who contributed to the literature search and acquisition process for this volume of the bibliography.

Countries Represented

The following countries have contributed the majority of the 764 works represented in this bibliography:

United States	395 entries	(52%)
United Kingdom	145 entries	(19%)
Australia	99 entries	(13%)
Canada	27 entries	(4%)
India	23 entries	(3%)
South Africa	15 entries	(2%)

The remaining works can be divided by continent or region as follows:

Europe	25 entries	(3%)
Asia	17 entries	(2%)
Africa	7 entries	(1%)
Caribbean	6 entries	(1%)
South Pacific	5 entries	(1%)

Percentages are rounded to the nearest whole number.

Arrangement of the Book

To bring together publications that concentrate on a particular issue or theme, the contents of this volume of the bibliography have been divided into chapters similar to those used in the first two bibliographies. Entries are arranged by year in reverse chronological subsections within each chapter and alphabetically by author within each year. Certain chapters are further divided by type of library, publication format, type of user, or geographic area.

In the five years between compilation of the second bibliography and preparation of this volume, emphasis in the literature has shifted dramatically from print-based resources and services to electronic resources and services. The following chapters in the second bibliography have been deleted from this volume due to lack of sufficient material: "Historical Studies," "Collection Management," "Information and Support Services," and "Document Delivery." The few works that do address these topics have been integrated into other chapters and can be identified through the Subject Index.

The scope of the first chapter, "Bibliographies, Literature Reviews, and Electronic Resource Lists," has changed somewhat since the second bibliography. When that volume was being compiled, documents and resource lists were not readily accessible via the World Wide Web, and the first chapter focused solely on works in print format. In the intervening five years, several online lists and bibliographies have been mounted on the Web. The first chapter in this volume includes, as well as print materials, selected online lists concerning remote access to library resources and services. The criteria for inclusion of these resources were relevance of the topic, breadth of coverage, and the apparent stability of the website. In addition to online resources, two authors conducted comprehensive literature reviews as part of larger projects. These have also been included in the first chapter.

The second chapter, "General Works," is divided into three sections by format/type of material. The first section provides the full entries for works of a monographic nature, primarily compilations of papers and volumes of conference proceedings. These listings contain cross-references to all the individual papers and chapters contained in the various works. The section for articles and papers contains a wide variety of general materials, including introductions to the field, overviews, and studies covering a range of topics and issues. Works that did not fit into one of the other chapters are also included in this section. The third section is new to this bibliography. In the previous volume, brief articles such as news items, announcements, and conference reports, were integrated into the various chapters. In this bibliography, those articles have been sorted out and amalgamated into a section called "News Items."

Most of the references listed in the third chapter, "Role of Libraries in Distance, Open, and Lifelong Learning," are of a philosophical or theoretical nature rather than reports of practical experience or research. Works that do not focus on any particular type of library are listed in the "General" section. Works dealing with academic libraries are included in the "College and University Libraries" section. Works focusing on the public library perspective are found under the heading "Public Libraries." The scope of this chapter has been expanded slightly to include works in which lifelong learning is discussed in relation to academic or public library services for the various types of adult learners.

The scope of the fourth chapter, "Organization, Planning, and Regulatory Issues," is different from the second bibliography. In that volume, there was sufficient content on guidelines and standards to warrant a separate chapter. Apart from the discussions of the revision of the ACRL *Guidelines for Distance Learning Library Services*, the number of works identified on this topic for the current bibliography is minimal. Therefore, the works concerning guidelines and standards have been folded into the fourth chapter. There are now three sections in Chapter 4. The first section, "Organization and Planning," focuses on the planning, budgeting, development, administration, and evaluation of library programs and services for distance learners. The section "Guidelines and Standards" covers the development and use of published guidelines, the need for or the implementation of quality standards, and matters concerning accreditation of academic programs. The third section lists those few items dealing with copyright issues in distance learning.

Replacing the chapters on collection management, information services, remote access to electronic resources, and document delivery is a new chapter, "Electronic Resources and Services." This fifth chapter contains four sections: general issues and specific initiatives, remote access to electronic resources, electronic reference services, and networked learner support. Many authors discuss general issues pertaining to the design and implementation of electronic libraries and services with regard to distance learning. Among the topics covered in the section "General Issues and Specific Initiatives" are the

World Wide Web browser as a user interface, differences between traditional and virtual libraries in terms of interface design, access to electronic databases, web page design, goals and objectives of a website, integration of library instruction into electronic libraries, use of Web guides and self-help aids, and help desk services.

The topic of remote access to electronic resources was well represented in the second bibliography, but the emphasis of most authors at that time was on access to online catalogues and networked CD-ROM products. Use of the World Wide Web for accessing library resources was not common in the early 1990s. Works from the middle and late 1990s tend to concentrate on use of the Web for delivering services to the remote user, who may or may not be a distance learner. For this reason, works dealing with remote access issues have been integrated into the larger chapter on electronic resources and services.

The third and fourth sections in Chapter 5 require some clarification. "Electronic Reference Services" is not strictly concerned with services for distance learners. However, the focus of the works abstracted is on the remote library user, and the issues covered are equally applicable to the distance learning environment. The title of the section "Networked Learner Support" is borrowed from a British research project. The term "networked learner support" (NLS) was introduced into the literature by researchers at the University of Sheffield through the NetLinkS Project in the Electronic Libraries (eLib) Programme. NLS refers to the educational role of library and information staff in support of online learning, including user education, information skills training, and reference assistance using current communication technologies such as e-mail and the World Wide Web. Works on NLS highlight the remote user and, for this reason, several papers and articles on the topic have been included in this bibliography.

The sixth chapter, "Instruction Issues," has also been divided into four sections to reflect the various emphases in the current literature. The type of material included in the chapter "Bibliographic Instruction" in the second bibliography has been listed in the first section of the larger chapter on instruction issues. This section, "Library Instruction," focuses on methodologies for educating distance learners and remote users in the use of libraries and library resources. Included are examples of programs developed or under development at specific institutions and reports on the use of various technologies for delivering user education.

The second section of Chapter 6, "Information Literacy," covers works on the ability to locate, interpret, critically evaluate, and communicate knowledge. Several current authors stress the importance of integrating information literacy skills into distance learning programs to help students think critically and evaluate resources found on the World Wide Web. In recent years, there have been sufficient writings produced on the topic to warrant a separate section on this concept.

The third and fourth sections of Chapter 6 pertain to library instruction provided through the Web. "Web-Based Instruction—General Works" lists works not specifically concerned with distance learners. This material was included because of the importance of the topic for librarians supporting distance learning programs. It was felt that most types of library instruction mounted on the World Wide Web would be of benefit to all types of library users, regardless of whether they were located on- or off-campus. The fourth section, "Web-Based Instruction for Distance Learners," does identify those few works that describe instruction on the Web specifically for the off-campus student.

The format and content of the seventh chapter, "Interlibrary Cooperation," is very similar to the chapter with the same title in the second bibliography. This chapter is concerned with the use of nonaffiliated libraries by distance learners. It brings together discussions of formal and informal cooperative arrangements among the various types of libraries. The chapter covers shared collections, joint-use libraries, franchising, reciprocal borrowing, and resource sharing. Following a general section, Chapter 7 is subdivided by type of library. One section is "Cooperation among Academic Libraries" and the other is "Public Library Cooperation with Academic Libraries."

Chapters 8–10 have a geographical orientation and are subdivided by country or region. Chapters 8 and 9 list research studies. "Library Surveys," the eighth chapter, includes studies of services for distance learners at various libraries. "User Studies," the ninth chapter, is concerned with the use and non-use of library materials and services by distance students and faculty. Chapter 10, "Library Case Studies," lists reports and publications that describe the library services and resources provided by specific institutions for their distance learning programs.

Indexes

This volume of the bibliography contains four indexes: an Author Index, a Geographic Index, an Institution Index, and a Subject Index.

The Geographic Index indexes publications by country and/or by province or state. For the United States, entries are indexed by the name of the state rather than by the name of the country. Only entries pertaining to the United States as a whole have been indexed under the name of the country. For Australia and Canada, entries are listed under both the name of the country and the names of individual states or provinces. For the United Kingdom, entries are listed both under this name and under the individual countries, namely England, Scotland, Wales, and Northern Ireland. All other countries are listed under the name of the country unless coverage is by region (e.g., the South Pacific, the Caribbean). There is no indexing for specific cities, towns, districts, or counties in the Geographic Index.

The Institution Index lists the names of colleges, universities, technical institutes, and public libraries that are the main subjects of the various publications included in this volume of the bibliography. If the name of the country, state, or province is not evident in the name of the institution, it has been added to the index entry. Where the name of a specific library has been used in a publication, a cross-reference is provided to the name of the institution (e.g., Perkins Library. *See* Doane College, Nebraska).

All four indexes are cumulative, including references from the first and second bibliographies as well as references in this volume. The indexes list references by item number rather than by page number. References to the first bibliography have (1) denoted after the entry number, and references to the second bibliography have (2) denoted after the entry number. All entries in this volume simply have their numbers listed following the first and second bibliographies' entry numbers.

Alexander L. Slade
Marie A. Kascus

February 2000

Introduction

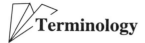

Terminology

Like its two precursors, this bibliography focuses on library issues in the broad field of distance learning. The introduction to the *Second Bibliography* noted that three terms were commonly used in the literature to label the library aspects of this field: *distance education library services*, *off-campus library services*, and *extended campus library services*. In the five years since publication of that work, the term *extended campus* has become less prominent in the literature, while the term *distance learning* is being used more frequently. There are two recent American examples of this shift in emphasis. The guidelines of the Association of College and Research Libraries (ACRL) used to be called *Guidelines for Extended Campus Library Services*. In the 1998 revision, they were renamed *Guidelines for Distance Learning Library Services* (#264). In the same year, the ACRL Extended Campus Library Services Section changed its name to Distance Learning Section (#76).

The term *open learning* was described in the *Second Bibliography* as referring to "courses or planned learning experiences offered by non-traditional educational or training institutions that attempt to remove barriers to education and training by minimizing admission requirements." Open learning activities may take place in a learning center or be carried out by independent study. While open learning is not quite the same as distance learning, many of the library concerns are similar. For this reason, references pertaining to library issues in open learning were included in the last bibliography. In the intervening five years, use of the term *open learning* has become more prominent in the literature, especially from Europe, to the point where it has been linked with distance learning into a new term, *open and distance learning* (ODL). To reflect this change and to acknowledge the relevance of this area, the title of the *Third Bibliography* has been altered to include the concept of open learning as well as that of distance learning.

New terms have expanded the parameters of open and distance learning in the past five years. These terms are connected with developments in the information and communication technologies and the increasing use of distance learning to complement or replace traditional classroom learning. One such term is *distributed learning,* which appears to have characteristics in common with ODL while at the same time implying the use of computer technology for course development and delivery. More specialized terms have been introduced into the literature, almost as subsets of *distributed learning.* *Synchronous learning* refers to real-time interaction, usually through computer-assisted communication, between instructors and students or between students and other students. *Asynchronous learning* involves computer communications that allow interactions and responses at separate times.

Other terms that have appeared recently to connote use of information and communication technologies for delivery of educational programs include *virtual learning, networked learning, Web-based learning, computer learning, online learning, independent learning,* and *tele-learning.* Broader terms like *virtual universities* and *virtual education* have also been introduced to represent the ultimate version of distance learning in which physical campuses are replaced by electronic resources and communication technologies.

The scope of this bibliography includes all the above-mentioned terms as well as the terms discussed in the previous edition: *off-campus education, extended campuses, open learning, flexible learning, flexible delivery, extended learning,* and *franchising.* The current array of confusing and overlapping terminology is indicative of a field in the process of change. Usage in context tends to delineate the various terms rather than universal agreements about standard definitions. It is important to realize that distance learning takes a variety of forms and utilizes a variety of terms and delivery mechanisms. In the context of this introduction, *distance learning* is used as a broad term to encompass most of the terms mentioned in this section. It is also the term that appears to be most widely recognized in the international library community.

Service Models

The literature indicates that there are four basic models for providing library services to distance learners. The first model involves on-site collections and library resources at remote centers, including extended campuses and regional, study, and local centers. The second model focuses on interlibrary cooperation, resource sharing, and student use of unaffiliated libraries. A third service model concerns the delivery of library materials to the student from the main campus of the parent institution. The fourth model pertains to the use of information and communications technologies to enable the distance learner to access electronic resources from remote locations. These four models are not necessarily independent or exclusive of one another, and many institutions employ two or more of them simultaneously in support of their distance learners.

In the first model, remote centers or extended teaching campuses provide some on-site access to library materials and resources, enabling students to meet at least the minimum requirements of specific courses taught in the off-campus or distance mode. Extended campuses are common in the United States, especially in areas of population density, and previous literature from this country has discussed various issues concerning these sites, including staffing, hours of service, physical space, facilities, collections, equipment, computer networking, and access to materials and electronic resources located at the main campus. However, compared to the sources included in the first two bibliographies, relatively little has been written about extended campuses in the recent American literature. This is largely due to the current emphasis on remote access to electronic resources.

Regional and study centers are evident in most countries, particularly those with open universities. In developing countries, these centers tend to be problematic because they are often the students' only means to access library materials for distance learning courses. Few institutions in developing countries can afford to deliver library materials directly to students due to transportation and other difficulties. Public libraries in these countries rarely have materials appropriate to distance education coursework. Common problems with study centers include insufficient funding, poorly trained staff, limited opening hours, inadequate collections that sometimes do not circulate, lack of equipment, and minimal reference materials. Students living in remote areas may be unable to visit these centers on a regular basis. The problems associated with regional and study centers have been particularly well documented in the literature from India (e.g. #137, #154).

Remote centers or extended campuses in developed countries often utilize other models of service and, despite some limitations, are generally effective in meeting the basic library needs of distance learners. A recent American work by Jurkowski (#289) indicates that libraries on extended campuses are becoming more powerful because of their ability to provide access via the World Wide Web to the same electronic resources available at the main library. In Australia, a new campus of the University of Queensland has been built specifically to facilitate the flexible delivery of courses, utilizing hi-tech resources, state-of-the-art computer rooms, and library facilities to support online teaching, learning, and research (#690).

In the second model, distance learners use unaffiliated libraries. Public libraries are often the libraries of first choice among these students (e.g., #637, #643). Use of public libraries for support of open and distance learning has been discussed at some length in the literature from the United Kingdom and other European countries (e.g., #208, #211). The United Kingdom has a well-developed public library system, and students enrolled at the Open University often use these libraries as their primary resource. Some institutions in the United States and elsewhere have entered into agreements with public libraries for support of their distance students (e.g., #582). In India and other developing countries, there has been considerable discussion about the role of the public library in supporting distance learning, and various authors call for improvements in the levels of service given by these libraries to distance learners (e.g., #224).

Use of unaffiliated academic libraries is an important issue in the second model and probably the most common means for distance learners to obtain access to materials in countries like the United States. A factor contributing to the popularity of this model in developed countries is the number of distance learners who live in urban areas and are close to one or more universities or colleges. The issue of access to these libraries has been discussed in countries such as Australia and the United Kingdom and has resulted in a number of cooperative borrowing schemes (e.g., #4, #169). Several examples can be found in the literature of formal cooperative agreements between academic institutions for support of off-campus and distance students. One example from the United Kingdom pertains to the franchising arrangements of the University of Central Lancashire with partner colleges (#642). In Canada, initiatives of the Association of Atlantic Universities Librarians Council (#567) and the British Columbia Electronic Library Network (#572) contribute to the improvement of library services to distance learners. Examples of formal cooperative arrangements and resource sharing in the United States are numerous (e.g., #565, #575).

In the third model of library services for distance learning, materials are dispatched from the campus library directly to the student or to a central pickup location. These delivery services are most common in developed countries with dispersed populations, such as Australia and Canada. Because it is difficult for many distance learners in these countries to use an academic library in person, the parent institution provides a publicized means for students to request materials from campus, designated staff to respond to requests, and an expedited method of delivering the materials to the student. Examples of Canadian institutions with this type of outreach service include the University of Victoria (#704) and the University of Calgary (#706). In Australia, Deakin University is cited as a model service for delivering library materials to off-campus students (#691). Many other examples of such services can be found in the literature from the United States (e.g., #736, #753). These types of delivery services are generally a phenomenon of developed countries. Few institutions in developing countries can afford to deliver library materials directly to students because of the number of students involved, the costs associated with sending materials by mail or courier, the limitations of the local postal/delivery systems, and general transportation difficulties within the country or region.

The fourth model of service involves the use of information and communications technologies (ICTs) and has been evolving rapidly in the past few years. The *Second Bibliography* indicated that distance learners at specific institutions in developed countries, such as Australia, the United Kingdom, and the United States, have had limited access to electronic resources from remote locations for some time. This access has increased dramatically since the *Second Bibliography* was published. Many distance learners now have the ability to search online catalogues, bibliographic databases, full-text materials, and the resources on the World Wide Web from home, office, or local centers. In many cases, this access complements the application of the other service models described above. However, there is currently a move in some areas to create virtual libraries and to reduce students' dependency on physical libraries. This topic is the focus of much debate and raises significant issues concerning library instruction and information literacy.

In developing countries, access to information and communications technologies is still relatively limited due to a variety of economic, political, and cultural factors. However, progress is being made in this regard (#12) and many institutions in developing countries see ICTs as the way of the future for distance education in general and library services in particular (e.g. #290).

The four models described in this section are applicable to both developed and developing countries. Within the models, shared areas of importance include interlibrary cooperation, library instruction for distance learners, administrative recognition and support of library services, and communication with faculty and course providers. However, in other areas there is differing emphasis on priorities. In developed countries, the topics that appear to be of most concern are access to ICTs and electronic resources, Web-based instruction for distance learners, information literacy, and methods of document delivery. The concepts of virtual campuses and virtual libraries have moved to the forefront of significant issues in distance learning due to political and institutional initiatives to capitalize on the use of current technologies for the delivery of educational programs.

In developing countries, topics of concern include the training of librarians and library staff, development of library collections at study centers and local libraries, expansion of physical facilities, access to basic equipment, and the lack of adequate funding for library services. Economic and cultural variables also influence the provision of library services in developing countries. Distance education in many of these countries is a means of national development and targets disadvantaged populations. Students from these groups are not likely to be technologically sophisticated or able to afford such devices as computers. Many of them live in remote areas and do not have easy access to study centers or local libraries. Where they do have access to library materials, the selection of appropriate materials written in their native language may be very limited. The use of ICTs to support distance learners in developing countries is an ideal goal but, in reality, many of these countries have a long way to go before they can reach it.

A Geographical View of Library Services for Distance Learning

United States

Continuing the pattern established in the first two bibliographies, the United States has contributed the largest number of entries to this volume. The proceedings of the seventh and eighth Off-Campus Library Services Conferences (#16, #22) were major additions to the literature. Also contributing to the U.S. publication output during this period were the theme issues of three journals: "Extended Campus Library Services" in *Colorado*

Libraries (#23), "Service to Remote Users" in *Library Trends* (#14), and the invited papers on "The Future of Library Services for Distance Education" in *Journal of Library Services for Distance Education* (#17). Two subsequent issues of the new peer-reviewed electronic journal, *Journal of Library Services for Distance Education* (*JLSDE*), also added to the U.S. publication output. The proceedings of the OCLC Symposium Distance Education in a Print and Electronic World: Emerging Roles for Libraries supplied a further four papers (#15), and a monograph entitled *Libraries and Other Academic Support Services for Distance Learning* added seven papers (#18). These publications alone contributed more than 100 entries to the bibliography and reported observations and findings on a broad spectrum of issues related to distance education in a rapidly evolving technological world. Other individual contributions were reported in dissertations, journals, newsletters, and chapters of monographs. Some of the prominent themes included in the U.S. literature are discussed below.

One of the more significant developments in the United States since publication of the last bibliography was the revision of the 1990 *ACRL Guidelines for Extended Campus Library Services*. The decision to revise the Guidelines was made by the ACRL Distance Learning Section (DLS), formerly the Extended Campus Library Services Section (ECLSS). Several articles describe the revision process, outlining the rationale for revising the Guidelines, the evolving terminology, and the process followed (#265-69). The revision process included extensive input from the extended campus community as well as individuals, consortia, and representatives of professional and accrediting bodies. The final version of the document, the *Guidelines for Distance Learning Library Services*, was approved by the ACRL Board of Directors at the 1998 Midwinter Meeting and by the ALA Standards Committee at the 1998 Annual Conference (#264). In the revised Guidelines, the term *extended campus* was replaced by *distance learning*. The "Definitions" section at the beginning of the Guidelines indicates that the phrase is inclusive of courses in all post-secondary programs designated as extension, extended, off-campus, extended campus, distance, distributed, open, flexible, franchising, virtual, synchronous, or asynchronous.

Copyright issues continue to be a topic of concern to American librarians. Fair use is an important ongoing consideration in the online environment, according to Bruwelheide (#274). Gasaway reviews the current state of the law in the United States regarding distance learning and copyright, pending amendments, and library services to distance learners (#273). A recent contribution to this area is James Neal's testimony at the hearings of the U.S. Copyright Office on Distance Education Through Digital Technologies (#272). Neal, who is Dean of University Libraries at Johns Hopkins University, represented the following associations at the hearing: Association of Research Libraries, American Association of Law Libraries, American Library Association, Association of College and Research Libraries, Medical Library Association, and Special Libraries Association.

Librarians serving distance learners are providing access to electronic reserve and delivering full-text readings to valid users, making authentication and authorization of remote users an emergent concern for library managers. Yott and Hoebeke identify three approaches to authentication to enable legitimate users to obtain remote access (#346). With the expansion of distance education programs and the demand for online resources to support them, Ogburn describes how one institution is formulating policies and guidelines on intellectual property and Web materials (#294). The issues of fair use and intellectual property rights are a prominent concern of all libraries supporting distance education.

Many American works discuss the changing role of the library in distance learning. Martin sees libraries as well positioned to assume a major responsibility for distance learning and to contribute to learning communities by forming partnerships with educators to design environments in which information technologies are integrated into the learning experience (#141). According to Snyder and Starratt, by convincing the university administration that the distance learning infrastructure should reside in the library, the academic library is poised to expand its role as the key campus learning support operation (#182). Saunders suggests that serving distance learners is bringing libraries together, with the result that students will use a combination of public libraries supplemented by academic libraries, which will be connected to global information via the Internet (#144). Lupro and Kennerly describe the Distance Learning Center at Fort Bend County Libraries' George Memorial Library, the only distance learning center in a public library in the United States (#204). The emphasis is on the growing need for libraries to redefine and adapt their services to assist tomorrow's users. One innovative approach to the future is provided by the Florida Distance Learning Library Initiative, a state-wide model of formal coordination in which multitype libraries cooperate to serve the needs of distance learners (#241).

The World Wide Web is making planning documents on library services for distance learning much more accessible to the library community. In addition to the report on the Florida Distance Learning Library Initiative cited above, references to several other planning documents on the Web have been included in this bibliography. Examples include Cornell University Library's *Distance Learning White Paper* (#231), City University of New York's *Report of the Subcommittee on Libraries and Open Learning* (#238), and the Consortium for Educational Technology for University Systems' *Information Resources and Library Services for Distance Learners: A Framework for Quality* (#240).

In the area of electronic resources and services, much is new and still evolving, but what is most evident is the increasing number of information sources that distance learners can access from remote sites. Electronic access is heightening the expectations of remote users and distance learners about what technology can do and what resources and services will be expected of libraries. The emphasis is on optimizing technology to enhance or extend existing services to remote users and distance learners. Rosseel describes innovations in supporting distance learners in general (#277), while Self, Wright, and Waugh describe how health sciences libraries have used advances in technology to enhance services to remote users (#343).

One prevalent example of optimizing technology for service delivery is by providing direct access to vendors' databases. Significant cost savings to member libraries can be realized for accessing vendor databases through a consortium. The larger the consortium, the greater the savings. In Lynch's 1996 survey of electronic services in academic libraries, almost all academic libraries reported making electronic reference databases available, with access to full-text journals common in all institutions (#324). The increased availability of electronic databases has fostered new services. Hightower, Reiswig, and Berteaux describe one such service, the Web-based Database Advisor, designed to facilitate research and help users decide which science database to choose for locating articles and resources (#287).

A second example of optimizing technology is in the area of electronic reference services. Examples of innovative reference service using e-mail are abundant in the literature, including Fishman (#376), Frank (#377), Schilling-Eccles and Harzbecker (#379), Staley (#382), Abels (#394), and Bristow (#398). The advantages and disadvantages of using computer-mediated communication technology for e-reference are discussed along with management and marketing issues for the service. With the growth of electronic reference, Sloan suggests that guidelines are needed to assist libraries in planning and formalizing their services (#380-81). Videoconferencing technology has been used to provide interactive reference assistance at some institutions, as described by Littman (#330), Folger (#388), Lessick, Kjaer, and Clancy (#391), and Pagell (#397). Another innovation is an Internet-based distributed reference service, the Internet Public Library, hosted by the University of Michigan School of Information and virtually operated using volunteer librarians and library students to serve global users, as described by Lagace and McClennen (#378).

Another example of utilizing technology is in the area of electronic reserve service. Cannon discusses a feasibility study on delivering course reserve materials over the Internet to distance education students at Binghamton University Libraries in collaboration with other New York libraries, noting the advantages as well as the disadvantages of the effort from her institution's perspective (#308). Schiller reports on a project at the State University of New York (SUNY) that explored the possibility of using the World Wide Web and the Internet to provide electronic access to course-related reserve materials (#299, #352-53). Copyright issues are of major importance in any effort to make course-related reserve materials available electronically.

The area of patron-initiated interlibrary loan and document delivery provides a fourth example of optimizing technology. At one reporting institution, remote users are being empowered to initiate their own requests. Preece and Kilpatrick describe how unmediated borrowing from 48 member libraries was made possible through a state-wide consortium using a shared online catalogue and circulation system in Illinois (#297). This effort reflects an emerging trend away from centralized mediated services to decentralized unmediated services for remote users and distance learners.

A fifth example of optimizing technology is found in connection to "networked learner support," with its emphasis on online professional development to enhance the educational role of library and information staff in support of online learning. Although it has been a prominent issue in the UK literature (see #407-39), this topic is just beginning to emerge in the U.S. literature under a variety of different headings. In the networked environment, Rapple anticipates new roles for librarians, including planning new services in collaboration with faculty, developing web pages, and designing information resources based on curricula needs (#422). In these networked learner support initiatives, librarians collaborate with faculty, computing professionals, and other campus personnel to extend electronic resources into the curriculum and other university activities, according to Williams and Zald (#425). In this context, McClure urges librarians to remain current with the new technology and library administrators to be sensitive to and supportive of the training needs of current staff (#434). According to McClure, what is at stake in the networked environment is whether the library will manage the use of information or be one of its many providers.

Technology is clearly heightening distance learner and remote user expectations of what resources are needed and what services are possible. This is making it necessary for libraries to offer electronic resources and a higher level of service, and influences what will be expected of librarians in terms of the technical skills needed to provide effective online support.

The area of library instruction, called bibliographic instruction in the *Second Bibliography,* continues to be of major significance in the distance learning environment. Delivery of instruction has been approached in a variety of ways, as exemplified by various authors. Bean (#442), Jaggers (#471), and Pederson (#479) describe the use of interactive television (ITV) as an instructional medium. Butros discusses the use of electronic mail to teach MELVYL MEDLINE (#450), and Burke reports on using e-mail and listservs to teach a 16-part library seminar (#455). Vishwanatham, Wilkins, and Jevec discuss the use of the Internet as a medium for online instruction (#454). Lance and Potter describe the integration of library instruction into the printed course modules (#474). Whitehead and Long discuss the use of an informal agreement with a cooperating institution to provide instruction for off-campus students (#481). Whyte describes the use of computer conferencing to team-teach a research/writing class (#482), and Pival and Tuñón outline the use of Microsoft's NetMeeting software as an inexpensive alternative to delivering face-to-face instruction (#445).

Information literacy, a prominent issue in the South African and Australian literature, is beginning to emerge in the U.S. literature as a challenge and an opportunity. Doherty, Hansen, and Kaya describe Montana State University's information literacy seminar, which emphasizes critical thinking and information skills (#485). Espinal and Geiger discuss the development of a course to link library information skills with management information skills and provide the course outline and syllabi (#502). At the University of Alaska-Fairbanks, library and information literacy is an essential component of the core undergraduate curriculum, according to Ruess and West (#506). Information literacy is course specific at Parkland College, where Hinchliffe and Treat discuss the integration of information literacy into an online introductory chemistry course (#480). Information literacy courseware and curriculum emphasize critical thinking and develop information skills. Harvey and Dewald (#494) and Lowe (#505) see collaboration with faculty and technical support staff as an opportunity for librarians to help learners become information literate in the asynchronous classroom.

Web-based instruction is an exploding theme in the U.S. literature. In the general literature, there are many exploratory examples of how libraries are using the World Wide Web as an extension of face-to-face classroom instruction (e.g., #511-13, #525-26, #528, #535). Specific examples of electronic and Web-based instruction for distance learners describe planning, developing, and testing basic and subject-specific Web-mounted tutorials. Jayne, Arnold, and Vander Meer outline Western Michigan University's experience in planning, creating, and testing two Web-mounted tutorials on library instruction (#531). Prestamo describes the development of Web-based tutorials for the ProQuest Direct online database (#547). Sedam and Marshall discuss the creation of course-specific web pages as part of a course-integrated instruction program at Northwestern University (#548).

In the area of interlibrary cooperation, state-wide cooperative resource sharing efforts represent a prominent theme in the literature of library support to distance learners. These mega consortia provide increased access to a larger body of resources and services than each library alone could afford to provide. Burdick (#552) and Madaus (#553-54) discuss the Florida Distance Learning Library Initiative, which represents a comprehensive, coordinated resource sharing effort directed at distance learners. Wang assesses Maine's state-wide collaboration for the provision of distance education through the Education Network of Maine (#751). Utah's state-wide technology initiative operates through the Utah Academic Library Consortium, which has developed cooperative programs that provide the infrastructure for delivering library services to distance learners, according to Morrison et al. (#573). Morrison describes academic resources available to help public libraries in Utah serve distance learners (#578). SWITCH, the Southeastern Wisconsin Information Technology Exchange, operates a joint library system for four Wisconsin institutions, combining resources and services to better meet distance learners' needs, according to Ruddy (#574).

Another form of cooperation involves contracting with an institution to provide library services to distance education programs and compensating the supporting library. Barsun and Weaver (#570) and Weaver and Schaffer (#575) describe one such agreement between Walden University, an accredited virtual university, and Indiana University of

Bloomington, a traditional higher education institution. A formal memorandum of understanding exists between the University of West Florida and Walton Junior College such that the collections, equipment, and furnishings placed in the joint use library can be reclaimed by the supplying institution if the partnership dissolves, according to Gilmer (#565). These types of formal and informal agreements have been undertaken to provide resources and services to distance learners and to satisfy accreditation requirements. While such agreements are used to provide library resources and services to distance learners, Rodrigues points out that they can supplement support but should not substitute as the main resource for distance learners (#172).

A prevalent theme throughout the literature is collaboration as an emergent challenge to bring together teams that will enable the information technology model to become a reality. The importance of librarians partnering with other constituencies is stressed. Librarians need to collaborate with computing services, faculty, and other libraries to optimize technology to its fullest. At the same time, the collaborative teaching and learning environment is affecting librarians' roles as facilitators and will necessitate continuing education for librarians to become adept at helping users in the application of the new technology. The trend toward disintermediation is enabling learners to use the library without the librarian and without physically visiting the library, creating new roles for librarians to provide technical support and navigation among the many websites. The provision of technical expertise and advice is seen as part of the future role of librarians.

Numerous research studies have been undertaken since publication of the *Second Bibliography.* Surveys of U.S. libraries include distance education course offerings in higher education, conducted by the National Institute on Postsecondary Education, Libraries and Lifelong Learning (#592); the extent and type of involvement ARL libraries play in distance learning, conducted by Snyder, Logue, and Preece (#593, #596); the level of library support provided by academic libraries for their off-campus programs in relation to the 1990 *ACRL Guidelines for Extended Campus Library Service,* conducted by Lahmon (#595); and coordination mechanisms between external degree programs and libraries, conducted by Corrigan (#598). User studies conducted in the United States include the role of the library of Nova Southeastern University in meeting the needs of distance education graduate students, conducted by Abate (#652); student use of OCLC's FirstSearch service across three university branch campus libraries, conducted by Burich, Gover, and Schwanz (#653); user satisfaction with the Florida Distance Learning Reference and Referral Center, conducted by Chavez et al. (#655); and citation analysis of journal usage of off-campus graduate students, conducted by Ruddy (#656).

United Kingdom

Compared to the sources cited in the *Second Bibliography,* the publication output from the United Kingdom in the area of library services for open and distance learning has increased in recent years. Following the United States, the United Kingdom has the next highest number of references in this bibliography. Contributing to the literature during this period are the proceedings from the first and second "Libraries Without Walls" conferences (#13, #21). Several papers from UK authors are included in these proceedings. A special theme issue of *Education for Information* on "Networked Learner Support" contributed seven papers on current initiatives in this area (#20). Other contributions are reported in news items, journal articles, research reports, book chapters, and monographs.

Authors from the United Kingdom echo some of the same concerns as their American colleagues regarding the role of libraries in distance, open, and lifelong learning. MacDougall predicts that, in the new academic environment, libraries will need to demonstrate their strengths for supporting distance learning and the librarian will need to become a hybrid manager utilizing professional knowledge, applying information technology, and contributing to curriculum design (#140). For the provision of adequate library services to distance learners, Cajkler advocates that a librarian should be involved in all stages of course development (#133). This comment is particularly relevant since the author is a tutor of distance education courses rather than a librarian.

A recurring theme in the UK literature is distributed libraries in the context of distributed higher education. Brophy identifies several ways in which libraries can support distributed education, including document and postal delivery systems, electronic links to networked services, delivery of packaged materials, use of the public library network, a national or regional library membership card, and wider use of full-text electronic products (#128). Stephens and Unwin report on the role of the library in postgraduate distance learning, noting that there is a conflict of values between the desirability of self-contained courses and the need for access to library resources (#164). According to Heery, academic libraries in the United Kingdom need to recognize the differences between traditional and non-traditional students and adapt their services to support the latter (#169).

Another recurring theme is that of lifelong learning. Brophy, Craven, and Fisher report on a study as part of the Electronic Libraries Programme (eLib) that examined models of lifelong learning and the role of libraries in relation to these models (#131). In separate papers, Brophy and Craven (#132) and Craven and Fisher (#134) comment further on the provision of library services for lifelong learners in UK academic libraries. Brophy uses three case studies to illustrate the provision of academic library services to lifelong learners: the Open University, the University of the Highlands and Islands Project, and the Virtual Academic Library of the North-West (VALNOW) (#149). Watkin reports on the role of the public library in supporting lifelong learning, with reference to developments in Clwyd Public Library (#198). Watkin also identifies staff expertise as a vital factor in the success of the Open Learning Service of the Clwyd Library and Information Service and describes a training program designed for librarians working with open learning customers and partnerships (#221). Several papers report on the South Ayrshire Libraries' project to enhance public library support for open and distance learning (#192-97), including the development of a Web-based information skills package for open learners (#194). Allred discusses the advances made by the "Open for Learning" project in the United Kingdom, including ease of access to learning materials and appropriate hardware, availability of trained staff to assist users, and collaboration between public libraries and local organizations such as colleges and open learning centers (#200).

In the area of remote access to electronic resources, Blackmore describes the Learning Web, which is used by Wirral Metropolitan College to provide remote learners with access to learning resources and support 24 hours a day regardless of time or location of the student (#717). Hunt reports on how the Open University plans to deliver electronic services to its distance learners, describing two electronic initiatives, the Resources for Open University Teachers and Students (ROUTES) Project and the Edbank Project to investigate the development of full-text databases for use by remote teacher training students (#719).

Although electronic reference services are discussed primarily in American publications, there are two British works that focus on this area. Davenport, Procter, and Goldenberg report on a collaborative reference service involving three higher education institutions cooperating to provide assistance to remotely located users over computer networks (#386). A question of concern in this experiment was the extent to which it is necessary to duplicate face-to-face interaction in designing remote reference service. Gleadhill describes NERD (Newcastle Electronic Reference Desk), which provides an inquiry function and a database of frequently asked questions (FAQs) and answers available 24 hours a day over the World Wide Web (#389).

The term "networked learner support" (NLS) was introduced into the literature by researchers at the University of Sheffield through the NetLinkS Project in the Electronic Libraries (eLib) Programme. NLS refers to the educational role of library and information staff in support of online learning, including user education, information skills training, and reference assistance using current communication technologies such as e-mail and the World Wide Web. The primary goal of the NetLinkS Project was to facilitate local and national development of NLS by examining its potential and providing appropriate professional development activities and resources. The focus of NLS is the remote user and, for this reason, several works on this topic have been included in this bibliography (see #407-39).

Two international symposia on NLS, held at the University of Sheffield in 1996 and 1997, account for many of the publications on this topic (#20, #409). Most of the papers from these symposia were prepared by authors from the United Kingdom. Themes addressed in the first symposium included the need for collaboration between information and technology specialists, the importance of user education and information skills training, the potential for videoconferencing in higher education, the importance of academics working in partnership with information specialists in planning curriculum, and the perceptions of library professionals about possible role changes in the networked environment. The second symposium focused on partnerships for supporting online learning, the potential of computer-mediated communications and the World Wide Web for the provision of information support, and the organizational and professional development issues associated with the role of networked learner support.

Interlibrary cooperation is a significant topic in the United Kingdom. Those attending the first "Libraries Without Walls" conference stressed the need for partnerships and other collaborative actions to help develop better services for distance learners. Brophy and MacDougall describe the kinds of cooperative activities recommended, including sharing experiences, identifying good practice, discussing problems, exchanging information on technology standards, transfer abilities, cooperative projects across Europe, and cooperation with the rest of the world (#557). Brophy reviews the issues affecting the provision of library services in partnerships between further and higher education institutions in the United Kingdom, noting that cooperation between learning resource services is a primary means to ensure that off-campus students have equitable access to library resources and is vital to the success of partnership arrangements (#568). Watkin describes the opportunities for public libraries to respond to the educational and training needs of society through PLAIL, Public Libraries and Adult Independent Learners, a European Commission Telematics Programme with partners in Wales, Scotland, Portugal, and Spain (#583).

A noticeable trend in the UK literature is that the number of distance education providers is increasing, and library services similar to those offered to off-campus students in North America are being introduced at some UK institutions. Examples of these services are Northern College in Scotland (#720), University of Surrey (#721), University of

Central Lancashire (#724), and Sheffield Hallam University (#725). Van der Zwan and Whitsed indicate that the mandate of the Open University (OU) has been extended to include development of a strategy for supporting distance students through networked access to information (#722). In a focus interview, Whitsed, the Director of Library Services at the Open University, discusses the OU strategy, the role of librarians in this strategy, and the impact of technology on services (#723). Hall reports on the University of Sunderland's efforts in supporting distance learning, including access to electronic resources via the Web, postal and fax delivery of materials, and telephone and e-mail help services (#718).

A far-reaching example of government support for research in the United Kingdom is the BIBDEL (Libraries Without Walls: The Delivery of Library Services to Distant Users) Project, which concluded in 1995. This project, coordinated by the Centre for Research in Library and Information Management (CERLIM) at the University of Central Lancashire, produced numerous reports and papers describing the research, the demonstration experiments, and the findings of the project (e.g., #21, #254, #360, #371). The VALNOW (Virtual Academic Library of the North-West) service at the University of Central Lancashire is one example of a service that developed out of the BIBDEL research (#236, #724). The project also produced a "tool kit" of techniques on the various aspects of providing library support to distance learners. The "tool kit" was developed as a hypertext package to facilitate its adaptation and modification by others to meet local needs (#262).

Research studies undertaken in the United Kingdom include two baseline surveys on open learning in public libraries conducted by Allred (#586, #589). The aim of the "Open for Learning" Project, which ran from 1992 to 1995, was for 90% of all public library authorities to have open and flexible learning centers. The 1996 survey (#586) found that 83% of public library authorities in the United Kingdom were providing open and flexible learning services. An evaluation report on the "Open for Learning" Project measured how well the project's target goals were met in making open and flexible learning available to adult learners through public libraries in England (#588).

The starting point for much of the UK research is the premise that library support to distance learners has been largely neglected. A number of user studies were undertaken to assess the information needs and resource requirements of these students. A significant contribution to the research literature from the United Kingdom is a large-scale project conducted through the University of Sheffield in 1994–1996 to investigate the use of libraries by postgraduate distance learning students. This two-year project consisted of five related studies: a questionnaire survey of 1,000 students, a diary study of 47 students, interviews with 11 course providers, a questionnaire survey of 116 university librarians, and a questionnaire survey of 134 public libraries to determine their role in supporting distance learning. The project resulted in a book reporting the results of the research (#637) and several articles and papers discussing the various findings and their implications for library practice (e.g., #631-32, #636, #643).

Another major research project originating in the United Kingdom was "Library Support for Franchised Courses in Higher Education," funded by the British Library and carried out by CERLIM (Centre for Research in Library and Information Management). Goodall and Brophy investigated the support for franchised higher education courses from the point of view of students, tutors, college librarians, and university librarians, focusing on user information needs and how students go about the process of identifying, locating, and using library and information resources. In addition to the final report on the project (#642), a number of journal articles describe various aspects of the research, including the library experiences of students enrolled in franchised courses (e.g., #638, #644, #648-49).

In other research, Bilby examined the extent to which UK universities were providing library services to their distance learners and the impact of information technologies on such services (#587). Farmer and others investigated the information needs of nursing staff in remote areas of Scotland (#639-41). Single-institution user studies were conducted by Mulvaney and Lewis at Birmingham University (#635), by Myhill and Jennings at the University of Exeter (#645), and by Owen at Leicester University (#646).

Australia and New Zealand

Australia has the third highest number of entries in this bibliography. The forms of publication from this country in the period since the *Second Bibliography* include journal articles, papers in conference proceedings, chapters in monographs, theses and dissertations, and short articles in the newsletter *DESIGnation*. DESIG, the Distance Education Special Interest Group within the Australian Library and Information Association, held a conference in Wagga Wagga in 1997 that produced several papers (#73). While proceedings of that conference were not published, transcripts of the papers are available from the editor of *DESIGnation*.

Two international studies examine Australian works on library services for distance learning. In a literature review prepared for the British Library funded project on "The Role of the Library in Distance Learning," Stephens examines publications from the United Kingdom, the United States, Canada, and Australia (#11). Particular attention is paid to research studies originating in these countries, with detailed commentary provided for selected works. As part of a paper on the international context of library services for distance learning, Slade and Kascus compare research studies from a number of countries, including Australia (#39).

Two Australian papers were contributed to the theme issue of *Journal of Library Services for Distance Education* on the future of this area. Cavanagh provides a vision of library services for distance learning that focuses on three issues: (1) who users will be, (2) how to provide optimal services for them, and (3) how better use of information technology will change the way things are done (#44). Orr and Appleton discuss their view of the future of library services for distance education from the perspective of Central Queensland University's initiatives in library instruction (#54).

A number of Australian works discuss the role of libraries in distance learning. In a general paper, Simpson examines a broad range of issues on the provision of library services for distance education (#65). Particular attention is paid in the paper to the role of the librarian in supporting the distance education curriculum and the relationship between lecturer, student, and librarian. The role of the librarian is also examined in a paper by Macauley and McKnight that focuses on postgraduate distance learners (#139). The authors propose that librarians assume the role of co-supervisor to ensure that the literature review component of a higher degree thesis is comprehensive and relevant. Small reports on an investigative tour of North America to study the role of libraries in virtual universities (#161-62). Based on her findings, the author offers an overview of pertinent issues concerning virtual universities and their libraries. These issues include information literacy, the role of the Internet as an information source, library services currently provided by virtual universities, the role of librarians in virtual universities, and the challenges for librarians in this context.

The topic of library support for open learning has generated much discussion in the Australian literature. A two-part report from the Senate Employment, Education and Training References Committee looks at the library needs of open learning students among other issues pertaining to the development of open learning in Australia (#120, #127). Booker reports on a statement drafted for the Australian Library and Information Association stressing equitable access to library resources for students engaged in open learning (#121). Three papers by Campbell discuss various issues regarding Open Learning Australia (OLA), the Open Learning Library and Information Service (OLLIS), and Open Net (#119), as well as the OLLIS Mark2 scheme for simplifying procedures for open learning students to access libraries (#174-75). Two works from South Australia provide examples of effective support services for open learning programs. Brittain describes the services offered by the OLTC (Open Learning Technology Corporation) Information Service to assist lecturers, course designers, developers of learning materials, and curriculum writers (#117, #123), while Booker describes the information and advisory services of OLIMCH (Open Learning Information and Materials Clearing House) that support flexible learning (#166).

The role of public libraries in supporting open learning students is the topic of three papers. Booker examines the findings of the PLAIL (Public Libraries and Adult Independent Learners) Project in Europe to determine their applicability to public libraries in Australia (#209). In response to this paper, Williams offers an educator's point of view on public library services for open learning in Australia (#215). The author suggests that networking among libraries, especially between libraries in different states, may be one means to increase support for open and distance learners. Van Dyk, in the context of providing an overview of library services for open learning, indicates that public libraries can become major players in supporting open learning students (#220).

As in the United States and the United Kingdom, electronic resources and services are areas of paramount concern in the Australian literature. McPherson describes the development and implementation of electronic library services at the University of Southern Queensland (#263, #419). Beaumont, Hicks, and Tucker report on the CIDER (CAVAL Information Delivery and Electronic Requesting) Project, which will provide a means for end-users at universities in the state of Victoria to electronically request and receive articles from journals held at participating libraries in the state (#280). Cavanagh discusses electronic library services for distance education students, with specific reference to the services offered by Deakin University (#309). He indicates that there is sufficient evidence that off-campus students will use electronic resources if these services are adequately promoted and the students see a benefit to themselves.

Remote access to electronic resources is considered by several authors. Beswick describes use of Edith Cowan University's Virtual Campus facility to provide library services to external students (#321). Stewart provides information on a collaborative trial between Southern Cross University and a number of publishers to make full-text legal materials available over the Internet via Web technology (#345). Neuhaus discusses two projects at Southern Cross University to establish a regional electronic network on the north coast of New South Wales (#351, #369). The aim of the projects was to make learning resources available to off-campus students through the regional university centers and by dial-up access throughout Australia.

Library instruction for distance learners continues be a major focus in the Australian literature. Three papers by McAlpine describe the development of a combined video- and computer-assisted learning (CAL) package to provide Open Learning Australia students with instruction in library use (#460, #476-77). The library instruction initiatives of Central Queensland University (CQU) are reported in a number of papers (e.g., #456, #461, #464). These initiatives include (1) a residential school on-campus where information literacy skills were taught in a face-to-face setting; (2) a virtual residential school that used a combination of desktop videoconferencing and teleconferencing to teach students at a distance; (3) two computer-assisted learning (CAL) programs, one on searching the online catalogue and the other on accessing and searching electronic databases; and (4) a series of courses on the Web to teach selected professional groups how to use the Internet effectively.

The concept of information literacy is frequently discussed in the context of library instruction programs at Australian institutions. Central Queensland University's commitment to helping its distance learners develop information literacy skills is well documented in the literature. Catts, Appleton, and Orr state that strategies for promoting information literacy as a component of lifelong learning are to be incorporated into all courses offered by the university, and CQU librarians work with faculty and lecturers to fulfil this objective (#492). Ward outlines CQU's projects for teaching information literacy skills to distance education students (#499). With a focus on teaching information literacy skills, Orr, Appleton, and Andrews describe the virtual residential school offered to both on- and off-campus students at Central Queensland University in 1995 (#500).

In a general paper, George and Luke argue that information literacy is pivotal in flexible teaching and learning because it enables individuals to engage in a variety of learning situations and opportunities in optimal ways (#503). George and Love further argue that librarians should encourage distance students to become involved in the process of information gathering so that these students can assume more control over their learning and research skills (#504). With reference to adult learning theory and independent learning, Wilson examines the development of information literacy skills among adult students in general and external students in particular (#507). Harrison outlines activities from a workshop intended to identify the key competencies associated with information literacy in open and flexible learning (#508).

Very little has been written in recent years on the topic of interlibrary cooperation to benefit distance learners in Australia. One exception is a paper by Humphreys and Cooper reporting that the University of Southern Queensland has established a joint-use academic/public library at its Wide Bay Campus in partnership with Hervey Bay City Council (#577). The joint library supports the flexible delivery of education and lifelong learning for students studying on-campus, by distance education, and through the enhanced delivery mode. The authors note that the Hervey Bay Library is the first joint-use academic/public library in Australia and one of the few in the world.

In the area of research, several user studies have been conducted by Australian librarians. Cavanagh reports on three studies conducted at Deakin University on electronic access to library catalogues and electronic ordering of library materials by off-campus students (#610, #617, #622). Macauley discusses the results of his research study on the information needs of postgraduate distance education students. In addition to the author's thesis on the topic (#619), several articles and papers describe various findings from the study and their implications for library practice (e.g., #611-14). In her thesis and two articles, Wilson reports on a study undertaken at Edith Cowan University to determine isolated students' acquisition of information literacy skills and levels of information literacy (#623, #525, #627). A thesis and a paper by Phelps discuss the results of a research study on the attitudes and perceptions of teaching staff at Southern Cross University toward the information needs of their distance education students (#620-21). Bowser's thesis reports on a study to identify, from a student perspective, critical support services and preferred support practices in distance education (#624).

Other publications from Australia describe library services for distance and flexible learning at specific institutions. Examples of institutional services described in the literature include James Cook University (#689), Deakin University (#691-92), Charles

Sturt University (#694, #698), Monash University (#695, #697), the University of South Australia (#696), and the University of Southern Queensland (#701).

New Zealand is also active in providing library services to distance learners, but there are comparatively few works describing developments and initiatives in that country. Only five works about New Zealand have been identified for this bibliography. Four of these works are about The Open Polytechnic of New Zealand (TOPNZ). Clover reports on the introduction of a service quality charter to improve services to distance education students at TOPNZ (#239). Smith outlines the process used by the Open Polytechnic to develop initial library services for its distance students (#246). Moore and others discuss a study conducted at TOPNZ to explore the implications of information literacy for staff involved in providing distance education (#496). A thesis by Mann examines the low use of academic libraries by undergraduate students, with a specific emphasis on the extent of library use by students in a TOPNZ distance education degree program (#707). The one work not concerned with TOPNZ is a research paper by Field, who investigated the client perspective on distance library services by surveying open learning students enrolled in the Master's of Library and Information Studies program at Victoria University of Wellington (#630).

Canada

Compared to the sources cited in the first two bibliographies, Canadian publication output in the area of library services for distance learning has been relatively modest in recent years. The primary vehicle for publication in this area has been the proceedings of the Off-Campus Library Services Conferences (#16, #22). Other forms of publications include journal articles and documents accessible via the Web.

Two international studies examine Canadian works on library services for distance learning. In the literature review for the British research project on "The Role of the Library in Distance Learning," Stephens reviews publications from the United Kingdom, the United States, Canada, and Australia (#11). Canadian research studies undertaken prior to 1996 are discussed in detail. In a paper on the international context of library services for distance learning, Slade and Kascus compare research studies from a number of countries, including Canada (#39).

Two Canadian papers were contributed to the "future trends" issue of *Journal of Library Services for Distance Education*. Adams looks at the future in terms of what is currently happening and what should be happening (#42). More service with less staff and funds is predicted, with technology bridging the gap. Slade views the future in relation to library services provided at the University of Victoria (#56). The author indicates that the next five years will see a continuation of traditional off-campus library services combined with a steady growth of student independence in the area of information access.

The role of libraries in distance learning is considered by a number of authors. Peters, in an online article directed to the Canadian Association of University Teachers, offers a general overview of various issues pertaining to library services for distance education (#55). The author warns that use of technology for teaching and learning may be an excuse for downsizing and that librarians may be replaced by technicians or support staff in the delivery of services to distance learners. In a position paper, Burge advocates that learner services for distance education should include adequately educated library staff and user-friendly information delivery and communication technologies (#118). In this context, Burge stresses the importance of formally educating librarians in adult learning principles. Three papers contributed to a Canadian monograph on open and distance learning mention library services in terms of their importance to effective teaching and learning and the obstacles to providing high-level support for research projects (#125). Small, an Australian librarian, reports on the role of libraries in virtual universities in North America, including the Open Learning Agency in British Columbia (#161-62).

In the area of electronic resources and services, Silva describes the design and implementation of an Internet resources course at McGill University (#300). Recent software to help libraries deliver more appropriate and successful online reference service is discussed by Vine (#385). The author provides brief descriptions of the functions of the ICQ and LiveContact software and comments that several libraries in Canada are planning trials of the software. Phelps, in an online paper prepared for the School of Library and Information Studies at University of Alberta, explores the various social and technological issues a library needs to consider in providing an electronic mail reference service (#393).

Library instruction is the focus of three Canadian papers. In an article primarily directed toward distance educators, Sexty examines the role of information literacy in an electronic environment (#498). The argument is advanced that educators and librarians need to work together to ensure that learners know why they need information, how to find and evaluate that information, and how to transform the information into knowledge for future use. A practical example of the application of Web technology to library instruction is provided by Sloan, who describes how librarians at the University of New Brunswick have designed a Web-based Virtual Pathfinder as a guide to library research (#536). Adams reports on the virtual library handbook prepared at the University of Saskatchewan to teach research skills to distance learners via the World Wide Web (#542).

The topic of interlibrary cooperation in Canada is highlighted in three works. Schafer describes NORALINK, the Northern Alberta Library and Information Network, which was intended to provide reference assistance, reciprocal borrowing privileges, and individual service for all postsecondary students in that part of the province (#560). An online report by the Distance Education Committee of the Association of Atlantic Universities Librarians Council recommends strategies for improving library services to distance learners in New Brunswick, Nova Scotia, Prince Edward Island, and Newfoundland (#567). An overview of the Electronic Library Network (ELN) in British Columbia is provided by deBruijn (#572). Two main objectives of ELN are to extend the collective resources of academic libraries in the province and to facilitate resource sharing among those libraries through the use of technology.

Only one Canadian research study has been identified for inclusion in this bibliography. In a conference paper, Schafer presents the findings of a focus group survey of student satisfaction with library services at Athabasca University (#628). Focus groups were found to be helpful in identifying areas in which the library was effective in its provision of services to students, while at the same time identifying areas of weakness.

Information on library services for distance learning at specific Canadian institutions can be found in the third edition of the *Off-Campus Library Services Directory,* prepared by Central Michigan University (#585). In addition, four papers discuss services at Simon Fraser University (#703), the University of Victoria (#704), the University of Northern British Columbia (#705), and the University of Calgary (#706).

Europe and Scandinavia

More works concerning Europe and specific European and Scandinavian countries are represented in this bibliography than in the previous two volumes. Contributing to the literature on Europe are the proceedings of the two "Libraries Without Walls" conferences (#13, #21) and various reports resulting from the BIBDEL Project (e.g., #21, #254, #360, #371). Papers from different conferences and journal articles comprise the other forms of publication about Europe and Scandinavia.

The role of libraries in open, distance, and lifelong learning is a central theme in many publications about this part of the world. In an address to an international seminar, Allred discusses the issue of library support for lifelong learning in Europe (#110). In another paper, Allred looks at the various electronic library programs underway in Europe (#111). Longworth suggests a role for libraries in the European Lifelong Learning Initiative (ELLI), an international professional association established to foster lifelong learning in Europe (#115). With particular reference to the United Kingdom and Europe, MacDougall discusses various issues affecting library support for distance learners in terms of opportunities, strengths, weaknesses, and threats (#140). Watkin reviews the objectives and contributions of the PLAIL (Public Libraries and Adult Independent Learners) Project, which investigated the library needs of adult learners in selected European countries (#198, #214). In two online documents, Kühne outlines various aspects of the DERAL (Distance Education in Rural Areas via Libraries) Project, which is intended to serve as a model for Europe-wide access to distance learning through public libraries (#190-91).

In addition to these general works, several papers discuss the role of libraries in specific countries. Garnes comments on the role of libraries in the lifelong and distance learning reform movement in Norway (#135). Lund considers how librarians can assume a more active role in the open learning activities of commercial colleges in Denmark (#138). Roza describes the involvement of two Hungarian county libraries, as well as the Distance Learning Center of the Technical University, in the European LISTED Project (#188). Allred remarks on the current status of open and distance learning in Germany and his role as an advisor on the development of open learning in German public libraries (#189). Stein describes how the Open University in the Netherlands created study centers in public libraries to provide its distance students with access to information (#212). A paper by Trohopoulos and Carpenter provides an overview of public libraries and mobile libraries in Greece, with a focus on the MOBILE project that identified user target groups in remote communities and their information needs (#213).

A number of papers from the "Libraries Without Walls" conferences pertain to the area of electronic resources and services. Sophoulis discusses the development of a new distributed university to serve the Aegean islands in Greece (#260). Pettman and Ward describe the UNIverse Project, funded by the European Commission, which was investigating the feasibility of a virtual union catalogue to enable end-users to access remote information sources (#296). A cooperative library network in the Antwerp region of Belgium is the topic of a paper by Van Borm, Corthouts, and Philips (#302). In another paper, Van Borm offers a progress report on HYPERLIB, the European Commission funded project of Loughborough University, United Kingdom and University of Antwerp, Belgium (#372).

Several works about the BIBDEL Project discuss the experiments conducted by the three partner institutions, the University of Central Lancashire in the United Kingdom, Dublin City University in Ireland, and University of the Aegean in Greece. Brinkley and OFarrell describe the two experiments at Dublin City University to investigate the delivery of library services to distance education students (#359). MacDougall compares the models of providing library services at the three partner institutions (#365-66). OFarrell reports on Dublin City University's progress in the BIBDEL Project at the midpoint in the project's duration (#370). Wynne discusses the issue of remote access to library resources in relation to the demonstration experiments at the partner institutions (#373).

The topic of networked learner support (NLS) has received attention in connection with a number of European initiatives. Fjällbrant and others describe the design and development of a networked end-user education program as part of the EDUCATE (End-User Courses in Information Access Through Communication Technology) Project of the European Union Telematics for Libraries Programme (#411, #431, #435). Langenbach and Bodendorf report that a project to create a virtual campus at the University of Erlangen-Nuremberg in Germany is integrating networked learner support into the software for the online courses (#415). Pye discusses the role of librarians in providing networked learner support as part of the European Union's Telematics for Teacher Training (T3) Project (#421).

The last area of concentration in the European literature is that of interlibrary cooperation. In two papers, Salvesen looks at the efforts of an inter-institutional committee established by the Norwegian Ministry of Culture to examine the role of public and academic libraries in supporting open and distance learning in Norway (#559, #580). Information on cooperative efforts in Sweden is provided by Kühne, who describes the "IT Education From a Distance" project, which involves 12 head libraries in Kalmar County and the University of Kalmar (#581).

Africa

Several conference papers and journal articles by African authors are included in this bibliography. As in the previous bibliographies, the majority of the literature from Africa on library services for distance learning originates in South Africa and concerns the University of South Africa (Unisa), a distance teaching institution.

Two papers discuss general aspects of distance learning in South Africa, with reference to Unisa's library services. Shillinglaw reflects on the change occurring in distance education in South Africa and the need for greater involvement of the librarian in the learning processes of distance students (#181). Suttie takes a critical look at post-apartheid education at Unisa, with emphasis on the links between the subject librarians and black postgraduate students (#716).

Five papers focus on the electronic services of the Unisa Library. A news item reports on Unisa's selection of the INNOPAC integrated library system to enhance library services for its 130,000+ distance education students (#708). Two papers by Raubenheimer describe document delivery services at Unisa in relation to Ariel software (#712) and use of overseas databases such as CARL Uncover (#714). Snyman discusses the installation of a CD-ROM network to enable teaching staff and distance education students to conduct their own literature searches (#715). Hartzer and others describe how Web-based information services were developed at Unisa to provide online support to remote library users (#711).

Three works by Grobler discuss library services for Unisa's remote business students. One paper offers a general overview of library and information support in place as of 1995 (#713). A journal article describes development of an electronic document delivery system using Lotus Notes to provide library support to students in the business program (#709). Another paper examines how the pilot project in computer-based distance education using Lotus Notes resulted in the reconceptualization of existing library and information support toward the virtual library (#710).

Library instruction and information literacy are the topics of the remaining two papers on Unisa. Fourie and Snyman describe how online searching skills are taught by distance education using a multimedia study package based on instructional design principles (#457). Behrens presents a case study on the development of a curriculum for an information literacy course for distance learners at Unisa (#486). To be considered as information literacy, the user education or library skills offered by the library must include learning how to synthesize and evaluate information related to a particular discipline.

Authors from Technikon SA, another South African postsecondary institution, also address issues concerning library instruction and information literacy. Henning and Oosthuizen use the term *information user education* to refer to all the components of the education process that lead to information literacy (#488). In this context, they discuss the results of a research study to determine what aspects of information user education should be offered to distance education students at Technikon SA, who should provide the training, and what methods should be used. In another paper, Van Vuren and Henning examine resource-based learning in relation to flexible learning in South Africa (#146). The authors see the provision of "information user training" as a way in which academic libraries can play a central role in supporting open and flexible learning in this country.

Library services for distance learning are considered in three general papers about Africa. With reference to developing countries, Gbade Oladokun reviews some of the barriers to the provision of library services in distance learning (#35). In another paper, Samuel Olugbade Oladokun discusses the role of the library in distance learning in relation to information technology and barriers to service in Africa (#159). The third paper, by Oladokun and Oyewumi, examines library services for African distance education programs, with particular reference to sub-Saharan Africa (#130).

Library user studies are reported in the final three papers from Africa. Benza and others report on a study conducted in three regions of Zimbabwe to critically assess the learner support services provided by the Zimbabwe Open University (#606). Mlotshwa discusses the results of a study to investigate the practice of "distance librarianship" and the provision of postal lending services to distance learners in Zimbabwe (#607). Kamau examines learner perceptions of the quality of study materials and support services provided by distance teaching institutions in Kenya, with particular attention to the External Degree Programme of the University of Nairobi (#608).

Asia

Of the Asian countries represented in this bibliography, India has the highest number of publications on library services for distance learning. The forms of publication from India include journal articles and conference papers. Most of the other literature about Asian countries can be found in the proceedings of the Asian Librarians Roundtable, held during the 12th annual conference of the Asian Association of Open Universities in Hong Kong (#12).

Several contributions from India are concerned with the role of academic libraries in supporting distance learners. General works in this area include three papers by Jagannathan on library systems in India open universities, barriers to service, and ways in which library services to distance learners can be improved (#137, #170, #556). Suggested measures to improve services include a Library Support Service Cell at each open university, learning resource centers at the regional and study centers, mobile library units to serve rural and isolated areas, networking of libraries, use of communication and information technologies, and resource sharing among all types of libraries. Gupta addresses similar issues and identifies the following means to improve library services to distance learners: cooperation between all types of libraries, improved communication between the library and the tutor, guidelines or standards for the functioning of the library system, appropriate training for library staff at study centers, and employment of more full-time librarians (#155). Papers by Gupta and Jain (#168) and Panchaly (#184) also reflect the need for enhanced library services to Indian distance learners and suggest further means to strengthen the support system.

Other Indian authors discuss the role of public libraries in supporting distance learners. Babu and Chandran recommend that public libraries in Tamil Nadu undertake a number of programs to support distance learners, including developing print and audiovisual collections relevant to distance education courses, establishing university study centers in public libraries, strengthening existing mobile library systems, establishing career guidance information centers, cooperating with other libraries, and establishing regional library systems (#224). A paper by Rao and Sujatha describes how Andhra Pradesh Open University established an "open university corner" in a public library (#226). Dev Nath, in a discussion of barriers to library services in India, indicates that public libraries have the potential to assist rural students, especially by providing access to audio-visual materials and by preparing bibliographies and abstracts for distance education courses (#124).

The topic of quality assurance has received attention in two Indian publications. Devi looks at the role of Dr. B. R. Ambedkar Open University Library in quality assurance for distance education and emphasizes that the library can contribute to quality assurance in the university by providing distance learners with easy access to information (#177). Saroja and Sujatha apply the concept of total quality management (TQM) to Indian distance education institutions and their library services and discuss the experiences of Dr. B. R. Ambedkar Open University in providing quality information services (#670).

Electronic resources and services are considered in the Indian literature more in terms of their potential to assist distance learners than in relation to current practice. Gupta sees automation of library operations and networking as ways in which open universities can provide better library services to distance learners (#154). A paper by Kanjilal indicates that self-sufficiency in library collections and service is no longer possible due to constraints in resources, and the open university libraries are looking to the concept of integrated digital libraries as the solution for the future (#290). It is pointed out that, while the backbone for developing digital libraries already exists in India, this development is presently in the nascent state. Sujatha notes that future plans for Dr. B. R. Ambedkar Open University include providing Internet services at the central library and giving distance students access to the Internet and the resources of the central library through a local area network (#679). Jagannathan indicates that future plans for Indira Gandhi National Open University include CD-ROM networking, online access to commercial databases, Internet services, participation in external library networks, development of a local area network, and involvement in a wide area network of distance teaching institutions (#674).

Library instruction and information literacy are examined in two papers from India. Rao and Sujatha discuss the topic of user education for distance learners and recommend that a number of studies be undertaken prior to designing instruction in this area (#484). The Travelling Workshop Experiment in the United Kingdom is suggested as a model for taking user education to the distance learners via a mobile van. An article by Mishra emphasizes the importance of information literacy for distance learners and offers a proposed syllabus for a credit course on this topic (#495).

Of the remaining works from India, three papers provide case studies of library services at Indira Gandhi National Open University (#48, #686-87), one paper looks at the library services of Dr. B. R. Ambedkar Open University, and one paper reports on a study to determine how distance learners at Indira Gandhi National Open University perceive the support services available to them (#629). In this study, it was found that the library facilities at the study centers were not well designed or convenient, and problems included a shortage of reference books and study materials, limited opening hours, and a lack of trained staff to assist the students.

Many of the publications from other Asian countries offer short summaries of library services for distance learners and progress reports on the computerization of library operations. Institutions represented in the papers presented at the Asian Librarians' Roundtable (#12) include Bangladesh Open University (#671); Universiti Sains Malaysia (#673); Korea National Open University (#675); Philippines Open University (#676); Sukhothai Thammathirat Open University, Thailand (#677); Institut Teknology Mara, Malaysia (#680); and Universitas Terbuka, the Indonesian Open Learning University (#681).

Several papers from various sources discuss the role of libraries in supporting distance learning in China. Yan Zhuang emphasizes the necessity for China's national Radio and TV Universities (RTVUs) to establish document information centers in their libraries to assist teachers, students, and alumni (#148). Xiao-chun examines the concept of lifelong learning in relation to information technology, libraries, and the concept of the virtual library in China (#305). In discussing the development of distance education in China via computer networks, Zhengbao emphasizes that academic libraries need to strengthen their services for distance learners (#306). Pourciau advances the argument that information literacy is essential to distance education and that educational institutions in China and elsewhere need to ensure that their graduates have acquired information literacy skills (#490). Ding indicates that the RTVUs in China are planning to develop an electronic library system with outreach services to support students who are studying on an independent basis (#672).

The Open University of Hong Kong (OUHK) appears to have the most sophisticated electronic library system in Asia. Two papers by Wong describe OUHK's electronic library (#682-83). The electronic library provides OUHK distance students with round-the-clock remote access, through a Web-based common user interface, to the online catalogue, bibliographic databases, reserve materials, and full-text products. In addition, a video server supplies on-demand instructional videos over the Internet to teach OUHK students how to use the electronic library services.

Conclusion

This bibliography, together with its precursors, provides a comprehensive record of both published and unpublished information on the subject of library support for open and distance learning. The majority of this information has come from the industrialized English-speaking countries, especially the United States, the United Kingdom, and Australia. Of the 764 references identified in this volume, 52% pertain to the United States, 19% to the United Kingdom, and 13% to Australia. The remaining 16% of the entries are divided among other countries of the world, with Canada, India, and South Africa accounting for many of these works.

The chapters in this book reflect themes common to most of the countries that have contributed to the literature during the past five years. The two chapters with the most entries in this bibliography are "Role of Libraries in Distance and Open Learning" and "Electronic Resources and Services." The consensus in the literature is that the paradigm of library service is changing in the new educational environment and that librarians need to refocus their role so that they are more involved in the teaching and learning process. The international literature of the middle and late 1990s shows a marked shift in emphasis from access to physical libraries and print materials to access to electronic libraries and electronic resources. With a growing number of remote users, including both distance learners and regular students and faculty, it is pointed out that libraries need to develop services to support people who are accessing electronic resources from locations other than the campus libraries.

This support is seen as a team effort, involving partnerships with various stakeholders, the two primary ones being teaching faculty and computing services staff. Some of the ways in which librarians can support distance learning courses are by working with faculty to integrate information resources into curriculum development, teaching students and faculty how to effectively use electronic resources, and generally attempting to foster information literacy skills in remote users. According to Miller (#158), the skills most needed by lifelong learners will be the ability to locate information, analyze it, and use it to solve problems. These are the information skills that librarians can foster in students as part of the new learning environment.

In addition to works on the role of academic libraries, there is also a significant body of literature on the role of public libraries in assisting people engaged in open and distance learning. Much of this literature revolves around specific British and European projects and programs such as the Open for Learning Project in the United Kingdom and the PLAIL (Public Libraries and Adult Independent Learners) Project. Authors such as Allred (#207) emphasize that the major function of the public library is to support adult learning and the concept of lifelong learning, and all other activities are either a byproduct of this function or incidental to it. Typical ways in which public libraries can offer support is through information provision, access to appropriate study materials, provision of adequate facilities and equipment, educational counselling, and information literacy support.

In developing countries such as India, the literature on the role of libraries in distance learning has a different emphasis. The common theme in this body of literature is "barriers to service," with many authors emphasizing that library services for distance learners are underdeveloped and need to be improved. Among the issues frequently discussed in this context are the need for cooperation between all types of libraries; enhancement of the public library system to support distance learners; the lack of adequate funding for library services; and, more recently, access to information and communications technologies.

As we move into the twenty-first century, many of the issues and trends identified in this bibliography will become more prominent. Due to the influence of the new information and communications technologies, the boundaries between on-campus and off-campus education are blurring, and initiatives developed to assist one user group will likely benefit the other group as well. Widening access to education through virtual learning is creating a new paradigm for library services that should place the needs of remote users on a par with their on-campus counterparts. The role of libraries in this new educational environment is changing, and the next five to ten years should see a shift toward support of all learning, regardless of location of the learner, the method of learning, or the institutional affiliation of the learner. Key concepts in this future will be information literacy and lifelong learning, with librarians acting as facilitators to help learners develop the skills to access, evaluate, and utilize information at any point where it is needed in their formal studies or throughout their lifespan. This bibliography marks a transition in the literature on library services for distance learning and points to a future in which remote access to information resources will be an issue paramount in the delivery of all library services.

Alexander L. Slade
Marie A. Kascus

February 2000

Library Services for Open and Distance Learning

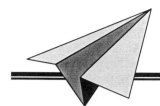

CHAPTER 1

Bibliographies, Literature Reviews, and Electronic Resource Lists

1. Ashton, Sarah. *Annotated Bibliography on Networked Learner Support*. Net-LinkS Project Resource Base. Online. Available: http://netways.shef.ac.uk/rbase/annbib.htm (Accessed April 13, 2000).

    One of the links on the NetLinkS website is to a Resource Base that provides an annotated bibliography on networked learner support (NLS). The bibliography, described as a work in progress, highlights NLS initiatives implemented in higher education institutions in the United Kingdom and other countries. The citations are to articles and papers available in either print or electronic format. Some listings include the author's postal and e-mail address. The entries are organized into three general sections: techniques and practices, organizational issues, and professional issues. Some citations are also listed in this volume, especially where the content is applicable to remote users of networked library resources. For further information on the NetLinkS Project, see entries in the Subject Index. A. Slade.

2. Lebowitz, Gloria. "An Extended Campus Resource List." *Colorado Libraries* 21, no. 1 (Spring 1995): 32.

    As part of the special issue of *Colorado Libraries* on extended campus library services, the author provides a selected list of resources relevant to the topic. Included are eight print resources, five directories of institutions offering programs, three listservs for keeping current, and two contacts for organizational involvement. M. Kascus.

3. Lorenzen, Michael. "Internet Resources: Distance Education: Delivering Instruction in Cyberspace." *College & Research Libraries News* 59, no. 5 (May 1998): 342-45.

    This is a list of electronic resources on distance education available on the Internet. The list is divided into the following categories: best starting points, discussion groups, newsgroups/usenets, electronic periodicals, organizations, and higher education sites. The author also provides a brief list of diploma mill warning signs to alert consumers to fake universities. M. Kascus.

4. Macauley, Peter. "The Information Needs of Australian Postgraduate Distance Learners: A Review of the Literature." [Charles Sturt University. Open Learning Institute]. *Occasional Papers in Open and Distance Learning*, no. 20 (November 1996): 15-26. Also online. Available: http://www.csu.edu.au/division/oli/oli-rd/ occpap20/macaul.htm (Accessed April 13, 2000).

The paper reviews some of the major studies and works on library services to distance learners, with particular attention to Australia. Most research literature in this area has concentrated on undergraduates. The author notes that the only relevant Australian study on library provision for postgraduate distance students is the 1993 survey undertaken by the University of Central Queensland (UCQ). Because there was so little written on this subject, the author made it the focus of his 1996 master's thesis by investigating the information needs of distance education higher degrees by research students at Deakin University. The findings from his study turned out to be similar to those from the UCQ survey. For more information on the author's thesis, see #619 in this volume. A. Slade.

5. NODE Learning Technologies Network. *Site Guide: Student Support*. Online. Available: http://node.on.ca/tfl/library/ (Accessed April 13, 2000).

This web page provides a list of resources pertaining to off-campus library services. It contains links to guidelines developed by library associations, practical examples of ways in which libraries are implementing library services for distance education, an annotated bibliography of online articles that discuss this issue, an annotated list of print resources, a selection of electronic mailing lists dedicated to various aspects of library service for distance education, and a list of special interest groups that examine this issue. A. Slade.

6. Preece, Barbara G. and Thyra K. Russell. "Selected and Annotated Bibliography." In *Libraries and Other Academic Support Services for Distance Learning*, edited by Carolyn A. Snyder and James W. Fox. Foundations in Library and Information Science, vol. 39. Greenwich, CT: JAI Press, 1997, 141-51.

This selected, annotated bibliography is part of an edited monograph on library support for distance learning (see #18 in this volume). It includes entries describing existing programs as well as entries focusing on various cultural and philosophical issues. The common thread throughout these works is a call for librarians to be more involved in the training of the patron and to use creative means to provide equal services to all. M. Kascus.

7. Reference and User Services Association. Machine-Assisted Reference Section. User Access to Services Committee. *Current User Research Bibliography*. Online. Available: http://staff.lib.muohio.edu/~shocker/mars/bib.html (Accessed April 13, 2000).

The User Access to Service Committee of the Machine-Assisted Reference Section (MARS) of the Reference and User Services Association is exploring the information-seeking behaviour of library users in the current electronic environment. This website lists a range of studies that focus on user behaviour in this environment, including Internet and Web behaviour. The focus is on studies that look at such questions as: How do users make choices among databases? How do they move from one interface to another? How do they decide what is an appropriate source of information? Excluded from this bibliography are catalogue use studies, surveys of use of the Internet or other databases by librarians, surveys about the kind of access offered in various libraries, surveys that deal with database tracking software, and studies dealing with only a single database. It is noted that this bibliography is an ongoing project. A. Slade.

8. Sloan, Bernie. *Librarian/Patron Collaboration in an Electronic Environment: Electronic Reference*. Graduate School of Library and Information Science, University of Illinois at Urbana-Champaign. Online. Available: http://alexia.lis.uiuc. edu/~b-sloan/e-reference.html (Accessed April 13, 2000).

   A list of print and electronic resources on collaboration between librarians and patrons in a digital/virtual/electronic library environment is provided at this website. The emphasis is on reference services for remote users and technologies that might assist in replicating the traditional reference environment electronically. Resources are grouped by the following headings: journal articles, Web papers, websites, and electronic reference service points. A. Slade.

9. Sloan, Bernie. *Library Support for Distance Learning*. Graduate School of Library and Information Science, University of Illinois at Urbana-Champaign. Online. Available: http://www.lis.uiuc.edu/~b-sloan/libdist. htm (Accessed April 13, 2000).

   The purpose of this site is to provide an informational resource for librarians interested in library support for distance learners. All of the resources listed are available via the World Wide Web. Sites are grouped by the following headings: (1) General Information on Distance Learning, (2) Regional Initiatives and Planning/Policy Documents, (3) Selected Papers on General Issues in Distance Learning, (4) Library-Specific Meta-Information on Distance Learning, (5) Selected Papers and Reports on Library Support for Distance Learning, (6) State and Regional Websites for Library Support for Distance Learning, (7) Individual Library Websites for Distance Learning Support, (8) Selected Papers on Electronic Reference Services, and (9) Evaluating Web Resources. A. Slade.

10. Sloan, Bernie. *Service Perspectives for the Digital Library: A Bibliography*. Graduate School of Library and Information Science, University of Illinois at Urbana-Champaign. Online. Available http://alexia.lis.uiuc.edu/~b-sloan/refbib.html (Accessed April 13, 2000).

    This bibliography accompanies the author's paper on remote reference services and service perspectives for the digital library (see #381 in this volume). Both print and electronic sources are included in the list. A. Slade.

11. Stephens, Kate. "The Role of the Library in Distance Learning: A Review of UK, North American and Australian Literature." *New Review of Academic Librarianship* 2 (Autumn 1996): 205-34.

    The literature review prepared for the British Library funded project on "The Role of the Library in Distance Learning" is reproduced in this article. The review focuses on literature from the United Kingdom, the United States, Canada, and Australia published or released prior to mid-1996. Particular attention is paid to research studies originating in these countries, with detailed commentary provided for selected works. The conclusion identifies a number of common themes that emerge from a comparison of the international literature. For the full report on the project, see #637 in this volume. A. Slade.

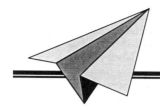

CHAPTER 2

General Works

This chapter includes compilations, news items, and articles and papers of a general nature that focus on library services for distance learning. Arrangement is by type of material rather than by topic.

Monographs, Proceedings, and Special Issues

1998

12. *Asian Librarians Roundtable: 12th Annual Conference of the Asian Association of Open Universities, 2-3 November 1998, The Open University of Hong Kong*. Hong Kong Sar, China: Open University of Hong Kong, 1998. 55 pp. Paper copy available from: The Library, The Open University of Hong Kong, 30 Good Shepherd St., Homantin, Kowloon, Hong Kong. Also online. Available: http://www.ouhk.edu.hk/~AAOUNet/ round/round.htm (in pdf format) (Accessed April 13, 2000).

Thirteen papers presented at the 1998 Asian Librarians Roundtable in Hong Kong were made available in both paper format as a compilation and electronic format as pdf files accessible through the Roundtable website. The Roundtable focused on the sharing of experience and knowledge in the use of communication and information technologies to enhance library outreach services. Subjects for discussion included the current status of library services in Asian open universities, the role of electronic library services in supporting distance education students, and current trends in library-related information technology. Twelve of the papers presented were written in English and provide information on library services for distance learning in the following countries: Bangladesh, China, Hong Kong, India, Indonesia, Korea, Malaysia, the Philippines, and Thailand. For information on the individual papers, see #671-82 in this volume. A. Slade.

13. Brophy, Peter, Shelagh Fisher, and Zoë Clarke, eds. *Libraries Without Walls 2: The Delivery of Library Services to Distant Users: Proceedings of a Conference Held on 17-20 September 1997 at Lesvos, Greece, Organized by the Centre for Research in Library and Information Management (CERLIM), Manchester Metropolitan University*. London: Library Association Publishing, 1998. 177 pp. ISBN 1-85604-301-0.

   The second European conference on library services for distance learning was held in Greece in 1997. Thirteen papers were presented by authors from the United Kingdom, Belgium, Australia, and the United States. The papers focused on theoretical perspectives on the role of libraries, descriptions of support for distance learners at specific institutions, outlines of European projects related to information access, and summaries of research studies on library services and user needs. For information on the individual papers, see the following entries in this volume of the bibliography: #107, #109, #134, #198, #236, #286, #296, #302, #636, #691, #717, #718, and #736. A. Slade.

14. Haricombe, Lorraine J., ed. "Service to Remote Users." [Theme issue]. *Library Trends* 47, no. 1 (Summer 1998): 1-184.

   This theme issue explores prospective challenges and newly created services at various libraries providing online support to remote users. The author introduces the topic of service to remote users, noting that remote users are challenging libraries to rethink their mission and services. The growth in technology has contributed to the increased numbers of people becoming independent users of information. In addition, technology has enabled librarians to enhance existing services to users. The author stresses that academic libraries, in particular, are rethinking their role because distance education students expect and are entitled to equal support from the parent institution. An overview is given for each contribution to this special issue. For the individual articles in this theme issue, see: #142, #147, #297, #336, #339, #341, #343, #381, #711, and #733 in this volume. M. Kascus.

15. OCLC Online Computer Library Center, Inc. *Distance Education in a Print and Electronic World: Emerging Roles for Libraries: Proceedings of the OCLC Symposium, ALA Midwinter Conference 1998, New Orleans, LA, January 9, 1998*. Dublin, OH: OCLC Online Computer Library Center, Inc., 1998. 20 pp. ISBN 1-55653-258-X. Also online. Available: http://purl.oclc.org/oclc/distance-1998 (Accessed April 13, 2000).

   OCLC sponsored this symposium on the topic of distance education for four reasons: the increased press given to the topic, the debate surrounding the topic, OCLC's stake in how virtual universities and libraries will relate, and how the World Wide Web and other technological innovations are helping to facilitate access and forcing a higher level of library service. Four presentations were made at this symposium. For the individual papers, see the following items in this bibliography: #28, #33, #553, and #742. M. Kascus.

16. Thomas, P. Steven and Maryhelen Jones, comps. *The Eighth Off-Campus Library Services Conference Proceedings: Providence, Rhode Island, April 22-24, 1998*. Mount Pleasant, MI: Central Michigan University, 1998. 350 pp.

Twenty-seven papers were published in the proceedings of the eighth Off-campus Library Services Conference sponsored by Central Michigan University. For information on the individual papers, see the following items in this volume: #39, #132, #232, #234, #235, #338, #384, #441, #442, #444, #486, #487, #542, #544, #548, #563, #564, #565, #628, #653, #654, #656, #710, #734, #735, #740, and #741. M. Kascus.

1997

17. Goodson, Carol, ed. "The Future of Library Services for Distance Education." [Theme issue]. *Journal of Library Services for Distance Education* 1, no. 1 (August 1997). Online. Available: http://www.westga.edu/~library/jlsde/jlsde1.1.html (Accessed April 13, 2000).

The first issue of *Journal of Library Services for Distance Education* was devoted to a discussion of the future of library services for off-campus and distance education. Selected international authors in this field were invited to contribute a summary of their views. Eleven papers appear in the issue, including five from the United States and two each from Australia, Canada, and the United Kingdom. For information on the individual papers, see the following entries in this volume: #41-44, #46-47, #49, #51, #54, and #56-57. A. Slade.

18. Snyder, Carolyn A. and James W. Fox, eds. *Libraries and Other Academic Support Services for Distance Learning*. Foundations in Library and Information Science, vol. 39. Greenwich, CT: JAI Press, 1997. 334 pp. ISBN 0-7623-0229-1.

The purpose of this monograph is to bring together models of library and other academic support services for distance learning. The models described are from different perspectives. Several of the contributions are from the administrator's perspective, describing library service roles, responses to political issues, and productive partnerships between faculty and librarians and between libraries and computing centers. One contribution focuses on collaborative learning in on-line courses, including costs and rewards. Another contribution is from a teacher's perspective, focusing on the development of distributed learning at the University of Alabama and library support for it. One chapter is a selected, annotated bibliography covering topics ranging from philosophical issues, such as access and equity, to examples of current programs of library support. This monograph has four substantial appendices: (1) Role of Libraries in Distance Education: Association of Research Libraries SPEC Flyer and SPEC Survey; (2) Master of Library and Information Science Program at the University of South Carolina; (3) Computer Access Survey of Distance Education Students at Monash University; and (4) Selected Web Pages for Distance Learning Programs. For the individual chapters in the monograph, see the following entries in this bibliography: #6, #493, #693, #745, and #747-49. M. Kascus.

19. Watson, Elizabeth F. and Neela Jagannathan, eds. *Library Services to Distance Learners in the Commonwealth: A Reader*. Vancouver, BC: The Commonwealth of Learning, 1997. 247 pp. ISBN 1-895369-47-9.

   This monograph contains 22 papers on library support services for distance education students. The following countries and areas of the Commonwealth are represented: Australia, Canada, the Commonwealth Caribbean nations, India, Kenya, New Zealand, South Africa, Tanzania, and the United Kingdom. The information dates from 1994, but publication was delayed until 1997. For information on the individual papers, see the following entries in the second bibliography: #20, #22, #43, #77, #158, #159, #160, #200, #202, #304, #338, #352, #412, #417, #419, #442, #457, #458, #460, #463, #464, and #467. A. Slade.

1996

20. Fowell, Sue and Philippa Levy, eds. "Networked Learner Support." [Special issue]. *Education for Information* 14, no. 4 (December 1996): 257-350.

   This special theme issue is a state-of-the art review on networked learner support (NLS). With teaching, learning, and research occurring across networks, what distinguishes networked learning is the use of computer-mediated communications (CMC) technologies to facilitate learner interactions. Networked learners can take part in online discussions and communicate with peers, instructors, and librarians by means of CMC. This issue explores the "scope and potential" of NLS through the perspectives of seven papers based on presentations made at the first International Symposium on Networked Learner Support at the University of Sheffield in June 1996. The papers represent current initiatives in NLS, describing the various learning, organizational, and professional issues that arise. Themes included are the need for collaboration between information and technology specialists, the importance of user education and information skills training, the need for careful planning, the potential for videoconferencing in higher education, the importance of academics working in partnership with information specialists in planning curriculum, curricular design, and the perceptions of library professionals about possible role changes in the networked environment. For the individual papers, see #427-30, #432, and #435-36 in this volume. M. Kascus.

1995

21. Irving, Ann and Geoff Butters, eds. *Access to Campus Library and Information Services by Distant Users: Proceedings of the First "Libraries Without Walls" Conference, Mytilene, Greece, 9-10 September 1995*. The fifth report from the BIBDEL Project (Libraries Without Walls: The Delivery of Library Services to Distant Users) funded by the Libraries Programme of the Commission of the European Communities. Preston, UK: Centre for Research in Library and Information Management, University of Central Lancashire, 1995. 91 pp.

This report is the fifth "deliverable" from the BIBDEL Project (Libraries Without Walls: The Delivery of Library Services to Distant Users). Twelve papers were published in the proceedings of the first "Libraries Without Walls" Conference sponsored by the Centre for Research in Library and Information Management (CERLIM), University of Lancashire, UK. For information on the individual papers, see the following entries in this bibliography: #176, #208, #213, #260, #327, #365, #372, #557, #559, #581, #583, and #648. For the other BIBDEL reports, see #284 and #285 in the second bibliography and #254, #262, #360, and #371 in this volume. M. Kascus.

22. Jacob, Carol J., comp. *The Seventh Off-Campus Library Services Conference Proceedings: San Diego, California, October 25-27, 1995*. Mount Pleasant, MI: Central Michigan University, 1995. 405 pp.

Thirty-eight papers were published in the proceedings of the seventh Off-campus Library Services Conference sponsored by Central Michigan University. For information on the individual papers, see the following entries in this volume of the bibliography: #67, #179, #181, #255, #256, #257, #259, #261, #271, #361, #402, #463, #466, #467, #469, #471, #474, #475, #483, #502, #505, #560, #573, #574, #576, #598, #600, #601, #603, #647, #663, #666, #668, #713, #757, #758, #760, and #761. M. Kascus.

23. Lebowitz, Gloria and Susan Potter, eds. "Extended Campus Library Services." [Special issue]. *Colorado Libraries* 21, no. 1 (Spring 1995): 5-32.

Guest editors provide a brief introduction as background for this special issue on the topic of extended campus library services. Two articles provide details about the types of programs and library services available from Colorado institutions. Two other articles discuss the impact that extended campus programs and students have on a public library and on a community college library. One article describes Access Colorado Library and Information Network (ACLIN), the State Library sponsored project to extend access to the collections of off-campus students' home institutions. Another article discusses student perceptions of library services based on an informal survey of students at three Colorado institutions. A selected resource list provides additional references for those who want to learn more about off-campus education and library support to off-campus students. For information on the individual articles, see the following entries in this volume: #2, #64, #178, #329, #582, #597, #602, #667, and #763. M. Kascus.

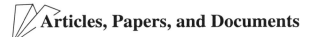Articles, Papers, and Documents

1999

24. Culpepper, Jetta. "Equivalent Library Support for Distance Learning: The Key to Staying in Business in the New Millennium." *Journal of Library Services for Distance Education* 2, no. 1 (July 1999). Online. Available: http://www.westga.edu/library/jlsde/vol2/1/JCulpepper.html (Accessed April 13, 2000).

In this guest editorial, the author offers her views on the quality of distance learning programs and the need for distance learners to receive library support equivalent to that available to their on-campus counterparts. Topics touched upon in this context include the research skills of distance learners, the characteristics of library support programs, the limitations of electronic resources, the need for print materials, and comparisons between distance learning and correspondence programs. The author emphasizes the importance of integrating information literacy skills into distance learning programs and warns that students lacking these skills may find themselves at a disadvantage in the current job market. A. Slade.

25.   Institute for Higher Education Policy. *What's the Difference? A Review of Contemporary Research on the Effectiveness of Distance Learning in Higher Education*. Prepared for the American Federation of Teachers and the National Education Association. April 1999. Online. Available: http://www.ihep.com/ PUB.htm (in pdf format) (Accessed April 13, 2000).

The American Federation of Teachers and the National Education Association commissioned the Institute for Higher Education Policy to conduct a review of the current research on the effectiveness of distance education to analyze what the research does and does not indicate about this area. This report suggests that there are many questions left unaddressed or unanswered in the research, making it difficult for policymakers, faculty, and students to develop properly informed judgments about key issues in distance education. One of the findings in the report is that "the research does not adequately address the effectiveness of digital libraries." The executive summary to the report states: "The library is at the core of the higher education experience and, especially at the graduate level, is an integral part of the teaching/learning process. Some digital libraries boast an enormous array of resources, with the implicit notion that they can provide the same service as the traditional library. But do digital libraries provide adequate services for the academic programs they are established to support?" A. Slade.

26.   Kirk, Elizabeth E. and Andrea M. Bartelstein. "Libraries Close in on Distance Education." *Library Journal* 124, no. 6 (April 1, 1999): 40-42.

This featured article in *Library Journal* highlights some of the prominent issues in the provision of library services for distance education in the United States. With reference to the growth of distance education programs, the authors discuss ACRL's revised guidelines, copyright issues, planning for library support of distance education, promoting the library's role, librarians as instructors, and fostering proactive services. Central Michigan University, SUNY-Plattsburgh, and Johns Hopkins University are cited as examples of institutions promoting library participation in distance learning development. The authors emphasize that distance education is not just a passing phase and that librarians need to play integral roles in developing and implementing a long-term plan for their respective institutions. A selected list of online distance education resources is included in the article as a guide for library staff involved in this area. A. Slade.

27. Watson, Elizabeth F. *Library Services to Distance Learners—The New Professional Paradigms*. Paper presented at the Pan-Commonwealth Forum on Open Learning, Brunei Darussalam, 1-5 March 1999: Empowerment through Knowledge and Technology. Online. Available: http://www.col.org/forum/casestudies.htm (in pdf format) (Accessed April 13, 2000).

> This paper examines several issues pertaining to the professional area of distance librarianship and the provision of quality library services to distance learners. These issues include a facilitatory institutional philosophy for library services to distance learners; new relationships between faculty, librarians, and other distance education personnel; the teaching role of librarians in distance education; the expanded use of technology to provide distance library services; and service delivery. The author emphasizes that the delivery of library and information services to distance learners has introduced a number of new paradigms into the library profession. The skills required to assist remote users also affect the delivery of library services to other clients, and distance librarianship is redefining what is common in today's practice of librarianship. A. Slade.

1998

28. Ehrmann, Stephen C. "Libraries and Distance Learning: A View From Outside." In *Distance Education in a Print and Electronic World: Emerging Roles for Libraries: Proceedings of the OCLC Symposium, ALA Midwinter Conference 1998, New Orleans, LA, January 9, 1998*. Dublin, OH: OCLC Online Computer Library Center, Inc., 1998, 11-14. Also online. Available: http://purl.oclc.org/oclc/distance-1998 (Accessed April 13, 2000).

> The expanded use of technology, particularly e-mail and the Web, in teaching and learning has affected libraries in a number of ways. First, telecommuting puts new demands on information services because users expect desktop delivery. Second, the pressure on colleges and universities for tighter coupling, both within institutions and with the outside environment, affects libraries. This stress on higher education, combined with advances in technology, has fueled a growing demand for information services. Library evaluation needs to encompass providers of the service, users of the service, and outcomes such as growth or failure of student skills in searching and using information. Those seeking guidance are encouraged to look at the Flashlight Project, which is developing toolkits for evaluating teaching, learning, and technology. M. Kascus.

29. Ferguson, Anthony W. "Back Talk: Is Distance Education in Our Future?" *Against the Grain* 10, no. 1 (February 1998): 85-86.

> The author offers his views on the future of distance education and its implications for libraries. With reference to the Western Governors University, he points to the growing popularity and expansion of distance education programs and notes a number of challenges that need to be addressed in providing services for the new remote user community. These challenges include the political problems with virtual universities, the cost of creating electronic campus infrastructures to serve remote users, the resistance of some faculty to teaching with technology, the need to provide students with Internet training, and the licensing

issues associated with electronic databases and full-text products. The author concludes that "distance education is in each of our futures" and libraries need to prepare for it. A. Slade.

30.   Goodram, Richard J. "Cooperation or Competition: An Entrepreneurial Question?" *Journal of Academic Librarianship* 24, no. 2 (March 1998): 155.

In this brief position paper, the author argues that the impact of the Internet and the proliferation of websites make it critical that librarians apply their skills to managing Internet-based information resources. This is particularly important because distance learning programs create and use Internet-based resources. Since librarians need to be involved in servicing distance learners, the author calls for libraries and librarians to cooperate in delivering services that respond to the changing needs of users. M. Kascus.

31.   Gorman, Michael. "Brave Music of Distant Drums: A Dissenting View on Distance Learning." *American Libraries* 29, no. 3 (March 1998): 54.

The author presents a dissenting view on distance learning, comparing the present "enchantment" with technology for delivering education to the "rhetoric" accompanying education by radio in the 1930s. According to the author, the difference between distance learning then and now is that library services and reading may be considered unnecessary if they do not fit into the technological structure on which distance learning depends. M. Kascus.

32.   Harris, David. "Distance Education and Its Technologies: From Correspondence Courses to the Net." In *Exeter '97: Virtual Libraries, Virtual Librarians: Proceedings of the CoFHE Annual Study Conference Held at the University of Exeter, 24-27 March 1997*, edited by S. R. Warrington. [London]: The Library Association. Colleges of Further and Higher Education Group, 1998, 29-34.

A number of broad issues affecting distance education are discussed in relation to the changes at the Open University (OU) in the United Kingdom. The discussion focuses on the educational implications of moving from a print-based correspondence course model to a more open and participatory model utilizing new technologies. Under the old model of OU education, library use was generally unnecessary because students received comprehensive course packages containing sufficient readings to complete the assignments. With the shift towards an electronic delivery model and the expansion of the Internet, students now have access to a wide range of resources. In the following statement, the author expresses concern about the students' abilities to effectively locate appropriate information through electronic sources: "Leave them to their own devices with electronic databases and they search too inefficiently or too promiscuously for academic purposes." He goes on to suggest that training in efficient search procedures is necessary in the new model of distance education. A. Slade.

33.   Jones, Maryhelen. "Future Fast Forward: Libraries and Distance Education." In *Distance Education in a Print and Electronic World: Emerging Roles for Libraries: Proceedings of the OCLC Symposium, ALA Midwinter Conference 1998, New Orleans, LA, January 9, 1998*. Dublin, OH: OCLC Online Computer Library Center, Inc., 1998, 1-5. Also online. Available: http://purl.oclc.org/oclc/distance-1998 (Accessed April 13, 2000).

From the author's perspective, the proliferation of distance education will challenge librarians in five ways. First is providing accelerated access to print and electronic course-related information. Second is providing instruction on identifying, accessing, and evaluating information for current courses and lifelong learning. Third is implementing assessment activities that reflect the value that collections, instruction, and other services have had for distance learning. Fourth is following intellectual property and copyright issues as they relate to the use of technologies and digital content in library services. Fifth is building relationships with review bodies to educate them about the complexities of providing library support to distance education programs. M. Kascus.

34.   NODE Learning Technologies Network. "Library Services for Distance Learners." *Networking* (June 1998). Online. Available: http://node.on.ca/networking/june1998/feature1.html (Accessed April 13, 2000).

The focus in this article is on the difficulties inherent in providing library services to distance learners. A wide range of issues is discussed, including collaboration among libraries, depository collections, student use of unaffiliated libraries, telephone and postal services from the home library, use of new technologies, copyright issues, administrative barriers to service, and the expense of providing services to distance learners. It is noted that while technology is beginning to have an effect on services to remote learners, much support is still provided by traditional means such as depository collections and books-by-mail programs. Despite the potential of technology to improve services to distance learners, it has so far done little more than improve the speed of access to library materials, leaving the extent of access unchanged. The argument is advanced that technology may be putting distance learners at a disadvantage because many of them are still without access to computers, and the funding being allocated for electronic services may be detracting from the resources needed to maintain traditional (non-electronic) services for the distance learners. A. Slade.

35.   Oladokun, Gbade. "Collaborative Effort Among Libraries/Information Centres in Aid of Distance Learning." In *Partners in Learning: Proceedings of the 14th Annual Conference of the Canadian Association for Distance Education, Banff, Alberta, 1998: Volume 2*, edited by Jon Baggaley, Terry Anderson, and Margaret Haughey. Athabasca, AB: Athabasca University, 1998, 273-75.

With particular reference to developing countries, this paper reviews some of the barriers to the provision of library services in distance learning. While information technologies are enhancing library support in developed countries, distance learners in developing countries, especially those in rural or remote areas, often lack the funds and/or the technological sophistication to take advantage of computer solutions to library access. The author advocates collaboration among all types of libraries as a means to reduce distance learners' disadvantages with regard to library support. A. Slade.

36.   Riggs, Donald E. *Library Services for Distance Education*. Paper presented at the International Conference on New Missions of Academic Libraries in the 21st Century, Beijing, China, October 25-28, 1998. Online. Available: http://www.lib.pku.edu.cn/98conf/proceedings.htm (Accessed April 13, 2000).

New models of distance education and library service are the focus of this paper. Library services for distance learners now include electronic delivery systems, compressed video transmission, contracting with local libraries, and sophisticated document delivery. Two key issues in the new electronic environment are instruction and training in the use of technology and the quality of library services. The author stresses that the distance learner has to be perceived in the same value structure as the on-campus learner. Riggs predicts that universities will continue to invest more resources in distance education and the delivery of library services and training to distance students will become more efficient and effective as technologies advance in sophistication. A. Slade.

37. Ryan, James H. "Measuring the Costs and Benefits of Distance Learning." Co-published simultaneously in *Journal of Library Administration* 26, nos. 1/2 (1998): 235-46, and *The Economics of Information in the Networked Environment*, edited by Meredith A. Butler and Bruce R. Kingma. New York: Haworth Press, 1998, 235-46.

In this conference address, the author discusses the growth and diversity of distance learning programs in the United States, examines their costs and benefits, and looks briefly at the role of librarians in distance education. Topics touched upon in this presentation include business and industry as distance education providers, the impact of technology on distance learning, information/knowledge as a commodity, competition in higher education, the increasing emphasis on learner-centered education, partnerships between educational institutions, and the implications of distance education in the future. The author predicts that by the year 2005, the largest percentage of professional degrees will be delivered at the workplace and undergraduates will do more work outside the classroom. Since technology is allowing people to become information navigators, librarians should concentrate on being information managers and finding creative ways to assist distance learners. In this context, the author advocates that librarians become involved in distance education planning teams to offer advice on what databases and resources can support the distance learner. A. Slade.

38. Slade, Alexander L. "Library Services for Distance Learning: What Librarians Need to Know!" *PNLA Quarterly* 63, no. 1 (Fall 1998): 19-21.

The focus of this conference paper is on the knowledge base for providing library services to off-campus and distance education students. To assist librarians in understanding and conceptualizing the knowledge necessary for providing effective support to distance learners, a framework is presented for identifying and organizing some of the major issues and variables in this area. The elements of the framework include terminology, characteristics of distance learners, models of service, and guidelines. Key issues in distance learning services are discussed under the headings of macro issues, external variables, logistical factors, planning and administrative issues, and service and instructional issues. The paper concludes with a list of points that summarize what librarians need to know about distance learning library services. The address for a web page that accompanied this presentation is included at the end of the article. A. Slade.

39. Slade, Alexander and Marie Kascus. "An International Comparison of Library Services for Distance Learning." In *The Eighth Off-Campus Library Services Conference Proceedings: Providence, Rhode Island, April 22 -24, 1998*, compiled by P. Steven Thomas and Maryhelen Jones. Mount Pleasant, MI: Central Michigan University, 1998, 259-97.

   To acknowledge the emerging globalism of distance learning, this paper examines the international context of off-campus library services as discussed in the literature. The paper focuses on the knowledge base of library services for distance learning, the factors influencing research and publication, and the topics and themes in the literature from the world community. Countries and geographic regions represented in the discussion include Australia, Canada, Europe, India, New Zealand, South Africa, United States, United Kingdom, and the Caribbean. Summaries of selected research are presented for each country or geographic region. Four models of service are identified: (1) use of remote centers or extended teaching campuses that provide some on-site access to library materials and resources, (2) use of unaffiliated libraries, (3) dispatch of materials from the campus library directly to the student, and (4) use of communication and information technologies for remote access to electronic resources. These models provide a framework for comparing international issues. The paper concludes by offering a glimpse of what the future holds for providing library services to distance learners. M. Kascus.

40. Watson, Elizabeth F. and Neela Jagannathan. *Library/Information Systems and Student Support: Summary and Closing Comments for the Second "Virtual Conference", 10-30 November 1998*. The Commonwealth of Learning Virtual Conferences: Pan Commonwealth Forum on Open Learning. Online. Available: http://www.col.org/forum/vc2_close.htm (Accessed April 13, 2000).

   The discussions and remarks posted on the Commonwealth of Learning's virtual conference on library services to distance learners are summarized at this website. The final report includes information on the characteristics of distance learning, management issues, services to distance learners, research, copyright issues, continuing education, and follow-up activities from the virtual conference. The contributions to the conference are archived at http://hub.col.org/li/index.html. A. Slade.

1997

41. Abbott, Thomas E. "Maine College Cyber-Programs Offered Internationally." *Journal of Library Services for Distance Education* 1, no. 1 (August 1997). Online. Available: http://www.westga.edu/~library/jlsde/vol1/1/TAbbott.html (Accessed April 13, 2000).

   In looking at the future of distance education, the author uses a fictitious news release dated 2017 about the University of Maine System's Educate the World Project to provide a framework for the discussion and to challenge our current assumptions about higher education. The Education Network of Maine is the University of Maine System's distance education operation. A recent System Telecommunication and Information Technology Task Force is providing leadership in planning the future development of distance education in Maine. The future the Task Force describes bears a strong resemblance to the scenario described in the fictitious news release. Among the topics discussed are the provision of a full range of library and information services and the technical help to make the services work. The scenario provides an opportunity to explore the changing role of future librarians. According to the author, the most valuable service that librarians can provide in the future will be training and education of faculty and students in accessing, evaluating, and applying information from the Internet. M. Kascus.

42. Adams, Chris. "The Future of Library Services for Distance Education: What Are We Doing, Where Are We Heading, What *Should* We Be Doing?" *Journal of Library Services for Distance Education* 1, no. 1 (August 1997). Online. Available: http:// www.westga.edu/library/ jlsde/vol1/1/CAdams.html (Accessed April 13, 2000).

   In discussing the future of library services for off-campus/distance education, the author gives a brief overview of what is currently happening and what should be happening. More service with less staff and funds is predicted, with technology bridging the gap. The influence politics has had on distance education is described. As libraries enter into agreements to underwrite the high cost of networked services, one element that will be especially important to the future of off-campus library services is the increasing number of cooperative ventures with other academic institutions. The issue of the growing disparity between technology-rich and technology-poor is a concern for the future. Other concerns are comparative statistics and cost analysis, the development of electronic reserves, copyright, and equitable access. M. Kascus.

43. Brophy, Peter. "Off-Campus Library Services: A Model for the Future." *Journal of Library Services for Distance Education* 1, no. 1 (August 1997). Online. Available: http://www.westga.edu/~library/jlsde/vol1/1/PBrophy.html (Accessed April 13, 2000).

   In the first issue of the *JLSDE*, the invited contributors were asked to project their views of the future of library services for distance education. The author predicts that the library of the future will be a hybrid institution in which electronic and traditional services operate in tandem. In this library of the future, librarians will need many new skills. The discussion focuses on a model being implemented in the United Kingdom, VALNOW (Virtual Academic Library of the North-West), located at the University of Central Lancashire but serving users across all of North-West England. VALNOW delivers materials, offers videoconferencing sessions with subject experts, and provides access to remote and local data sets through a cooperative network. Based on the author's experience with the VALNOW model, he comments that "we have seen the future and it works." M. Kascus.

44. Cavanagh, Tony. "Library Services for Off Campus Students: At the Crossroads?" *Journal of Library Services for Distance Education* 1, no. 1 (August 1997). Online. Available: http://www.westga.edu/~library/jlsde/vol1/1/TCavanagh.html (Accessed April 13, 2000).

   This view of the future of library services for distance education is from an Australian perspective, but has broad applicability. The vision focuses on three issues: (1) who users will be, (2) how to provide optimal services for them, and (3) how better use of information technology will change the way things are done. In the area of users, the author points to the recent emphasis on flexible delivery and lifelong learning in Australia and indicates that more students than ever before are studying off-campus. He predicts that more services will be fee-based, user satisfaction and flexible delivery will become more important, and client-centered services will be the norm. In providing optimal service, one suggestion is that libraries may choose to outsource the provision of services to other institutions. To be successful in supporting distance education in the future, libraries need to allocate adequate budget and staff for off-campus services, publicize services targeted toward various categories of users, be proactive in obtaining information and support from faculty, and provide users with a wide variety of means to request and receive information and materials. In terms of information technology, the author emphasizes that libraries will have to use a combination of electronic and traditional resources to provide optimal services to remote users. M. Kascus/A. Slade.

45. English, Julie. "The LL.B. (Distance Learning) Degree of Nottingham Law School: The Student's Perspective." *The Law Librarian* 28, no. 4 (December 1997): 207-10.

   The author recounts her experiences as a student in a distance learning law program in England. Lack of access to library resources is mentioned several times as a disadvantage or problem in the program. Nottingham Law School did not provide any access to library facilities, and local libraries were limited in their usefulness. On residential weekends, students took every opportunity to use the law school's main library but sometimes found that the librarian was unavailable and the library was locked. The author got around this problem by telephoning the librarian in advance. She observes that distance learners do like to read widely in particular subject areas but the lack of easy access to a law library does not allow for this. To compensate, many distance law students tend to purchase textbooks and additional readings. A. Slade.

46. Goodson, Carol. "I Have Seen the Future, and It Is Us!" *Journal of Library Services for Distance Education* 1, no. 1 (August 1997). Online. Available: http://www.westga.edu/~library/jlsde/vol1/1/CGoodson.html (Accessed April 13, 2000).

   In this contribution to the theme issue of *JLSDE* on the future of library services for distance education, the emphasis is on customizing library services to meet user needs. As distance education is increasingly viewed as the model for higher education in the future, so library services for distance learners will become the prototype for the future of all library service. Librarians experienced in serving remote users will lead the rest of the library world into the future, according to this author's vision. M. Kascus.

47. Jones, Maryhelen. "High Five for the Next Five: Libraries and Distance Education." *Journal of Library Services for Distance Education* 1, no. 1 (August 1997). Online. Available: http://www.westga.edu/~library/jlsde/vol1/1/MJones.html (Accessed April 13, 2000).

   In this view of the future presented in the first issue of *JLSDE*, the author begins with the premise that the mix of technologies is shaping the future of distance education. Five major trends/issues that will occur during the next five years are discussed. Trend one predicts that librarians will engage in collaborative activities with instructional and technical teams responsible for delivering distance education. Trend two predicts that copyright issues related to the new technologies will remain legally clouded in the United States. Trend three predicts that library vendors offering electronic access will seek the cooperation of librarians in tapping the market potential of distance education. Trend four predicts a radical change in higher education's institutional framework toward virtual universities. Trend five predicts that librarians will become more comfortable with asynchronous electronic sources for professional development. M. Kascus.

48. Kanjilal, Uma. "Reaching Out to Distance Learners in Library and Information Science at the Indira Gandhi National Open University." *Information Development* 13, no. 1 (March 1997): 19-22.

Multimedia-based distance teaching is used to deliver library and information science programs at Indira Gandhi National Open University (IGNOU) in India. To facilitate the students' access to CD-ROM databases and information technologies, the university has developed the concept of work centers located in different libraries and information centers throughout the country that have the basic infrastructural facilities. Details are provided about IGNOU's library and information science programs, the multimedia method of instruction, a profile of the students, and the university's efforts to instil quality into its library and information science education. A. Slade.

49. Kascus, Marie. "Converging Vision of Library Services for Off-Campus/Distance Education." *Journal of Library Services for Distance Education* 1, no. 1 (August 1997). Online. Available: http://www.westga.edu/~library/jlsde/vol1/1/MKascus.html (Accessed April 13, 2000).

In the first issue of the *JLSDE*, the invited contributors were asked to project their views of the future of library services for distance education. In this contribution, the author begins with three assumptions: (1) distance education is a growth industry for higher education, (2) off-campus students are at a disadvantage compared to their on-campus counterparts, and (3) powerful and pervasive technologies will continue to improve the delivery of education and library support at a distance. What this author predicts is a convergence of off-campus library service with the library's need to serve a growing number of remote users. The extended campus will be part of every library's future for two reasons. First, there will be a paradigm shift to the electronic library and with it will come the need for a client-centered philosophy that includes both remote users and distance learners. Second, as technology is used to further connectivity, there will be advances in the delivery of library support minimizing the physical disadvantages previously encountered. In the next five years, economies of scale will result from statewide cooperation, making it possible to achieve even greater strides in library service to the extended campus. M. Kascus.

50. Krentz, Roger F. "Library Issues in Distance Learning." *New Jersey Libraries* 30, no. 2 (Spring 1997): 11-13.

Based on his experience as a library director and a former college professor who has taught off-campus classes, the author discusses a number of current issues in providing library services to distance learners. To ensure that distance students have access to equitable library services, the author indicates that libraries need to perform the following functions: become involved in the curriculum development process, make remote access to electronic resources as seamless as possible, teach distance learners to think critically about information access and use, encourage students to integrate electronic resources into their normal research procedures, establish guidelines for document delivery and electronic reserves to make material available to distance learners while complying with copyright law, and allocate sufficient staff to adequately assist distance students. Two additional issues are identified: the need to obtain increased funding to support the use of technology and electronic resources, and the need to deliver library services to students without access to a computer. The author advocates that librarians must become partners with faculty in the curriculum development process and assume a proactive role in integrating electronic resources into the curriculum to meet the information needs of students and faculty in distance learning programs. A. Slade.

51. Lebowitz, Gloria. "After the Millennium: Library Services to Distance Education." *Journal of Library Services for Distance Education* 1, no. 1 (August 1997). Online. Available: http://www.westga.edu/~library/jlsde/vol1/1/GLebowitz. html (Accessed April 13, 2000).

   This contribution to the first issue of the *JLSDE* looks at the future in terms of the importance of library instruction, which will be provided via print, electronically, on websites, and via e-mail. When developing library services for extended campus students, the issue to be decided is whether these services will be administered independently or integrated seamlessly into existing library departments. Budget and finances will be key determining factors in making that decision. The need for economy of finances or space will cause some libraries to include the document delivery function within one unit of the library. Also discussed is the view that librarians will work more collaboratively with teaching faculty in the electronic classroom of the future. M. Kascus.

52. Lebowitz, Gloria. "Library Services to Distant Students: An Equity Issue." *Journal of Academic Librarianship* 23, no. 4 (July 1997): 303-8.

   In this discussion of the reasons for providing library services to distant students, the issue of equity is prominent. Two external influences are considered important when planning and developing extended campus library services: (1) regional and specialized accreditation and (2) guidelines for extended campus library services as established by ACRL. Also considered important is a philosophical and economic commitment on the part of the academic institution. Three models for providing library support are discussed: a department or unit dedicated to providing services, integrated or decentralized services, and branch campus structure. A recent addition to these models is the approach of providing a library home page specifically for off-campus/distant students. Preference is given to the dedicated unit structure with a librarian assigned to work with off-campus students. The author stresses that, regardless of the model chosen, institutions and libraries need to recognize that distance education/off-campus students are entitled to library service comparable to that available to on-campus students. M. Kascus.

53. Lewington, Valerie. "Finding the Fulcrum: Designing a Library Support System for Distance Learners." In *Belfast '96: Designs on Learning: Proceedings of the CoFHE Annual Study Conference Held at Stranmillis College, Belfast, 1st-4th April 1996*, edited by D. J. D. Mitchell. [London]: The Library Association. Colleges of Further and Higher Education Group, 1997, 55-58.

This paper contains the author's notes from a workshop conducted at the 1996 CoFHE conference. The workshop examined user education sessions for distance learners, the distance learner's motivation, ways to provide library services to distance learners, and how library staff would like the services to be seen by clients, the employing institution, and colleagues. A. Slade.

54. Orr, Debbie and Margaret Appleton. "New Opportunities for Remote Students." *Journal of Library Services for Distance Education* 1, no. 1 (August 1997). Online. Available: http://www.westga.edu/~library/jlsde/vol1/1/DOrr_MAppleton.html (Accessed April 13, 2000).

The authors discuss their view of the future of library services for distance education from the perspective of Central Queensland University (CQU) in Australia. At CQU, there are many methods of providing library instruction to distance education students, including printed guides, computer-assisted learning (CAL) programs, and electronically mediated tutorials that use CU-SeeMe videoconferencing software. The World Wide Web is being explored as another way of delivering instruction. CQU's Virtual Residential program shows potential for the delivery of distance education in the future. Projects conducted at the CQU Library have indicated that it is possible to offer information literacy programs to all off-campus students, and the library is more intimately involved in the teaching and learning process and its design than ever before. M. Kascus.

55. Peters, Diane. "Delivering Distance Education: The Evolving Nature of Post-Secondary Education." *CAUT Bulletin Online* (Canadian Association of University Teachers) 44, no. 10 (December 1997). Online. Available: http://www.caut.ca/English/Bulletin/97_dec/distance.htm (Accessed April 13, 2000).

This short article outlines various issues pertaining to library services for distance education. The topics covered include resource sharing among libraries, library involvement in program planning, use of technology, financing library services, delivery services from the campus library, and bibliographic instruction. The author cautions that use of technology for teaching and learning may be an excuse for downsizing and that librarians may be replaced by technicians or support staff in the delivery of services to distance learners. This could result in a focus on techniques of information retrieval without providing students with adequate training in the assessment and evaluation of the information retrieved. A. Slade.

56. Slade, Alexander L. "Some Observations on the Future of Library Services for Off-Campus and Distance Learning." *Journal of Library Services for Distance Education* 1, no. 1 (August 1997). Online. Available: http://www.westga.edu/~library/jlsde/vol1/1/ASlade.html (Accessed April 13, 2000).

The author's views on the future of library services for distance learning are discussed in relation to services provided at the University of Victoria (UVic). A conservative perspective of the future is offered, reflecting the author's experience with distance learners. Because there is presently no requirement for UVic's off-campus students to have electronic access to the university, he predicts that it will take several years before the students are fully hooked up to the Internet and able to search independently for information resources. In addition to requirements of the institution, other factors influencing students' use of information technology will be developments in the home entertainment and communications industries, the provision of clear instructions to the students on how to obtain remote access to information resources, the availability of low-cost or no-cost access to electronic resources, the availability of appropriate computer resources and access privileges at local educational centers, and the provision of effective bibliographic instruction on how to conduct effective searches of electronic products. The author indicates that the next five years will see a continuation of traditional off-campus library services combined with a steady growth of student independence in information access. A. Slade.

57. Stephens, Kate and Lorna Unwin. "The Heart of the Matter: Libraries, Distance Education and Independent Thinking." *Journal of Library Services for Distance Education* 1, no. 1 (August 1997). Online. Available: http://www.westga.edu/~library/jlsde/vol1/1/KStephens_LUnwin.html (Accessed April 13, 2000).

The authors' position on the future of library services for distance education is that advances in technology will not necessarily help distance learners become more autonomous. They may lead to further student isolation as more emphasis is placed on prepackaged programmed learning and less emphasis is placed on reading and critical thinking. The vision described is one of increased collaboration between academics and librarians in integrating electronic access with traditional learning. The importance of a learning agenda that includes critical thinking is stressed. The librarian will need to play a central role in the learning process of the future, if there is to be a balance between the marketplace and a commitment to the development of students as self-directed learners. M. Kascus.

58. Watson, Elizabeth F. *Distance Librarianship: What, Why, How?* Paper presented at the Commonwealth Library Association Workshop on Library Services to Distance Learners, Harare, Zimbabwe, August 6, 1997. Available from: Learning Resource Centre, University of the West Indies, Cave Hill Campus, Bridgetown, Barbados.

Distance librarianship is concerned with the provision and delivery of quality library and information services to anyone associated with distance education. This paper provides a broad overview of important issues within the practice of distance librarianship. These issues include philosophy and mission, standards and guidelines, management issues, resources, information and library support services, reference services and bibliographic instruction, document delivery, interlibrary cooperation, and professional sources to support the practice of distance librarianship. The paper also examines distance librarianship in relation to the characteristics of distance education, the literature on library services for distance learning, and Third World issues. See #20 in the second bibliography for a related paper and #19 in this volume for updated information on the source of that paper. A. Slade.

1996

59. Kascus, Marie A. "Library Support for Quality in Distance Education: A Research Agenda." In *Distance Education Symposium 3: Instruction: Selected Papers Presented at the Third Distance Education Research Symposium, The Pennsylvania State University, May 1995*, edited by Michael F. Beaudoin. Research Monographs No. 12. University Park, PA: American Center for the Study of Distance Education, The Pennsylvania State University, 1996, 72-82.

This paper begins with the assumption that library support is central to the design, delivery, organization, and administration of quality distance education programs. A brief historical perspective on library support for distance learners is followed by a review of the literature in terms of content, change, and trends. While the body of literature is growing at a rapid pace, it remains largely descriptive and non-analytical, as is true of much of the literature of distance education itself. The majority of the publications report practice and application rather than research findings. The three principal research methods that have been used are user studies, library surveys, and case studies. What is needed is a greater emphasis on developing an analytical framework that can be used to make broad generalizations about improving practice. In looking to the future of library support for the distance learner, the research focus needs to be on (1) establishing evaluative criteria that can be used to measure performance, (2) collecting data and testing assumptions through carefully planned research, and (3) using the results of that research to forge a common methodology that is valid across institutions. M. Kascus.

60. Stephens, Kate. "The Tale of the Autonomous Distance Learner: Just Another Legitimating Narrative?" In *Going the Distance: Teaching, Learning and Researching in Distance Education*, edited by Nicki Hedge. Sheffield: Division of Education, University of Sheffield, 1996, 50-60.

This paper questions the validity of a theory of learner autonomy in distance learning that does not include some element of independent library use. The author contends that such a theory is academically suspect and may be regarded as a "legitimating narrative" for distance learning rather than a sound basis for educational practice. Various works on educational theory, distance learning, and discourse analysis are used as the basis for a critical examination of autonomous learning. A need is identified for empirical research to test how the theoretical constructs of learner autonomy correspond to reality. Several questions are posed about library use in distance learning in relation to the practices of course providers, librarians, and students. The author indicates that a research project underway at the University of Sheffield (see #637 in this volume) may provide some provisional answers to these questions and shed some light on the issue of autonomous learning as a justificatory discourse in distance learning. A. Slade.

61. Watson, Elizabeth F. *Distance Librarianship: New Partnerships and Changing Relationships*. Paper presented at the 26th Conference of the Association of Caribbean University Research and Institutional Libraries (ACURIL), May 19-24, 1996, St. Martin. Available from: Learning Resource Centre, University of the West Indies, Cave Hill Campus, Bridgetown, Barbados.

The term "distance librarianship" is used to connote the practice of providing library services to distance learners. This area of librarianship is examined in terms of its knowledge base, the partnerships important for the delivery of quality services, the growth of distance education, the library and information needs of distance learners, relationships with distance educators and distance administrators, the provision of library services in the Third World, and professional education to support distance library services. Partnerships in distance librarianship involve a variety of stakeholders, including academics, course developers, instructional designers, computer specialists, and other libraries. Non-traditional partnerships with entities such as courier companies, commercial information providers, and telecommunications carriers are also significant relationships for the delivery of services to distance learners. It is emphasized that distance librarianship differs from traditional library services in many respects and requires librarians to be innovative and proactive in developing new partnerships, strengthening existing relationships, and delivering information and materials in a timely manner, to support the learning needs of distance students. See #20 in the second bibliography for a related paper and #19 in this volume for updated information on the source of that paper. A. Slade.

1995

---

62. Behrens, Shirley J. "Lifelong Learning in the New Education and Training System." *Mousaion* 13, nos. 1/2 (1995): 250-63.

    The concept of lifelong learning is discussed in relation to policy documents and frameworks in South Africa, its context in formal education and training systems, the characteristics of lifelong learners, and the significance of information literacy. South African policy documents that emphasize lifelong learning fail to mention the importance of information skills in the learning process. The author notes that provincial education departments will need to incorporate information literacy into their definitions of lifelong learning for curriculum development purposes; otherwise the concept of lifelong learning is relatively meaningless in the new South African education and training dispensation. A. Slade.

63. Heseltine, Richard. "End-user Services and the Electronic Library." *OCLC Newsletter*, no. 215 (May/June 1995): 19-21.

    In a speech at the OCLC Europe Users' Forum, the author looks at trends that will affect academic libraries in the future. These trends include increasing enrollments, more older students with a wider range of qualifications and academic backgrounds, more part-time students, an expansion of distance learning programs, and a shift to a more flexible educational system. Heseltine predicts a total transformation of the teaching and learning environment, which will in turn affect the provision and use of information. In this new environment, libraries will need to focus on actual user needs and develop more extensive end-user services that are not restricted by time or location. Emerging from this will be an organizational structure based on functionally oriented, collaborating teams in which individuals perform specific rather than generic roles in areas such as resource management, user support, document supply, network management, and external relations. A. Slade.

64. Lebowitz, Gloria. "What Is This Thing Called ...?" *Colorado Libraries* 21, no. 1 (Spring 1995): 6-8.

   The terminology applied to extended campus library services is discussed, and similarities and differences between off-campus and distance education are noted. A historical perspective is provided that traces off-campus education in the United States back to 1873, when Anna Eliot Ticknor established correspondence programs for women known as the "Society to Encourage Studies at Home." The various stages in the development of distance education are described as correspondence courses, delivery by voice via radio, video, and computer. Also discussed are the opportunities available through off-campus education, the characteristics of the people who are taking advantage of these opportunities, the types of support services that are available, and how off-campus and distance education affect us as librarians. M. Kascus.

65. Simpson, Cathy. "Issues in the Provision of Library Services to Distance Learners." In *Language in Distance Education: How Far Can We Go? Proceedings of the Joint NCELTR/WA AMES Working Conference, Edith Cowan University, Perth, 10-12 July 1994*, edited by Sandra Gollin. Sydney, NSW: National Centre for English Language Teaching and Research, Macquarie University, 1995, 126-37.

   Drawing on the published literature, the author examines a broad range of issues on the provision of library services for distance education, including library services to distance learners in Australia and overseas, equity of access for remote students, document delivery, technological options in remote services, staffing issues, planning and management, and costs involved in providing remote library services. In terms of costs, the author estimates a cost of $118.70 (Australian) to process a transaction for a distance student. Particular attention is paid to the role of the librarian in supporting the distance education curriculum and the relationships between lecturer, student, and librarian. It is stressed that communication is vital in this context and that librarians need to explain how the tools available to them can help users solve their problems, talk to lecturers as well as students, and get more involved in the design of courses and the development of curriculum. A. Slade.

66. Slade, Alexander L. "North American Research Priorities." *DESIGnation*, no. 8 (August 1995): 4-5.

   This contribution to the newsletter of the Australian Distance Education Special Interest Group summarizes the results of a survey conducted in 1994 by the Research Committee of the ACRL Extended Campus Library Services Section. Respondents to the survey itemized a total of three dozen research topics they would like to see addressed. The top two priorities that emerged from the survey were (1) bibliographic instruction for distance learners and (2) use of new technologies to enhance library support for off-campus students. For a related article, see #67 below. A. Slade.

67. Slade, Alexander L. "Open Hearing on Research Priorities: A Background Paper." In *The Seventh Off-Campus Library Services Conference Proceedings: San Diego, California, October 25-27, 1995*, compiled by Carol J. Jacob. Mount Pleasant, MI: Central Michigan University, 1995, 403-5.

To establish a context for the Open Hearing on Research Priorities held at the Seventh Off-campus Library Services Conference, this paper outlines the background and results of a survey conducted in 1994 by the Research Committee of the ACRL Distance Learning Section (formerly Extended Campus Library Services Section). A questionnaire was developed to allow librarians to select five important areas of extended campus library services requiring research. Thirty-one potential research topics were identified and are listed. For a related article, see #66 above. M. Kascus.

1994

68. Cleveland, Patricia L. and Elaine K. Bailey. "Organizing for Distance Education." In *Proceedings of the Twenty-Seventh Hawaii International Conference on System Sciences: Volume IV: Information Systems: Collaboration Technology, Organizational Systems and Technology*, edited by Jay F. Nunamaker, Jr. and Ralph H. Sprague, Jr. Los Alamitos, CA: IEEE Computer Society Press, 1994, 134-41.

Two academics from the College of Business Administration at the University of Hawaii present a "field-tested" case illustration of the problems and opportunities inherent in developing complex distributed educational systems through distance education technologies. In the context of examining logistical issues related to distance education course delivery, the authors discuss library support in terms of the problems in providing adequate resources to students. Enabling the students to have remote access to electronic resources is seen as a solution to these problems. This paper is noteworthy in that it is one of the few works by academic staff to include library services in a discussion of distance education. A. Slade.

1993

69. Fabian, K. and L. Elias. "Distance Teaching and Library Services for Universities in Central Slovakia." In *Teleteaching: Proceedings of the IFIP TC3 Third Teleteaching Conference, Teleteaching 93, Trondheim, Norway, 20-25 August 1993*, edited by Gordon Davies and Brian Samways. Amsterdam: Elsevier Science, 1993, 223-27.

The objective of the Networking for Universities in Central Slovakia project, funded by the European Community, was to build an elementary networking infrastructure for three university institutions in one city in Central Slovakia: College of Education, College of Economics, and Institute of Automation and Communication. Following connection of the sites via leased lines, the project intends to add distance teaching and library applications to the network infrastructure.

Computer equipment and library software will have to be acquired to support the distance teaching program. A. Slade.

News Items

1999

70. Buckstead, Jonathan. "Conference Circuit: Are You Looking for a Good Distance Learning Library Support Model?" *College & Research Libraries News* 60, no. 6 (June 1999): 443-44.

One of the sessions at ACRL's 9th National Conference was titled "Going the Distance: Library Services to a Global Community." This brief report summarizes the content of the session. One speaker emphasized the increase in distance learning throughout the world and the characteristics of adult learners. A second presenter outlined the steps in developing an effective distance learning library service program. These steps include establishing a task force to oversee goal setting, offering as many resources and services as possible, and promoting the resources and services that are offered. A. Slade.

71. Orgeron, Elizabeth. "Conference Circuit: An Integrated Approach to Supporting Distance Education." *College & Research Libraries News* 60, no. 7 (July/August 1999): 552.

Webster University's library support for distance learners was highlighted in a session at ACRL's 9th National Conference. This short report summarizes some of the main points of the session. Presenters discussed the Web-based module "Passports," which provides students and faculty with access to online full-text databases, instructional tutorials, connections to other libraries, and the basics of searching the Internet. According to the presenters, the crux of integrating traditional with technological services is careful evaluation of needs, setting goals, and creating a Request for Proposal (RFP) to define what is needed from a vendor and a product. A. Slade.

72. Weiser, Allison. "PA Approves Phoenix Campus." *Library Journal* 124, no. 8 (May 1, 1999): 19-20.

This news item reports that the University of Phoenix, a for-profit institution, has received approval to open campuses in Pennsylvania. Pennsylvania students will have access to the university's virtual library of databases and full-text resources. Some people in the library field are skeptical about the University of Phoenix's ability to provide adequate services through its virtual library. The article notes that University of Phoenix students are being encouraged to use local libraries and refers to the concern expressed by an author in a previous issue of *Library Journal* (#26 above) about the strain being placed on the collections, services, and staff of non-profit libraries by for-profit institutions. A. Slade.

1998

73. Bannister, Marion, Jennifer Vaughan, Beverley Broad, and Carol Mills. "ALIA DESIG Conference: Charles Sturt University-Wagga Wagga Campus, Wagga Wagga NSW, December 5-6, 1997." *DESIGnation*, nos. 15-16 (September 1998): 2-5.

   A two-day conference on library services for distance education was held in 1997 in Wagga Wagga, Australia. The theme of the conference was "Shifting Sands," reflecting the concern about the increasing use of technologies in library services. Nine papers were presented at the conference, covering a range of topics including support issues in online teaching, library services for postgraduate distance education students, an electronic delivery management system, library services for prisoners, organizational restructuring, and remote access to electronic resources. For information on seven of the papers, see #150, #156, #312, #616, #688, #694, and #695 in this volume. A. Slade.

74. Burich, Nancy J. "Conference Circuit: Library Services to Distant Students." *College & Research Libraries News* 59, no. 9 (October 1998): 679.

   This news report highlights the panel discussion "Library Services to Distant Students: Values, Ethics, and Cooperation" held at the 1998 American Library Association conference. The following topics were covered by the panelists: the development of Web-based courses at the University of Maryland University College, the Florida Distance Learning Library Initiative, and copyright issues in distance learning. A. Slade.

75. Clarke, Zoë. "Distance No Object in Delivering Services." *Library Association Record* 100, no. 2 (February 1998): 93.

   The "Libraries Without Walls 2" conference was held in Greece in 1997. The conference attracted 52 participants from 14 countries and gave delegates an opportunity to exchange information about library services for distance and life-long learning. The conference objectives and presentations of the various speakers are summarized in this news article. For the proceedings of the conference, see #13 in this volume. A. Slade.

76. Davis, Mary Ellen. "News from the Field: ACRL Section Renamed Distance Learning Section." *College & Research Libraries News* 59, no. 7 (July/August 1998): 485-86.

   This news item announces the mail ballot approval of the Extended Campus Library Services Section (ECLSS) name change to Distance Learning Section (DLS). The name change is intended to update the image of the section and to clarify the nature of its programs. It is a reflection of the marked shift that has taken place in the area of extended campus, off-campus, and distance education in the decade since ECLSS was formed in 1990. M. Kascus.

77. Hinchliffe, Lisa Janicke. "Conference Circuit: From Black-and-White TV to Rich Interactive Learning Environments: The 14th Annual Conference on Distance Teaching and Learning." *College & Research Libraries News* 59, no. 9 (October 1998): 683-85.

The 14th Annual Conference on Distance Teaching and Learning held in Madison, Wisconsin, in 1998 attracted over 1,000 international participants from the areas of education, business, industry, and government. The activities and presentations at the conference are summarized in this report. The author notes that libraries were well represented in the concurrent sessions, with three papers focusing on the opportunities and challenges in providing access to library services and resources for remote users. Three additional papers addressed issues concerning online instruction in library research skills. For information on the individual papers, see #446, #489, #514, #543, #731 and #738 in this volume. A. Slade.

78. "InterLibrary Lending for Distance Learning." *Document Supply News* (British Library), no. 59 (September 1998): 1.

This news item reports that the University of Newcastle has approached British Library Document Supply Centre (DSC) to discuss the provision of interlibrary loan services to distance learning students. The DSC has two options for providing these services: a simple package based on the ARTEmail format allowing requests to be channelled through to the Automated Request Processing system and use of the Inside Web database, which provides integrated search and direct order facilities on the Web. A one-year project is now being considered to develop the e-mail option for handling ILL requests for distance learners by integrating it within existing automated ILL systems and procedures in UK universities. It is noted that the proposed DSC service to distance learners has generated considerable interest from other universities, especially those with students in overseas countries. For further information on the DSC service, see #303 in this volume. A. Slade.

79. LaGuardia, Cheryl. "Conference Circuit: The Eighth Off-Campus Library Services Conference: A Look at One of the Major Growth Areas in Academic Libraries." *College & Research Libraries News* 59, no. 6 (June 1998): 418, 431.

A short report is given on the Eighth Off-Campus Library Services Conference sponsored by Central Michigan University (CMU) and held in Providence Rhode Island April 22-24, 1998. Conference attendees came from the United States, Canada, South Africa, and the United Kingdom. Among the off-campus services issues discussed at the conference were remote service program planning, partnerships with individuals and institutions, copyright and licensing, telelearning, electronic reserves, staffing, outcomes assessment, and marketing. Additional topics included in the concurrent paper presentations were course-specific web pages, Web tutorials, Picture-Tel-based instruction, partnerships among libraries to serve remote clientele, and collaboration between faculty and librarians for information literacy. For the conference proceedings, see #16 in this bibliography. M. Kascus.

80. Pettman, Ian. "Conference Report: Libraries Without Walls 2: The Delivery of Library Services to Distant Users, The Second Conference, 17-20 September 1997, Hotel Delfinia, Molyvos, Lesvos, Greece." *New Library World* 99, no. 1139 (1998): 43-44.

The "Libraries Without Walls 2" conference, held in Greece in 1997, attracted 52 delegates from 14 countries. The themes underlying the conference papers included collaboration among libraries, commitment to services, practicality in service delivery, lifelong learning, equity in access to services, human factors, negotiation, use of technology, professionalism, innovation in services, and vision. For the proceedings of the conference, see #13 in this volume. A. Slade.

81. Thomas, P. Steven. "Library Services Conference Spotlights Access Needs of Off-Campus Users." *Library Hi Tech News*, no. 153 (June 1998): 15, 17.

The Eighth Off-Campus Library Services Conference, held in Providence, Rhode Island, in April 1998, attracted a record-breaking 220 participants from five countries. Three themes emerged from the 27 presentations: bibliographic instruction and information literacy, user access, and program development and evaluation. This news item highlights the activities and presentations at the conference and comments on issues discussed at previous Off-Campus Library Services Conferences. A. Slade.

82. "UNM Virtual Library: The University of New Mexico Provides Distance Library Services to College Students from 15 States." *Hispanic Outlook in Higher Education* 8, no. 21 (June 19, 1998): 10-11.

The University of New Mexico General Library (UNMGL) won the contract to provide library services to students of the Western Governors University (WGU), a virtual university involving 16 states in the United States. UNMGL will be responsible for the creation and ongoing operation of WGU's Central Library Resource. In that role, UNMGL has created a library web page for WGU students and faculty that provides access to electronic library resources including UNMGL's online catalogue, OCLC's FirstSearch service, and the H. W. Wilson full-text database. Other services will include library instruction guides, a delivery service for books and photocopies of articles, telephone and e-mail reference services, and electronic reserve materials. A. Slade.

83. York, Vicky. "Libraries and the Western Governors University [Part 2]." *MPLA Newsletter* (Mountain Plains Library Association) 42, no. 4 (February 1998): 7.

In the continuation of this news article (see #98 below), it is noted that Texas became the 17th state to participate in the Western Governors University. In December 1997, the University of New Mexico was selected to establish and operate the WGU Central Library Resource. The role of the Central Library Resource will be to provide comprehensive library services to WGU students. These services will include four basic components: a website with links to consortia resources; online access to full-text and citation databases; Internet service accounts; and reference, document delivery, interlibrary loan, and technical assistance. A. Slade.

1997

84. Barton, Mary Ann. "Distance Learning Issues." *College & Research Libraries News* 58, no. 6 (June 1997): 391.

This brief news article reports on two presentations on distance learning given at ACRL's 8th National Conference in Nashville. The first, "Determining User Needs in Order to Provide Library Services," is a report on an electronic survey of distance education students at Nova Southeastern University. The second, "Expanding the Role of the Library in Teaching and Learning: Distance Learning Initiatives," is a report of the examination of distance education issues by three librarians at Southern Illinois University. M. Kascus.

85. Davis, Mary Ellen. "News from the Field: ECLSS Develops Data Collection Form." *College & Research Libraries News* 58, no. 1 (January 1997): 7.

An announcement is made about the development of a standardized form for collecting data on library services provided to distance students. This form, the Uniform Statistics Data Collection (USDC) form, was piloted by members of the Extended Campus Library Services Section (ECLSS), now called the Distance Learning Section (DLS). The document collected data in three parts: materials transactions (aspects related to students' requests and how filled), information transactions (referral/reference questions and instruction sessions), and information collected by branch libraries. M. Kascus.

86. Davis, Mary Ellen. "News from the Field: NCES Issues Report on Distance Education." *College & Research Libraries News* 58, no. 10 (November 1997): 689.

This news item announces the National Center for Education Statistics (NCES) report "Distance Education in Higher Education Institutions." The report is referred to as the "first comprehensive national survey of distance education by colleges." Findings from the report are that access to library resources varied depending on type of library resource, 56% of the institutions offered an electronic link to the library, 62% had cooperative agreements for students to use other libraries, 45% assigned library staff to help distance education students, and 39% made library collections available at remote sites. M. Kascus.

87. Eberhart, George M. "U of Northern Colorado Cuts Extended Services." *American Libraries* 28, no. 7 (August 1997): 22-23.

This brief news item announces the decision of the University of Northern Colorado to eliminate its Extended Campus Library Services program effective June 30, 1997. The rationale for the cut was the fact that the service had been funded by the College of Continuing Education, which faced a budget reduction that year, according to the Associate Dean. M. Kascus.

88. "Florida Libraries, OCLC, SOLINET to Build Distance Learning Library." *Advanced Technology Libraries* 26, no. 11 (November 1997): 5-6.

The development of the Florida Distance Learning Library Initiative is announced in this news item. The project involves a partnership between Florida community college, university, and public libraries together with the Southeastern Library Network (SOLINET) and OCLC. The intention is to create an electronic library that will include access to online catalogues, bibliographic databases, electronic journals, online class reserve materials, electronic course syllabi, patron-initiated interlibrary loan, and computerized reference and referral services. For details on the Distance Learning Library Initiative, see #247 in this volume. A. Slade.

89. Jones, Maryhelen. "DE Library Leaders Deliver Instruction Differently—Creatively!" *College & Research Libraries News* 58, no. 7 (July/August 1997): 485-86.

The ACRL program "Library Instruction for Off-Campus Students: Four Views of Services and Support" is described in this news item. One view (Indiana University-Purdue University-Columbus) gives a branch librarian's perspective. A second view (Central Michigan University) describes introducing off-campus students to OCLC's FirstSearch databases on the Web. A third view (Oregon State University) describes a Web tutorial used for instruction. A fourth view (Linfield College) reports on a teaching reference librarian support initiative in an English writing course. M. Kascus.

90. "Library Service for Distance Learning." *Library Systems* 17, no. 11 (1997): 87.

This is one of the many news announcements about the development of the Florida Distance Learning Library Initiative. For the general details of the announcement, see #88 above. For details on the Distance Learning Library Initiative, see #247 in this volume. A. Slade.

91. Miller, William and Thomas E. Abbott. "Improving Distance Learning Through Technology." *College & Research Libraries News* 58, no. 6 (June 1997): 394-95.

A short report is given on a preconference workshop entitled "Improving Distance Learning Through New Applications of Technology," held at the 1997 meeting of the American Association for Higher Education. At this preconference, librarians described to the audience of deans and teaching faculty how libraries fit into the asynchronous classroom. Librarians from George Washington University Virginia Campus, National-Louis University, and the University of Maine System described their experiences providing distance library services. An open discussion on a variety of distance education issues followed the workshop. M. Kascus.

92. "OCLC and SOLINET Build Distance Learning Library in Florida." *Library Hi Tech News*, no. 148 (December 1997): 26.

This is one of the many news announcements about the development of the Florida Distance Learning Library Initiative. For the general details of the announcement, see #88 above. For details on the Distance Learning Library Initiative, see #247 in this volume. A. Slade.

93. "OCLC and SOLINET Building Electronic Library." *Library Journal* 122, no. 20 (December 1997): 27.

This is another of the many news announcements about the development of the Florida Distance Learning Library Initiative. For the general details of the announcement, see #88 above. For details on the Distance Learning Library Initiative, see #247 in this volume. A. Slade.

94. Senior, Karen. "Libraries Without Walls 2: The Delivery of Library Services to Distant Users." *SCONUL Newsletter* (Standing Conference of National and University Libraries), no. 12 (Winter 1997): 22-23.

The papers delivered at the "Libraries Without Walls 2" conference, held in Greece in 1997, addressed principal strategic issues in the provision of library services to distant users. Emphasis was on international, regional, and sectoral approaches to best practice, delineating how participants were attempting to achieve their particular vision of support to distance learners. Conference themes included service development, use of information technology, research project work, human resources issues, and lifelong learning. The presentations of the various speakers are grouped by theme and summarized in this article. For the proceedings of the conference, see #13 in this volume. A. Slade.

95. Storey, Tom. "Florida Libraries, SOLINET and OCLC to Build a Distance Learning Library." *OCLC Newsletter*, no. 230 (November/December 1997): 5-7.

OCLC announces the development of the Florida Distance Learning Library Initiative in this news report. OCLC's contributions to the Initiative include access to databases of the FirstSearch service via a dedicated link and the Internet, and SiteSearch software for managing local and remote resources. For more details on the Distance Learning Library Initiative, see #88 and #247 in this volume. A. Slade.

96. "The University of South Florida Tampa Campus Library Awarded Grant." *Information Outlook* 1, no. 2 (December 1997): 8.

This news item announces that the University of South Florida Tampa Campus Library has been awarded a $100,000 grant by the Florida Distance Learning Initiative to establish a Reference and Referral Center that will act as a library service for students and faculty participating in distance learning across the state. For details on the Distance Learning Library Initiative, see #247 in this volume. A. Slade.

97. Weber, Dave. "Distance Education Workshop Held at AACL." *Letter of the LAA* (Library Association of Alberta), no. 111 (November 1997): 8.

The Alberta Association of College Librarians sponsored a half-day workshop on library services for distance learning in 1997. Topics covered in the workshop included characteristics of distance learners, financing library initiatives, lobbying for campus and client support, service delivery, and recommendations for libraries embarking on distance programs. The workshop concluded with the prediction that the future of library service to distance learners will be a hybrid of methods, with telephones, answering machines, and postal delivery working alongside website development, online request forms, and remote access to research databases. A. Slade.

98. York, Vicky. "Libraries and the Western Governors University [Part 1]." *MPLA Newsletter* (Mountain Plains Library Association) 42, no. 3 (December 1997): 9-10.

This news item outlines the development and mandate of the Western Governors University (WGU), a virtual university formed through a collaboration of 16 states in the western United States. It is noted that, from the beginning, the designers of WGU have sought input and involvement from the library community. Through those discussions it was made clear that library services needed to be an integral part of the WGU. At the time of writing, an RFP (Request for Proposals) to provide a central library service for the WGU had been developed and distributed. For the second part of this article, see #83 above. A. Slade.

99. Young, Ann-Christe. "Grants and Acquisitions: The Tampa Campus Library." *College & Research Libraries News* 58, no. 11 (December 1997): 816.

An announcement is made about a grant to the University of South Florida Tampa Campus to establish the state's Distance Learning Library Initiative Reference and Referral Center. The Center will serve as a library for students participating in distance learning programs who have reference questions. The Center will make information available through a variety of communication modes, including a toll-free number, e-mail, and the World Wide Web. M. Kascus.

1996

100. Bean, Rick. "Conference Circuit: Off-Campus Services: From the Margins to the Center." *College & Research Libraries News* 57, no. 1 (January 1996): 35-36.

This brief news article is a report on the Seventh Off-campus Library Services Conference held in San Diego, October 25-27, 1995. The conference attracted participants from the United States, Canada, England, South Africa, India, Ireland, New Zealand, Sweden, and Australia. Among the major conference themes and issues were the relationships between accreditation agencies and institutions with extended campuses, how off-campus librarians support their institutions' international programs, and the need for off-campus librarians to teach students and faculty about electronic resources as well as research and library use skills. M. Kascus.

1995

101. Cavanagh, Tony. "Some Notes on an Overseas Study Tour." *DESIGnation*, no. 8 (August 1995): 5-6.

In 1994, the author visited the United States and England to investigate document supply services at CARL UnCover and the British Library Document Supply Centre. While in the United States, the author also visited the University of Wyoming to learn about its library services for off-campus students. In England, he contacted the University of Central Lancashire to inquire about the European BIBDEL project on the delivery of academic library services to distant users. In this brief article, he reports on the findings of his visits and inquiries, noting comparisons in the provision of off-campus library services between Australia and other countries. A. Slade.

102. Dancik, Deborah. "Conference Report: Distance Education: A Fad or the Future?" *College & Research Libraries News* 56, no. 4 (April 1995): 243.

This news item reports on three presentations at the Association of College and Research Libraries (ACRL) University Libraries Section (ULS) Current Topics Discussion Group program. One presenter raised the question of whether distance education is a fad or the future. A second presenter made a distinction between distance learning and distance education, the latter implying a particular pedagogy rather than having focus on the learner. A third presenter saw distance education as an opportunity for new delivery methods and collaboration. It was evident from the discussion that there is a growing awareness of distance education. Issues that need further discussion are the need for partnerships for improving access, issues of accreditation, and strategies for funding support for distance learning. M. Kascus.

103. Sandore, Beth. "LITA Telecommunications Interest Group. American Library Association Conference, Miami Beach, June 1994." *Technical Services Quarterly* 13, no. 1 (1995): 43-46.

This is a concise report of the LITA Telecommunications Interest Group program on developments in electronic networks and the challenges of providing distance education and library services to a diverse group of learners. Following the introductory remarks, three speakers addressed different aspects of networking and its effect on distance education. A lively discussion followed the formal program. This program integrated technical discussion with groups interested in using technology to enhance library service and programs. M. Kascus.

104. Watson, Elizabeth. "Jamaica Hosts COMLA Workshop: Library Services to Distance Learners." *COMLA Newsletter* (Commonwealth Library Association), no. 86 (February 1995): 7-8.

The Commonwealth Library Association sponsored a workshop on library services to distance learners in Kingston, Jamaica, in 1994. Forty librarians, distance educators, and administrators from 13 countries attended the two-day workshop. Themes addressed in the workshop included macro issues in supporting distance learners, user services and needs, experiences at specific institutions, and the library/distance education interface. Three small group sessions focused on service delivery, collection development, and user services. For further information, see #4 in the second bibliography. A. Slade.

1994

105. "Open Learning Update: Support for Public Libraries." *APLIS* 7, no. 4 (December 1994): 184.

This brief news item reports that the Open Learning Agency of Australia (OLA) has undertaken a review of the library service implications of OLA university programs. Of OLA students surveyed in 1994, 56% used public libraries while 46% used academic libraries. A number of recommendations have been made to encourage OLA students to use university libraries and to therefore reduce the demand on public libraries. A. Slade.

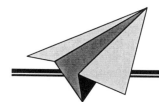

CHAPTER 3

Role of Libraries in Distance, Open, and Lifelong Learning

This chapter includes works that focus primarily on the role of academic and public libraries in supporting distance learning, open learning, and lifelong learning.

General

For other general works that pertain to the role of the library, consult the Subject Index under the headings: "flexible learning," "lifelong learning," "open learning," and "role of the library in distance learning."

1998

---

106. Allen, Margaret (Peg). "Library Services for Nurses in School: Where Do You Draw the Line?" *National Network* 22, no. 4 (April 1998): 7, 25.

With reference to discussions on the Medlib-L listerver, the author examines the topic of hospital libraries providing services to staff nurses who are enrolled in nursing education programs, especially those offered by distance education. The issues covered include the model of nursing education in the United States, access to nursing education, the benefits of serving nurses through hospital libraries, the budget and staff problems faced by hospital libraries, standards of service and the need for an information management plan, the considerations of academic libraries regarding support of distance education students, and multitype library solutions. The author recommends collaboration and partnerships between academic and hospital libraries to improve services for nurses engaged in higher education. A. Slade.

107. Brophy, Peter. "Libraries Without Walls: From Vision to Reality." In *Libraries Without Walls 2: The Delivery of Library Services to Distant Users*, edited by Peter Brophy, Shelagh Fisher, and Zoë Clarke. London: Library Association Publishing, 1998, 6-13.

The introductory paper in the proceedings of the second "Libraries Without Walls" conference discusses the vision of the conference, the purpose of libraries, the functions of the electronic library, and the concept of the hybrid library. The vision of the conference was "every user, regardless of his or her physical location, should be able to use all library services." The purpose of libraries is viewed in terms of the transformation of data to information to knowledge and the reverse process of knowledge to information to data. The concept of the hybrid library is illustrated by a brief description of the University of the Highlands and Islands Project in Scotland. A. Slade.

108. McManus, Mark G. R. "The Way I See It: Neither Pandora nor Cassandra: Library Services and Distance Education in the Next Decade." *College & Research Libraries News* 59, no. 6 (June 1998): 432-35.

In this futuristic view of library services in support of distance education, it is suggested that libraries may not be a key player in distance education. Technology mediated distance education, as exemplified by the virtual university (i.e., the Western Governors University), cannot be ignored by libraries. Several suggestions are made to assure that libraries and librarians play a role in distance education in the current technological environment. Librarians must be involved early in the development process for the distance education program. They need to work with distance education faculty to extend library instruction to the electronic environment. Librarians also need to view the library as a learning place and not a warehouse, and library service needs to be seen as more than pointing to resources. Librarians must demonstrate the added value of the library to the educational process. "Libraries must be active, political, and effective builders of learning *knowledge structures* " for their survival. M. Kascus.

109. Owen, Maurice. "Hyperlinks to Reality and the Knowledge Matrix." In *Libraries Without Walls 2: The Delivery of Library Services to Distant Users*, edited by Peter Brophy, Shelagh Fisher, and Zoë Clarke. London: Library Association Publishing, 1998, 47-51.

In this theoretical paper, the author considers the role of libraries in the "knowledge matrix" that is being shaped by the current electronic technologies. A significant question in this regard is how libraries will interface with other information providers or "knowledge keepers." Using the visual arts as an example, four key elements in the knowledge matrix are identified: the discipline (e.g., visual arts), librarianship, pedagogy, and Internet-related technologies. Discipline-specific World Wide Web guidance systems or conceptual indices integrated into library networks are suggested as a means to link all four elements as well as to promote distance learning and encourage library usage. A. Slade.

1997

110. Allred, John. "Bibliotheken—Offen fur Lebenslangen Lernen." [Libraries—Open for Lifelong Learning]. *Bibliotheksdienst* 31, no. 1 (1997): 36-46.

    The author's lecture at an international seminar addresses the issue of library support for lifelong learning. A wide range of open learning and correspondence courses exists in Europe. Libraries can offer a large selection of media and advice to support these courses. However, many European libraries are unclear about their role in this area and need to examine their priorities. A. Slade.

111. Allred, John. "Open Learning Via the Electronic Library." *Open Learning Today*, no. 35 (January/February 1997): 4-6.

    Using a case study of an independent learner seeking information on the World Wide Web and an outline of various electronic library programs underway in Europe, the author briefly examines the role of the electronic library in open learning. One way that libraries can support open learning is by providing the learners with "maps" to guide them through the maze of electronic resources and lead them from a relevant resource to other items that reinforce, develop, or contrast the ideas and skills under study. A. Slade.

112. Hensley, Randy Burke. "Virtual Education Environments." *PNLA Quarterly* 62, no. 1 (Fall 1997): 25-26.

    The author identifies five themes pertaining to the role of libraries in the new distance learning and virtual education environments: tools, learning, community, communication, and narratives. Tools for virtual education environments are discussed in terms of appropriateness, supportability, upgrading, training, and experimentation. Learning is considered in relation to user learning styles, learning needs, and library instruction. The discussion of community is concerned with libraries providing the attributes of a physical community in a virtual environment and participating in group learning settings known as learning communities. The section on communication is concerned with asynchronous and synchronous forms of interaction as well as the use and value of text materials in an electronic context. In examining the theme of narratives, the author identifies the need for libraries to create a new "story" to explain their role in the emerging virtual educational environments. A. Slade.

113. Holmes, Geraldine H. "Diversity and Distance Learning: A Challenge for Distance Educators." *Quarterly Bulletin of the International Association of Agricultural Information Specialists* 42, nos. 3/4 (1997): 284-88.

    This article, written by an educator, is noteworthy due to its brief remarks on library resources in the context of a discussion of strategies for successful distance learning and diversity issues that may create barriers in this learning environment. The author refers to an unpublished study on the needs of distance learners, which indicated that lack of local library resources was a problem. She goes on to say: "The distance educator must be aware of this and be prepared to send needed instructional/informational material to the students or to identify and recommend resources that students can personally acquire (such as subscriptions to selected journals)." This comment accentuates the need for librarians to inform educators about the types of library services that can be provided to distance learners. A. Slade.

114. Holowachuk, Darlene. *The Role of Librarians in Distance Education*. 1997. Online. Available: http://www.slis.ualberta.ca/598/darlene/distance.htm (Accessed April 13, 2000).

This paper by a graduate student at the University of Alberta examines selected issues surrounding the role of libraries in distance education. These issues are trends in education, needs of the distance learner, challenges faced by librarians, and strategies to meet the challenges. Included among the challenges discussed are document delivery and cost and access issues. Among the solutions considered are resource sharing, partnerships with faculty members, and relevant technology. The appendix includes a list of print and Internet resources. M. Kascus.

115. Longworth, Norman. "An International Professional Association for Lifelong Learning." *The Electronic Library* 15, no. 5 (October 1997): 371-75.

ELLI (European Lifelong Learning Initiative) is an international professional association established in 1992 to foster lifelong learning in Europe. As a result of this initiative, lifelong learning concepts and practice have become much better known. ELLI treats lifelong learning as a process that develops individuals throughout a lifetime. To achieve its mission, ELLI runs conferences; publishes a lifelong learning magazine; participates in European education and training programs; works with other professional organizations to improve knowledge and practice; and constructs ELLInets, networks of interested organizations in each country of Europe. The goals of ELLI are described in detail in this article. It is suggested that libraries and information centers can contribute to ELLI beyond their usual role in education by being current with the movement, stocking books on the subject, and taking an active role in their organizations to increase awareness of lifelong learning. M. Kascus.

116. Sigurdardottir, P. S. "Bokasafns-og Upplysingaponusta Fyrir Fjarnema." [Library and Information Services to Distance Learners]. *Bokasafnid*, no. 21 (April 1997): 18-24.

This article reports the results of a survey conducted in 1995 to determine the use of libraries by students in a distance education teacher training program offered by Kennarahaskoli Islanda University College of Education (UCE) in Reykjavik, Iceland. The survey also investigated the students' evaluation of the UCE Library. A. Slade.

1996

117. Brittain, Jane. "Managing Information in Distance and Open Learning." In *Introduction to Information Management*, edited by J. Michael Brittain. Occasional Monographs, no. 16. Wagga Wagga, NSW: Centre for Information Studies, Charles Sturt University—Riverina, 1996, 239-48.

The Open Learning Technology Corporation Limited (OLTC) in South Australia provides a national information and advisory service on open learning technologies to the education and training community. It is supported by the OLTC Information Service, which disseminates information and offers value-added services to OLTC's customers. These services include current awareness services, locally developed non-bibliographic databases, a website, distribution of OLTC publications and other products, an inquiry service, and customized information services on a fee-for-service basis. Every request to the OLTC Information Service is logged for evaluation purposes and to plot the inquiry trends and statistics on the use of staff time. The OLTC Information Service emphasizes transferable skills, project management, and entrepreneurial approaches, with less emphasis on traditional librarianship. A. Slade.

118. Burge, Elizabeth J. "Inside-Out Thinking About Distance Teaching: Making Sense of Reflective Practice." *Journal of the American Society for Information Science* 47, no. 11 (November 1996): 843-48.

In this position paper, the author uses the Kolb experiential learning cycle to organize reflective thoughts about her work as a distance educator. Included are some common sense ideas relevant to designing learner services when institutions offer distance mode courses. Learner services include adequately educated library staff and user-friendly information delivery and communication technologies. The implication here is that the librarian who has studied adult learning principles will be able to act more appropriately when serving the distance education learner. According to Burge, learners need to be encouraged to regard the librarian as the nearest person to whom they can talk "safely." She stresses the importance of formally educating librarians in adult learning principles. M. Kascus.

119. Campbell, Helen and Clark Quinn. "Connecting Students to Information and Learning: Open Learning Australia, Open Net and Open Access." In *Public Libraries— What Are They Worth? Proceedings of the 2nd National Public Libraries Conference, Sydney, 12-15 November 1995*, edited by Alan Bundy. Adelaide, SA: Auslib Press, 1996, 22-30.

This paper covers a wide range of issues regarding Open Learning Australia (OLA), the Open Learning Library and Information Service (OLLIS), and Open Net. OLA is discussed in terms of its mandate, model of education, flexible structure, and accomplishments to date. OLLIS is examined in relation to the Open Learning Library Review in 1994, the change in administration following the review, the introduction of OLLIS Mark2 to simplify students' access to libraries, library instruction programs for OLA students, the creation of the Open Learning Electronic Support Service (OLESS), and the OLESS pilot projects in electronic communication. Open Net, a private service provider, was created as a result of the OLESS pilot studies. Its mission includes the provision of local access points so OLA students can connect to the Internet and locate online information relevant to their studies. The paper concludes by reflecting on the role of public libraries in assisting OLA students. Since OLLIS Mark2 will encourage OLA students to borrow from academic libraries, the role of public libraries will be to provide information about OLA and OLLIS Mark2 and serve as local access points for Open Net. For more information on OLLIS Mark2, see #174-75 in this volume. A. Slade.

1995

120.   Australia. Parliament. Senate. Employment, Education and Training References Committee. *Inquiry into the Development of Open Learning in Australia, Part 2*. Canberra: Senate Employment, Education and Training, References Committee, 1995. 117 pp.

   Pages 33-37 in Part 2 of the government report on open learning in Australia expand on the brief comments in Part 1 (see #127 below). Submissions to the Committee are summarized and the issue of student support for open learning students is discussed in relation to library services and access to information not included with course materials. The report concludes that open learning students are putting pressure on the Australian library system and recommends that administrators devise a funding system that "recognizes that their client base may be much wider than the host institution." A. Slade.

121.   Booker, Di. "Draft Statement on Libraries and Open Learning." *DESIGnation*, no. 8 (August 1995): 3-4.

   This statement, drafted for the Australian Library and Information Association, stresses equitable access to library resources for students engaged in open learning. Library and information service personnel can support open learners by providing advice and guidance to facilitate the development of lifelong learning skills and by providing access to, and assistance in locating, appropriate information sources, facilities, and equipment. A number of principles and beliefs about open learning library services are listed at the end of this short statement. A. Slade.

122.   Boyce, Judith I. and Bert R. Boyce. "Library Outreach Programs in Rural Areas." *Library Trends* 44, no. 1 (Summer 1995): 112-28.

   Library outreach programs in rural areas are examined in terms of their use. Rural areas are served by national and state information agencies, local public libraries, and libraries of colleges and universities. Special efforts have been directed at supporting distance learning activities and health information needs. New technologies such as video and digital media are augmenting but not replacing the services provided by traditional delivery systems such as local libraries or branches, bookmobiles, deposit collections, and books-by-mail programs. Public libraries remain the backbone of rural outreach programs, with technology just beginning to have an impact. M. Kascus.

123.   Brittain, Jane. "Open Learning Technology Corporation Information Services." *DESIGnation*, no. 7 (April 1995): 4.

   The author provides a brief summary of the services offered by the OLTC (Open Learning Technology Corporation) Information Service in South Australia. The services include a quarterly newsletter to provide managers of education and training with information highlights of developments in open learning and distance education, a directory of consultants and other professionals with specific expertise who are able to undertake elements of open learning projects, a database of current research in open learning, and a dissemination service for OLTC products and publications. For more information on the OLTC Information Service, see #117 in this chapter. A. Slade.

124. Dev Nath, Wooma Sankar. "Preparing Libraries for Distance Education." In *Preparing Libraries for the 21st Century: Seminar Papers: Fortieth All India Library Conference, Goa University Library, Goa, January 5-8, 1995*, edited by C. V. Subbarao, A. P. Gakhar, and O. P. Sharma. Delhi, India: Indian Library Association, 1995, 260-67.

Following a brief review of the history and characteristics of distance education in India, this paper focuses on barriers to library services for distance learning programs. Relatively few distance learners have the opportunity to use library resources, and those who live in isolated areas usually have no access at all. Financial and geographic factors act as barriers to the expansion of library networks. Study centers have limited space for library materials and lack experienced staff. Since the task of providing library materials to thousands of distance learners cannot be accomplished by the distance teaching universities alone, collaboration between academic, public, and special libraries is needed to meet the demands of a diverse learner population. Public libraries have the potential to assist rural students, especially by providing access to audio-visual materials and by preparing bibliographies and abstracts for distance education courses. However, the public library system requires additional funding, trained staff, and appropriate equipment to take on this role. A. Slade.

125. Roberts, Judith M. and Erin M. Keough, eds. *Why the Information Highway? Lessons from Open and Distance Learning*. Toronto: Trifolium Books, 1995. 276 pp. ISBN 1-895579-39-2.

This book focuses on Canadian distance education in the 1990s and its relationship with information technologies. Library services are mentioned briefly in three papers. In the paper by Jane Bradley, "Learners and Learner Services: The Key to the Future," the author uses library services as an example of a learner service that contributes to the encouragement of independent learning. Later in the paper, Bradley mentions that open distance learning appears to be taking advantage of librarians' abilities to navigate through networks, access electronic resources, and interpret the information retrieved. The guidelines of the Canadian Library Association are mentioned in this context. In the paper by Noel Thomas and Donald McDonell, "The Role(s) of Technology in Minority Group Distance Learning," the authors comment that providing complete library services remains an obstacle to be overcome in distance learning. They acknowledge the access and delivery services currently provided by Canadian academic libraries and go on to state that this is still not sufficient for high-level research projects. The authors see the solution being the mass storage of library materials in digitized form. Judith Tobin, in "Evaluation and Research: What Do We Need to Know?," indicates that libraries are crucial in providing the support needed by distance learners and expresses disappointment that distance learning library services are minimally represented in the curriculum of library schools. A. Slade.

1994

126. Arfield, John. "Flexible Learning and the Library." In *Flexible Learning in Higher Education*, edited by Winnie Wade, Keith Hodgkinson, Alison Smith, and John Arfield. London: Kogan Page, 1994, 68-75.

This chapter examines a wide range of issues pertaining to the impact of flexible and distance learning programs on libraries. After considering changes and trends in teaching and learning in higher education, the author discusses the following aspects of library services in relation to flexible learning: course reading lists, book stock, non-print media, computer-based services, and information-handling skills. The argument is advanced that library staff should be involved at all stages in the development of flexible and distance learning so that they can contribute to the development process and prepare for the impact of these programs on the library, A. Slade.

127.   Australia. Parliament. Senate. Employment, Education and Training References Committee. *Inquiry into the Development of Open Learning in Australia, Part 1*. Canberra: Senate Employment, Education and Training, References Committee, 1994. 148 pp.

This government report on open learning in Australia contains a short commentary on libraries on p. 52. The capacity of libraries to meet the needs of open learning students emerged as an important issue during the Committee's inquiry. The submissions received from libraries and library associations are acknowledged, and the support provided to open learning students by Open Learning Australia and Deakin University is mentioned. Further comments on libraries are contained in Part 2 of the report (see #120 above). A. Slade.

1992

128.   Brophy, Peter. "Distributed Higher Education—Distributed Libraries?" *New Library World* 93, no. 1099 (1992): 22-23.

In this first installment in a series of "vision statements" in *New Library World*, Peter Brophy examines the concept of distributed libraries in the context of distributed higher education. He argues that a better way of providing higher education in a climate of lifelong learning is to take the education to the customer. A current example of this approach is the provision of franchised courses in the United Kingdom. Ways in which libraries can support distributed education are through document and postal delivery systems, electronic links to networked services, delivery of packaged materials, use of the public library network, a national or regional library membership card, and wider use of full-text electronic products. The result could be a reduction in the number of physical libraries, with regional libraries supporting high-level research and the British Library Document Supply Centre acting as the major supplier of materials not available at regional centers. A. Slade.

College and University Libraries

For other works that discuss this topic, see the following heading in the Subject Index: "role of the library in distance learning—college and university libraries."

1999

129. Ali, Anthony. *Evaluation of Some Distance Learning Programmes at Nigerian Universities*. Paper presented at the Pan-Commonwealth Forum on Open Learning, Brunei Darussalam, 1-5 March 1999: Empowerment through Knowledge and Technology. Online. Available: http://www.col.org/forum/casestudies.htm (in pdf format) (Accessed April 13, 2000).

A study was conducted to evaluate the human and material facilities available for teaching and administration at the distance learning centers of two universities in Nigeria. One of the facilities investigated was library support. In the findings, neither of the two distance learning centers had a library or had negotiated with the owners of the centers for enhancing the existing secondary school libraries at the two locations. The author notes that "the need for a library at those two centers may well be both an academic and administrative oversight." In the discussion of results, he further remarks that the lack of any library facilities is "a very serious lapse since a well-equipped library is a university's dream of what a center of academic excellence should have." A. Slade.

130. Oladokun, Samuel Olugbade and Olatundun O. Oyewumi. *Coping with the Tyranny of Library Service at a Distance: A Typical African Case*. Paper presented at the Pan-Commonwealth Forum on Open Learning, Brunei Darussalam, 1-5 March 1999: Empowerment through Knowledge and Technology. Online. Available: http://www.col.org/forum/casestudies.htm (in pdf format) (Accessed April 13, 2000).

Following an outline of the history and status of distance education in Africa, the authors discuss library services for African distance education programs, with particular reference to sub-Saharan Africa. Their remarks are prefaced with the statement, "generally, in most African countries, library support service to distance learners leaves so much to be desired." In many cases, students are expected to use local library facilities without consideration as to whether those libraries have relevant materials or will allow students from other institutions to use their resources. While technology holds promise for improving library services, the authors note that most African countries are not keeping pace with technological developments. Two examples of institutions that do have "hi-tech" libraries are the University of South Africa and the University of Botswana. The authors indicate that these institutions offer some hope for improved library services in the rest of Africa and offer the following recommendations to facilitate such improvement: collaboration and reciprocal borrowing between universities, establishment of sub-regional groupings of libraries, appeals for government aid, provision of delivery services using trains and commercial vehicles, requests for assistance from international organizations, and the inclusion of distance librarianship in the curriculum of African library schools. A. Slade.

1998

131. Brophy, Peter, Jenny Craven, and Shelagh Fisher. *The Development of UK Academic Library Services in the Context of Lifelong Learning*. Manchester, UK: Centre for Research in Library and Information Management, Manchester Metropolitan University, 1998. 74 pp. ISBN 1-900508-40-0.

This report is an outcome of a study commissioned by the Joint Information Systems Committee (JISC) of the UK Higher Education Funding Councils (HEFC) as part of the Electronic Libraries Programme (eLib). The study was intended to examine models of lifelong learning and the role of libraries in relation to these models. The first sections of the report look at the background and context of lifelong learning in the United Kingdom; the development of UK lifelong learning policy; and the implications of the Dearing, Kennedy, and Fryer reports and the Green Paper, "The Learning Age." Following these discussions, the report considers the role of academic and public libraries in the lifelong learning process, the problems in providing library and information services to lifelong learners, and the provision of library services for lifelong and distance learning outside the United Kingdom. The conclusions in the report focus on thirteen areas, including basic library services for lifelong learning, the content of information services, the concept of hybrid libraries, converged services, information quality, electronic resources, and help desk services. The report concludes with 23 specific recommendations directed to JISC and HEFCs, to institutions and their libraries, and to the library community as a whole. A. Slade.

132. Brophy, Peter and Jenny Craven. "Lifelong Learning and Higher Education Libraries: Models for the 21st Century." In *The Eighth Off-Campus Library Services Conference Proceedings: Providence, Rhode Island, April 22-24, 1998,* compiled by P. Steven Thomas and Maryhelen Jones. Mount Pleasant, MI: Central Michigan University, 1998, 47-61.

Lifelong learning is becoming an important issue for many countries of the world as a strategy in coping with change. In this paper, the authors define lifelong learning and place it in the context of learning theories. The focus is on an analysis of current support in UK academic libraries for non-traditional and distance learning. The authors conclude with an action plan that includes (1) development of basic service, (2) development of hybrid libraries, (3) a focus on content, (4) converged services, (5) multi-agency provision, (6) integration of library services into learning, (7) libraries as social centers, (8) information quality, (9) electronic resources, (10) information skills, (11) help desk services, (12) lifelong relationships, and (13) dynamic management. The concept of lifelong learning implies major changes to the traditional pattern of higher education and poses challenges and opportunities for libraries. M. Kascus.

133. Cajkler, Wasyl. "Distance Learning: The Tutor's Experience." *Education Libraries Journal* 41, no. 1 (Spring 1998): 13-20.

The role of the librarian in distance education course development is examined through the eyes of a tutor. The author's remarks are based on experience with distance education courses, consultations with librarians, information provided by conference participants, and questionnaire feedback from distance learners. Librarians are often not consulted in the development of distance education courses because of a range of pressures on the course team, including inexperience in the design of distance courses, time-restrictions, poor organization, procedural requirements, inadequate resourcing, and challenges with technology. The exclusion of librarians from the course development process is discussed in relation to the expectation that access to library resources is necessary for successful completion of assignments in some courses. To investigate the provision of library support to distance learners, a questionnaire survey was sent to a sample of postgraduate students. The majority of the respondents indicated that access to library resources was important for their studies. For the provision of adequate library services to distance learners, the author advocates that a librarian should be involved in all stages of course development. The advantages and challenges associated with this involvement are outlined. A. Slade.

134. Craven, Jenny and Shelagh Fisher. "The Provision of Library Services for Lifelong Learners in UK Academic Libraries." In *Libraries Without Walls 2: The Delivery of Library Services to Distant Users*, edited by Peter Brophy, Shelagh Fisher, and Zoë Clarke. London: Library Association Publishing, 1998, 94-108.

The focus of this paper is on the role of the library in supporting the concept of lifelong learning. The first part of the paper examines the nature and definitions of lifelong learning with reference to developments in the United Kingdom, the characteristics of lifelong learners, their motivations for learning, the content of their learning, and the locations where lifelong learning can take place. The second part discusses library services to lifelong learners, considering both non-traditional students and individuals who are engaged in learning activities that are not connected to a formal academic program. Non-traditional students include distance learners, part-time students, and people taking franchised courses. The library services available to this group of learners are outlined using examples from a number of universities in the United Kingdom. Library support for learners who are not students of an institution is less clearly defined in the United Kingdom and depends on the policies of the various libraries. Three examples are provided of academic libraries that provide some services to non-members of the university. The paper concludes by considering potential ways in which libraries could enhance services to lifelong learners, including networked learner support, increasing access to electronic information resources, and developing library and information managers. A. Slade.

135. Garnes, K. "Universitetsbibliotekene: En Sareptas Krukke for All; Men Hvem Betaler for Tjenestene?" [University Libraries: A Sarepta's Jar for All; But Who Pays for the Services?]. *Synopsis* 29, no. 3 (June 1998): 172-76.

The lifelong and distance learning reform in Norway will demand greater flexibility and cooperation in university libraries and will depend on the development of electronic network services. Since the costs of electronic and printed material are rising and interlending fees do not cover costs, the author urges that resources be earmarked for library services to decentralized learning. A. Slade.

136. Hahn, Bessie K. and Canchuan Li. *The Role of the Academic Library in Distance Education*. Paper presented at the International Conference on New Missions of Academic Libraries in the 21st Century, Beijing, China, October 25-28, 1998. Online. Available: http://www.lib.pku.edu.cn/98conf/proceedings.htm (Accessed April 13, 2000).

Several broad issues are examined in this conference paper, including distance learning in higher education today, the types of distance learning, library services for distance learning, the academic library in the new information age, the new functionality of the academic library, and the advantages of the library and librarians in supporting distance education. It is stressed that librarians' skills and knowledge in using information technology will be of great benefit to distance learning programs and that academic libraries need to take advantage of their strengths in this area to support both distance learners and educators. A. Slade.

137. Jagannathan, Neela. "Libraries in Distance Teaching Universities." In *50 Years: Library and Information Services in India*, edited by M. K. Jain, P. B. Mangla, D. R. Kalia, and Neela Jagannathan. Delhi, India: Shipra, 1998, 65-76.

The following topics are discussed in this paper: the growth of distance education in India, the Indian scenario of library services to distance learners, the requirements of distance learners, the problems faced by these students, the problems encountered by Indian open universities in providing library and information services, and suggested measures to provide outreach services to distance learners. The measures include a Library Support Service Cell at each open university, learning resource centers at the regional and study centers, mobile library units to serve rural and isolated areas, networking of libraries, use of communication and information technologies, and resource sharing among all types of libraries. A. Slade.

138. Lund, M. "Abne Laeringsmiljoer." [Open Learning Centres]. *Bibliotekspressen*, no.1 (January 1998): 4-5.

Representatives from the Danish Commercial Colleges Library Association visited selected English colleges in 1997 to study open learning centers. The centers visited were well staffed by librarians, but these staff members lacked interaction with lecturers. In Danish commercial colleges there is a willingness to involve the library in the learning process. Models from abroad can help influence a more active role for librarians. A. Slade.

139. Macauley, Peter and Sue McKnight. "A New Model of Library Support for Off-Campus Postgraduate Research Students." In *Quality in Postgraduate Research: Managing the New Agenda: Proceedings of the 1998 Quality in Postgraduate Research Conference, Adelaide, April 23-24*, edited by Margaret Kiley and Gerry Mullins. Adelaide, SA: Advisory Centre for University Education, University of Adelaide, 1998, 95-106. Also online. Available: http://www.deakin.edu.au/library/staff/newmodelliboc.html (Accessed April 13, 2000).

The authors suggest the need for a new model of library support for postgraduate distance learners that involves librarians collaborating with academic staff on supervisory teams. Based on the results of a Deakin University research study (see #619 in this volume), the authors propose that librarians assume the role of co-supervisor to ensure that the literature review component of a higher degree thesis is comprehensive and relevant. Librarians can also ensure that the students and their supervisors are kept up-to-date on new information resources in their research areas. Some of the advantages of adopting this model may be faster degree completions, higher standards of research, increased information literacy skills in both students and supervisors, improved research collections in university libraries, and reduced isolation for off-campus researchers. For a related paper, see #156 in this chapter. A. Slade.

140. MacDougall, Alan. "Supporting Learners at a Distance." *Ariadne: The Web Version,* no. 16 (July 1998). Online. Available: http://www.ariadne.ac.uk/issue16/main/ (Accessed April 13, 2000).

With particular reference to the United Kingdom and Europe, this article discusses various issues affecting library support for distance learners in terms of opportunities, strengths, weaknesses, and threats. Academic libraries are particularly well placed to support distance learning, drawing on their infrastructure for serving on-campus populations. A challenge for librarians is to rethink the level and type of information services that can be offered to support new modes of course delivery in a cost-effective and efficient manner. Sheffield Hallam University is cited as an exemplary provider of library services for distance learning in the United Kingdom. A weakness and threat for libraries is the failure of administrators to recognize the implications of the growth of distance learning and to allocate the necessary resources to support it. Another threat is that distance educators will bypass libraries and "spoonfeed" students with packaged material. In the new academic environment, libraries will need to demonstrate their strengths for supporting distance learning, and the librarian will need to become a hybrid manager utilizing professional knowledge, applying information technology, and contributing to curriculum design. A. Slade.

141. Martin, Rebecca R. *The Library as a Partner in Creating a Dynamic Learning Community*. Paper presented at the International Conference on New Missions of Academic Libraries in the 21st Century, Beijing, China, October 25-28, 1998. Online. Available: http://www.lib.pku.edu.cn/98conf/proceedings.htm (Accessed April 13, 2000).

The role of academic libraries in serving as resources for new ways of teaching and learning through technology is highlighted in relation to the concept of learning communities. Learning communities comprise specific academic programs with linked courses, coordinated study across disciplines, and targeted student groups. These communities center on student learning and the design of educational experiences that reflect individual student interests. Libraries are well positioned to contribute to these communities because their emphasis on information competencies and resource-based learning is consistent with the focus of student-centered learning. One primary contribution would be for librarians to form partnerships with educators to design environments in which information technologies can be integrated into the learning experience. Another contribution would be the delivery of information services to students at a distance, providing the arena for interaction among members of the learning community in a technologically supported environment. A. Slade.

142. Niemi, John A., Barbara J. Ehrhard, and Lynn Neeley. "Off-Campus Library Support for Distance Adult Learners." *Library Trends* 47, no. 1 (Summer 1998): 65-74.

Adult learners in higher education at remote sites are described in terms of their needs and expectations. Case studies centered on these adult learners at Northern Illinois University are discussed. Based on the literature reviewed, distance adult learners' expectations of library service demonstrate a great need. A list of potential online resources for distance adult learners is included. The authors conclude by discussing the implications for library services to enhance this nontraditional learning environment. A goal is to optimize the technology to support the new emerging mode of higher education in the online environment. M. Kascus.

143.   "Ny Kompetanse: Grunnlaget for en Helhetlig Etter-og Videreutdanningspolitikk." [New Competence: The Foundation for a Comprehensive Further Education Policy]. *Synopsis* 29, no. 1 (February 1998): 8-9.

With reference to the Buer Committee report in Norway, this article stresses that educational institutions should assume responsibility for planning library services for their distance learning students. In addition, libraries should be involved in the planning of distance education courses at an early stage. Institutions with key subject responsibilities for developing access to electronic resources should be given funding to extend such access to distance learners. A. Slade.

144.   Saunders, Laverna. "Distance Learning Challenges Us to Adapt Our Services." *Computers in Libraries* 18, no. 5 (May 1998): 45.

This editorial discusses three ways in which distance learning challenges libraries. First, remote learners are entitled to the same services that on-campus students receive. Such services include online catalogue access, e-mail, reference service, document delivery, telephone assistance, and instructional materials available through web pages. Second, the growing demand for full-text information has an impact on licensing that restricts access to a building or a campus and eliminates the option of authentication. Third, the effort to serve the learner is bringing libraries together in new ways. It is suggested that users will use a combination of libraries, including public libraries supplemented by the academic library, all of whom will connect to global information via the Internet. The Florida Distance Learning Library Initiative is given as a model of formal coordination that can serve as an example to libraries of how to redefine and adapt their services to assist tomorrow's users. M. Kascus.

145.   Starr, Leah K. "Reference Services for Off-campus Students." *OLA Quarterly* (Oregon Library Association) 4, no. 3 (Fall 1998). Online. Available: http://www.olaweb.org/quarterly/quar4-3/starr.shtml (Accessed April 13, 2000).

The author reviews a number of issues pertaining to library support for off-campus students, especially those living in rural areas. With reference to Eastern Oregon University, three general areas requiring special attention in serving distance learners are identified: (1) remote access to the catalogue and other electronic resources; (2) research guidance, publicity, and marketing of services; and (3) contact points for students such as e-mail, telephone, and computer conferencing. It is pointed out that off-campus students have different library needs from on-campus students and that reference librarians need to respond to those differences by providing traditional services in non-traditional ways. A. Slade.

146. Van Vuren, A. J. and J. C. Henning. *User-Education in a Flexible Learning Environment—An Opportunity to Stay Relevant in the 21st Century.* Paper presented at the 1998 IATUL (International Association for Technological University Libraries) Conference held in Pretoria, South Africa, July 1998. Online. Available: http://educate.lib.chalmers.se/IATUL/proceedcontents/pretpap/vuren.html (Accessed April 13, 2000).

Definitions of "flexible learning" vary but generally focus on three aspects: delivery methods, a learner-centered approach, and the role of resource-based learning. Each of these aspects is examined in relation to flexible learning in South Africa. The concept of resource-based learning is discussed in terms of definitions, information literacy, and implications for academic libraries. A number of strategies are identified for how academic libraries can support learning activities in open and flexible learning. Provision of "information user training" is one such strategy and is seen as a way for the library and information profession to play a central role in education in South Africa. Academic libraries should do the following if they want to remain relevant in the twenty-first century: promote their services to make academic staff aware of the need for information user training in flexible learning programs; become involved in the curriculum development process; and actively develop information user training materials in different formats, including print-based materials and interactive computer programs. A. Slade.

147. Wolpert, Ann. "Services to Remote Users: Marketing the Library's Role." *Library Trends* 47, no. 1 (Summer 1998): 21-41.

Libraries should approach distance education as a new business opportunity, using market evaluation and analysis techniques. If academic libraries align themselves closely with faculty and administrators and develop performance measures, they can provide educational support while improving awareness of the importance of libraries as a competitive advantage. Libraries need to become more sophisticated about packaging, advertising, and promoting their valuable resources. They have to develop meaningful performance measures that document costs and contributions in this new environment. The all-digital library is problematic, and the Internet is not a substitute for high-quality library support to distance learners. According to the author, those institutions that take advantage of the experience of libraries will have a competitive advantage in satisfying the needs and interests of distance education students. M. Kascus.

148. Yan, Zhuang. *Thinking on Setting Up the Document Information Centre in TV Universities.* Paper prepared for the '98 Shanghai International Open and Distance Education Symposium, Shanghai TV University, Shanghai, China, April 15-17, 1998. Shanghai, China: Open Education Research Institute, Shanghai Television University, 1998. Full text on CD-ROM. Available at: International Centre for Distance Learning, The Open University, Walton Hall, Milton Keynes MK7 6AA, United Kingdom.

The author indicates that it is necessary for TV universities in China to establish document information centers in their libraries to assist teachers, students, and alumni. The main purpose of a document information center is to collect the publications and academic documents of its own school. The centers that have already been established in Chinese universities can serve as models for the TV universities. The administrative conditions for these centers include developing a long-term development plan, cooperating with the academic departments, establishing a system of legal deposit, cataloguing materials for easy access, and making documents accessible to teachers and students outside the campus. To promote the exchange of information through document information centers, the following conditions should be met: establishing complete files and records of publications and documents, publicizing the collections, and sharing information with other appropriate universities. A. Slade.

1997

149. Brophy, Peter. *Distributing the Library to the Learner*. Paper presented at Beyond the Beginning: The Global Digital Library: An International Conference Organised by UKOLN on behalf of JISC, CNI, BLRIC, CAUSE and CAUL, 16th and 17th June 1997 at the Queen Elizabeth II Conference Centre, London, UK. Online. Available: http://www.ukoln.ac.uk/services/papers/bl/blri078/content/repor~22.htm (Accessed April 13, 2000).

   With reference to projects undertaken by the Centre for Research in Library and Information Management (CERLIM) at the University of Central Lancashire, this paper discusses the concept of lifelong learning in terms of its benefits and effects and its implications for academic library services. The following brief case studies are presented to illustrate the provision of academic library services to lifelong learners in the United Kingdom: the Open University, the University of the Highlands and Islands Project in Scotland, and the Virtual Academic Library of the North-West (VALNOW). The principles and issues involved in library support of lifelong learning include the need for libraries to move toward service on demand to all users, to provide services through cooperative arrangements with other libraries, and to deliver services in a variety of locations. The challenge for libraries is to deliver a full range of services, including value-added services, to a high number of customers before other competitors step in to fill the needs of lifelong learners. A. Slade.

150. Cavanagh, Tony. *Off Campus Library Services for Prisoners*. Paper presented to the Australian Library and Information Association Distance Education Special Interest Group National Conference: Shifting Sands, Charles Sturt University, Wagga Wagga, December 5-6, 1997. Available from: Christine Cother, Editor DESIGnation, University of South Australia Library, Holbrooks Road, Underdale, South Australia 5032.

   Prisoners who enroll in distance education courses face a number of problems in obtaining access to library resources, including the lack of academic material in prison libraries, lack of computer and telephone access, delays in receiving materials by mail, prison security regulations, and lack of peer group support. The author argues that a good library service can make a significant difference to the success of these students and lists a number of ways in which academic institutions and libraries can improve support for students who are inmates of penal institutions. A. Slade.

151. Diller, Karen and Nancy Huling. "Distance Learning: Opportunities and Challenges." *ALKI: The Washington Library Association Journal* 13, no. 3 (December 1997): 10-13. Also online. Available: http://www.wla.org/alki/dec97/distance.html (Accessed April 13, 2000).

  The focus here is on the importance of collaborative efforts in providing effective leadership to statewide constituencies. In this context, the issues involved in the organization, management, and delivery of library services are discussed. These issues are grouped into three broad areas: access, services, and administration. Access to online catalogues and databases involves issues of licensing and authentication as well as a procedure for requesting and delivering needed materials. Access is also an issue with the use of reserve materials, prompting some libraries to offer electronic reserves. Another issue is the attitude of students in the current electronic environment. Students may want resources and services provided without the expectation that they will develop independent information skills. E-mail is an option for reference service, as well as Web-based tutorials and desktop videoconferencing. M. Kascus.

152. Fidishun, Dolores. *Can We Still Do Business as Usual? Adult Students and the New Paradigm of Library Service*. Paper presented at the ACRL 8th National Conference: Choosing Our Futures: Nashville, Tennessee, April 11-14, 1997. Online. Available: http://www.ala.org/acrl/paperhtm/c25.html (Accessed April 13, 2000).

  As the number of adult students increases, librarians need to be more aware of the learning styles and characteristics of these students. Of particular concern in serving adult learners are hours of service, remote access to services, and understanding of technology. Librarians need to market their services and collect feedback from adult students regarding additional needs. The message here is that libraries need to be made more user-friendly for adult students. M. Kascus.

153. Goodson, Carol. "The Way I See It: Putting the 'Service' Back in Library Service." *College & Research Libraries News* 58, no. 3 (March 1997): 186-87.

  In this opinion paper, the author suggests that the role of the librarian is not to make users independent learners, but rather to give them what they want. The traditional view of teaching students how to do research and not doing it for them is considered less relevant in the current business climate. It is suggested that users are willing to pay for services and that they want and expect librarians to do the work for them and deliver a finished product. The implication is that librarians are on their way to extinction if they do not change their way of doing things. It is further suggested that librarians are misleading users by implying that they can acquire the same search skills as librarians through a brief instructional session. M. Kascus.

154. Gupta, Dinesh Kumar. "Library and Information Access to Distant Learners: New Opportunities Through Information Technology." In *Information Technology Applications in Academic Libraries in India with Emphasis on Network Services and Information Sharing: Papers Presented at the Fourth National Convention for Automation of Libraries in Education and Research (CALIBER-97) at Patiala, 6-8 March 1997*, edited by A. L. Moorthy and P. B. Mangla. Ahmedabad, India: Information and Library Network Centre, 1997, 40-42.

The provision of library services to distance education students is a special challenge for open universities in India. Their study center libraries have limited usefulness because books do not circulate and must be used on the premises, opening hours are restricted to weekends, there is no liaison with local libraries, and the centers are too distant for students living in remote areas. Automation of library operations and networking are seen as ways that open universities can provide better library services to distance learners. Information technology, digital libraries, and the Internet will offer new opportunities for libraries, and distance students will be the beneficiaries. A. Slade.

155. Gupta, Dinesh Kumar. "Library as Support Service in Distance Education." In *Library and Information Science: Parameters and Perspectives: Essays in Honour of Prof. P. B. Mangla. Volume One: Library and Information Science: Basic*, edited by R. G. Prasher. New Delhi, India: Concept, 1997, 352-59.

This paper examines the library as a support service in Indian open universities. The topics covered include the main tasks of the regional and study centers, the media available to distance learners, and barriers to library services. The following needs are identified as issues for consideration in improving services to distance learners: cooperation between all types of libraries, improved communication between the library and the tutor, guidelines or standards for the functioning of the library system, appropriate training for library staff at study centers, and employment of more full-time librarians. It is stressed that the library has a central role in distance education and librarians need to create awareness of this role with the proper authorities. A. Slade.

156. Macauley, Peter. *A Proposed Model of Library Support for Distance Education Research Students*. Paper presented to the Australian Library and Information Association Distance Education Special Interest Group National Conference: Shifting Sands, Charles Sturt University, Wagga Wagga, December 5-6, 1997. Available from: Christine Cother, Editor DESIGnation, University of South Australia Library, Holbrooks Road, Underdale, South Australia 5032.

Based on the results of his research project at Deakin University (see #619 in this volume), the author proposes a model of library support for distance education higher degree by research students. The essential feature of this model is the inclusion of a librarian on each student's supervisory team to assist with and assess the literature review portion of the candidate's dissertation. The author points out that this is one research area in which academics are often found wanting. The proposed model is discussed in terms of its educational and professional objectives, the library skills of postgraduate students and academic staff, typical duties that a librarian might perform as a member of a supervisory team, and other considerations such as staffing issues, attitudes of academics, and the willingness of the stakeholders to support the model. For a related paper, see #139 in this chapter. A. Slade.

157. Machovec, George S. "Key Elements in Using Technology for Library Support in Distance Education." *Online Libraries and Microcomputers* 15, no. 12 (December 1997): 1-6. Also online. Available: http://www.infointelligence.com/sampolm.htm (Accessed April 13, 2000).

With reference to the development of distance education in the United States, this article briefly outlines the role of the library in distance learning and identifies key service elements in library provision. Examples of some of the larger distance programs currently operational are the University of Phoenix On-line Campus, Nova Southeastern University, and the Western Governors University. Key elements in library services for distance education are reference services, arrangements with nearby libraries, document delivery, access to databases and electronic journals, a database of subject specialists who can be contacted for assistance, and access to resources on the World Wide Web. A. Slade.

158. Miller, Gary E. "Distance Education and the Emerging Learning Environment." *Journal of Academic Librarianship* 23, no. 4 (July 1997): 319-21.

In this position paper, the author discusses the new environment for teaching and learning brought about by technology. Distance education is one way in which education is responding, but it is viewed as only part of a broader change process. The learning environment is more flexible and responsive to student needs. The characteristics of the new learning environment are that it will be life-long, learner-centered, and collaborative. The new learning environment will also emphasize individual inquiry using original data and sources rather than lectures and prepared texts. It will be structured so learners get experience in problem solving, decision making, and value exploration. Pennsylvania University is cited as an example of the new learning environment that stresses active and collaborative learning. The concept of virtual universities is discussed from both the profit-making and non-profit making perspectives. Virtual universities are acknowledged as representing an important way in which higher education institutions can respond to the rapidly changing needs of society and the workforce. These universities recognize the importance of support services that lifelong learners will need. The skills most needed will be the ability to evaluate information, analyze it, and use it to solve problems. These are the information skills that librarians can foster in students as part of the new learning environment. M. Kascus.

159. Oladokun, Samuel Olugbade. "Information Dispensation in Distance Learning: The Advent of a New Dawn." In *Open, Flexible and Distance Learning: Education and Training in the 21st Century: Selected Papers from the 13th Biennial Forum of the Open and Distance Learning Association of Australia, University of Tasmania, Launceston, 29 September-3 October 1997*, edited by Jo Osborne, David Roberts, and Judi Walker. Launceston, Tasmania: University of Tasmania, 1997, 350-53.

The role of the library in distance learning is discussed in relation to information technology (IT) and barriers to service in Africa. While advances in IT have benefited developed countries, most African countries are lacking the resources and infrastructure to utilize computer technologies in distance learning. The republics of South Africa and Botswana are examples of two countries that have been able to introduce IT and use facilities like the Internet and e-mail. The University of Botswana Library has Internet access and is in the process of connecting its branch libraries to the Internet. It is advocated that developed countries assist Africa in acquiring access to IT and that African academic libraries work collaboratively to share resources and acquire modern technologies to support distance learning. A. Slade.

160. Sherron, Gene T. and Judith V. Boettcher. *Distance Learning: The Shift to Interactivity*. CAUSE Professional Paper Series, no. 17. Boulder, CO: CAUSE, 1997. 39 pp.

This CAUSE Professional Paper examines fundamental issues in the provision of distance education programs, discussing the development of these programs in the United States and other countries, the technologies used for distance learning, and the processes in planning and designing for distance learning. Libraries and library services are discussed in this latter section under the heading "Information Resources Support." The authors identify three ways in which library staff can expand their support of distance learning programs: developing a more immediate mechanism to supply articles to students; purchasing duplicate copies of books; and sending library materials to students by fax, mail, or e-mail. Data on library support for distance education programs collected in two e-mail surveys of American institutions is reported in this context and in Appendix A of the paper. Among the findings from the second survey conducted in 1995, 71% of the responding institutions provided library services to distance learners and 34% offered remote access to electronic resources available through the campus libraries. A. Slade.

161. Small, Margaret. "Virtual Universities and Their Libraries: A Comparison of Australian and North American Experiences." *Advances in Librarianship* 21 (1997): 25-46.

The author received a study grant in 1996 to investigate the role of libraries in virtual universities in North America. After examining the status of virtual universities in Australia and the relationship between distance teaching universities and their libraries, the author discusses the findings from her visits to the following institutions: the Extension Center for Media and Independent Learning at the University of California, Berkeley; the National Technological University; the Mind Extension University; the University of Phoenix Online Campus; the Western Governors University; and the Open Learning Agency in British Columbia. Based on her findings, the author offers an overview of pertinent issues concerning virtual universities and their libraries. These issues include information literacy, the role of the Internet as an information source, library services currently provided by virtual universities, the role of librarians in virtual universities, and the challenges for librarians in this context. For a related paper, see #162 below. A. Slade.

162. Small, Margaret. "Virtual University Libraries: A Report of ALIA's 1996 Study Grant." *Australian Library Journal* 46, no. 4 (November 1997): 409-19.

The author reports on the results of her project to investigate the role of libraries as electronic services and as physical facilities in virtual universities. Following a discussion of virtual universities in general, the author looks at this type of university in Australia and North America, with particular reference to the library services at the following institutions: Open Learning Australia; the Extension Center for Media and Independent Learning at the University of California, Berkeley; the National Technological University; the Mind Extension University; the University of Phoenix Online Campus; the Western Governors University; and the Open Learning Agency in British Columbia. The paper concludes with an examination of the role of libraries and librarians in virtual universities. For further information on this project, see #161 above. A. Slade.

163. Spille, Henry A., David W. Stewart, and Eugene Sullivan. *External Degrees in the Information Age: Legitimate Choices*. American Council on Education/ Oryx Press Series on Higher Education. Phoenix, AZ: Oryx Press, 1997. 239 pp. ISBN 0-89774-997-9.

The purpose of this book is to provide a guide to accredited external degree programs in the United States. In the introductory chapters, libraries are mentioned in three contexts. In discussing an appropriate academic base for external degree programs on p. 28, the authors state that "there should be an adequate library or learning resource center, or arrangements should be in place for students to use other appropriate library facilities." On p. 35, in the chapter "Diploma Mills: What They Look Like and How to Avoid Them," one of the characteristics of a "diploma mill" is identified as follows: "the organization does not maintain a library of sufficient breadth and depth to support its programs, nor is there provision for access to non-owned libraries." In listing principles to consider when choosing a degree program on p. 37, the authors indicate that "learner support should provide convenient access to such services as counselling, financial aid information, and library resources." In the second part of the book, 140 legitimately accredited external degree programs are listed by state. Each listing includes a narrative program description containing information supplied by the institution about essential program elements. Many of the institutional descriptions include some mention of library services. The remarks vary in length from brief phrases to three or four sentences. A. Slade.

164. Stephens, Kate and Lorna Unwin. "Postgraduate Distance Education and Libraries: Educational Principles versus Pragmatic Course Design." *Teaching in Higher Education* 2, no. 2 (1997): 153-65.

As part of a research project funded by the British Library, 11 course providers were interviewed about their views on the role of the library in postgraduate distance learning. The authors discuss these views in relation to the expansion of postgraduate distance learning programs in the United Kingdom and the differences in expectations about library use between students and course providers. Selected comments from five interviews are included in this paper. Based on the findings of the research project and the interviews with course providers, a provisional typology of distance learning courses is presented to reflect various combinations of the requirements for and attitudes toward library use. It is pointed out that there is a conflict of values in distance learning between the desirability of self-contained courses and the need for access to library resources. The importance of library use is stressed as a means to foster critical thinking in teaching and learning. For the full report on the survey, see #637 in this volume. A. Slade.

165. Stephens, Kate and Lorna Unwin. "Revisiting 'Openness and Closure in Distance Education': A Critical Look at the Access Image of Distance Learning in the United Kingdom." In *Research in Distance Education 4: Revised Papers from the Fourth Research in Distance Education Conference, Deakin University, 1996*, edited by Terry Evans, Viktor Jakupec, and Diane Thompson. Geelong, Victoria: Deakin University Press, 1997, 79-93.

With reference to the findings of the British Library funded research project on the role of the library in postgraduate distance learning (see #637 in this volume), the authors take a critical look at the concepts of "openness" and equal opportunity in distance learning. In this context, various issues are discussed, including subject choice and student participation, recent developments in information technology, access to libraries, the virtual library, and the globalization of education. Findings from the research project revealed that library use is a clandestine activity for many distance learners due to the lack of support from staff at public libraries and restrictive access privileges at other university libraries. A case is made for more critical understanding of the complexities of distance learning in relation to openness and library use. A. Slade.

1996

166. Booker, Di. "Flexible Delivery Resources." In *Introduction to Information Management*, edited by J. Michael Brittain. Occasional Monographs, no. 16. Wagga Wagga, NSW: Centre for Information Studies, Charles Sturt University-Riverina, 1996, 229-37.

The Open Learning Information and Materials Clearing House (OLIMCH) supports flexible learning in South Australia by providing information and advisory services to TAFE SA lecturers, course designers, developers of learning materials, and curriculum writers. OLIMCH services and products include production of bibliographies on specialized topics, compilation and distribution of the Clearing House database, and contribution of holdings to the Australian Bibliographic Network (ABN). OLIMCH management strategies involve teamwork, a customer-centered philosophy, developing partnerships and strategic alliances with other clearinghouses, and a commitment to quality services. The Clearing House has established a reputation as a significant service that has contributed to increased productivity for flexible delivery development at TAFE SA. A. Slade.

167. Derlin, Roberta L. and Edward Erazo. *Distance Learning and the Digital Library: Transforming the Library into an Information Center*. 1996. 14 pp. ERIC ED 400 832. Reprinted in *Teaching and Learning at a Distance: What It Takes to Effectively Design, Deliver, and Evaluate Programs*, edited by Thomas E. Cyrs. New Directions for Teaching and Learning, no. 71. San Francisco: Jossey-Bass, 1997, 103-9.

In this futuristic view, the transformation of the library from a repository of print to a digital information center enables distance learners to obtain support for their educational goals. The challenges to this transformation include the growth of the World Wide Web, copyright and fair use issues, electronic mail, and electronic publications. Also discussed in this context is the future role of the librarian as information specialist. The factors determining whether or not libraries will be transformed into this vision of the future depend on technology and information issues. The authors note that it will be essential for librarians to learn new technologies and new skills to keep pace with technological developments in distance learning. M. Kascus.

168. Gupta, Dinesh Kumar and S. L. Jain. "Open University and Library: Concept and Relationship." *University News* (New Delhi) 34, no. 30 (July 22, 1996): 9-11, 17.

The role of the library in fulfilling the objectives of open universities in India is discussed in relation to the limitations of the study center libraries and the need to improve services to distance learners. To outline the current Indian scene, brief descriptions are provided of library services at Indira Gandhi National Open University, Kota Open University, and Dr. B. R. Ambedkar Open University. Cooperation between all types of libraries and computerization of open university libraries are highlighted as means to enhance services to distance learners. A. Slade.

169. Heery, Mike. "Academic Library Services to Non-Traditional Students." *Library Management* 17, no. 5 (1996): 3-13.

The premise of this paper is that academic libraries in the United Kingdom need to recognize the differences between traditional and non-traditional students and adapt their services to support this latter group of students. Four categories of non-traditional students are identified: students with disabilities, students from overseas countries, part-time students, and distance learners. Each type of student is discussed in relation to their characteristics, library needs, and ways that academic libraries can improve services to meet those needs. It is noted that one of the greatest challenges facing academic libraries is that of providing library services to the growing numbers of distance learners. Sheffield Hallam University and Northern College, Aberdeen, are cited as examples of UK academic libraries providing services to distance learners similar to those provided in North America. Drawing on the international literature, the following library services for distance learning are discussed: a designated staff member to coordinate services, provision of deposit collections or book boxes, borrowing privileges at local libraries, access to library catalogues, postal delivery services, enquiry services, library instruction, and promotion of services. A. Slade.

170. Jagannathan, Neela. "Taking Stock of Library Services to Distance Learners." *Kakatiya Journal of Open Learning* 2, no. 2 (December 1996): 29-52.

Following a summary of the growth of distance education in India, the topic of library support to off-campus students is examined from both an international and an Indian perspective. The library system in Indian open universities is discussed in relation to the regional and study centers, the requirements of distance learners, the problems faced by these students, the problems encountered by the open universities in providing library services, and evaluation studies of library facilities for distance learners at Indira Gandhi National Open University. A number of recommendations are offered on how to reach distance learners, including both manual services and services provided though multimedia technologies. The conclusion is that open university libraries in India need to provide a judicious mix of manual and technology oriented services to distance learners, and libraries of all types should assume responsibility for supporting these students. A. Slade.

171. Joy, Finbarr. "The LE Club Project: A Synergy of Systems for the 'Learning Environment'." *The Electronic Library* 14, no. 5 (October 1996): 405-10.

This is a review of the requirements and issues identified by the LE Club (Learning Environment Club) project for the development of a computerized learning environment. The project involves ten colleges of Further Education in the United Kingdom, with the library automation company Fretwell-Downing (FD) as technical leader and Sheffield Hallam University as research partner. The goal of the project is "managing the learning experience" with reference to distance learning over networks using digital materials. The development of an integrated distance learning system that links directly to library catalogues raises issues about the role of the library. The assumption is that by placing the library at the heart of the framework, the LE Club project is galvanizing the role of the library in the learning process and ensuring the continued importance of library services. Early indications are that the project is fostering collaboration between faculty and librarians in delivering integrated services. For a related paper, see #410 in this volume. M. Kascus.

172. Rodrigues, Helena F. "The Role of the Library in Distance Education." *Microcomputers for Information Management* 13, no. 1 (1996): 21-29.

The role of the library in distance education is seen as evolving in the current networked environment. This paper focuses on the influence of accreditation commissions' standards on library service to off-campus and distance education students and the library needs of these learners. Library expectations for distance education programs require institutions to develop an adequate base of resources and facilitate access to them, maintain an ongoing assessment strategy, provide adequate staff, ensure library services are provided to all users regardless of where they are located, and provide training and encouragement to faculty and students in the use of library resources. One solution to providing services to distance learners is to develop cooperative agreements with other libraries, but a library should not depend on agreements as the main resource for distance learners. The following policies and procedures currently in effect by libraries with distance education programs are discussed: state or regional borrowing cards, consortium membership, a toll-free telephone number, fax services, communication, networks, and the Internet. Planning should be the first item on the agenda, if the goal is service to distance learners. M. Kascus.

173. Walling, Linda Lucas. "Going the Distance: Equal Education, Off Campus or On." *Library Journal* 121, no. 20 (December 1996): 59-62.

Library education delivered via distance learning by the University of South Carolina is equal to that delivered by any other means in any other place, according to the author. In finding library resources, instructors and students identify appropriate, accessible collections, but students do travel to major libraries to complete assignments. Strong support, including some collection development activity, has occurred in many libraries in the states involved. Interlibrary loan, fax, and the Internet are major resources. The number and types of resources used for distance education programs were examined, and no obvious differences were found between those used by students in Columbia and those used by off-campus students. M. Kascus.

1995

174.   Campbell, Helen. "OLA's Open Learning Library and Information Services: OLLIS Evolving." *DESIGnation*, no. 7 (April 1995): 7-10.

Following a review of its services and administration, the Open Learning Library and Information Service (OLLIS) of Open Learning Australia (OLA) introduced a new scheme called OLLIS Mark2 to simplify procedures for open learning students to access libraries. This article summarizes the findings of a student survey and a survey of OLLIS Support Libraries conducted as part of the review, examines the review's recommendations, and looks at the objectives for OLLIS Mark2. The surveys found that OLA students' use of libraries was low and that most partner libraries were unaware of use by these students. It is hoped that OLLIS Mark2 will encourage library use through its simplicity and standardized approach to access, service, and cost management. For more information on OLLIS Mark2, see #175 below. A. Slade.

175.   Campbell, Helen. "OLLIS Mark2: Equity and Parity for Students—for Libraries." In *Access Through Open Learning: With a Major Focus on Networked Learning*, edited by Allan Ellis and Julie Burton. 2nd Edition. [Southern Cross University] Occasional Papers in Open Learning, vol. 5. Lismore, NSW: Norsearch, 1995, 31-37.

The Open Learning Library and Information Service (OLLIS) of Open Learning Australia (OLA) introduced in 1995 a revised approach to library services called OLLIS Mark2. The recommendations from a number of reviews and the Senate Inquiry into the Development of Open Learning in Australia (see #120 and #127 in this volume) prompted a new system of library service to open learning students based on operational simplicity, financial limitations, and responsiveness for all the parties involved. The basic structure of OLLIS Mark2 eliminates the need for library vouchers and includes a simplified process for students to enroll at an OLLIS Support Library at no charge, with the exception of a delivery fee for those students who enroll as off-campus borrowers. OLA underwrites the student enrollment fees, paying the OLLIS Support Libraries a standard fee for each enrollment. OLLIS Mark2 aims to provide equitable access to library services for all OLA students and parity of funding across a range of partner libraries. A. Slade.

176.   Curran, Chris. "University Distance Teaching: Library Support and the New Technologies." In *Proceedings of the First "Libraries Without Walls" Conference, Mytilene, Greece, 9-10 September 1995*, edited by Ann Irving and Geoff Butters. Preston, UK: Centre for Research in Library and Information Management, University of Central Lancashire, 1995, 4-12.

This paper begins with the assumption that distance teaching at the university level is a substantial and well-established component of higher education in a growing number of countries. The advantages, nature, and cost structure for distance education are discussed as well as library access, the area that has historically been poorly developed. The emphasis shifts to the potential of technology to help with the challenge. The problem of implementing the new technologies is discussed in terms of the availability of facilities for student access and the constraints of copyright. The author concludes that technology offers a viable solution to the delivery of library services to remote users, but it is still rare in tertiary institutions because of the inherent problems in universal access and copyright. M. Kascus.

177.   Devi, V. Rama. "The Role of Dr. B. R. Ambedkar Open University Library in Quality Assurance in Distance Education." In *Quality Assurance in Distance Education*, edited by M. Satyanarayana Rao. Hyderabad, India: Centre for Evaluation, Dr. B. R. Ambedkar Open University, 1995, 178-80.

   The central library of Dr. B. R. Ambedkar Open University (BRAOU) in India provides services to its 92 study centers, including collection development, acquisitions, and maintenance. The central library is also responsible for providing referral services to BRAOU distance learners and input into course development. The library has recently changed its role from that of storehouse to being an active information center. In its new role, the library has created a computer network to link universities, colleges, and research institutions, and has developed a media library. The next step is to initiate resource sharing with libraries of other open universities and build an effective network of distance education libraries. With this structure in place, the central library would be able to transmit information quickly to BRAOU study centers. By providing distance learners with easy access to information, the library can contribute to quality assurance in the university. A. Slade.

178.   Gardner, W. Jeanne. "Community Colleges Serving Branch Campuses." *Colorado Libraries* 21, no. 1 (Spring 1995): 15-17.

   Four Colorado college libraries and resource centers are described in terms of how they serve distance learners at branch campuses and their perceptions of that service. The community colleges described are Arapahoe Community College, Front Range Community College Westminster Campus, Pikes Peak Community College, and Pueblo Community College. The ability of community colleges to offer services to branch campus sites is facilitated by the Access Colorado Library Information Network (ACLIN), which provides access to the automated systems and online catalogues of over 120 Colorado libraries as well as to online databases, and the CARL Corporation. M. Kascus.

179.   Kincaid, Ramona, Lillian Mangum, Paula Mochida, and Ellen Okuma. "STARS: Navigating Distance Education Library Services Between Islands." In *The Seventh Off-Campus Library Services Conference Proceedings: San Diego, California, October 25-27, 1995*, compiled by Carol J. Jacob. Mount Pleasant, MI: Central Michigan University, 1995, 213-20.

   The Hawaii Interactive Television System (HITS) provided an opportunity for distance education librarians to participate in the University of Hawaii's outreach program. "STARS" provided the priorities for library support and a plan of action. An information brochure was developed to inform distance education faculty of the newly coordinated services available to them and their students. Included among the services are reference assistance at the remote site or via a toll-free number; access to collections and borrowing privileges; document delivery via telefacsimile, full-text databases, or other electronic format; library instruction via HITS and/or on-site; and core collections. Other efforts to improve the quality of service to distance education programs included meeting with students and attending cohort program meetings, teaching students search strategies and describing resources and services, and administering surveys to get input from students and faculty in these programs. For a related paper, see #289 in the second bibliography. M. Kascus.

180.   Moore, Michael G. "Editorial: The 1995 Distance Education Research Symposium: A Research Agenda." *American Journal of Distance Education* 9, no. 2 (1995): 1-6.

  This editorial reports on the Third Distance Education Research Symposium held at Penn State University in 1995. Research presentations were organized into four groups: course design, instruction, policy and administration, and learners and learning. In the area of research on instruction, one presentation related to the role and future of the library in the distance learning environment. Issues discussed include the importance of remote access and the role of electronic resources in contributing to the quality of distance education. Future research needs recommended in this presentation are a comparison of attitudes and performance of off-campus and on-campus students regarding library use and skills, measurement of student learning outcomes in terms of information literacy, and a determination of how best to include library information skills in the distance education curriculum. Four monographs were produced based on the presentations of the four research groups and are available from the American Center for the Study of Distance Education. M. Kascus.

181.   Shillinglaw, Noel. "Academic Transformation and Library and Information Service at the University of South Africa." In *The Seventh Off-Campus Library Services Conference Proceedings: San Diego, California, October 25-27, 1995*, compiled by Carol J. Jacob. Mount Pleasant, MI: Central Michigan University, 1995, 341-53.

  This study argues for greater involvement of the librarian in the learning process of distance students in South Africa, where information resources and the use of the library are important to tertiary education. The distinction between the dedicated distance teaching university and the off-campus extensions of conventional universities is breaking down. The term "transformation" is used in this paper in connection with the change process operating in distance education in South Africa to express radical change and the reconstruction of the system. The need for academic libraries in South Africa to investigate regional or national collaboration in the areas of information systems, resource sharing, and provision of service is stressed. This renewal process, with its reassessment of national educational policies and resources, is seen as signaling a new direction that will also place distance education clearly in its African context rather than emulating foreign models. M. Kascus.

182.   Snyder, Carolyn A. and Jay Starratt. "Distance Learning and the Academic Library." In *Continuity and Transformation: The Promise of Confluence: Proceedings of the Seventh National Conference of the Association of College and Research Libraries, Pittsburgh, Pennsylvania, March 29-April 1, 1995*, edited by Richard AmRhein. Chicago: Association of College and Research Libraries, 1995, 317-20.

By convincing the university administration that the distance learning infrastructure should reside with the library, the academic library is poised to expand its role as the key campus learning support operation. This view is based on experiences at Southern Illinois University at Carbondale. Several aspects of the academic library structure are examined in terms of the needs of distance learning programs. Several reasons are given to demonstrate that libraries can move easily into distance learning. First, libraries have considerable knowledge and experience in working with all departments, schools, and campus-wide academic programs. Second, libraries have demonstrated their effectiveness in supporting the learning process through reserve books, media rooms, library instruction, and point-of-need assistance at the reference desk. Third, library deans and directors have demonstrated their leadership and management ability in organizing technology-based learning services. Fourth, libraries are heavily involved in networks and other technological developments. Fifth, libraries have demonstrated leadership in multitype library networks, cooperative borrowing, and other consortia activity. For all of these reasons, libraries are well positioned to assume a major responsibility in distance learning. M. Kascus.

183. Unwin, Lorna, Neil Bolton, and Kate Stephens. "The Role of the Library in Distance Learning: Implications for Policy and Practice." *Library and Information Briefings*, no. 60 (May 1995): 1-9.

A progress report is provided on the British Library funded study, entitled "The Role of the Library in Distance Learning," which was underway at the University of Sheffield in 1995. The study, conducted between 1994 and 1996, was close to its mid-point at the time of writing. With reference to the scope and methodology of the research project, this "briefing" examines a number of current issues in the provision of library services to distance learning students, including the scale of distance learning, characteristics of the distance learner, access to libraries, and the role of information technology. For the full report on the project, see #637 in this volume. A. Slade.

1994

---

184. Panchaly, Nalini. "Distance Education System and Library Service." In *Distance Education in India: Studies in Quality and Quantitative Aspects*, edited by K. Murali Manohar. IDEA Publications no. 1. Warangal, India: Indian Distance Education Association, 1994, 154-61.

Following an outline of the distance education system in India, the role of the library is considered. The author advocates that, in addition to traditional library functions, libraries in Indian distance education institutions need to organize the following services to reach the common people: career information centers, mobile units, facilities in study centers, collection development to fight illiteracy, and extension activities such as lecture groups and reading circles. Future goals in this area include strengthening the public library system and connecting libraries via computer networks. A. Slade.

185. Wade, Winnie. "Flexible Learning in Higher Education: Implications for Librarians." *Education Libraries Journal* 37, no. 2 (1994): 5-10.

After providing a general examination of the concept of flexible learning, this article discusses the Flexible Learning Initiative at Loughborough University of Technology and the implications of flexible learning for librarians. The main objective of the Flexible Learning Initiative is to develop a strategic approach to the promotion and support of innovative methods of teaching and learning. The increased emphasis on resource-based learning has placed considerable pressure on academic libraries in terms of collection development, space, and technology. The author stresses that the key element for librarians with regard to flexible learning must be close collaboration and cooperation with tutors and teaching staff so that services can be planned and resources acquired at an early stage in the program. A. Slade.

1992

186. Sharifabadi, Saeed Rezaei. *Information Gathering Behaviour of Students Studying in Distance Education and Off-Campus Programs at University Level*. Originally prepared as a course paper in November 1992. Online. Available: http://wilma.silas.unsw.edu.au/students/R-REZAEI/off-camp.htm (Accessed April 13, 2000).

Four surveys have been selected for examination in this review of the information-gathering behaviour of university distance education students. In addition, several models of information provision through library services are discussed. The surveys selected are the Open University Survey (England, 1978), the University of Wyoming Survey (United States, 1983), the Chinook Educational Consortium (Canada, 1985), and the Deakin University Survey (Australia, 1987). The reports of these studies are discussed individually, followed by a comparative evaluation. All four studies are limited because of the problems associated with the use of questionnaires only and the fact that the data gathered are broad and generalized. The concern is that the surveys do not measure the amount of use of informal channels in gathering information. The studies show that distance learners gather information through other students, faculty, and course-tutors in addition to using library resources and consulting librarians. It is noted that the biggest barrier to student information gathering is faculty perception of student needs, because they assume that all student information needs are met by course packages. M. Kascus.

Public Libraries

For other works that discuss this topic, see the following headings in the Subject Index: "open learning—public libraries" and "role of the library in distance learning—public libraries."

1999

187. McCormick, Angela and Audrey Sutton. "Independent Learning Online." *Scottish Libraries*, no. 73 (1999): 14-17.

The authors report on South Ayrshire Libraries' project to investigate use of the World Wide Web as a means of accessing online courses for independent learners. Interim successes in the project included the introduction of information skills support to the public library environment and the provision of Web-based support materials for learners who are pursuing independent study courses. This article focuses on the following issues in the project: practical implementation, local partnerships, staff training, cost, and models of future provision. The authors note that this research has highlighted a number of areas of interest to public libraries, and other local authorities have expressed interest in adapting the information skills interface for their own public library situations. For the final report on the project, see #193 below. A. Slade.

188. Roza, Frank. [Distance Education and Public Library Supply]. *Tudomanyos es Muszaki Tajekoztatas*, no. 3 (March 1999): 101-5.

The purpose of the European LISTED project is to involve public libraries in open and distance education systems aided by individual learning and new information technology tools. This involvement includes making learning packages available for individual learning, providing literature for reference purposes, and managing consultation opportunities and support for orientation in distance learning programs. When LISTED was extended to Central and Eastern Europe in 1998, Hungary was the first country to join the project. This paper describes the involvement of two Hungarian county libraries in LISTED, as well as the participation of the Distance Learning Center of the Technical University. A. Slade.

1998

189. Allred, John. "Open Learning in Germany: Laying the Foundation for Learning." *Library Association Record* 100, no. 1 (January 1998): 15.

The author comments on the current status of open and distance learning in Germany and his role as an advisor on the development of open learning in German public libraries. Allred indicates that opportunities exist for public libraries to support open learning and some librarians seem willing to collaborate with educational and training providers. However, he stresses that many public librarians will need to change their attitudes about being supporters of learning as opposed to deliverers of information. Allred also remarks that a well-managed national government program is necessary in Germany for successful development of public library support for open learning. A. Slade.

190. Kühne, Brigitte. *DERAL: Distance Education in Rural Areas via Libraries. Workpackage 1: State of the Art. D1.1/D1.2 Report on Existing Studies*. October 29, 1998. Online. Available: http://deral.infc.ulst.ac.uk/ (can be downloaded in Word 97) (Accessed April 13, 2000).

   DERAL (Distance Education in Rural Areas via Libraries) is a project under the Telematics for Libraries initiative in Europe, which aims to encourage the role of public libraries in the transfer of information, knowledge, and education to users who have difficulty following normal courses of study. The goal of the DERAL project is to develop guidelines for public librarians throughout Europe on support for library users wishing to participate in distance learning and related information searching. A set of tools based on Internet technology and videoconferencing will be developed to allow libraries to act as brokers between the providers of distance learning courses and users. DERAL is intended to serve as a prototype in five regions of Europe and, if successful, will become a model for Europe-wide access to distance learning through public libraries. This report documents the current position with regard to distance-learning provision in the five DERAL regions (Sweden, Austria, Spain, the United Kingdom, and the Republic of Ireland) and describes current and previous studies in the field. A. Slade.

191. Kühne, Brigitte. *DERAL: Distance Education in Rural Areas via Libraries. Workpackage 1: State of the Art. D1.3 User Responses*. October 29, 1998. Online. Available: http://deral.infc.ulst.ac.uk/ (can be downloaded in Word 97) (Accessed April 13, 2000).

   As part of the DERAL Project (see #190 above), the needs and aspirations of learners, public libraries, and education providers were measured in a survey of the DERAL regions of Europe. The aim of the survey was to answer the following questions: (1) Who are the students who require distance education facilities in public libraries and why? (2) Why do public libraries want to support distance learning? and (3) Why do educational institutions want to support distance learning by providing courses? This report summarizes the methods used in the survey and the findings. A. Slade.

192. McCormick, Angela and Audrey Sutton. "Logging On at the Library." *Adults Learning* 9, no. 10 (June 1998): 12-14.

   This article outlines interim findings of the British Library funded "Open Learning and the Internet" Project of South Ayrshire Libraries. In this project, the term "open learning" covered a range of independent learning approaches, including distance learning. South Ayrshire Libraries established a network of links with the local university, local colleges, and the business community to investigate how the public library can best support a diverse group of learners. The partners were given responsibility for identifying representative groups to participate in the project. In determining the learning needs of the participants, it was found that learners wanted training on the Internet as well as improved information retrieval skills and specific information resources to support courses. To meet these needs, the project highlighted a role for public libraries in providing Internet training. To this end, a Web-based information skills tutorial was mounted on South Ayrshire Libraries website. At the time of writing, the project had seven months to run and the next step was to concentrate on the practical implementation of work already done. For the final report on the project, see #193 below. A. Slade.

193.   McCormick, Angela and Audrey Sutton. *Open Learning and the Internet in the Public Library*. British Library Research and Innovation Report 135. Wetherby, UK: British Library Research and Innovation Centre, 1998. 74 pp. ISBN 0-7123-97299. Also online. Available: http://www.south-ayrshire.gov.uk/blric/Contents.htm (Accessed April 13, 2000).

The aim of the South Ayrshire Libraries' "Open Learning and the Internet" Project, which took place in 1997–1998, was to demonstrate how open learning materials available on the Internet could be integrated with the provision of open learning services in public libraries to provide an enhanced learning environment. The specific objectives of the project were to establish an online directory of information skills resources for independent learners in public libraries, integrate maintenance of the directory with normal staff duties, add subject-specific units to the online directory and organize this material on the project website, identify groups of independent and distance learners to take part in information skills training courses, create profiles of these learners through questionnaires and interviews, develop and deliver the in-house training courses, and evaluate the training courses and subject directories. The report provides details on the project objectives and methodologies, the analysis of the research results, the technical issues and staff training implications, the conclusions of the project, and areas identified for further research. A. Slade.

194.   Newton, Robert, Audrey Sutton, and Mike McConnell. "Information Skills for Open Learning: A Public Library Initiative." *Library Review* 47, no. 2 (1998): 125-34.

South Ayrshire Libraries, in collaboration with Robert Gordon University, developed a Web-based information skills package for open learners as part of a British Library funded project to enhance public library support to users engaged in open or distance learning. One of the main aims was to provide access to learning resources, as opposed to information about the Internet. The project was not intended to duplicate existing electronic resources, but rather to identify and classify a range of learning resources and make them accessible through a Web-based directory. This directory could then be used as the basis for developing information skills courses to be made available locally by public library staff. Details are provided on the procedure and rationale for developing the information skills website and the progress on the project to date. For the final report on the project, see #193 above. A. Slade.

195.   Sutton, Audrey, Robert Newton, and Mike McConnell. *Open Learning and the Internet in Public Libraries—An Information Skills Approach*. Online. Available: http://www.south-ayrshire.gov.uk/blric/webartic.htm (Accessed April 13, 2000).

A progress report is provided on South Ayrshire Libraries' project to enhance public library support for open and distance learners. This report outlines information on the background of the project, objectives, progress, the directories of subject-specific open learning materials, and interim conclusions. For the final report on the project, see #193 above. A. Slade.

196. Sutton, Audrey. "Open Learning and the Internet in the Public Library." *OLS News* (Open Learning Systems), no. 64 (June 1998): 4-5.

South Ayrshire Libraries initiated a project to identify the needs of open and independent learners who draw upon the resources of public libraries. This article is a progress report on the project at the halfway point, outlining information on the website developed for learners, interim findings, evaluation of the research, implications for staff and learners, and interim conclusions. The website was intended to assist learners by providing an information skills tutorial, a Web-based open learning directory, and a list of subject directories on a range of learning resources. For the final report on the project, see #193 above. A. Slade.

197. Sutton, Audrey, Robert Newton, and Mike McConnell. "Open Learning and the Net." *Public Library Journal* 13, no. 2 (March/April 1998): 26-29.

The progress of a British Library funded project to enhance public library support to users engaged in open or distance learning is reviewed in this article. The project was initiated by South Ayrshire Libraries in Scotland, in collaboration with Robert Gordon University. The objective was to identify and classify a range of learning resources that could be accessed via the Internet. This was to be accomplished by designing and developing a Web-based directory to support open learners. Details are provided on the proposal submitted to the British Library, the model of information skills teaching developed for the project, the parameters established for learners and resources, recent progress, future challenges, and interim conclusions. For the final report on the project, see #193 above. A. Slade.

198. Watkin, Alan. "The Public Library: The Local Support Centre for Open and Distance Learners." In *Libraries Without Walls 2: The Delivery of Library Services to Distant Users*, edited by Peter Brophy, Shelagh Fisher, and Zoë Clarke. London: Library Association Publishing, 1998, 143-50.

The role of the public library in supporting lifelong learning is considered with reference to developments in Clwyd, Wales, and to two projects funded by the European Commission. There are three foci in the Clwyd public library initiative: provision of information on learning opportunities, development of learner support, and direct delivery of learning activities through open and distance learning. The PLAIL (Public Libraries and Adult Independent Learners) Project, which ended in 1995, demonstrated the contributions of the public library to the personal development of its customers and identified the barriers that prevent adults from accessing conventional educational and training opportunities. The LISTED (Library Integrated System for Telematics-based Education) Project, still in progress at the time of writing, seeks to address the issue of user services based on the identification and retrieval of resources and the establishment of pilot sites for library-mediated access to learning opportunities. An outcome of both projects has been the identification of the needs of open and distance learners. These needs involve access to information on learning opportunities, appropriate study materials, adequate facilities and equipment, and counselling/guidance services. A. Slade.

1997

199. Osborne, Elizabeth. "Open Learning in Public Libraries: The Experience of Three Counties." *Open Learning* 12, no. 1 (February 1997): 62-65. Abbreviated version published as "Open Learning in Public Libraries: Creating Community Learning." *Adults Learning* 7, no. 7 (March 1996): 162-63.

These articles describe the open learning services of three public library authorities in the United Kingdom: Clwyd Library and Information Service, Cambridgeshire Libraries and Information Service, and Staffordshire Library Service. Each of the authorities has attempted to develop a comprehensive open learning service with access to appropriate equipment, general guidance, and direct tutorial support. Each authority has also adopted a proactive policy in relation to networking, publicity, and working with the local community. A. Slade.

1996

200. Allred, John. "Public Libraries and Open Learning." *Open Learning Today*, no. 29 (January/February 1996): 7-9.

Public libraries are well placed and suited to support adult learning and the concept of lifelong learning. The advances made by the Open for Learning Project in the United Kingdom to provide open learning services in public libraries include ease of access to learning materials and appropriate hardware, the availability of trained staff to assist users, and collaboration between public libraries and local organizations such as colleges and open learning centers. An example of public library staff helping a user to get started in open learning illustrates the success of the project. A. Slade.

201. Donaghy, Pauline. "Lessons in Learning." *Scottish Libraries*, no. 57 (1996): 14-15.

Shetland Library's open learning service for remote island communities has proved popular. The author describes her experience in establishing the service. Training of library staff was an important component in the development process, providing background information about the service and product awareness. The aim of the service is to encourage customers to engage in further learning. Staff routinely follow-up with learners by telephone to determine how they are doing with the open learning materials and whether they need any assistance. Ideas in progress at the time of writing include a questionnaire to help determine customer needs, development of a computer/AV center, temporary employment of a tutor/counsellor, further staff training, and a mobile open learning service for the remote island communities. A. Slade.

202. Donald, Arthur. "Open Learning: An Issue of Quality." *Scottish Libraries*, no. 59 (1996): 10-11.

With reference to the Open for Learning Project in the United Kingdom, the author describes the production of a guide and video to assist public library staff in determining the best methods for providing open learning services. The guide identifies a number of quality issues that should be taken into account, including materials, equipment, promotion, learner support, staff development, evaluation, management, and planning. The guide is intended to help library staff understand who are the typical users of an open learning service, how to support these users, how to establish links to career and educational guidance, and ways to access technical and tutorial support and other library resources. The film that accompanies the guide demonstrates how library staff can apply some of the approaches described in the guide. A. Slade.

203. Langhorn, K. "Open Distance Learning: Endnu et Udkald til Fremtiden?" [Open Distance Learning: Yet Another Call to the Future?]. *Bibliotekspressen*, no. 1 (January 1996): 10-11.

The role of public libraries in supporting Open Distance Learning (ODL) in Denmark is discussed. The author argues that public libraries are appropriate bodies to assume this role due to their experience in providing materials to different user groups. The position of Danish public libraries will be strengthened if they agree to act as intermediaries in managing ODL resources and materials. A. Slade.

204. Lupro, Linda and Joyce Claypool Kennerly. "Cutting the Public Library/Distance Learning Edge." *Texas Library Journal* 72, no. 4 (Winter 1996): 166-69. Also online. Available: http://www.txla.org/pubs/tlj-4q96/lupro.html (Accessed April 13, 2000).

A historical perspective is given on the Distance Learning Center at Fort Bend County Libraries' George Memorial Library, the only distance learning center in a public library in the United States. The authors discuss how the library was approached by Texas A & M University to participate in a successful grant proposal to fund a demonstration project that would bring distance learning, the Internet, and electronic literacy and information services to unserved populations in five Texas communities. The Distance Learning Center has been used in many ways. There are links to the academic world, providing a variety of opportunities for staff development and public education, including adult education and literacy volunteers. Continuing education short courses have included study skills and re-mediation classes. Examples of staff development activities directly involving the Distance Learning Center are given. Fort Bend County Libraries is in the forefront of a development in public libraries that is helping to provide opportunities for others. M. Kascus.

1995

205. Aldrich, Rona and Alan Watkin. "Public Libraries and Open Learning Service Delivery—Accrediting the Librarians Contribution." *Public Library Journal* 10, no. 1 (January/February 1995): 28-31.

With reference to the Open for Learning Project involving open learning and public libraries in the United Kingdom, the staff training initiatives of the Clwyd and Gwynedd public library authorities in Wales are discussed. The authorities sought financial and training support in 1992 to accredit a pilot group of librarians in the provision of services to open learners through the public library network. The accreditation process was intended to bring librarians' skills and competencies in line with the standards established for a NVQ (National Vocational Qualification) in Flexible and Open Learning. The experimental program was undertaken in partnership with local councils and produced positive outcomes in terms of meeting customer needs, enhancing the confidence of library staff, and establishing closer working relationships between library authorities and training and enterprise councils. A. Slade.

206. Allred, John. "Making Learning Truly Open." *Library Association Record* 97, no. 5 (May 1995): 267-69.

The author reviews some of the findings of the Open and Flexible Learning in Public Libraries Second Baseline Survey (see #589 in this volume), concentrating on major developments in public libraries between 1992 and 1994, the characteristics of learners who use open learning materials, the involvement of library staff in learner support, and the potential of library technology to assist learners. Additional information is provided on definitions of open and flexible learning, bibliographic information systems that list and evaluate open learning materials, European research programs that are concerned with open learning and libraries, and the training of library staff in the delivery of open learning. A. Slade.

207. Allred, John. "The Managing of Libraries for Adult Education." *An Leabharlann, The Irish Library* 11, no. 3 (1995): 129-37.

With reference to the Open for Learning Project in the United Kingdom, this article looks at the public library as a learning place. The argument is advanced that the major function of the public library is to support adult learning and all other activities are either a by-product of this function or incidental to it. Some inadequate paradigms about public libraries are identified and an alternative paradigm is proposed. This view puts the public library at the center of self-directed learning, providing customers with a set of "maps" to determine their information needs and ways to fulfil those needs. A. Slade.

208. Allred, John and Joyce Allred. "Open and Distant Learning in Public Libraries." In *Proceedings of the First "Libraries Without Walls" Conference, Mytilene, Greece, 9-10 September 1995*, edited by Ann Irving and Geoff Butters. Preston, UK: Centre for Research in Library and Information Management, University of Central Lancashire, 1995, 67-69.

The Library Association, in partnership with Information for Learning, has been monitoring the UK's Open for Learning Project for three years. This paper focuses on the experiences of two distance learners, illustrating how the public library can provide opportunities for individual learning. The open learning functions that a public library can perform are identified as awareness of open learning, confidence in learning, information and guidance about learning opportunities, assessment and support, access and referral to learning resources for independent learning, and progression to formal education and training. M. Kascus.

209. Booker, Di. "Open Learning and Public Libraries." *Australasian Public Librar-ies and Information Services* 8, no. 1 (March 1995): 4-9.

Because Australasian public libraries are expected to assist open learning students and other independent learners, the author examines the findings of the PLAIL (Public Libraries and Adult Independent Learners) Project in Europe to determine their applicability to public libraries in her part of the world. Five areas identified by the PLAIL report in which public libraries can support adult learners are information provision, access to appropriate study materials, adequate facili-ties and equipment, educational counselling, and information literacy support. The author poses a number of questions under each of the five areas to begin a de-bate about what services and resources Australasian public libraries can and should provide to independent learners. An annotated list of publications high-lighting relevant issues in this area is included at the end of the article. A. Slade.

210. Brophy, Peter, John Allred, and Joyce Allred. *Open Distance Learning in Public Libraries: Final Report*. (PROLIB/ODL 10117). Preston, UK: Centre for Re-search in Library and Information Management, University of Central Lancashire, 1995. Online. Available: http://www.mmu.ac.uk/h-ss/cerlim/projects/odinhp.htm (in MSWord format) (Accessed April 13, 2000).

This is the final report on the Open Distance Learning in Public Libraries (PROLIB/ODL) project of the Centre for Research in Library and Information Management (CERLIM) in the United Kingdom. The topic, open distance learning in public libraries, was investigated through a four phase study. Phase one exam-ined the responsibilities for open learning in the European Union. Phase two exam-ined how public libraries were already contributing to distance learning or might contribute in the future. Phase three investigated ways in which open distance learn-ing in public libraries could be coordinated with other European Union projects. Phase four investigated requirements and specifications for support systems to fa-cilitate use of open distance learning technology by library users. M. Kascus.

211. Green, Andrew. "Open and Flexible Learning Opportunities." *Public Library Journal* 10, no. 5 (September/October 1995): 123-26.

With reference to the Open Learning in Public Libraries initiative in the United Kingdom, the development of open learning services in Staffordshire is described. Since receiving funding from the Employment Department in 1993, Staffordshire Library Service has successfully expanded its open learning net-work in public libraries and prisons. It has also developed complementary advice and guidance services and instigated the formulation of a policy for teleworking in libraries and a telematics strategy in partnership with the Youth and Commu-nity Education Service. Details are provided on the beginnings of the project, planning the open learning center, the production of a video promoting the serv-ice, expansion of the network of centers, the provision of open learning services in local prisons, the introduction of adult guidance and support services, publicity for the services, and current developments. A. Slade.

212. Stein, F. "Afstandsonderwijs Dichter Bij de Burger: Open Universiteit Vestigt Steunpunten in Openbare Bibliotheken." [Bringing Distance Learning Closer to the Public: The Open University Creates Study Help Centres in Public Libraries]. *Bibliotheek en Samenleving* 23, no. 3 (March 1995): 29-31.

To provide distance students of the Open University in the Netherlands with access to information, 18 study centers were created, three of which were located in libraries. In 1993, a network of smaller centers was established, with four of them situated in public libraries. The author indicates that students value the link with the public library and that its designation as an Open University support center underlines the contribution that libraries can make to distance learning. A. Slade.

213. Trohopoulos, Ioannis and Julie Carpenter. "Extending European Information Access Through Mobile Library Services: Some First Results." In *Proceedings of the First "Libraries Without Walls" Conference, Mytilene, Greece, 9-10 September 1995*, edited by Ann Irving and Geoff Butters. Preston, UK: Centre for Research in Library and Information Management, University of Central Lancashire, 1995, 47-54.

An overview of public libraries and mobile libraries in Greece is given, with a focus on the MOBILE project. The MOBILE research project identified user target groups in remote communities and their information needs. The project had three library authority partners located in Greece, Scotland, and the Netherlands. The purpose of the project was to investigate the technical feasibility of introducing a range of information and document delivery services into the existing public library network using telecommunications technology and the mobile library environment. The problems and issues involved in extending end-user services are outlined. The three field trials included a locally designed monitoring and evaluation component. M. Kascus.

214. Watkin, Alan. "Public Libraries and Adult Independent Learners (PLAIL)—New Technology to Meet a New and Old Customer Need." *Program: Automated Library and Information Systems* 29, no. 4 (October 1995): 433-43.

The 1994–1995 European Commission funded project, called PLAIL (Public Libraries and Adult Independent Learners), was led by the Clwyd Library and Information Service in partnership with institutions and agencies in Scotland, Spain, and Portugal. The objectives of the project were to conduct research into the needs of adult independent learners, define the services required to meet those needs, and outline to what extent those services would rely on existing and new technology. This paper examines the progress and some of the findings of the project and discusses the under-utilization of technology in public libraries. Three potential ways to improve public library services for adult independent learners are identified: (1) developing technologically based staff training, (2) investing in cost-effective technology, and (3) adopting internationally recognized specification standards for multimedia and technology. The paper concludes by outlining a program for delivering staff training through use of audio-visual media, print materials, CD-ROM, and multimedia computer software. A. Slade.

215. Williams, Richard. "Open Learning and Public Libraries: An Educator's Perspective." *Australasian Public Libraries and Information Services* 8, no. 2 (June 1995): 51-56.

In response to an article in a previous issue of this journal (see #209 in this chapter), the author offers an educator's point of view on public library services for open learning in Australia. The argument is advanced that the concept of the adult independent learner is flawed in its realization and very few independent learners actually exist due to a lack of appropriate support mechanisms. It is emphasized that public libraries have a central role in supporting independent learning and helping learners become information literate. The author recognizes that the Australian public library system is overextended and suggests that networking among libraries, especially between libraries in different states, may be one means to increase support for open and distance learners. A continuing education program for library staff on strategies for assisting independent learners is recommended as another way to enhance public library support in this area. A. Slade.

1994

216. Allred, John. "Library-Based Open Learning." In *Open Learning in the Mainstream*, edited by Mary Thorpe and David Grugeon. Harlow, UK: Longman, 1994, 74-86.

This chapter reviews the history and development of open learning in public libraries in the United Kingdom, with a comparison to the United States. The topics discussed include the characteristics of the learners, open learning packs, educational guidance, self-help resources, referral networks, the UK Open for Learning Project, the role of academic libraries in open learning, and the training of library staff. A. Slade.

217. Brent, Jocelyn. "Opportunities for Libraries in Rural and Isolated Communities." In *Public Libraries: Trading in Futures: Proceedings of the 1st National Public Libraries Conference, Melbourne, 1-3 February 1994*, edited by Alan Bundy. Adelaide, SA: Austlib Press, 1994, 114-16.

The author observes that people in rural and isolated areas of Queensland are engaging in open and distance learning programs and need access to library resources. The libraries in these communities have both advantages and disadvantages. The advantages of rural libraries are that they are recognized as the community center; the librarian is able to provide personalized attention to users; and the libraries can link via the State Library into the state, national, and international library systems. The disadvantages are the time taken to satisfy requests mostly due to a lack of technology, limited hours of access, and lack of adequate support from local authorities. To strengthen these libraries, the author recommends that they form partnerships with other libraries, government agencies, and businesses. The development of distance learning opportunities for public library staff may attract qualified librarians to isolated areas and offer an opportunity for teaching institutions and public libraries to work together to provide technology and assistance for people engaged in self-directed learning in remote centers. A. Slade.

218. Bundy, Alan. "Redefining Remoteness in the Learning Society." In *First National Conference on Building a Better Future for Regional Australia, Whyalla, South Australia, 20-22 April 1994: Proceedings*, edited by Alan Bundy. Whyalla: University of South Australia Library, 1994, 230-37.

Participation in open learning and distance education programs is increasing in rural areas of Australia. The libraries in these remote centers are poorly equipped to respond to the needs of adult learners. Among the problems facing rural libraries are lack of qualified staff, difficulties in providing staff training, dependence on interlibrary loans to meet information needs, and demands for outreach services from people who cannot easily visit the library. To make rural libraries more accessible and useful, the author recommends establishing joint use libraries with other institutions such as schools, regionalizing collections, using more technology, installing a toll-free telephone number for out-of town users, and providing speedy mechanisms such as courier service and fax to deliver library resources to isolated areas. Also recommended are a formal review and evaluation to determine ways of providing better access to library services and development of a local information policy that takes into account community needs, available resources, and options for cooperation with other organizations and institutions. A. Slade.

219. Oakley, David, John Allred, Peter Shufflebotham, and Keith Lindsay. *Open for Learning: Physical Environment in Public Library Open Learning Centres*. London: Employment Department, 1994. 13 pp. ISBN 0-8639-2407-7.

Intended as a checklist of good practice, this guide offers suggestions for public libraries on the layout of open learning centers. The following topics are covered: location, lighting, workspace, hardware, software, signs and directions, getting started, and potential problems and their effects. A. Slade.

220. Van Dyk, Marie-Thérèse. "Open Learning: Open Information Access." In *Public Libraries: Trading in Futures: Proceedings of the 1st National Public Libraries Conference, Melbourne, 1-3 February 1994*, edited by Alan Bundy. Adelaide, SA: Austlib Press, 1994, 105-13.

With an emphasis on the role of public libraries, this paper provides a broad overview of library services for open learning in Australia as of 1994. The topics covered include the characteristics of open learning, the Open Learning Agency of Australia, the Open Learning Library and Information Service (OLLIS), funding for open learning library services, the library voucher scheme, the role of public libraries in the open learning network, public library funding, and electronic access issues in public libraries. The author emphasizes that the Open Learning Agency of Australia has created new educational options for students and that libraries must undergo a paradigm shift and adopt new strategies and technologies to meet the information needs of these students. With some modifications of policies and participation in electronic networks, Australian public libraries can become major players in supporting open learning students. A. Slade.

221. Watkin, Alan. "Open and Successful: Open Learning and the Clwyd Library and Information Service." *Open Learning Today*, no. 23 (November 1994): 7-10.

Staff expertise is identified as a vital factor in the success of the Open Learning Service of the Clwyd Library and Information Service. Library staff in Clwyd attempt to offer comprehensive support to their open learning customers by helping them identify their educational/training goals, providing appropriate information, selecting other resources to support a specific study program, assisting in programming the course of studies, acting as a general advisor during the learning program, helping to alleviate potential problems of isolation, providing effective referral advice when tutorial or subject support is needed, and assisting in the accreditation process. Other factors contributing to the success of Clwyd's service are a training program designed for librarians working with open learning customers and partnerships with local colleges and other agencies. A. Slade.

1993

222. Library Association. "Clwyd Leads Way in European Project." *Library Association Record* 95, no. 10 (October 1993): 545.

   The Clwyd Open Learning Service in Wales is playing a leading role in the Public Libraries and Adult Independent Learners (PLAIL) Project, a European initiative to develop adult independent learning through public libraries. The major results of the project will focus on standards of performance, use of technologies to attain these standards, guidelines on the training needs of public librarians, and a dissemination program across Europe. A. Slade.

1991

223. Allred, John. "Open Learning—The Future." *Northern Librarian* 7 (December 1991): 18-20.

   The author offers his views on the future of open learning in the United Kingdom. He points to the expansion of open learning opportunities and indicates that the public library is well placed to offer information about the choices available to users. Following a discussion about learner qualifications and assessment of prior learning, Allred predicts that emerging technologies will affect the range of learning opportunities available to the general public. A. Slade.

224. Babu, B. Ramesh and D. Chandran. "Distance Education and Public Libraries in Tamil Nadu: Some Considerations." In *Education Through Public Libraries— A Practical Approach: Proceedings of the National Seminar on Public Library Movement: Concepts and Strategies: April 19-21, 1991: Madras*, edited by C. Palanivelu and K. S. Raghavan. Madras, India: Government of Tamilnadu, Directorate of Public Libraries, 1991, 311-20.

   Distance education has become popular in the state of Tamil Nadu in India because job-oriented and professional courses are difficult to find in traditional day colleges. Since many distance learners cannot easily access university study centers, the public library system is best suited to meet the library needs of these students. The authors suggest that public libraries in Tamil Nadu undertake a number of programs to support distance learners, including developing print and audio-visual collections relevant to distance education courses, establishing university study centers in public libraries, strengthening existing mobile library systems, establishing career guidance information centers, fund raising to expand services, cooperating with other libraries, and establishing regional library systems. Several barriers to implementing these recommendations are identified, including lack of funding, lack of interest among public librarians, lack of coordination between public libraries and academic libraries, and lack of an effective policy to encourage development of the public library system to support distance learning. A. Slade.

225. Barnes, Carole and John Allred. *Educational Guidance for Adults and Public Libraries: Report of the 1989/90 Survey Undertaken by the National Educational Guidance Initiative and the Library Association*. Leicester, UK: National Institute of Adult Continuing Education, 1991. 34 pp. ISBN 1-872941-81-8.

This report provides information from a 1989/90 survey on educational guidance for adults and public libraries in the United Kingdom. It offers an overview of the relationship between educational guidance services and libraries, highlights management issues for public libraries identified in the survey, provides four case studies of good practice in this area, and makes recommendations for enhancing educational guidance activities in public libraries. A. Slade.

226. Rao, V. Chandrasekhar and G. Sujatha. "Developing Public Library Services for Distance Learners." In *Education Through Public Libraries—A Practical Approach: Proceedings of the National Seminar on Public Library Movement: Concepts and Strategies: April 19-21, 1991: Madras*, edited by C. Palanivelu and K. S. Raghavan. Madras, India: Directorate of Public Libraries, Government of Tamilnadu, 1991, 321-31.

To provide library support to its distance education students, Andhra Pradesh Open University established an "open university corner" in a public library. Based on the success of this pilot project, the authors recommend that all the distance teaching institutions in India collaborate with the Department of Public Libraries in their state to plan and develop public library services for distance learners. These services could include collection development specifically for distance learners; reading, lending, and audio-visual facilities; information services; mobile services; extension services; and staff training in various aspects of distance learning systems. It is noted that the success of developing public library services for distance learners depends on government support. The authors recommend that at least 10% of the public library system's budget be allocated for support of neoliterates and distance learners and that three-quarters of this amount should go toward services for distance education. A. Slade.

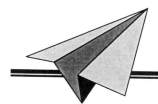

CHAPTER 4

Organization, Planning, and Regulatory Issues

This chapter includes works that focus on library planning, administration, organizational issues, guidelines and standards for library services, and copyright issues.

Organization and Planning

For other works that discuss aspects of organization or planning while emphasizing other topics, see the following headings in the Subject Index: "administration," "budget and finance," "extended campuses—staffing," "library buildings," "marketing," "paraprofessionals," "performance measurement," "personnel," "planning of library services," "standards of library service," "staff selection," and "training of library staff."

1999

227. Canepi, Kitti. "Implementing Library Services for an Off-Campus Site: Evolution, Not Revolution." *Journal of Library Services for Distance Education* 2, no. 1 (July 1999). Online. Available: http://www.westga.edu/~library/jlsde/vol2/1/reports/KCanepi.html (Accessed April 13, 2000).

This "Report from the Field" discusses the planning process for the implementation of library services at the Bristol, Tennessee, off-campus location of East Tennessee State University (ETSU). ACRL Guidelines were used as the basis for the plan of action and a new position was established with the title "Extended Campus Services Librarian." The author describes the planning process in terms of factors considered and hurdles identified. The chosen strategy in the process was cooperation, especially with the following stakeholders: staff at the extended campus, the main library, other local libraries, and technology innovators at ETSU. The author notes that building the service was a gradual process, with improvements being added each semester until a full off-campus library service finally became available. A. Slade.

228. Davidson, Laura. "Starting a New Service to Distributed Learners." *Journal of Library Services for Distance Education* 2, no. 1 (July 1999). Online. Available: http://www.westga.edu/~library/jlsde/vol2/1/reports/LDavidson.html (Accessed April 13, 2000).

The author's presentation at the 1998 WILS World Conference is reproduced in this "Report from the Field." Written in the first person, the paper offers practical advice on establishing a library service for off-campus programs. Four categories of issues are identified as part of the planning process: (1) determining what off-campus programs and classes will be offered, (2) learning the locations of the classes and what local resources are available, (3) defining what "equivalent" services will be provided, and (4) deciding whether services for distance learning will be an independent unit in the library or integrated into other operations. The author stresses the importance of the ACRL Guidelines in the planning process and summarizes her interpretation of the philosophy behind the Guidelines as a basis for defining the issues. A variety of topics are touched upon in the context of this paper, including communication with faculty, working with local libraries, remote access to electronic resources, the GALILEO project in Georgia, limits on photocopying, reserves, reference services, and library instruction. A. Slade.

229. Metz-Wiseman, Monica, Tina Neville, Ardis Hanson, Kim Grohs, Susan Silver, Edward Sanchez, and Margaret M. Doherty. "Building a Virtual Library: How the University of South Florida Did It." *College & Research Libraries News* 60, no. 4 (April 1999): 267-69.

The development of a virtual library at the University of South Florida is described in terms of the planning and implementation processes. One of the goals of the project was support for the university's 10,000 distance education students. The planning process involved a survey of of eight peer libraries and focus group sessions with library users. The implementation process concentrated on a common user interface, integration of SiteSearch software into the user interface, selection of electronic resources, metadata, digitization, electronic reserves, document delivery, marketing, and staff training. A cross-functional team approach was used to coordinate the project, and details are provided on the tasks and interrelationships of the various groups involved in building the virtual library. A. Slade.

1998

230. Caballero, Cesar and Henry T. Ingle. "Thousands Still Shoeless: Developing Library Services in Support of Distance Education: A Case Study." *Journal of Library Services for Distance Education* 1, no. 2 (June 1998). Online. Available: http://www.westga.edu/~library/jlsde/vol1/2/CCaballero_HIngle.html (Accessed April 13, 2000).

This is a case study of the methods, procedures, concepts, and resources used to develop library service in support of distance education at the University of Texas at El Paso (UTEP). Among the strategic goals for the library was expanded teaching partnerships between librarians, faculty, and computer technologists. An

Information Services Team was formed to coordinate the review of new electronic resources and services. In planning for library services, UTEP included relevant accreditation and library standards considerations from the Southern Association for Colleges and Schools (SACS) and the Association of Colleges and Research Libraries (ACRL). The Information Services Team conducted a needs assessment, informed the library staff about distance education curriculum developments and library service needs, and developed and implemented new services. Among the services developed were access to the online catalogue and online databases, document delivery, reference service, and library instruction. A Wide Area Network was put into place to provide distance students and faculty with needed resources. M. Kascus.

231. Cornell University Library. *Distance Learning White Paper*. Final Revision, April 21, 1998. 6 pp. ERIC ED 418 705. Also online. Available: http://www.library. cornell.edu/staffweb/Distance.html (Accessed April 13, 2000).

      This is the final revision of the Distance Learning White Paper at Cornell University (CU). Potential issues that the library might face in supporting distance learning are identified in this paper, and some solutions are recommended. The CU Library is an integral part of the education of residential students and considers itself well positioned to serve non-residential learners. By working closely with faculty and the Office of Distance Learning, the library hopes to overcome barriers to distance learning. Among the issues discussed are network access and authentication, acquisition and collection development, document delivery services, reference and instruction services, faculty support, and the library's relationship to other departments. A selective bibliography of further readings and helpful URLs are provided. M. Kascus.

232. Fritts, Jack. "Administrative Structures for Extended Campus Library Services: A Survey of Institutional Operations." In *The Eighth Off-Campus Library Services Conference Proceedings: Providence, Rhode Island, April 22-24, 1998*, compiled by P. Steven Thomas and Maryhelen Jones. Mount Pleasant, MI: Central Michigan University, 1998, 147-54.

      A study was conducted to examine the library organizational structure designed to support extended campus educational programming. The study involved a survey in which a request for participation was sent to the OFFCAMP discussion list asking for volunteers to answer questions about their administrative structure. Thirty-five respondents expressed an interest and 17 people with unique position titles completed the survey. The list of questions asked of the participants and the list of institutions are included in the appendices. The emphasis here is on how academic libraries deal with change, focusing on how these libraries administer library services to distant students. The goal is to refine the survey instrument and increase the size of the population for future study. M. Kascus.

233. Haricombe, Lorraine J. "Users: Their Impact on Planning the Agile Library." In *Creating the Agile Library: A Management Guide for Librarians*, edited by Lorraine J. Haricombe and T. J. Lusher. Westport, CT: Greenwood Press, 1998, 81-93.

      The author looks at broad trends affecting higher education and academic library services, including the development of information technologies, the growing number of adults returning to higher education, the expansion of distance education programs, the changing patterns and new paradigms in teaching and learning environments, and increases in interdisciplinary research. These trends are discussed in relation to challenges for future planning in academic libraries. The author notes that libraries tend to be service-oriented without being very user-centered and argues that academic libraries need to know their users, especially their remote users, and be flexible enough to adapt to their needs. Planning to meet users' needs will require feedback from the users themselves and attention in the following areas: student demographics; support services to off-campus students; location of remote sites; available technology and agility; partnerships with other campus constituents, such as faculty and computing centers; and commitment of library support on the part of the university administration. A. Slade.

234.　Lebowitz, Gloria. "Promoting Off-Campus Library Services: Even a Successful Program Needs a Marketing Plan." In *The Eighth Off-Campus Library Services Conference Proceedings: Providence, Rhode Island, April 22-24, 1998*, compiled by P. Steven Thomas and Maryhelen Jones. Mount Pleasant, MI: Central Michigan University, 1998, 213-20.

The author stresses the need for and development of a marketing plan to promote off-campus library services. The marketing plan as described includes the following activities: (1) assessment of the audience and the environment, (2) analysis of user needs and current marketing practices, (3) development of a mission statement, (4) development of objectives and goals that fulfill the mission, and (5) evaluation of the effectiveness of the solutions and audience satisfaction. A survey was sent to 29 willing participants representing institutions that provide off-campus library services. Of those responding, one-half indicated that their organizations have an institutional as well as a library mission statement that made reference to serving off-campus students, but only one-third have such a mission statement at the unit level. To some extent, all have material by which they publicize or promote their services to their users. M. Kascus.

235.　Wykoff, Leslie W. "Merging Library, Educational Television, and Computing Services in an Extended Campus Environment." In *The Eighth Off-Campus Library Services Conference Proceedings: Providence, Rhode Island, April 22-24, 1998*, compiled by P. Steven Thomas and Maryhelen Jones. Mount Pleasant, MI: Central Michigan University, 1998, 313-20.

A description is given of an administrative structure that involved the merger of library, educational television, and computing services at Washington State University (WSU) at Vancouver. This is a case study representing a current trend in higher education in the United States. The presentation focuses on leadership styles, professional cultures, group process models, team decision making, and staffing. The integrated information service concept is credited with the success of the WSU approach to delivering information technology services to students. The importance of staff willingness to join in the collaborative effort is considered essential to achieving success when merging existing information services. M. Kascus.

236.　Wynne, Peter M. "Fools Rush In: Key Human Factors in Operationalizing Service Delivery to Remote Users." In *Libraries Without Walls 2: The Delivery of Library Services to Distant Users*, edited by Peter Brophy, Shelagh Fisher, and Zoë Clarke. London: Library Association Publishing, 1998, 109-21.

The Virtual Academic Library of the North-West (VALNOW) service of the University of Central Lancashire is based on the BIBDEL demonstration project undertaken in 1994–1995 (for further information on BIBDEL, see the entries in the Subject Index). VALNOW provides library support to colleges in the Northwest of England that offer University of Central Lancashire franchised courses. The services include catalogue access, book loans, provision of periodical articles, reference enquiries, and access to external information resources. Requests are conveyed to VALNOW by e-mail, fax, phone, or mail. Material is delivered to the college libraries by mail or fax. A number of human factors contributed to a different development approach to VALNOW as opposed to the BIBDEL project. The lessons learned from BIBDEL include approaching the initiative as an equal partnership between the college and the university, conducting needs assessments prior to introducing services, identifying key personnel for communication purposes, being sensitive to differences in library administration in the two types of institutions, tailoring services to the college's technical level, getting agreement among partners, and publicizing the service effectively. For a related paper, see #724 in this volume. A. Slade.

1997

237. Bing, JoAnn, Susanne Flannelly, Jessica Goodwin, and Michael T. Hutton. *The Design of a Distance Library Service System*. A paper presented to the Ed.D Program in Instructional Technology and Distance Education in partial fulfillment of the Requirements for the Degree of Doctor of Education, Nova Southeastern University, 1997. Online. Available: http://www.fcae.nova.edu/~huttonm/isd2.html (Accessed April 13, 2000).

The authors describe a systems approach to the design of distance library services (DLS) to support the adult independent learner. This model of library support includes the following: (1) access to electronic resources, (2) reference and referral services/support, (3) library user training, (4) borrowing privileges, (5) document delivery, and (6) course reserve service. Seven inputs to the DLS system are identified: operating budget, student requests, faculty requirements, librarians, library policy and practice, library connectedness, and course assignments. Feedback into the system would come from program evaluations conducted by librarians as well as cost benefit data collected. The internal reviews would be used to revise the procedures and policies of the distance library services to ensure that they are user friendly. A cost benefit analysis of an unspecified DLS system indicates that the cost to provide these services to distance learners is $2,598 per student. Six benefits to students are delineated. M. Kascus.

238. City University of New York. University Library and Educational Technology Task Force. *Report of the Subcommittee on Libraries and Open Learning*. 1997. Online. Available: http://www.osc.cuny.edu/resources/taskforce/ra_new/ra_intro.html (Accessed April 13, 2000).

At the City University of New York (CUNY), the Board of Trustees authorized the creation of the University Library Educational Technology Task Force to prepare a university-wide plan for expanding the role and use of educational technology in support of teaching, learning, and research. Four subcommittees were established, including one on Libraries and Open Learning. Each subcommittee conducted research using surveys, focus groups, and outside experts as needed. The findings of each of the subcommittees are reported and recommendations are made in an executive summary. Recommendations called for the university to "reaffirm the central role libraries play in instruction and scholarly research; assure that all CUNY libraries are equipped with adequate technological resources to serve their communities; and review skills requirements for library support positions with an eye toward assuring that incumbent support staff are trained to use technology to assist the user community and that newly hired staff possess requisite skills." Other recommendations include establishing formula-based library funding with the Digital Library as a priority to expand existing facilities, giving additional attention to links to the Internet, and improving interlibrary loan and document delivery. M. Kascus.

239. Clover, David. "Committing to Customer Service: Development of a Service Charter at The Open Polytechnic Library." *New Zealand Libraries* 48, no. 12 (December 1997): 239-43.

The Library of the Open Polytechnic of New Zealand (TOPNZ), a distance education provider, introduced a service quality charter in 1997 to improve services to library users. The charter was written from the perspective of a library user and outlined service standards that users could expect to be met. This article discusses the concept of service quality in relation to published standards and describes the process used to create the charter for the TOPNZ Library. The participation of library staff in developing the service quality charter was a key element in the process. It resulted in customer service being placed high on the library's priorities, increased awareness among library staff of the service component of their work, and created a willingness to critically examine library procedures with the aim of removing barriers to customer service. A. Slade.

240. Consortium for Educational Technology for University Systems. *Information Resources and Library Services for Distance Learners: A Framework for Quality.* C.E.T.U.S., 1997. Online. Available: http://www.cetus.org (in pdf format) (Accessed April 13, 2000).

A Joint Committee of Chief Executive Officers from California State University (CSU), the State University of New York (SUNY), and the City University of New York (CUNY) agreed that library services to distance learners is a central issue that will have an impact on quality. This document is the product of the Consortium for Educational Technology for University Systems (CETUS), which developed from the Joint Committee's efforts. The document contains recommendations on guidelines for information resources and library services for distance learners. The overall intent is to provide "sample" principles as a resource for developing, enhancing, and endorsing standards and guidelines for distance learners. Topics covered in the document include an overview of current practices in providing information resources and library services; existing policies on accreditation for library services for distance learners; statements of principles, fair use, and ownership; illustrative scenarios; recommendations for implementation; and suggested steps for policy formulation. M. Kascus.

241. Florida Institute on Public Postsecondary Distance Learning. Library Subcommittee. *Final Report*. 1997. Online. Available: http://dlis.dos.state.fl.us/dlli/report.html (Accessed April 13, 2000).

This report updates Florida's statewide plan to meet the library needs of distance learners. The effort is coordinated by the Florida Institute on Public Postsecondary Distance Learning and the Florida Distance Learning Network (FDLN). Seven areas in need of programmatic and financial support are identified: (1) access to electronic resources, (2) reference and referral services, (3) library instruction, (4) borrowing privileges, (5) document delivery, (6) course reserve services, and (7) access to library equipment and facilities. Brief definitions are provided for each of the seven services. An overall budget and program summary are provided, projecting budgeted amounts through 2001 for each of the seven services as well as budget summary specifics for each service. M. Kascus.

242. Goodson, Carol F. "Performance Standards for Library Personnel: Extension/Off-Campus Services Librarian." In *The Complete Guide to Performance Standards for Library Personnel*. New York: Neal-Schuman, 1997, 132-34.

A section of this monograph focuses on performance standards for professional staff working in off-campus library services. The performance measures for off-campus services librarians are based on effectiveness in the following areas: publicizing and marketing library services to ensure that distance education instructors and users are aware of available library services and have access to them, providing library materials and services that are appropriate to the off-campus classes, writing grant proposals, negotiating with other departments and local agencies to provide services, and securing extra-institutional support. Assessment criteria for distance librarianship include instructor/peer feedback, supervisor observation, and self-evaluation. M. Kascus.

243. Goodson, Carol F. "Performance Standards for Paraprofessional Staff: Off-Campus Services/Extension Assistant." In *The Complete Guide to Performance Standards for Library Personnel*. New York: Neal-Schuman, 1997, 81-85.

One section of this monograph provides performance standards for paraprofessionals working in the area of off-campus library services. The performance criteria relate to the following: supplying material in response to student requests, supervising student workers, mailing publicity materials, preparing material for reserve collections, interfacing with regional cooperative borrowing systems, and other related duties. Assessment measures are provided for each set of performance standards. For paraprofessionals working in off-campus library services, performance assessment should be based on feedback from peers and cooperating libraries, supervisor observation, self-evaluation, and portfolio items. It is recommended that both employee and supervisor document specific examples illustrating successful (or unsuccessful) performance. M. Kascus.

244. Peterson, Billie. "Tech Talk." *LIRT News* 19, no. 3 (March 1997). Online. Available: http://web.uflib.ufl.edu/instruct/LIRT/1997/mtechtalk.html (Accessed April 13, 2000).

In this position piece, the author raises questions about what local libraries can do when faced with an influx of students affiliated with another institution's distance education program. It is recommended that the library director of the institution involved establish policies and practices to provide needed services to their distance education students. In developing these policies, four areas of service to be addressed are (1) access to electronic resources such as online catalogues, networked databases, full-text resources, and Internet resources; (2) instructional services such as electronic handouts, e-mail, tutorials, interactive video instruction, course packages, Internet, and online searching; (3) document delivery services such as mail, fax, and interlibrary loan; and (4) reference services such as e-mail, telephone information and request services, CD-ROM, and end-user searching. Conducting user studies before and after library services are established may be necessary. Libraries can also establish relationships with other libraries and may need to consider compensation to other libraries for access and support. As an aid in identifying the issues surrounding library support to distance learners, a list of resources is provided. M. Kascus.

245.   Riggs, Donald E. "Distance Education: Rethinking Practices, Implementing New Approaches." *College and Research Libraries* 58, no. 3 (May 1997): 208-9.

Because Nova Southeastern University (NSU) is one of the pioneers in distance education, library services have been monitored and improved. This is evidenced by a recent survey of distance education students, which found that 97% were satisfied with library materials and 91% were satisfied with the timeliness of the receipt of materials. What is stressed is that distance education library services require considerable planning, and it is important that the library be involved from the very beginning in any new distance education program. An evaluation focusing on both quantitative and qualitative aspects is needed. In addition to monitoring the services provided, it is suggested that face-to-face contact with students at distant sites is a good way for librarians to gather information about user needs. The goal is to provide students who are taking courses at remote sites with the same level of library service as that provided on-campus. It is suggested that current and emerging technologies offer a positive environment for improving library support to distance learners. M. Kascus.

246.   Smith, Alan. "Self-Directed Learning Off-Campus: The Open Polytechnic's Approach to Knowledge Access for Distance Students." *New Zealand Libraries* 48, no. 12 (December 1997): 235-39.

In 1992, the Open Polytechnic of New Zealand developed a library service for its distance students. The steps in the process, from policy formation to implementation, are described in a historical context. The development of the service was influenced by two factors in the institution's educational philosophy: self-directed learning and equity of access to all services and resources. The policy framework adopted was underpinned by four key principles: library access would be available to all enrolled students; copies of every item recommended or referenced in course materials would be available for loan; full library services, not just document delivery services, would be provided to distance students; and the costs would be included in tuition, with no separate transaction charges. Details are provided on the conceptual model developed for the service, the planning phase, and implementation of the service. It is noted that the service model was not designed to be dependent on advanced technologies, but rather was based on use of common tools such as the telephone, fax machine, and the postal system. A. Slade.

247. University of South Florida. Tampa Campus Library. *A Proposal to Establish and Provide the Services of the Distance Learning Library Initiative Reference and Referral Center*. Tampa, FL: University of South Florida, Tampa Campus Library, 1997. Online. Available: http://www.lib.usf.edu/~ifrank/distance/rrcproposal.html (Accessed April 13, 2000).

This is a proposal to locate the Distance Learning Library Initiative Reference and Referral Center at the University of South Florida's Tampa Campus Library. The library's goal is to provide Florida university and community college distance learners with remote access to the same quality reference services available to on-campus students. Among the service standards the Center is committed to meeting is 24-hour-per-day, seven-day-per-week access to the Center through an 800 number, e-mail address, and Web request forms. A summary of the proposal is given, outlining the library's commitments for developing, maintaining, and expanding the services of the Center. Also discussed are the rationale for locating the Center at the University of South Florida, the timeline, and the budget. M. Kascus.

248. Wynne, Peter M., Peter Brophy, and Geoff Butters. "An Examination of the Costs and Benefits of an Experimental Extension of Academic Library Services to Remote Users." *New Review of Academic Librarianship* 3 (1997): 25-37.

The demonstration experiment undertaken by the University of Central Lancashire as part of the BIBDEL (Libraries Without Walls: The Delivery of Library Services to Distant Users) Project is described, with specific emphasis on its costs and benefits. The experiment involved the delivery of library services to Newton Rigg College, which offers higher education courses validated by the University of Central Lancashire. This paper discusses the philosophy of the BIBDEL Project, the networking solutions adopted in the experiment, and the library services provided to the college. A priority in the project was the use of inexpensive, off-the-shelf products. An analysis of the costs involved in the experiment is presented in tabular form, including costs for computer hardware and software, telecommunications, specialist services, postage, fax transmission, file transfer, staff time at the host site, and staff time at the remote site. A discussion of the benefits from the experiment in relation to the costs includes confirmation that students and teaching staff found the services to be valuable. A. Slade.

1996

249. Northwest Missouri State University. Resource Group for a Telecommunications-Based Delivery System. *Recommendations for a Telecommunications-Based Delivery System: Presented to the Coordinating Board for Higher Education*. Maryville, MO: Northwest Missouri State University, 1996. 115 pp. ERIC ED 403 793.

This report is the product of a cooperative planning effort by a group of leaders in higher education across Missouri. The goal was to summarize available resources and make recommendations for increasing access. This report urges that any higher education telecommunications-based delivery system should emphasize access to library resources, be learner-centered, be faculty supported, provide high quality instruction, support the institution's mission, emphasize educational partnerships, use integrated evaluation and improvement strategies, and use appropriate technology. Six principles are applied to the planning of library services. First, all library collections in the state are viewed as one resource for learners. Second, every academic library should provide circulation privileges to any student taking a course in the state. Third, training programs in information retrieval should be developed and made available to all students. Fourth, academic libraries should organize state-wide to provide remote reference services. Fifth, accountability for the existence of adequate library resources for distance education programs should be assigned to the originating institution. Sixth, higher education institutions should adopt the ACRL *Guidelines for Extended Campus Library Services*. A view of the current distance learning picture in Missouri is given along with recommendations. M. Kascus.

250. Rosenquist-Buhler, Carla. "New Partners in Distance Education: Linking Up to Libraries." *Library Administration and Management* 10, no. 4 (Fall 1996): 220-25.

Libraries need to be a visible and active partner in the planning and implementation process so universities can provide distance education programs that are comparable to on-campus programs. Three kinds of services that libraries offer are identified: (1) remote access to electronic resources, (2) assistance and instruction, and (3) document delivery. Other services provided by most libraries include access to online catalogues, electronic journal indexes, and online databases. What is stressed is the importance of training and instruction in the use of these electronic resources and services for all users, but especially remote users. Handouts can be provided in print and electronic format. Instruction can be provided on-site via satellite or video. Communication can take place via e-mail, telephone, fax, or mail. Several important things not provided by technology are noted: access to resources not available electronically, instant results, point-of-need help, serendipity, and browsability. In looking to the future, the needs of distance learners will have to be identified, licensing agreements will have to be negotiated, instruction at the point-of-need will have to be developed, and seamless access to technology will have to be provided. M. Kascus.

1995

251. Bazillion, Richard J. and Connie L. Braun. "Building Virtual - and Spatial - Libraries for Distance Learning." *CAUSE/EFFECT* 18, no. 4 (Winter 1995): 51-54. Also online. Available: http://www.educause.edu/ir/library/text/cem9549.txt (Accessed April 13, 2000).

This paper discusses the design implications of new technologies that libraries may use in support of distance learning. The space needs in new library buildings are of two kinds: (1) a large classroom equipped for the teaching of electronic research skills and (2) an information "common" where students may create new documents from electronic versions. Distance learning imposes demands on library services in two areas: user training and reference assistance. The use of interactive television (ITV) is discussed in terms of its potential for teaching and delivering information resources. New buildings have to be designed as teaching instruments through which libraries can reach off-campus students where and when library services are needed. From the library design perspective, the goal is to simplify contact between librarian and distance learner. M. Kascus.

252. Bazillion, Richard J. and Connie Braun. "Service to Distance Learners." In *Academic Libraries as High-Tech Gateways: A Guide to Design and Space Decisions*, edited by Richard J. Bazillion and Connie Braun. Chicago: American Library Association, 1995, 157-59.

This is part of a chapter titled "Academic Libraries at the Millennium." The library's role in the future will be to bring together researchers and their services regardless of distance. Libraries are likely to maintain a physical presence for years to come, but that does not mean that the structures are fixed. According to the authors, distance learning is achieving new stature for a variety of reasons. Contemporary library buildings need to incorporate information technology as an element of the building fabric, but one that has the potential to make a teaching instrument of the building itself. The assumption is that a properly designed library can contribute significantly to the educational process. It can keep faculty and students in touch with the world of learning that abounds over the Internet and help students to acquire the information skills they will need to take with them into the workplace. M. Kascus.

253. Bazillion, Richard J. and Connie Braun. "The Teaching Library and Distance Education." In *Academic Libraries as High-Tech Gateways: A Guide to Design and Space Decisions*, edited by Richard J. Bazillion and Connie Braun. Chicago: American Library Association, 1995, 143-46.

This section in a chapter titled "The Library Becomes a Teaching Instrument" begins with the premise that the potential for developing library research skills at a distance can be realized using online sources along with e-mail, fax, and interactive video. Distance education students will still need instruction in accessing and searching online resources. While the technical problems of providing library service to off-campus courses are solvable, two questions remain: (1) Will teaching faculty take advantage of the technology to enhance their courses? and (2) Are there implications for the design on new library buildings? The importance of information literacy and building flexibility are stressed in planning for off-campus library services. The authors conclude that the teaching library of the future will remain a campus center and retreat for students, even if the emphasis shifts to distance learning. M. Kascus.

254. Butters, Geoff, Monica Brinkley, Panayiotis Papachiou, and Ellie Viachou. *Access to Campus Library and Information Services by Distant Users: General Issues*. The fourth report from the BIBDEL Project (Libraries Without Walls: The Delivery of Library Services to Distant Users) funded by the Libraries Programme of the Commission of the European Communities. Preston, UK: Centre for Research in Library and Information Management, University of Central Lancashire, 1995. 55 pp.

This report is the fourth "deliverable" from the BIBDEL Project (Libraries Without Walls: The Delivery of Library Services to Distant Users). The report explores the management issues surrounding distant access and delivery from the perspective of both users and providers. The issues include costs, copyright, staff and user training, and library cooperation. It is stressed that an essential part of providing library services to remote users must be the delivery of training in how to access these services and make the best use of them. One important management issue is that of controlling resources when services are delivered remotely. Examples of control issues include licenses for computer software and electronic documents and authentication of remote users. Also discussed in this report are mobile libraries. It is suggested that mobile libraries, equipped with both print materials and CD-ROM workstations, could extend the reach of the academic library to cover remote users. For the other BIBDEL reports, see #284 and #285 in the second bibliography and #21, #262, #360, and #371 in this volume. M. Kascus.

255. Wilson, Christine. "Work in Progress: Development of Academic Library Outreach Services on the High Plains." In *The Seventh Off-Campus Library Services Conference Proceedings: San Diego, California, October 25-27, 1995*, compiled by Carol J. Jacob. Mount Pleasant, MI: Central Michigan University, 1995, 111-20.

The development, assessment, and implementation of off-campus library services at Fort Hays State University in Kansas are described in this paper. The assessment included several areas: (1) a view of the history of the university and its continuing education program, (2) a study of the demographics of the region, (3) a survey of continuing education students, and (4) visits with area libraries and continuing education faculty. The user study and other data collected in the assessment stage were used for the design and development stage. Policies emerged from the mission and goals, from the survey analysis, and from practice. Assessment is an ongoing part of the process of implementing this evolving program. M. Kascus.

256. Gover, Harvey R., David L. Pappas, and Leslie Wykoff. "Branch Campus Library Needs Assessment: A Follow-up Study for Continued Program Planning." In *The Seventh Off-Campus Library Services Conference Proceedings: San Diego, California, October 25 -27, 1995*, compiled by Carol J. Jacob. Mount Pleasant, MI: Central Michigan University, 1995, 127-62.

This study reports on the library needs assessment at the Spokane, Vancouver, and Tri-Cities branch campuses of Washington State University (WSU). This is a follow-up to an earlier study and is an instrument for ongoing program planning. The original survey was used with some modifications to facilitate comparison of the 1995 and 1991 results. The survey results indicated (1) the need for greater emphasis on enhanced bibliographic instruction programs, (2) that the students are not yet comfortable with electronic access, and (3) the disparity in services between institutions and its potential impact on how users view those services as a whole. Appendices include the 1991 questionnaire, the 1995 questionnaire, and detailed survey responses from WSU Spokane, WSU Tri-Cities, and WSU Vancouver. For the earlier study, see #175 in the second bibliography. M. Kascus.

257. Lebowitz, Gloria. "Starting an Off-Campus Library Services Program—from Scratch!: A Process." In *The Seventh Off-Campus Library Services Conference Proceedings: San Diego, California, October 25 -27, 1995*, compiled by Carol J. Jacob. Mount Pleasant, MI: Central Michigan University, 1995, 241-46.

An overview of the process of starting-up an off-campus program is presented in this paper. Four phases in the process are identified: (1) needs assessment, (2) program design, (3) program implementation, and (4) program evaluation. Elements important in the needs assessment are the target audience, environment, course needs of students, library skills of students, faculty usage of library services, and faculty attitudes and perceptions regarding student need for library services. Elements important in program design include staffing, format, services, document delivery, use of technology, and publicity. In terms of program implementation, it is recommended that a pilot program be undertaken to eliminate potential problems. Program evaluation is as important as needs assessment because meeting the needs of the target audience is critical to the program's success. Program evaluation provides the opportunity to assess needs and to modify the program design. M. Kascus.

258. Oregon State System of Higher Education. Interinstitutional Library Council. *Library Support for Distance Education Programs: A Report Prepared and Submitted by the Interinstitutional Library Council, Oregon State System of Higher Education*. 1995. Online. Available: http://www.osshe.edu/dist-learn/library.htm (Accessed April 13, 2000).

According to the Interinstitutional Library Council of the Oregon State System of Higher Education (OSSHE), two issues are central to a consideration of library support for distance learning programs: (1) the need for planning and (2) the recognition that library services involve more than marginal costs. In addition to adequate planning and budgeting, the specific issues common to distance learning in general are identified in four broad areas: availability of library resources, use of technology, personnel, and copyright issues. Responses to each of these issues are addressed. The need for local agreements for access and support include a range of areas such as staffing, facilities, and on-site resources. A sample agreement is attached at the end of the report. The importance of acknowledging cost considerations and allocating funds is stressed. Also stressed is that no one way works for all and there are good models to follow, such as Linfield College (Oregon) and Central Michigan University. Among the recommendations in the summary is that the ACRL *Guidelines for Extended Campus Library Services* be used to guide the planning process for distance learning library support. M. Kascus.

259. Pettingill, Ann. "Distance Education Library Services at Old Dominion University." In *The Seventh Off-Campus Library Services Conference Proceedings: San Diego, California, October 25-27, 1995*, compiled by Carol J. Jacob. Mount Pleasant, MI: Central Michigan University, 1995, 303-16.

A summary is provided of the planning and implementation steps taken over a two-year period in establishing Old Dominion University's distance education program. The library's efforts in establishing both formal and informal methods of communication with all of its partners (students, faculty, site personnel, and university administration) are described in detail. The planning process, which included the library, involved identifying user groups, user needs, and phased service levels. Phase one included patron registration, document delivery, interlibrary loan, reserve, and library instruction. Phase two included access to the online catalogue, library instruction programs, reference assistance, access to periodical indexes, and expanded documentation. This phase resulted in the expansion and reorganization of staff to manage the increased workload. Phase three involved upgrades to services and products, including the development of Internet service, e-mail, instructional products, and core collections. The fact that every aspect of the library program has been subjected to the evaluation process is stressed. M. Kascus.

260. Sophoulis, Costas. "The Needs of Remote Communities." In *Proceedings of the First "Libraries Without Walls" Conference, Mytilene, Greece, 9-10 September 1995*, edited by Ann Irving and Geoff Butters. Preston, UK: Centre for Research in Library and Information Management, University of Central Lancashire, 1995, 13-15.

The author begins with a discussion of the development of a new distributed university to serve the Aegean islands in Greece. The organizational structure for the University of the Aegean consisted of a network of interconnected units. Along with this structure came the need for a library service to serve the various units. The university library service was developed by networking the library, so there was one single entity with locally organized activities on the individual islands. Participation in the BIBDEL Project was seen as a way of solving some of the technical problems in establishing a networked library service for the new distributed university. M. Kascus.

261. Tucker, Joan. "Management Issues for Off-Campus Library Delivery Services, Particularly in a Multicampus Environment." In *The Seventh Off-Campus Library Services Conference Proceedings: San Diego, California, October 25-27, 1995*, compiled by Carol J. Jacob. Mount Pleasant, MI: Central Michigan University, 1995, 363-73.

Following a change in government policies in Australia, many institutions previously operating as a single campus are now part of large multicampus universities, thus creating management issues for off-campus library delivery service. The author draws upon the experience of Deakin University, which operates Australia's largest off-campus library delivery service, in discussing the management issues considered in developing its current model of service. The issues are centralization versus decentralization, integration with other library services, collection management, and technology utilization. The author concludes by noting that the multicampus environment provides many opportunities for Deakin University to offer better service and to introduce operational efficiencies. M. Kascus.

262. University of Central Lancashire. Centre for Research in Library and Information Management. *The Libraries Without Walls Toolkit*. The sixth report from the BIBDEL Project (Libraries Without Walls: The Delivery of Library Services to Distant Users) funded by the Libraries Programme of the Commission of the European Communities. 1995. Online. Available: http://www.dcu.ie/library/bibdel/ (Accessed April 13, 2000).

This "toolkit" is a Web-based guide designed to assist librarians in planning and developing library services for distance learners. It is a product of the European BIBDEL Project, 1994–1995. The web pages in the toolkit provide detailed advice and guidance on a wide variety of topics organized under the following general headings: management issues; transport and communications issues; issues related specifically to home-based users; the use of electronic documents;

the provision of specific services to distant users; legal issues, including copyright; and issues related to the cost of providing services. For the other BIBDEL reports, see #284 and #285 in the second bibliography and #21, #254, #360, and #371 in this volume. A. Slade.

1994

263. McPherson, Madeleine. "Necessity and Invention in a New Regional University." *LASIE* (Library Automated Systems Information Exchange) 24, nos. 4/5 (January/February & March/April 1994): 70-76.

The process of transforming a college library into a university library is described in relation to strategic planning and distance education. The University College of Southern Queensland became the University of Southern Queensland (USQ) in 1992. As a college, there was little need for library services to support distance education because the courses were designed to be self-contained and everything the students needed was included in their course packages. Many of the new university's students are external and more library support was needed. The strategic plan developed for the library had three main emphases: development of a quality collection to support teaching, the rapid implementation of electronic information services, and staff development. Development of electronic library services was recognized as the only affordable way in which the library could keep pace with increasingly diverse demands and meet the needs of external students. Details are provided on the implementation of USQ's electronic library services, staffing, organizational change, infrastructure, collection development, and relations with other libraries. A. Slade.

Guidelines and Standards

For other works that mention guidelines or standards, see the following headings in the Subject Index: "accreditation," "evaluation of library programs—quality assessments," "guidelines and standards," "quality in off-campus and distance learning programs," and "standards of library service."

1998

264. Association of College and Research Libraries. Distance Learning Section. "Guidelines for Distance Learning Library Services: The Final Version, Approved July 1998." *College & Research Libraries News* 59, no. 9 (October 1998): 689-94. Also online. Available: http://www.ala.org/acrl/guides/distlrng.html (Accessed April 13, 2000).

This is the final version of the ACRL *Guidelines for Distance Learning Library Services*, approved July 1998. The original guidelines were published in 1982 and revised in 1990. Distance learning library services are defined and a philosophy is given to establish a framework for the guidelines. Areas covered by the guidelines are management, finance, personnel, facilities, resources, and services.

The essential services for distance learners are reference, computer-based information services, access to networks, consultation services, library instruction, assistance with non-print media and equipment, document delivery, reciprocal borrowing, reserve materials, adequate hours of service, and promotion of library services. For related articles, see #265-69 below. M. Kascus.

265. Gover, Harvey. "Revising the Guidelines." *College & Research Libraries News* 59, no. 9 (October 1998): 690.

The background to the revision of the ACRL Guidelines is outlined in this companion piece to #264 above. The groups and organizations that provided input into the Guidelines are listed, and the individuals who contributed significantly to the cycle of revision are acknowledged. For related articles, see #266-69 below. A. Slade.

1997

266. Association of College and Research Libraries. Extended Campus Library Services Section. "Guidelines for Extended Academic Library Services: A Draft." *College & Research Libraries News* 58, no. 2 (February 1997): 98-102.

This news article provides a draft revision of the 1990 ACRL *Guidelines for Extended Campus Library Services*. The draft was based on extensive input from the extended campus community as well as other individuals, consortia, and representatives of professional and accrediting bodies. The article discusses the rationale for revising the guidelines, the evolving terminology in this area, and the process followed in arriving at what best reflects the scope and purpose of the guidelines. For the final version, *Guidelines for Distance Learning Library Services*, see item #264 above. For related articles, see #267-69 below. M. Kascus.

267. Gover, Harvey. "Racing the Winds of Change: Revision of the 1990 ACRL Guidelines for ECLSS." *College & Research Libraries News* 58, no. 2 (February 1997): 99.

The author discusses the revision of the 1990 ACRL *Guidelines for Extended Campus Library Services*, focusing on the challenge posed by the terminology chosen for the document. "Extended campus" has been replaced by "extended academic" throughout the document, beginning with the title. With the current revisions and new title, ACRL *Guidelines for Extended Academic Library Services*, the guidelines will serve libraries, librarians, and students of electronic universities now and in the future. For related articles, see #264-66 above and #268-69 below. M. Kascus.

1996

268. "Boom in Distance Education Spurs Concern Over Library Support." *Chronicle of Higher Education* (5 July 1996): A15.

A brief news item in the *Chronicle of Higher Education* reports that a committee of the Association of College and Research Libraries has been charged with developing guidelines that would prompt institutions to be more responsive to the library needs of remote students. Comments from the committee chair are quoted and readers are invited to provide advice on the guidelines. For related articles, see #264-67 above and #269 below. A. Slade.

269. Davis, Mary Ellen. "News from the Field: Revisions Under Way for ECLSS Guidelines." *College & Research Libraries News* 57, no. 8 (September 1996): 477.

This news item announces the efforts of the ACRL Extended Campus Library Services Section (ECLSS), now the Distance Learning Section (DLS), to gather input for revising the *Guidelines for Extended Campus Library Services.* All engaged in providing library support to academic programs in non-residential campus settings are asked to review the guidelines and contribute feedback. For related articles, see #264-68 above. M. Kascus.

270. Jones, Maryhelen. "Leadership in the Wild Blue Yonder." *College & Research Libraries News* 57, no. 1 (January 1996): 24-26.

How academic librarians partner with Air Force educators and librarians with the United States Air Force's Quality Education System (QES) process is described as one example of "every librarian a leader." The QES process is based on the concept of using a defined group of educational partners that will make continuous improvements in their own base-level situations. QES fosters continuous improvement in education programs, staff, and facilities, including library support and services. This process is neither accreditation nor military inspection, but it uses Air-Force developed standards tied to quantified measurements for faculty, programs, student services, and library support. M. Kascus.

1995

---

271. Gilmer, Lois C. "Accreditation of Off-Campus Library Services: Comparative Study of the Regional Accreditation Agencies." In *The Seventh Off-Campus Library Services Conference Proceedings: San Diego, California, October 25-27, 1995*, compiled by Carol J. Jacob. Mount Pleasant, MI: Central Michigan University, 1995, 101-10.

The standards of regional accreditation agencies for off-campus library services are compared, and changes in the standards, occurring during the period from 1989 to 1994, are noted. Results of this comparison show that all of the accreditation agencies except the Western Association of Schools and Colleges, which had previously addressed the issue, have revised their standards, with greater emphasis on the provision of off-campus library services. What is evident from the comparison is the diversity in the standards and the general reliance on the guidelines produced by the American Library Association. M. Kascus.

Copyright Issues

For other works that discuss this topic, see the following heading in the Subject Index: "copyright issues."

1999

---

272. Neal, James G. *Testimony of James G. Neal, Dean, University Libraries, Johns Hopkins University*. Hearings on Distance Education Through Digital Technologies, U.S. Copyright Office, Library of Congress, January 26, 1999. Online. Available: http://www.arl.org/info/letters/neal.html (Accessed April 13, 2000).

James Neal's testimony at the hearings of the U.S. Copyright Office on Distance Education Through Digital Technologies is reproduced at this website. Neal represented the following associations at the hearing: Association of Research Libraries, American Association of Law Libraries, American Library Association, Association of College and Research Libraries, Medical Library Association, and Special Libraries Association. Four key recommendations are emphasized in Neal's presentation: (1) updating the current distance education exemption to facilitate use of the latest technologies and pedagogical practices; (2) balancing the interests of users and owners of copyrighted works so that educational institutions, including libraries, can realize the benefits of information technologies and networked environments; (3) ensuring that the statute is sufficiently flexible to incorporate new technologies not yet developed; and (4) providing a modern distance learning limitation and statutory language in keeping with educational needs and technological opportunities to permit parties to engage in licensing discussions that complement the law. In the testimony, examples are provided of selected institutions that use digital technologies to support distance learners. A. Slade.

1998

---

273. Gasaway, Laura. "Distance Learning and Copyright." *Journal of Library Services for Distance Education* 1, no. 2 (June 1998). Online. Available: http://www.westga.edu/~library/jlsde/vol1/2/LGasaway.html (Accessed April 13, 2000).

Issues surrounding distance learning and copyright are crystallizing and coming to the forefront. In this paper, the author reviews the current state of the law in the United States regarding distance learning and copyright, pending amendments to the law, and library services to distance learners. The law is not clear on whether the use of copyrighted works permitted in face-to-face teaching is also permitted in the distance learning environment. According to the author, pending amendments to copyright law that would redefine the meaning of face-to-face teaching in U.S. law will make it easier in the future to use copyrighted works in distance learning. Libraries can qualify for the library exemption by meeting three requirements: (1) reproduction and distribution must not be for direct or indirect commercial advantage, (2) the library must be open to the public or to researchers doing research in the same or similar field, and (3) copies must contain a notice of copyright. It is assumed that libraries may also provide an electronic copy of an article to a user, if the copy meets the requirements of current law. It is suggested that as libraries develop electronic reserve collections, they will have a need to develop policies that conform to fair use. M. Kascus.

1997

274.   Bruwelheide, Janis H. "Copyright and Distance Education." *Library Acquisitions: Practice and Theory* 21, no. 1 (Spring 1997): 41-52.

Distance educators are concerned about copyright and uncertain about how U.S. copyright law applies in a distance learning environment. Although no guidelines currently exist, scenarios have been developed by the Working Group on Intellectual Property Fair Use Conference Subcommittee on Distance Learning. This paper presents an overview of U.S. copyright law and distance education issues, defines fair use and identifies the factors to determine eligibility, suggests scenarios that probably are/probably are not fair use, and points out selected resources available to assist distance educators for understanding copyright and intellectual property issues. The appendix lists copyright sources, resources available via the Internet, and Internet sources on distance education. M. Kascus.

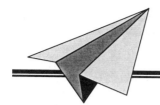

CHAPTER 5

Electronic Resources and Services

This chapter includes works that focus on electronic libraries, electronic resources, electronic library services, remote access issues, electronic reference services, and support for networked learners. Related terms subsumed under "electronic libraries and library resources" include "digital libraries" and "virtual libraries."

General Issues and Specific Initiatives

Numerous terms in the Subject Index relate to general issues and specific initiatives in electronic resources and services. Some of the more pertinent terms are "CD-ROM," "computer interfaces," "computer literacy," "computer networks," "computer programs," "computerization of libraries," "digitization," "electronic gateways," "electronic libraries and library resources," "electronic library services," "electronic mail," "electronic reference services," "electronic reserve materials," "evaluation of library programs and services—web pages," "front-ends (user-system interface)," "information kiosks," "Internet," "Intranet," "library instruction—computer-assisted instruction," "online catalogues," "online search services," "scanning (electronic)," "technical support for electronic services," "technology," "telematics," "videoconferencing," "web pages," and "World Wide Web."

1999

275. Barnard, John. "Web Accessible Library Resources for Emerging Virtual Universities." *Journal of Library Services for Distance Education* 2, no. 1 (July 1999). Online. Available: http://www.westga.edu/~library/jlsde/vol2/1/JBarnard.html (Accessed April 13, 2000).

The author provides an overview of significant issues related to electronic libraries and virtual universities. Institutions described in this context are the Western Governors University, National Technological University, California Virtual University, and the University of Phoenix. A number of design and implementation issues of an electronic library are discussed, including the World Wide

Web browser as a user interface, differences between traditional and virtual libraries in terms of interface design, access to electronic databases, web page design, goals and objectives of a website, integration of library instruction into electronic libraries, use of Web guides and self-help aids, and help desk services. Other issues covered include integration of library resources into Web-based courses, electronic reserve materials, database licensing issues, and conversion of print materials into electronic format. It is noted that a model of Web-based library resources can be divided into three areas: the information resources themselves, the means of delivering them to users, and some method for users to interact with a live information professional. A. Slade.

276. Metcalf, Judith. "On My Mind: Full Circle, Back to Selecting and Organizing." *American Libraries* 30, no. 5 (May 1999): 42.

In this opinion paper, the author comments on the recent growth of distance education and World Wide Web technology and delineates the need for librarians to develop and organize services for users they may never see in person. To assist remote users, librarians should select online databases that are user-friendly, provide clear directions on their use, and communicate with vendors to insist that they provide effective help screens. The library's role in online instruction is also stressed in this context. A. Slade.

277. Rosseel, Trish. "Supporting Distance Learners: Innovations in the Field." *Leading Ideas: Issues and Trends in Diversity, Leadership and Career Development*, no. 6 (February 1999). Online. Available: http://www.arl.org/diversity/leading/issue6/rosseel.html (Accessed April 13, 2000).

This "Leading Ideas" paper, produced by the Association of Research Libraries (ARL), looks at definitions of distance education, the remote classroom and networked learning approaches to distance education, and library support for distance learners. Three brief case studies are presented to illustrate library services being offered via the Internet. The University of Maryland University College (UMUC) offers access to reference librarians through asynchronous computer conferencing, live chat sessions, and e-mail. The University of Maine System Network (UNET) conducts library instruction sessions using interactive television. The University of South Florida-Tampa houses the Reference Referral Center for the Florida Distance Learning Library Initiative. Other electronic library services offered by various institutions include electronic reserve materials and full-text database searching and document delivery through OCLC FirstSearch and CARL UnCover services. Current issues in distance learning library services include authentication and authorization of remote users, vendor licensing agreements, intellectual property and copyright issues, professional development for librarians in areas connected with information technology, and networked learner support. A. Slade.

1998

278. Barker, Philip. "The Role of Digital Libraries in Future Educational Systems." In *Online Information 98: Proceedings of the 22nd International Online Information Meeting, London, 8-10 December 1998*, edited by Brian McKenna, Catherine Graham, and Jane Kerr. Oxford: Learned Information Europe, 1998, 301-10.

Digital libraries are seen as important for supporting electronic course development (ECD) and the development of virtual university environments to facilitate lifelong learning. Three types of electronic resources form the basis for digital libraries: electronic books, electronic journals, and network-based facilities and services. Following a discussion of these resources, this paper focuses on end-user interface issues and architectures for a virtual university. To illustrate some of the possibilities of electronic resources, a case study is presented that involves recent work on applying ECD and virtual reality techniques within a conventional university. It is noted that the availability of electronic resources alone is not adequate for successful learning, and a virtual support system with interactive tutorial assistance is needed to accompany them. This virtual university paradigm is attractive for lifelong learning because access to the resources and support structure can be provided in any location with access to the Internet, including homes, offices, libraries, and community centers. A. Slade.

279. Beagle, Don. "Asynchronous Delivery Support for Distance Learning: A Strategic Opportunity for Libraries." *Journal of Library Services for Distance Education* 1, no. 2 (June 1998). Online. Available: http://www.westga.edu/~library/ jlsde/vol1/2/ DBeagle.html (Accessed April 13, 2000).

Strategic opportunities exist for libraries with the asynchronous (Web-based) delivery, as opposed to synchronous (real-time video) delivery, of distance learning. Libraries can leverage their strengths, reaping benefits in terms of instructional visibility and relevance. Future distance learning would benefit from not delivering a classroom lecture using remote technology but rather using an array of "knowledge media" to design interactive individual learning environments for remote users. In making the transition from teaching-centered to learner-centered, there is a need to develop an assessment process to measure student reactions to library media support instead of student reactions to the remote classroom. What is advocated is the development of flexible learning environments in which staff can use an array of knowledge media in response to the needs of individual patrons. M. Kascus.

280. Beaumont, Anne, Craige Hicks, and Joan Tucker. "CIDER: CAVAL Information Delivery and Electronic Requesting." In *Robots to Knowbots: The Wider Automation Agenda: Proceedings [of the] Victorian Association for Library Automation Inc. 9th Biennial Conference and Exhibition, January 28-30, 1998, Melbourne Convention Centre*. [Melbourne, Victoria: Victorian Association for Library Automation, 1998], 67-78.

Assisted by a government grant, the CAVAL consortium in Australia is developing an electronic document delivery service. The CIDER (CAVAL Information Delivery and Electronic Requesting) Project, which began in 1997, will provide a means for end-users at universities in the state of Victoria to electronically request and receive articles from journals in the social sciences, arts, and humanities held at participating libraries in the state. Integral to the project is the use of Ariel software as enhanced through the JEDDS (Joint Electronic Document Delivery Software) Project administered by the Australian Vice-Chancellors Committee. This paper is a progress report on CIDER, describing its administration, philosophy, strategies, and electronic infrastructure. Due to its complex nature, CIDER is using innovative software and technology, which was still undergoing development and testing at the time of writing. Major issues to be addressed in the project include the beta testing of software, user authentication, and copyright matters. A. Slade.

281. Brooks, Monica and Lynne Edington. "Planning Strategies for Cooperative Library Programs for Rural and Distance Learners in West Virginia." *Resource Sharing and Information Networks* 13, no. 2 (1998): 3-13.

A merger of Marshall University and Marshall University Graduate College included an integration of library services for rural and distance learners in West Virginia. The integration strategy involved combining CD-ROM subscriptions on a Web-accessible network, sharing costs for a subscription to full-text resources such as Proquest Direct to run on the same network, and providing document delivery between the two institutions. Other initiatives will include a library instruction program on the use of electronic resources, enhanced collaboration with faculty, and a staff training program. Web forms and surveys will be used to evaluate services. A. Slade.

282. Butler, John and Bill DeJohn. *Library and Information Services for the Minnesota Virtual University: A Status Report and Needs Assessment*. MVU Committee on Quality of Learning Resources, 1998. Online. Available: http://kinglear. lib.umn.edu/dejohn/servicesmvu.htm (Accessed April 13, 2000).

A needs assessment was conducted to determine how well Minnesota institutions are providing library services for distance learners. A 1995 University of Minnesota study revealed that both faculty and distance learners "tended to avoid circumstances that required the use of library resources." It was determined that a program of quality library support to distance/virtual learners would include provisions in five areas: (1) networked information resources, (2) document delivery, (3) borrowing privileges, (4) reference and referral service, and (5) information literacy and user training. Each area is discussed in terms of the infrastructure in place, initiatives in the planning and development stage, and gaps and challenges. In terms of networked information services, extensive licensing of bibliographic and full-text resources has been achieved at the institutional level, but also through some state-wide and consortial licensing. Appendix A includes a sample of networked information resources currently available throughout the state. Appendix B includes a library web page sampler. M. Kascus.

283. Cain, Mark. "The Way I See It: Only Change Is Constant." *College & Research Libraries News* 59, no. 8 (September 1998): 602-3.

In this column, three librarians offer their views on what their jobs will be like in five years. One of the librarians, Mark Cain, remarks that distance learning will become more prominent and he will have to devote more time to supporting the development of online academic programs. This will affect the library in that the staff will have to plan for electronic reserves, home delivery of monographs and other hard-copy materials, and Web-based instruction for remote library users. A. Slade.

284.   Carty, Susan Kinnell. "The Challenge of the Educated Web." *Searcher* 6, no. 4 (April 1998). Online. Available: http://www.infotoday.com/searcher/apr98/story2.htm (Accessed April 13, 2000).

This is a philosophical discussion of the World Wide Web and the challenges it poses. The issue of librarians as middlemen raises the question of the need for librarians in the future. The way research and learning used to be and the way they are today are compared, focusing on how they affect the library as a physical place. The roles of online learning and distance learning are also discussed. In looking to the future of libraries, the author raises important issues about the long-term impact of the democratization of resources that the Web is bringing about. Virtual universities are discussed, including the Western Governors University and the Southern Regional Electronic Campus. The projection is that learning will become a lifelong endeavor and librarians and information professionals will make the difference in tomorrow's world. A list of selected websites for tracking changes on the Web is given. A sidebar gives a capsule timeline for the Internet, the Web, and schools. M. Kascus.

285.   Chepesiuk, Ron. "Internet College: The Virtual Classroom Challenge." *American Libraries* 29, no. 3 (March 1998): 52-55.

With the shift to the virtual classroom, libraries are expected to deliver online resources to students wherever they are located. This is the philosophy of the "Internet College," as exemplified by such institutions as the University of Maryland University College (UMUC), Embry-Riddle Aeronautical University Extended Campus, Case Western Reserve Network Education, Nova Southeastern University School of Computer and Information Sciences, Cornell University Site for Distance Learning, and Colorado Electronic Community College. Web addresses are provided for each of these institutions. The following issues are discussed as important for information delivery in the future: the need for additional staff to handle increased patron demand, the need for librarians to complete tasks for online students that resident students could perform themselves, the differing technological skill levels of students, the need for faculty to understand the library's role in online education, copyright issues, digitization issues, and network security. M. Kascus.

286.   Hendry, Joe. "The Genesis Project: Cumbria's Lifelong Education Project." In *Libraries Without Walls 2: The Delivery of Library Services to Distant Users*, edited by Peter Brophy, Shelagh Fisher, and Zoë Clarke. London: Library Association Publishing, 1998, 151-58.

The Genesis Project, a partnership initiative among business and industry, local communities, local government, and the educational sector, is intended to address the educational, economic, and social needs of the people of Cumbria (United Kingdom) through use of information technologies. The program identifies a range of services that will benefit the citizens of Cumbria. These services include networking educational institutions and linking them to local schools;

disseminating information from public sector agencies; networking services to business and commerce; providing new opportunities for higher education through distance learning; creating a digital library facility that can provide access to the resources of the networked educational institutions; and utilizing schools, colleges, libraries, and village halls as community facilities for continuous learning. As part of the planning process, an opinion survey was commissioned to profile the local community and identify its requirements. The results of the survey indicated that there was "overwhelming" support for the project. A Phase I implementation strategy is planned that will provide 140 access points to information at 20 sites throughout Cumbria. A. Slade.

287. Hightower, Christy, Jennifer Reiswig, and Susan Berteaux. "Introducing Database Advisor: A New Service That Will Make Your Research Easier." *College & Research Libraries News* 59, no. 6 (June 1998): 409-12.

Database Advisor (DBA) was introduced at the University of California at San Diego (UCSD) to facilitate research by helping the user decide which science databases to use for locating articles and other resources. The development process for this Web-based tool is described. Interviews were conducted with students and public services staff to solicit recommendations for improving the functionality of the interface. Findings indicated that students are discovering databases that were previously unknown to them. Technical information is provided on running DBA to assist others interested in providing a similar service. M. Kascus.

288. Jones, Mark, Karen Kear, and Andy Reilly. "The Design, Development and Use of a CD-ROM Resource Library for an Open University Course." *British Journal of Educational Technology* 29, no. 3 (1998): 241-54.

A multidisciplinary team at the Open University (OU) in the United Kingdom produced a CD-ROM containing a large collection of articles for students in a course on "Information Technology and Society." Documents to be included on the CD-ROM, called a resource library, were selected by the academic members of the course team and copyright clearance was obtained by the OU. The documents were then scanned into electronic form and the files converted to bitmaps suitable for use on a personal computer. Students were encouraged to search the contents of the CD-ROM to find materials relevant to course topics. To facilitate this searching, the articles were electronically indexed using a set of course-related themes. Details are provided on the development of the CD-ROM and various production issues including editing, graphics, copyright, cost, quality assurance, and the roles of staff. Feedback from students indicated that the CD-ROM was well received, but some students found that reading large amounts of text from a computer screen was uncomfortable and inconvenient. It is interesting to note that there is no mention of library involvement in this project and the development of the CD-ROM appears to have been an attempt to eliminate the need for library use in the course. A. Slade.

289. Jurkowski, Odin L. "The Evolution of Academic Branch Libraries." *Illinois Libraries* 80, no. 1 (Winter 1998): 27-28.

Academic branch libraries on extended campuses are becoming more powerful through their ability to provide access via the World Wide Web to the same electronic resources available at the main library. In terms of branch resources, these libraries can now design their own websites and reduce the number of print materials acquired. However, the branch library must depend more on the main library for prompt delivery of print materials identified through the electronic resources. Reference materials and some circulating books will still need to be collected. In terms of management, branch libraries will continue to need an on-site librarian to assist patrons, provide effective public relations, represent the main library, manage the budget, and maintain the website and the day-to-day operations of the library. A. Slade.

290.   Kanjilal, Uma. *Digital Libraries for Distance Learners: Prospects for India*. Paper presented at the International Conference on New Missions of Academic Libraries in the 21st Century, Beijing, China, October 25-28, 1998. Online. Available: http://www.lib.pku.edu.cn/98conf/proceedings.htm (Accessed April 13, 2000).

Factors limiting the provision of library services to open university students in India include restrictive services at the regional and study centers, increasing enrollments, an increasing number of distance courses, rising costs, and a declining book-to-student ratio. Due to constraints in resources, self-sufficiency in library collections and service is no longer possible, and the open university libraries are looking to the concept of integrated digital libraries as the solution for the future. The utility of digital libraries for distance learners is examined in terms of the services that could be provided and the advantages from the point of view of distance learners. The prospects of developing digital libraries for distance learners in India are discussed in relation to current networking initiatives. It is pointed out that, while the backbone for developing digital libraries already exists in India, this development is presently in the nascent state. A. Slade.

291.   Li, Jie. *Distance Education in Health Sciences and Library Services*. Paper presented at the International Conference on New Missions of Academic Libraries in the 21st Century, Beijing, China, October 25-28, 1998. Online. Available: http://www.lib.pku.edu.cn/98conf/proceedings.htm (Accessed April 13, 2000).

Following a discussion of asynchronous and synchronous distance education, this paper focuses on telemedicine and library services for distance learners in the health sciences. At present, medical libraries are providing three basic services to distance learners: (1) remote access to electronic databases, (2) document delivery, and (3) electronic assistance and instruction. Topics mentioned in this context include end-user searching of bibliographic databases, web pages maintained by medical libraries, interlibrary loan services, and remote reference services. Resource sharing and collaboration among libraries are identified as issues currently requiring more attention to improve assistance to distance learners. A. Slade.

292.   Morrison, Rob. "The Virtual Library: Myths, Issues, and Reality." In *Virtual Learning Environments: Cases from the Field*, compiled by Daren Bakst. Washington, DC: American Association of Collegiate Registrars and Admissions Officers, 1998, 155-60.

The concept of the virtual library is discussed in relation to definitions of the term, misperceptions, issues, services, and the delivery of distance education. The following myths about the virtual library are examined and refuted: all information is available online, all online information is free, librarians will become unnecessary, and technology reduces costs. Virtual services and issues identified include organizing online information, evaluating electronic information, information literacy, computer literacy, collaboration with faculty and computing services staff, policies of accreditation agencies, resource sharing, and standardization of technology. Responsibility of the "home" institution and partnerships with other libraries are key components to the success of the virtual library in distance learning. These two components are emphasized in the ACRL *Guidelines for Distance Learning Library Services*. A. Slade.

293. Nesta, Frederick N. "The Remote Reference Room." In *IOLS '98: Proceedings of the 13th National Conference on Integrated Online Library Systems, New York, May 13-14, 1998*, compiled by Pamela R. Cibbarelli and Carol Nixon. Medford, NJ: Information Today, 1998, 121-30.

At Saint Peter's College, a web page serves as the Reference Room for off-campus users and for all students when the library is closed. The web page primarily provides links to the online catalogue and Web versions of selected periodical indexes. This paper discusses various issues associated with developing and maintaining the website, including selection criteria, collection development tools, page design, cataloguing and classification of resources, and updating links to ensure currency. The author notes that the same tools and techniques used to maintain currency of print collections can also be used to keep Internet collections up-to-date. A. Slade.

294. Ogburn, Joyce L. "Acquiring Minds Want to Know: Information Policies and Intellectual Property." *Against the Grain* 10, no. 3 (June 1998): 88, 93.

The integration of technology with content in libraries has prompted the merger of policies on information technology and intellectual property rights. In view of the expansion of distance education programs and the demand for online resources to support these programs, Old Dominion University is developing guidelines on intellectual property and Web materials. The author notes that distance education classes strain the concepts of fair use and librarians need to be cognizant about protecting intellectual property rights. A. Slade.

295. O'Sullivan, Una. "ROUTES." *Ariadne: the Web Version*, no. 15 (May 1998). Online. Available: http://www.ariadne.ac.uk/issue15/routes/ (Accessed April 13, 2000).

ROUTES is an electronic gateway project being undertaken by the Open University (OU) Library. Its principal aim is to bring librarians and academic staff together to select Internet resources for OU students. The academic staff evaluate the websites while library staff handle the indexing and retrieval of the resources and deal with the issues concerning access, copyright, and performance. An important objective of the OU Library is to enhance students' learning experience by using networked environments to create a feeling of belonging to the university. As part of the ROUTES project, help files and guidelines are being developed to assist students in using online resources, evaluating information on the Internet, and managing information retrieved. At the time of writing, priorities for ROUTES were to develop a training program in electronic information retrieval, pilot it with two student groups, refine the database, and publicize the project. A. Slade.

296. Pettman, Ian and Suzanne Ward. "The UNIverse Project: Global, Distributed Library Services." In *Libraries Without Walls 2: The Delivery of Library Services to Distant Users*, edited by Peter Brophy, Shelagh Fisher, and Zoë Clarke. London: Library Association Publishing, 1998, 159-70.

The UNIverse Project, funded by the European Commission for the period 1996 to 1999, is based on the concept of a virtual union catalogue that will enable end-users to access remote information sources. The UNIverse Consortium comprises six full partners, including the British Library and the National Library of Greece, and 11 associate partners, including the Norwegian Technical University and the University of Sheffield Library. This paper examines the aims and objectives of the project, presents a technical perspective on the operation of the system, discusses the services to be provided to users, describes the procedures to be used for evaluating UNIverse, and outlines the progress in the project to date. The objectives of UNIverse include the production of software to merge distributed library catalogues into an effective union catalogue and to integrate services related to the use of this catalogue. The four core services to be provided to end-users are record supply, search and retrieve, multimedia document delivery, and interlibrary loans. Evaluation of the project will involve consultation with both librarians and end-users. A. Slade.

297. Preece, Barbara G. and Thomas L. Kilpatrick. "Cutting Out the Middleman: Patron-Initiated Interlibrary Loans." *Library Trends* 47, no. 1 (Summer 1998): 144-57.

Interlibrary loan at Southern Illinois University, Carbondale, has undergone a major transformation in the direction of empowering patrons to initiate their own requests. The library began facilitating unmediated borrowing from the 48 members of a statewide consortium through a shared online union catalogue and circulation system. The turnaround time for interlibrary loan transactions was reduced dramatically, resulting in increased patron satisfaction with the process. This article discusses the rationale for the redesign in conjunction with the North American Interlibrary Loan and Document Delivery (NAILDD) Project, the use of technology, and the impact on staffing. Included among the reasons for the redesign were increased patron demand, revision of the library's mission statement, and reallocation of funds to support purchase of photocopies and borrowing fees. In terms of staffing, less professional staff time is needed to process the increased number of items borrowed, but unmediated borrowing results in a better service. M. Kascus.

298. Sandelands, Eric. "Creating an Online Library to Support a Virtual Learning Community." *Internet Research: Electronic Networking Applications and Policy* 8, no. 1 (1998): 75-80.

International Management Centres (IMC), an independent business school in the United Kingdom, created a virtual library in partnership with Anbar Electronic Intelligence, a database publisher, to support faculty and students participating in IMC's online programs. The online library of management literature enables users to download full-text articles or request print copies to be forwarded by fax or express mail from the British Library. Books can be ordered online from partner bookshops in the United Kingdom. Dissertation abstracts for all IMC final projects are available as a searchable database. Information is provided in this article on the partnership with Anbar Electronic Intelligence, IMC's virtual university model, the process of designing virtual library resources, and the benefits of the online "action learning" library. For a related article, see #326 below. A. Slade.

299.   Schiller, Nancy and Nancy Cunningham. "Delivering Course Materials to Distance Learners over the World Wide Web: Statistical Data Summary." *Journal of Library Services for Distance Education* 1, no. 2 (June 1998). Online. Available: http://www.westga.edu/~library/jlsde/vol1/2/NSchiller_NCunningham.html (Accessed April 13, 2000).

An $85,000 grant to conduct a feasibility study on delivering library resources over the Internet to distance learners was awarded by the Office of Educational Technology (OET) to the Buffalo, Binghamton, and Plattsburgh campuses of SUNY. The project had two goals, the first of which is discussed in this paper. The first goal was to determine the technical requirements for developing and operating a Web-based distance learning service. For statistical purposes, a project log was kept that included optical scanning equipment for this type of work, optimal file format, submission format and deadlines for faculty, and types of materials for inclusion. The second goal of the project was to determine if the Internet was the most effective way to deliver instructional materials. That goal will be discussed in a paper in preparation. The OET project designed and maintained a website for students to access course related material (instructional material as well as reserve reading), electronic resources and services, electronic journals, electronic reference services, interlibrary loans, and online catalogue access. Course related Internet sites were incorporated into the website. M. Kascus.

300.   Silva, Marcos. "Creating Electronic Environments for Learning." *Argus* (Montreal) 27, no. 1 (Spring-Summer 1998): 24-28.

Following a discussion of the implications of networked technologies on learning environments, this paper describes the design and implementation of an Internet resources course at McGill University. The objective of the Web-based course is to give teachers and school librarians knowledge of basic Internet applications and resources so they can implement networking projects in their classrooms or libraries. Students in the course have access to a virtual library that contains over 25 full-text journals. The library also offers access to a McGill librarian to help students with reference questions. Use of bibliographic resources is integrated into the course. In one assignment, students must search the ERIC database on a topic of interest, save the file, and send it by e-mail to their instructor. A. Slade.

301.   Smith, Gary. "Distance Learning: Perspectives from a Library Technologist and Student." In *National Online Meeting Proceedings—1998: Proceedings of the 19th National Online Meeting, New York, May 12-14, 1998*, edited by Martha E. Williams. Medford, NJ: Information Today, 1998, 365-74.

A distance learning student enrolled in a bachelor's degree program at the University of Phoenix offers his perspectives on the pros and cons of online instruction. For this author, the advantages clearly outweigh the disadvantages. Contributing to his positive experience is the availability of online library resources from a variety of information providers. He indicates that these sources of information, which are accessible from any location through a secure website, fulfil nearly all his information needs and enable him to successfully complete his course assignments. A. Slade.

302. Van Borm, Julien, Jan Corthouts, and Richard Philips. "ANTILOPE, BRONCO, IMPALA and ZEBRA: All Animals Running for Regional Library Provision in the Antwerp Library Network." In *Libraries Without Walls 2: The Delivery of Library Services to Distant Users*, edited by Peter Brophy, Shelagh Fisher, and Zoë Clarke. London: Library Association Publishing, 1998, 72-93.

The University of Antwerp serves as the hub for a cooperative library network in the Antwerp region of Belgium. The university's online catalogues and databases and the World Wide Web form the basis for the virtual library and document delivery services provided to distant users and the libraries in the regional network. The catalogues and systems that support these services are ANTILOPE, the Antwerp union catalogue of periodicals; ZEBRA, the union catalogue of the libraries in the regional network; BRONCO, a database containing the tables of contents of scientific journals; and IMPALA, the Belgian electronic document ordering system. The following topics are discussed in this context: the design of the Web OPAC, interfaces to CD-ROM bibliographies, authorization and authentication of users, electronic document ordering and delivery services, functions of the local request processing system, and billing mechanisms. Problem areas are identified as copyright issues, user assistance, performance measures and indicators, the Internet as a knowledge base, and staff training in electronic information provision. A. Slade.

303. Vassie, Roderic. *Access to Library Resources: A Blindspot in Distance Learning*. A report on the proceedings of a one-day seminar on "ILL for Distance Learning" held at the British Library Document Supply Centre on 20 November 1998. Available from: Roderic Vassie, Regional Marketing Manager (Middle East and Africa), The British Library Document Supply Centre, Boston Spa, West Yorkshire, England LS23 7BQ.

A one-day seminar on interlibrary loan for distance learning, organized by the British Library Document Supply Centre (BLDSC) and the University of Newcastle, focused on three main themes: technical issues, copyright issues, and marketing. The underlying aim of the seminar was to discuss ways that the BLDSC can supply materials to distance learners, especially overseas students, on behalf of other institutions. Among the technical issues examined were an integrated search and ordering facility, a simple Web interface, electronic delivery, tracking and security of loans, access to databases and electronic journals, access to information technology (IT), user training, and secure credit card payment. Discussion of copyright issues centered on copyright declaration forms versus electronic signatures, responsibilities of librarians with regard to similar or related orders, and definition of the term "pupil." Marketing issues included market research, benchmark websites, product differentiation, customer service, pricing of the service, the role of the BLDSC, and the role of the British Council. Concluding remarks stress that it would not be cost-effective for each UK university to establish its own library or document delivery system in each overseas country. A. Slade.

304.   Wang, Peiling. *Distance Education and Virtual Digital Teaching Laboratory*. Paper presented at the International Conference on New Missions of Academic Libraries in the 21st Century, Beijing, China, October 25-28, 1998. Online. Available: http://www.lib.pku.edu.cn/98conf/proceedings.htm (Accessed April 13, 2000).

Following a description of the author's experience in teaching a distance education graduate course via a two-way audio and two-way video system at the University of Tennessee at Knoxville, a virtual digital laboratory is proposed as a means to support distance teaching and learning. The proposed model utilizes the Internet and the World Wide Web to offer a digital library, a course web page, an online virtual office hours module, a course e-forum, digitally-recorded class sessions, and an assignment submission and distribution system. The digital library is a main component in the model, serving the function of an academic library in providing access to electronic resources and reserve materials. A. Slade.

305.   Xiao-chun, Ge. *Long Distance Open Education, Lifelong Education and Virtual Library*. Paper prepared for the '98 Shanghai International Open and Distance Education Symposium, Shanghai TV University, Shanghai, China, April 15-17, 1998. Shanghai, China: Open Education Research Institute, Shanghai Television University, 1998. Full text on CD-ROM. Available at: International Centre for Distance Learning, The Open University, Walton Hall, Milton Keynes MK7 6AA, United Kingdom.

This paper examines the concept of lifelong learning in relation to information technology (IT), libraries, and the virtual library. Distance education has a long history in China and IT will aid libraries in supporting this type of education. In this regard, the following topics are discussed: construction of the virtual library, networking of libraries, multi-symbol computer technology, hypermedia systems, hypertext technology, virtual reality technology, and technical services provided by the virtual library. In planning for the virtual library, the author recommends strong leadership; standardization in database construction; and a collaborative team approach involving library, computer, and technology specialists. Access to the virtual library in distance education should help to break down cultural barriers and enhance lifelong learning. A. Slade.

306.   Zhengbao, Zhang. *Chinese Academic Libraries and the Development of Distance Education*. Paper presented at the International Conference on New Missions of Academic Libraries in the 21st Century, Beijing, China, October 25-28, 1998. Online. Available: http://www.lib.pku.edu.cn/98conf/proceedings.htm (Accessed April 13, 2000).

With reference to the development of distance education in China via computer networks, the author emphasizes that academic libraries need to strengthen their services for distance learners. In this regard, librarians should undertake a number of activities such as evaluating, selecting, and organizing networked resources for distance learners; providing training in search techniques; and preparing navigation guides to the Internet. Librarians also need to work together with teaching staff to integrate information resources into distance education courses. It is noted that providing information resources for distance education is a new mission for Chinese academic libraries. The China Academic and Library Information System (CALIS), coordinated by Peking University, will assist with this goal by providing access to digitized and networked documents and information resources. A. Slade.

1997

307. Banks, Ronald A., Ramona H. Thiss, Gabriel R. Rios, and Phyllis C. Self. "Outreach Services: Issues and Challenges." *Medical Reference Services Quarterly* 16, no. 2 (Summer 1997): 1-10.

Virginia Commonwealth University/Medical College of Virginia has planned and implemented four one-year outreach service projects funded by the National Library of Medicine and the National Network of Libraries of Medicine Southeastern/Atlantic Region. All four projects utilized Grateful Med as either the sole or major means of electronic access to health sciences information resources. The focus of the project is on information access for public health nurses, HIV/AIDS information access, and circuit librarian services in rural southern Virginia. The issues and challenges identified from the project and ways to resolve them are documented here. M. Kascus.

308. Cannon, Nancy. *Distance Learning and Electronic Reserves*. SUNYLA Preconference on Library Services for Distance Learning: Focus Session on Electronic Reserves, June 4, 1997. Online. Available: http://www.oneonta.edu/~libweb/cannon/disted.html (Accessed April 13, 2000).

Binghamton University Libraries, in collaboration with other libraries in New York state, conducted a feasibility study on delivering course reserve materials over the Internet to distance education students. The advantages of using electronic reserves were immediate access 24 hours per day from any computer with an Internet connection, continuous availability of materials, and easy password access through the Adobe Capture software. The problems with electronic reserves were the amount of staff time to scan materials not already in electronic format, the need for high-end computer equipment and Internet access, slow downloading time for scanned images, and copyright issues. A number of questions about electronic reserves are posed for consideration. The conclusion is that, due to the time necessary to scan documents for Web availability, it is unlikely electronic reserves will ever become the main method for supplying supplementary course-related materials to distance education students. A. Slade.

309. Cavanagh, Anthony. "Electronic Access to the Library: What It Can Offer Distance Education Students." In *Open, Flexible and Distance Learning: Education and Training in the 21st Century: Selected Papers from the 13th Biennial Forum of the Open and Distance Learning Association of Australia, University of Tasmania, Launceston, 29 September-3 October 1997*, edited by Jo Osborne, David Roberts, and Judi Walker. Launceston, Tasmania: University of Tasmania, 1997, 64-69.

This paper discusses electronic library services for distance education students, with specific reference to the services offered by Deakin University. Deakin provides multiple means for its off-campus students to request library materials, including phone, fax, e-mail, Web forms, and dial-in ordering from the online catalogue. Between 1993 and 1996, electronic ordering increased by approximately 16% but still only accounted for 19% of the total number of requests received from off-campus students. Several possible barriers to electronic access are identified: cost and inconvenience of access, time commitments, student inertia, lack of awareness of benefits, cultural and attitudinal factors, and lack of technical knowledge. The following suggestions are made to raise student awareness and increase use of electronic technology: more publicity and instructional materials, reciprocal arrangements with other institutions, and a gradual introduction of technology-based assignments into the distance education courses. The paper concludes by indicating that there is sufficient evidence that off-campus students will use electronic resources if these services are adequately promoted and the students see a benefit to themselves. A. Slade.

310. Eastmond, Dan and Dan Granger. "Using Technology as a Course Supplement." *Distance Education Report* 1, no. 5 (September 1997): 3-7.

Written from the perspective of a distance educator, this article is a practical guide to using computer network technology as a supplement to distance education courses. The article focuses on course design issues and, in the context of discussing online research to support course instruction, suggests learning activities or assignments that involve the use of online library catalogues, bibliographic databases, and electronic journals. A. Slade.

311. Goodwin, Wayne. "Serving Remote Students in Distance-Learning Programs." In *Summary of Proceedings of the Fiftieth Annual Conference of the American Theological Association, Iliff School of Theology, Denver, Colorado, June 21-24, 1996*, edited by Melody S. Chartier. Evanston, IL: American Theological Association, 1997, 25-50. Responses: 51-58.

This historical perspective on theological education provides a framework for understanding the current interest in new models of teaching and learning such as distance education. The three models of theological education in America identified provide background for the discussion of the theological library. The issues of importance to the theological library of the future are access rather than collections, cataloguing, copyright, electronic conversations and resources, user training, and upgrading librarians' skills for their new educational role. Gordon-Conwell Theological Seminary serves as a case study of distance learning opportunities for students, including a discussion of resources to support the curriculum. The role of technology is discussed, noting that the Charlotte Campus has led the way in introducing computer-assisted instruction into the classroom and the library. Two responses to this presentation are given. John Bracke points out that the resources of distance learning—electronic library resources, websites, and the Internet—serve and enhance the educational effort rather than drive it. John Dickason sees remote access to online catalogues giving students more flexibility and technology augmenting good collections, but he stresses the importance of those resources and services provided by libraries that are irreplaceable. M. Kascus.

312. Gorman, Lyn. *Academic Forum: Online Teaching and Library Service*. Paper presented to the Australian Library and Information Association Distance Education Special Interest Group National Conference: Shifting Sands, Charles Sturt University, Wagga Wagga, December 5-6, 1997. Available from: Christine Cother, Editor DESIGnation, University of South Australia Library, Holbrooks Road, Underdale, South Australia 5032.

The rapid growth in online education has implications for libraries and librarians, particularly at Charles Sturt University. The author identifies a number of significant issues and questions about library support for online teaching, including priorities in converting holdings into electronic formats, copyright issues pertaining to electronic resources, and resource sharing and networking among libraries. Other issues include training library staff as facilitators in an electronic environment and collaboration between librarians and academic staff. A. Slade.

313. Hutton, Michael T. *An Analysis of Distance Library Service Systems*. A paper presented to the Ed.D Program in Instructional Technology and Distance Education in partial fulfillment of the Requirements for the Degree of Doctor of Education, Nova Southeastern University, 1997. Online. Available: http://www.fcae. nova.edu/~huttonm/isd1.html (Accessed April 13, 2000).

Library services for distance learning are examined from a systems perspective in this paper. The distance library service system (DLS) is discussed in terms of input, outputs, and feedback within the academic environment. The inputs, along with their outputs and feedback, are graphically represented as a model. Further discussion focuses on boundaries and processes within the system, illustrated by a process flow chart representing how the online student accesses library services. The author concludes that the current distance library services system is adequate to meet student needs, but DLS will have to change as distance education changes. M. Kascus/A. Slade.

314. Miller, Mark. "Supporting Independent Learners Through Telematics." *Learning Resources Journal* 13, no. 2 (June 1997): 4-7.

To support students in its Individually Negotiated Learning Route (INLR), the University College of Suffolk (UCS) is developing and evaluating telematics applications. As part of this initiative, UCS is developing a website that will include an access gateway to provide students with INLR information and assistance. Staff in the UCS Library Learning Resources Centre are compiling an online directory of subject or discipline-based websites to include on the gateway. It will offer students a "pre-validated" range of relevant sites for information and learning resources. Academic staff are assisting in the development of the directory by recommending sites useful for their subject areas. A. Slade.

315. Skinner, Robert. "Distributed Education and Libraries." Co-published simultaneously in *Collection Management* 22, nos. 1/2 (1997): 71-80, and *Collection Development: Access in the Virtual Library*, edited by Maureen Pastine. New York: Haworth Press, 1997, 71-80.

Libraries face the challenge of providing the same quality of service to all students and faculty whether on-campus or off-campus. This paper explores how faculty and students are using electronic conferencing, and gives examples of how libraries can take advantage of electronic conferencing with regard to collections. No one method of electronic conferencing is best for all purposes. An overview is given of the principal technologies being used in the classroom. For each technology, the advantages and disadvantages are given as well as the ways in which libraries are using or might use the technology. The free technologies discussed are e-mail, mailing lists, Usenet, Chat, and the World Wide Web. Two examples of commercial conferencing products are provided: FirstClass and Lotus

Notes. Online services used to deliver distributed information, such as AOL and CompuServ, are also discussed. As electronic communication becomes more familiar to students and faculty, it becomes a viable means for academic librarians to use in communicating with patrons. M. Kascus.

316.   Susman, Mary Beth. "Where in the World Is the Colorado Electronic Community College?" *Community College Journal* 68, no. 2 (October/November 1997): 16-20.

Colorado Electronic Community College is a virtual college that uses telecommunications technology to deliver curriculum created by the Colorado college system. Library support is mentioned briefly in the context of a description of college services. It is noted that library access is provided through various Internet library resources, interlibrary loan, and by CARL. A. Slade.

317.   Warm, Julie J. "Electronically Providing Instructional Support Services for the Distance Learner." *Library Hi Tech News*, no. 139 (January/February 1997): 31.

This short article describes the author's reaction to a presentation on the University of Phoenix (UOP), a virtual university with over 2,000 distance learning students. The author reports that UOP students have full library resources online through three different providers: EBSCOhost, SearchBank, and UPI Electronic Products. A. Slade.

318.   Zastrow, Jan. "Going the Distance: Academic Librarians in the Virtual University." In *Computers in Libraries '97: Proceedings of the Twelfth Computers in Libraries Conference, March 10-12, 1997, Arlington, Virginia*, compiled by Carol Nixon, Heide Dengler, and John Yersak. Medford, NJ: Information Today, 1997, 171-76. Also online. Available: http://lama.kcc.hawaii.edu/staff/illdoc/DE/DEpaper.htm (Accessed April 13, 2000).

Librarians are well positioned to take a leadership role in Internet-delivered computer-mediated education. Two main roles librarians can play are identified as support services and technology advisers. Among the support services outlined are (1) reference assistance involving use of e-mail, the Internet Public Library, electronic pathfinders, World Wide Web, and online catalogues; (2) library instruction, including use of videocassettes and online guides; (3) research assistance; (4) interlibrary loan and document delivery; and (5) electronic reserves. As technology advisers, librarians can assist faculty in creating distance education sites. Some ideas given for working with faculty in designing and implementing electronic courses are educating faculty about current technologies, conducting literature searches, consulting on fair use and copyright, and giving input in designing user-friendly interfaces for computer-mediated education. M. Kascus.

1996

319.   Adams, Kate and Sara Martin. *Distance Education Clearinghouse Web Site*. Lincoln: University of Nebraska Lincoln, 1996. 10 pp. ERIC ED 399 966.

A website was developed by the University of Nebraska-Lincoln Information Services staff using a grant funded by NEB*SAT, Nebraska's multiple-channel satellite and optical fiber educational telecommunications network. The website provides a clearinghouse of distance education, Internet, and web page development information useful to librarians and educators throughout Nebraska. This paper includes a discussion of the goals and objectives of the project, the implementation process involved, and how the project will benefit Nebraskans. A description is given of the criteria for resource selection, resource categories used for the clearinghouse home page, and record format. Other issues discussed are responsibilities of team members, cataloguing workflow, placing records on the Web server, the evaluation process, and maintenance issues. M. Kascus.

320.   Besser, Howard. "Issues and Challenges for the Distance Independent Environment." *Journal of the American Society for Information Science* 47, no. 11 (November 1996): 817-20.

Among the issues and challenges for distance independent education is instructional support. In this article, the author outlines the changes in the infrastructure that are needed when moving from the same time/same place educational model to the distance independent environment. The author suggests that libraries need to consider how to change their services to accommodate distance learners. The importance of having curricular support materials online is stressed while acknowledging that copyright is an issue when placing materials online. Additionally, delivering materials already online may not permit delivery to a distance learner in another state. Many university libraries are exploring the use of electronically delivered reserve materials, while others are helping teaching faculty organize online delivery of all curricular support material. M. Kascus.

321.   Beswick, Jillian. "Overcoming the Hurdles: The Development of Electronic Library Services on the Virtual Campus." In *Electronic Dream? Virtual Nightmare: The Reality for Libraries: Conference Proceedings: 1996 VALA Biennial Conference and Exhibition, 30 January to 1 February 1996, World Congress Centre, Melbourne*. Melbourne, Victoria: Victorian Association for Library Automation Inc., 1996, 39- 45.

In 1992, Edith Cowan University established a computer-based communication facility called the Virtual Campus to support its external students. Library services were added in 1994, providing a means for the students to submit requests by e-mail; search online catalogues; and access the FirstSearch, Uncover, and Current Contents databases. Low use of the electronic library services prompted a survey of the external students. While 69% of those surveyed knew about the Virtual Campus, only 11% of these students had used it. In response to the survey findings, the library implemented a number of new strategies to improve usage. These included an active promotional campaign, providing remote access to the CD-ROM network, and offering real-time user education sessions via the chat facilities on the Virtual Campus. As a result of these changes, use of the library services on the Virtual Campus increased. Future plans include providing online request forms on the World Wide Web and offering self-paced information literacy programs. A. Slade.

322.   Faulhaber, Charles B. "Distance Learning and Digital Libraries: Two Sides of a Single Coin." *Journal of the American Society for Information Science* 47, no. 11 (November 1996): 854-56. Also online. Available: http://www.carl-acrl.org/ Archive/Conference95/faulhaber.html (Accessed April 13, 2000).

Distance learning enables the University of California to pool students from various campuses, decreasing pupil cost and allowing specialized resources to be shared. The author's experience with a multi-point distance learning course at the Berkeley campus stresses the need for digital library support. The technology used in presenting the class is described and the administrative and technical difficulties experienced are discussed. The author concludes that distance education without a digital library is not possible. Instead of providing digital services directly, libraries will collaborate with other partners, such as the computer center and instructional technology programs, to provide the tools for faculty and students to create digital resources themselves. The role of the library in the future will be to take information directly from its creator, the faculty, and put it on the World Wide Web for students. This will require considerable staff time. M. Kascus.

323.   Latta, Gail F. *The Virtual University: Creating an Emergent Reality*. Lincoln: University of Nebraska-Lincoln, 1996. 44 pp. ERIC ED 399 970.

According to the author, information technologies are transforming the educational enterprise, and the success of higher education in the virtual universe will depend on the creative application of these technologies. Entrepreneurial efforts by other providers to create virtual learning environments are expanding. Using examples of virtual universities, insight is provided into the competitive marketplace in which academic institutions are delivering their unique product. Changes in student demographics and expectations are discussed as part of the rapidly shifting educational landscape. The success of higher education in the current virtual environment will depend, in part, on providing access to reference, study, and research resources. Librarians have a key role to play in this process, and several areas in which they can work collaboratively with faculty are discussed. By providing a range of support services, librarians can help faculty who are trying to improve their teaching and student learning through effective use of information technology. Librarians can also support faculty in the task of adapting curriculum to the new presentation and delivery media. Finally, librarians can assist faculty to incorporate technology into the design of online curriculum to help students become information literate. M. Kascus.

324.   Lynch, Mary Jo. *Electronic Services in Academic Libraries*. ALA Survey Report. Chicago: Office for Research and Statistics, American Library Association, 1996. 41 pp. ISBN 0-8389-7865-7.

In 1996, the American Library Association and Ameritech Library Services collaborated on a survey of electronic services in academic libraries. A questionnaire was mailed to a sample of 1,132 academic libraries in the United States. Respondents were asked to indicate whether or not they offered various electronic services by responding to 22 questions. Among the findings were that doctorate-granting institutions are most likely to offer electronic services; electronic public catalogues are available in the majority of academic libraries; almost all academic libraries make electronic reference databases available; electronic journals providing full text of already published material are common in all institutions; and lists of reserve materials are available electronically fairly often, especially in doctorate-granting institutions, but text of reserve materials is much less available electronically. Other findings revealed that Internet access is likely to be available to campus faculty, students, and staff outside the library; many libraries have home pages on the World Wide Web; electronic document delivery services are widely used by libraries in doctorate-granting institutions and somewhat less often in others; and almost all academic libraries offer informal assistance and formal training in the use of electronic services to students and faculty. A. Slade.

325. Mirza, Javaid S. "On-Line Support for Research Projects." In *Innovations in Distance and Open Learning: Proceedings of the 10th Annual Conference of the Asian Association of Open Universities, November 14-16, 1996, Tehran*. Tehran, Iran: Payame Noor University, 1996, 126-28.

Distance education programs in science and engineering present problems from the point of view of laboratory access and library support. The author notes that most distance education institutions solve the problems by seeking support from local tertiary institutions and arranging for use of their laboratory and library facilities. In cases where local resources are not adequate or the cost is prohibitive, the author suggests use of information and communication technologies to provide the students with access to experienced tutors and enriched library support. A. Slade.

326. Sandelands, Eric. "Virtual Libraries for Virtual Students." *Online and CD Notes*, no. 7 (September 1996): 3-5.

The focus of this paper is on the role of virtual libraries in learning and the contribution of Anbar Electronic Intelligence to the concept of the virtual university. One characteristic of the virtual university is access to the best possible library of published information, which must be accessible via the World Wide Web as well as having courseware and reading material available on CD-ROM. Two examples are given of pioneering institutions that are using the Internet for distance learning and designing their structures around this aim. Both Business School Nederland (Holland) and International Management Centres (IMC) have adopted electronic support services. The Anbar Management Intelligence Database is used by both institutions. This database provides a virtual library, with abstracts delivered to the desktop and full-text articles available for purchase. For a related article, see #298 above. M. Kascus.

1995

327. Brophy, Peter. "The Concept of 'Libraries Without Walls'." In *Proceedings of the First "Libraries Without Walls" Conference, Mytilene, Greece, 9-10 September 1995*, edited by Ann Irving and Geoff Butters. Preston, UK: Centre for Research in Library and Information Management, University of Central Lancashire, 1995, 16-21.

The author begins with a discussion of the concept of "Libraries Without Walls," focusing on how the library can be taken to the user so the user does not have to go to the library. An overview is given of the key issues that will affect the delivery of library services to users at a distance, including electronic networking, desktop delivery, and access versus collections. A new role for librarians that focuses on becoming an "information tour guide" is described. Users are discussed in terms of the need for independence in their information skills. Electronic archives are discussed in relation to the need for preservation and bibliographic control. Electronic texts are considered in terms of the following opportunities: dynamic systems, multiple sources, information skills, reference services, and resource sharing. The key issues to resolve are equity of provision, partnerships, telematics, copyright, electronic services, user training, and cost. M. Kascus.

328.   Erazo, Edward and Roberta L. Derlin. "Distance Learning and Libraries in the Cyberspace Age." In *CHECS '95: The Internet—Flames, Firewalls and the Future: Council for Higher Education Computing Services: Proceedings for the 1995 Conference, New Mexico Military Institute, Roswell, New Mexico, November 8-10, 1995*, edited by Martha Suiter. [Las Cruces, NM]: Council for Higher Education Computing Services, New Mexico State University, [1995], 51-56. ERIC ED 398 917. Also online. Available: http://dns1-checs.nmsu.edu/95conf/PROCEEDINGS/erazo.html (Accessed April 13, 2000).

This paper presents two success stories in "digitizing" libraries and explores various options in developing electronic library support for distance learning. The role of the library in the distance learning environment should be similar to on-campus library services, including interlibrary loan, reference, document delivery, and electronic database services. Additional services should include a toll-free number, telephone reference, and telefacsimile. Librarians need to expand their traditional roles and work closely with instructors and students. Two institutional leaders, Nova Southeastern University in Florida and the University of Alaska, Fairbanks, are discussed. The author concludes that the future of distance learning is tied to the future of higher education and libraries will need to plan to meet the challenges of cyberspace. M. Kascus.

329.   Fayad, Susan. "ACLIN Expansion Grant Project: Expanding Library Services Within the State." *Colorado Libraries* 21, no. 1 (Spring 1995): 22-24.

Access Colorado Library and Information Network (ACLIN) brings the major library resources of the state within easy reach for residents and, as such, the network has the potential to play a key role in supporting extended campus library services. Funding for ACLIN improved considerably with the receipt of two major grants, one from the U.S. Department of Education and the other from the U.S. Department of Commerce. Both grants had the same four goals: (1) increase access to ACLIN, (2) expand content on ACLIN, (3) provide audience development and education, and (4) influence public policy in the formation of a state-wide information structure. An important issue is the sustainability of ACLIN and the need for ongoing operating funds, because the grants can only be used for research and development. M. Kascus.

330.   Littman, Marilyn Kemper. "Videoconferencing as a Communication Enhancement." *Journal of Academic Librarianship* 21, no. 5 (September 1995): 359-64.

Videoconferencing is discussed, first in terms of its capabilities, advantages, and disadvantages and, second, as a planning strategy and technique to accommodate library needs. Examples of library uses of videoconferencing are given, including direct instruction in the use of online information retrieval strategies and techniques to remote students. Delivery of remote personalized service via this technology can accommodate individual learning styles and preferences. Criteria to consider in evaluating and selecting a videoconferencing system include cost, features and format, system power and performance, ease of learning and use, sound and video quality, operating environment, adherence to industry standards, and vendor reputation. Academic librarians are encouraged to facilitate the design of videoconferencing applications that contribute to the establishment of virtual collaborative relationships and the enrichment of library services. M. Kascus.

331. Taylor, Warren G. "Distance Education on the Internet at Front Range Community College." *Colorado Libraries* 21, no. 3 (Fall 1995): 14-16.

Distance learning is taught via the Internet at Front Range Community College (FRCC) in Colorado. The key components of the Internet course program are instructional design and library support. The library/media center has been an integral part of the program from its inception. Library/media center staff are competent in Internet functions and operations. They provide Internet reference service either on-site at the library or by e-mail. Student response to the online courses has been positive. FRCC intends to continue to offer Internet courses and plans to rely on the library and other college support services to achieve student success over the Internet. M. Kascus.

1994

332. Atkinson, Roger. *How Can AARNet Support Openness in Open Learning?* 1994. Online. Available: http://cleo.murdoch.edu.au/asu/edtech/pubs/atkinson/ Atkinson-Netwkshp93.html (Accessed April 13, 2000).

The Open Learning Electronic Support Services (OLESS) network in Australia is discussed in relation to two projects, ADENet (Australian Distance Education Network) and the "Electronic Access to Library Services for Distance Education and Open Learning" proposal. This latter proposal was based on the belief that electronic access to libraries is a key change agent in preparing for the development of online universities. The project proposed to offer solutions to core problems in making new information technologies available via AARNet (Australian Academic Research Network) to remote library users. However, the proposal encountered difficulties due to a perception that it conflicted with government plans for open learning electronic support services and, as a result, was eventually rejected for funding. After reporting this rejection, the author identifies some dilemmas and uncertainties that need to be resolved in the OLESS initiative. A. Slade.

Remote Access to Electronic Resources

For subject access to other works that pertain to remote access, consult the following headings in the Subject Index: "authentication of library users," "CD-ROM," "computer networks," "electronic reserve materials," "end-user searching," "Internet," "licensing (computer products)," "local area networks," "online catalogues—remote access," "online search services," "remote access to electronic resources—for distance learners," "remote access to electronic resources—general works," "transaction log analysis," "wide area networks," and "World Wide Web."

1999

333. Duffy, Anne. *Remote Control: Creating a Technology-Centered Library in Rural Alaska.* Paper presented at the ACRL 9th National Conference: Racing Toward Tomorrow: Detroit, Michigan, April 8-11, 1999. Online. Available: http://www.ala.org/acrl/pdfpapers99.html (in pdf format) (Accessed April 13, 2000).

The University of Alaska Fairbanks-Kuskokwim Campus is a major partner in the Distance Delivery Consortium (DDC), which was created "to promote distance education, telemedicine, and telecommunications for rural Alaska." The DDC facilitates access to information and resources for students and the general community in southwest Alaska and works with schools, the regional consortium library, and other agencies to assist with telecommunication support. This paper describes the following aspects of the DDC: its history, structure, and membership; funding; use of technology; and relationships with local agencies. The author observes that through outsourcing and networking, the DDC has fostered an information community that benefits the entire state of Alaska. A. Slade.

334. Hulshof, Robert. "Providing Services to Virtual Patrons." *Information Outlook* 3, no. 1 (January 1999): 20-23.

Virtual patrons are library users who access electronic resources and request assistance without visiting the library in person. These users require services that are immediate, useful, and easily accessible. The author argues that the most significant additional service that virtual patrons need is technical support. Important tasks for libraries preparing to offer technical support to electronic library users include establishing clear parameters for service, developing written policies and procedures, involving staff in the development of a technical support plan, and providing guides and self-help aids for users. Additional requirements are staff training and access to appropriate hardware and software. The author emphasizes that remote access is becoming an increasingly significant element of library service and libraries need to prepare and plan for it in terms of resources, time, and staff. A. Slade.

335. Noble, Steve. *Delivering Accessible Library Services in a Distance Learning Environment.* Paper presented at CSUN 99: Technology and Persons with Disabilities: the 14th annual conference of the California State University, Northridge, Center On Disabilities, Los Angeles, March 15-20, 1999. Online. Available: http://www.dinf.ch/csun_99/session0151.html (Accessed April 13, 2000).

The focus in this extended abstract of the author's conference presentation is on how the library needs of students with disabilities in distance learning programs can be met. Typical library services for distance learners are described and the problems in supporting students with disabilities are discussed. While document delivery is problematic in serving the library needs of students with print disabilities, books are the weakest link in this process. One initiative to address this weakness is a test project in the United States that is examining various methods of delivering accessible educational information to students with visual and learning disabilities. In particular, the study will explore the delivery of Audio-Plus books via digital methods in a networked environment of five local and distance education sites. A. Slade.

1998

336. Cooper, Rosemarie, Paula R. Dempsey, Vanaja Menon, and Christopher Millson-Martula. "Remote Library Users—Needs and Expectations." *Library Trends* 47, no. 1 (Summer 1998): 42-64.

Defining remote users and their needs will help library staff to provide relevant services. Customer satisfaction is correlated with knowledge at a distance. Distance learning at DePaul University is offered as a case study to emphasize the elements needed to support distance education faculty and students. The services recommended for remote users and distance learners are described along with the implications for library staff roles. To promote user satisfaction, library staff need to better understand users and their needs. Faculty and student needs and expectations at DePaul are discussed. Recommendations are divided into two categories: those dealing with remote users in general and those dealing with distance learners. According to the author, remote users need (1) constant, around-the-clock access to online databases mounted on user-friendly systems; (2) 24-hour help desk or technical support; (3) a personal relationship with library staff; and (4) extensive information describing specific resources and the full range of services available at the "home" library. According to the author, the distance learner needs (1) a greater range of services provided by the library staff, such as conducting online searches and preparing packets of information, with less emphasis on self-service; (2) to use a variety of libraries in addition to the "home" library; and (3) to learn what other libraries can do for them. M. Kascus.

337. Eustis, Joanne and Gail McMillan. "Libraries Address the Challenges of Asynchronous Learning." *JALN: Journal of Asynchronous Learning Networks* 2, no. 1 (March 1998). Online. Available: http://www.aln.org/alnweb/journal/vol2_issue1/eustis.htm (Accessed April 13, 2000).

The two innovative information delivery initiatives described in this paper are examples of how academic libraries are meeting the challenge of the extended campus. VIVA, the Virtual Library of Virginia, is a consortium of 39 state-assisted colleges and universities. VIVA was established to encourage collaboration among Virginia institutions of higher education and to support the electronic dissemination of information. Cooperative electronic collection development has led to financial benefits for both the institution and the distance student. Authentication of library users has become a recurring issue. A complement to VIVA resources is Electronic Theses and Dissertations (ETDs), available through Virginia Tech's Scholarly Communications Project (SCP). In a partnership with the graduate school, SCP developed and implemented procedures for online student submission of approved theses and dissertations. Although the ETD initiative began at Virginia Tech, it is being adopted by other universities. M. Kascus.

338. Furniss, Kevin A. and Doug Kariel. "Library Catalogs, the World Wide Web, and Serving the Off-Campus User: Boon or Bust?" In *The Eighth Off-Campus Library Services Conference Proceedings: Providence, Rhode Island, April 22-24, 1998*, compiled by P. Steven Thomas and Maryhelen Jones. Mount Pleasant, MI: Central Michigan University, 1998, 155-58.

According to the authors, library catalogues can be enhanced to meet the information needs of the remote user. Specific ways in which the off-campus library services librarian can work with catalogue librarians are suggested. One way to improve access through the catalogue is to enhance the description of certain types of materials such as conference proceedings and collections of articles in a book. This could be done by including contents notes in the MARC 505 field of the bibliographic records for these elusive materials. Another way to enrich bibliographic access for remote users through the catalogue is the addition of subject headings and cross-references. Analysis of OPAC transaction logs to identify unsuccessful searches would provide decision support for how catalogers can enhance access. World Wide Web-based library catalogues provide links to Internet access resources by connecting via a Uniform Resource Locator (URL), which can be added to the bibliographic record. Enhancing bibliographic records is important to ensure that remote users are getting a level of catalogue access adequate to their needs. M. Kascus.

339. Gulliford, Bradley. "Making Choices in the Virtual World: The New Model at United Technologies Information Network." *Library Trends* 47, no. 1 (Summer 1998): 158-71.

This article discusses the transformation of the United Technologies Corporation Information Network (IN) from a traditional library system to a virtual system of websites, document delivery, telephone and e-mail reference, and desktop technical support. This change has brought about the need to educate and empower its customers who are now forced to make decisions, choose resources, and develop their own information strategy. The Information Network negotiates "site licenses" with vendors and publishers to allow access to publishers' servers from employees' desktops. As a result of the shift to an electronic library, many roles of IN staff are shifting. There is a need to find a middle ground between doing the work for customers and insisting that customers fulfil their own information needs. M. Kascus.

340. Luther, Judy. "Distance Learning and the Digital Library or What Happens When the Virtual Student Needs to Use the Virtual Library in a Virtual University." *Educom Review* 33, no. 4 (July/August 1998): 22-26.

Various issues pertaining to distance learning and remote access to electronic resources are discussed in this article, including the changing nature of distance learning, the characteristics of the electronic library, licensing requirements for electronic resources, authentication of remote users, and new models of distance learning as exemplified by the Western Governors University in the United States. A. Slade.

341. Peters, Thomas A. "Remotely Familiar: Using Computerized Monitoring to Study Remote Use." *Library Trends* 47, no. 1 (Summer 1998): 7-20.

Computerized monitoring has been used as a tool for libraries to gather information about the behaviour of remote users. The emphasis in this article is on what libraries have learned about remote use from computerized monitoring and what larger issues have been raised by remote access. The older method of trans-action log analysis is now complemented by the use of Web server log analysis to unobtrusively study how remote users navigate into and through library websites. One of the major issues raised is whether uninformed, unobtrusive computerized monitoring is an ethical way of treating remote users. Three service challenges posed by remote access in the foreseeable future are identified: (1) more informa-tion is available offline than online; (2) online presents formidable service issues for libraries, assuming that putting full-text online is easy compared to developing usable, useful, used online services; and (3) there is a threat of diurnal diffusion of use of library collections and services with the prospect of digital collections available 24 hours a day. Remote access and computerized information sources are altering the way in which people interact with information. M. Kascus.

342.   Rockman, Ilene F. "Challenges and Opportunities in Reaching the Remote User." In *Recreating the Academic Library: Breaking Virtual Ground*, edited by Cheryl LaGuardia. New York: Neal-Schuman, 1998, 241-55.

The following four elements are identified as important in serving the needs of remote library users: services, staffing, security, and infrastructure. Included under services are the types of instructional programs and support materials of-fered. Staffing involves the range of competencies in subject fields and the part-nerships with nonlibrary personnel to address the technical needs of remote users. Security refers to the protection, integrity, accuracy, and reliability of data to be accessed and delivered. Infrastructure pertains to the ability to deliver informa-tion through a variety of network configurations and typologies. In discussing each of these elements, this book chapter looks at collaboration between institu-tions as a means to pay for access to electronic resources, the impact of distance learning on library services to remote users, creative solutions to remote access problems at selected institutions, and the significance of bandwidth capabilities and ATM (asynchronous transfer mode) for remote access. It is argued that li-brarians must adapt to changes in information technologies and assume proactive roles to meet the present and future needs of the remote user. A. Slade.

343.   Self, Phyllis C., Barbara A. Wright, and Jessica L. Waugh. "Remote Users of Health Sciences Libraries." *Library Trends* 47, no. 1 (Summer 1998): 75-90.

This article explores the various innovations in service models over three decades to extend health sciences library and information services beyond the walls of the library. Remote users of health sciences information are identified as more demanding, informed consumers, and their expectations are discussed. Also discussed are the ways in which health sciences librarians have used advances in technology to enhance library services. An overview is given of the few evalua-tion studies performed on remote user services. The article does not discuss copy-right issues, but notes that "fair use" of health information is threatened by the proposed copyright legislation and poses a new challenge in reaching the remote user. M. Kascus.

1997

344. Hensley, Kelly, Martha F. Earl, Janet S. Fisher, Marcellus Turner, and Rita Scher. "Providing Library Services to a Remote Non-Traditional Program for Health Career Students: The Kellogg Experience." *Bulletin of the Medical Library Association* 85, no. 1 (January 1997): 48-51.

East Tennessee State University received a grant from the Kellogg Foundation to support a non-traditional program for health care students in a community-based curriculum. One focus of the proposal was to encourage students to practice in rural areas. To provide information resources, librarians relied on technology. Resources included CD-ROM databases, document delivery, an on-site collection of books, reference services, and library instruction. A standard evaluation was conducted each time a library instruction or database training session was provided, focusing on course content and librarian performance. Since the original model to provide library services was developed, the technology has evolved and the Internet will further facilitate access. M. Kascus.

345. Stewart, Des. "Delivering Full-Text Legal Information to Remote Clients Via the World Wide Web." In *On the Edge: Proceedings of the Seventh Asian Pacific Specials, Health and Law Librarians' Conference, Perth, 12-16 October 1997*. [Perth, WA] : Special Libraries Section, Health Libraries Section of the Australian Library and Information Association and Australian Law Librarians Group, 1997, 503-15.

To support its off-campus law students, Southern Cross University (SCU) initiated a collaborative trial between the university and a number of publishers to make full-text legal materials available over the Internet via Web technology. Permission was received in 1996 to mount selected products on SCU's Web server to determine if networking the products to remote users was a viable option. Part of the project was to evaluate the usefulness of the service for remote clients by surveying users as well as monitoring the technical capabilities of server software and hardware. The results of the survey showed that most off-campus law students found the Web version of the products easy to search and the majority preferred the electronic version to the print format. The trial confirmed that there is a need to offer legal information from commercial publishers via the World Wide Web to off-campus students, and SCU is pursuing this through negotiations with selected publishers of legal materials. A. Slade.

346. Yott, Patrick and C. H. Hoebeke. "Improving Valid Access to Site-Licensed Resources." *College & Research Libraries News* 58, no. 10 (November 1997): 698-700.

The issue of remote service authentication is discussed with reference to the University of Virginia. To protect site licenses, libraries usually restrict access to databases and other electronic resources on the basis of the institution's IP domain. The authors identify three approaches to authentication that can enable patrons to obtain remote access to these resources: (1) establishing a go-between server that requires the user to log in with ID and password to convince the vendor's computer that the remote user is in the valid domain, (2) implementing a

Z39.50 system allowing users to log in to a client machine that will send a hidden ID and password to the vendor's system, and (3) using a simple cgi script that validates users against a local database. The latter approach is used at the University of Virginia and details are provided on its application, including an example of how members of a valid subset of the university population are authenticated against a local database on a server maintained by the university's central computing division. A. Slade.

1996

347. Commings, Karen. "Libraries of the Future: Two 'All in One' Workstation Projects." *Computers in Libraries* 16, no. 5 (May 1996): 26-27.

This short article reports on two examples of how libraries are using online technology to expand access to their services by bringing the library to the user's desktop. At Drake University, a CD-ROM local area network provides remote wide area network access that supports 20 concurrent users: eight local and 12 remote users. Thirty-two CD-ROMs are accessible campus-wide. Howard County Library in Maryland provides a "Data Depot," a one-stop resource for local library and government information. The Data Depot is a cooperative project involving Howard County government, Patuxent Publishing Company, and the Mall in Columbia. This public information kiosk provides a direct connection to the library's online public access catalogue. Using the Data Depot, many residents can request copies of different applications, fill them out, and fax them back without leaving the information kiosk. M. Kascus.

348. Huesmann, James and Deb Downing. "Extending Access and Delivery (Far) Beyond the Library Walls." *Computers in Libraries* 16, no. 5 (May 1996): 28-31.

Linda Hall Library (LHL), an independently funded public library of science, engineering, and technology in Kansas City, has extended its virtual reach via the Internet to its new branch in New York. Through LEONARDO, the online catalogue and information system, LHL now provides world-wide access to its collection and document delivery services. An overview is provided of LEONARDO, which uses the Ameritech Library Services client/server, Horizon. Both public and staff can access LEONARDO. OCLC and LEONARDO windows open on the desktop, so library staff can export from OCLC and import to the online catalogue. M. Kascus.

349. Larsen, Ronald L. "Extending Library Services to the Distance Learner: Baby Steps." *Linkages* (Institute for Distance Education, University of Maryland) 4, no. 2 (Winter 1996). Online. Available: http://www.umuc.edu/ide/linkwi96.html#extending (Accessed April 13, 2000).

Extending library services to distance learners is important but, because these services are new to academic libraries, progress in this area is measured in "baby steps," according to the author. The University of Maryland System (UMS) has invested heavily in electronic databases, indexes, and remote delivery services. A multi-year grant to UMS expanded access to 150 databases through the library's online catalogue. Side effects of this expanded access included incompatible indexes for some of the databases loaded. The solution was to join the University of Massachusetts (Amherst) Center for Intelligent Information Retrieval (CIIR), which has developed an information retrieval environment called INQUERY. This enabled UMS libraries to mount discipline-specific databases. M. Kascus.

350.   Lusher, T. J. "Support Services for Campus Remote Users." *Public & Access Services Quarterly* 2, no. 1 (1996): 5-11.

Campus remote users are defined as users who have access to libraries and databases from their on-campus departments and dormitories. The assumption is that these remote users require support services that blend services provided to patrons who come into the library and those who are long distance users. The following suggestions are made for those planning library support services to campus remote users: a traditional print hand-out designed with the remote user in mind, real-time search assistance, telephone reference, and electronic reference services. M. Kascus.

351.   Neuhaus, John and Geoff Hill. "Library and Computer Centre Convergence in a Regional Setting: The Regional Network Infrastructure Project at Southern Cross University." In *Electronic Dream? Virtual Nightmare: The Reality for Libraries: Conference Proceedings: 1996 VALA Biennial Conference and Exhibition, 30 January to 1 February 1996, World Congress Centre, Melbourne*. Melbourne, Victoria: Victorian Association for Library Automation Inc., 1996, 47-54.

Two projects at Southern Cross University to establish a regional network are described. The aim of the projects was to make learning resources available to off-campus students through the regional university centers and by dial-up access throughout Australia. The resources included full access to the Internet, university file servers and minicomputers, a Web-based electronic library, the university's online catalogue, CD-ROM databases, and Ariel document transmission. The projects also provided the infrastructure necessary for delivering courses in an electronic networked mode, including remote audiographic tutorials. This paper reports on the outcomes of the projects, focusing on the areas of cooperation between the library and the computing center. Initial student reaction to the new system was positive, especially with regard to the full-text databases. For a related paper, see #369 below. A. Slade.

352.   Schiller, Nancy, Nancy Cannon, and Carla Hendrix. *Distance Learning Project Proposal: Collaborative WWW Support of Distance Learning: Library Delivery of Electronic Course-Related Materials and Resources*. 1996. Online. Available: http://ublib.buffalo.edu/libraries/course/proposal.htm (Accessed April 13, 2000).

A project is proposed to investigate the feasibility of delivering library resources and services via the Internet to distance education students enrolled in engineering and nursing programs within the State University of New York (SUNY). SUNY libraries at Binghamton, Buffalo, and Plattsburgh will work together to develop prototype services that will allow them to explore issues concerning access to online course materials and support services. The components of the project are designing models for collaborative innovative library services, constructing web pages and linking course-related material, integrating web pages with other electronic services, exploring copyright issues, experimenting with hardware and software to deliver electronic library material across the Internet, and disseminating the expertise gained to other SUNY institutions. The project is intended to serve as a demonstration of the capabilities of the World Wide Web in a way that can be expanded to other SUNY campuses. The project can help answer questions about copyright, authentication policy, and digitization technology. The requested budget support for the project is provided. For a related paper, see item #353 below. M. Kascus.

353.   Schiller, Nancy. "World Wide Web Library Support for Distance Learning at the State University of New York at Buffalo." *MC Journal: The Journal of Academic Media Librarianship* 4, no. 1 (Summer 1996): 25-37. Also online. Available: http://wings.buffalo.edu/publications/mcjrnl/v4n1/schiller.html (Accessed April 13, 2000).

At the Binghamton, Buffalo, and Plattsburgh campuses of the State University of New York (SUNY), a project has been developed that uses digitizing technology and the World Wide Web to provide access to course-related material as well as electronic library services and Internet-based resources. Engineering and nursing students are the target population. Adobe Capture software has been used to prepare course materials for the Web. Copyrighted materials are excluded from the present experiment. Faculty and librarians at these three SUNY campuses undertook a year-long project to test the feasibility of delivering services via the Internet. As part of the project, these sites experimented with providing access through the system to reserve materials. Other key components included designing models for innovative library services for distance learners as a collaborative effort, exploring issues related to copyright, and experimenting with hardware and software to provide remote access to multimedia materials. The benefits of the project are described. For a related document, see #352 above. M. Kascus.

354.   Stewart, Des and Rosemary Blakeney. "Information Highway or Dirt Track: Challenges in Delivery of Electronic Information Products to Isolated Clients." *Quarterly Bulletin of the International Association of Agricultural Information Specialists* 41, no. 2 (1996): 211-13.

A Wide Area Network (WAN) was installed at New South Wales Agricultural Institute to link locations across the state. This paper outlines the challenges in delivering electronic information products and services to geographically remote users. Included among the challenges discussed are the structure of licensing agreements, the technical problems of networking across large distances, the development of a client education program, the change in the librarian's role from that of provider to trainer and/or facilitator, and the problems associated with trying to provide equal service to all clients wherever they are located. The services delivered over the WAN include e-mail, document delivery, and information resources. M. Kascus.

355.   Sylvia, Margaret. "Remotely Possible? Simple Remote Access to the Network." *Computers in Libraries* 16, no. 10 (November/December 1996): 63-67.

The experiences of St. Mary's University (San Antonio, Texas) in providing remote access to the network are discussed. In exploring the options for providing remote access, the goal was to have a simple solution. Among the remote access issues discussed are TCP/IP support, DOS support, multitasking capability, and CD-ROM drive support. Among the options considered were J&L Chatterbox, Omniware, and Everywhere Access (EA/2). Another type of remote access solution considered was bulletin board systems (BBS) and Doorway software. The decision was to go with EA/2, a software only solution from Supro. The process of installing EA/2 and printing remotely are also discussed. M. Kascus.

356. Wynne, Peter M. "Experimentation with Electronic Document Delivery in the BIBDEL Project at the University of Central Lancashire." *The Electronic Library* 14, no. 1 (February 1996): 13-20.

As part of the European BIBDEL (Libraries Without Walls: The Delivery of Library Services to Distant Users) Project, each partner institution undertook a demonstration experiment appropriate to its local environment. This article focuses on the University of Central Lancashire's experimentation in providing electronic document delivery to remote users at Newton Rigg College. Agreement was reached with a publisher to supply in electronic format a number of journals to which the university already subscribed. Information is provided on the technical difficulties encountered in establishing electronic access to these journals, the methods for viewing and downloading articles, service costs, and management issues. Issues that need to be addressed before the experimental delivery of electronic journals can be made into an operational service include staff costs, system maintenance, cost of publications, and copyright compliance. The author reports that the experiment has shown that it is possible to deliver electronic journals to a remote site, preserving all the visual cues that users take from the printed page. A. Slade.

1995

357. Ackerson, Linda G. and Adam Szczepaniak. "Using Local Area Networks to Achieve Remote Access: Some Lessons from a Pilot Test." *Journal of Academic Librarianship* 21, no. 3 (May 1995): 195-97.

The University of Alabama (UA) used a local area network (LAN) to provide networked access to CD-ROM bibliographic and full-text literature. A pilot test was designed, implemented, and evaluated to enable the UA libraries to observe the feasibility of providing remote access through the LAN and to predict the effect of implementing this plan for all libraries. Among the issues discussed are connectivity, publicity, education, and support. The importance of publicity is stressed not only to inform library users, but also to encourage interest in remote access. Faculty were given the option of requesting either individual or group instruction sessions. Graduate students were trained using a computer classroom. Support issues are important in terms of providing a safety net. M. Kascus.

358. Brigham, Carole J., Kay Hodson, Ann C. Hanson, and Judith Graves. "Electronic Library: A Collaborative Venture for Education, Sigma Theta Tau and Health Care Agencies." *Reflections* 21, no. 1 (Spring 1995): 20-21.

A collaborative project involving Ball State University and Sigma Theta Tau provided distance education nursing students with electronic access to the

Virginia Henderson International Nursing Library. Students in selected courses received laptop computers fully loaded with the appropriate software and modems to connect to the library. Assignments were given to familiarize the students with the library's electronic resources and to enable them to practice their searching skills. One assignment required the students to demonstrate the library's electronic functions to supervisors and peers in their workplace. The demonstrations, along with other components of the program, helped to increase the awareness of health care agency administrators and practicing clinicians about the value of information technology. A. Slade.

359. Brinkley, Monica and Jack OFarrell. "Delivery of Library Services to Distance Education Students: The BIBDEL Research Project at Dublin City University Library." *The Electronic Library* 13, no. 6 (December 1995): 539-46.

Dublin City University (DCU) Library was one of the partners in the BIBDEL (Libraries Without Walls) research project in Europe. As part of the project, the DCU Library conducted two experiments to investigate the delivery of library services to distance education students. One experiment involved delivery of library services directly to the home; the other provided delivery via a local study center or library. For the first experiment, students were provided with e-mail accounts and access to the DCU online catalogue. Information or reference inquiries and loan requests could be made by e-mail. Requested books and articles were sent by post from the library. Scanning of articles and file transfer were tested as a means of document delivery but not used due to copyright uncertainties. In the second experiment, the Library of Dundalk RTC (regional technical college) was used as a local center for DCU distance students. A dedicated personal computer was installed in the library and connected to the college network, providing a gateway into the DCU online catalogue. Apart from using the local center as an access point, the library services offered in the second experiment were identical to those in the first experiment. The experiments established the technical feasibility of remote delivery of services, and work on the BIBDEL project shifted to management issues that would have to be addressed if the services became operational. For a related article, see #370 below. A. Slade.

360. Butters, Geoff, Monica Brinkley, Panayiotis Papachiou, Ellie Viachou, and Ann Irving. *Access to Campus Library and Information Services by Distant Users: Evaluations of Three Demonstration Experiments*. The third report from the BIBDEL Project (Libraries Without Walls: The Delivery of Library Services to Distant Users) funded by the Libraries Programme of the Commission of the European Communities. Preston, UK: Centre for Research in Library and Information Management, University of Central Lancashire, 1995. 170 pp.

This report is the third "deliverable" from the Commission of the European Communities funded project known as BIBDEL (Libraries Without Walls: The Delivery of Library Services to Distant Users). The report includes evaluations of three demonstration experiments carried out by the University of Central Lancashire in the United Kingdom, Dublin City University in Ireland, and the University of the Aegean in Greece. Each experiment provided selected library services to distance learners, including access to their online public access catalogues (OPAC's). Evaluations are given on user reactions to the services, the interface, modes of access, types of use made, capabilities of the technology, the impact on library staff, and training needs. For the other BIBDEL reports, see #284 and #285 in the second bibliography and #21, #254, #262, and #371 in this volume. M. Kascus.

361.   Glass, Ron P. "Providing Off-Campus Library Service Using Notebook Computers for Remote Access of Electronic Information Systems." In *The Seventh Off-Campus Library Services Conference Proceedings: San Diego, California, October 25-27, 1995*, compiled by Carol J. Jacob. Mount Pleasant, MI: Central Michigan University, 1995, 121-25.

Notebook computers are used to provide library services to remote MBA students at Le Tourneau University in Longview, Texas. The four types of notebook computers and software used by the students to complete course requirements and to access library resources are described. A library CD-ROM local area network provides access to various databases such as Ebsco's Academic Abstract Full-text Elite. A one-day seminar, "Electronic Information Systems," taught by librarians, is a required part of the curriculum. It includes a 100-page manual containing information on the library and information resources available to off-campus students in the MBA program. Notebook computers with modems and CD-ROM networks are two tools that can provide information to students at a distance and enable the library to know and better serve them. The importance of libraries seizing the opportunity provided by new technology is stressed. M. Kascus.

362.   Heck, Jeff and Gayle Baker. "The Scholar's Workstation Project at the University of Tennessee." *Library Hi Tech* 13, no.3, issue 51 (1995): 55-66.

The Scholar's Workstation Project at the University of Tennessee, Knoxville, tested a model of library services in which workstations act as an electronic branch library to provide the user with timely and convenient remote access to information. Environmental sciences was chosen as an appropriate multidisciplinary subject for developing a Scholar's Workstation. The specific goals of the project were to make electronic resources available on microcomputer workstations at remote sites, identify and install software and develop menus for access to electronic resources, train users to become self-sufficient in searching and accessing online resources, involve library school students in training users and resolving routine technical problems, provide document delivery, and describe usage patterns. Helpful suggestions are provided for those interested in establishing a similar remote service. M. Kascus.

363.   Holborn, Robert, Andrea Savas, Angie Ward, and Larry Hudson. "Support Services for Adult Learners Enrolled in Distance Education Courses." *Journal of Educational Media and Library Sciences* 32, no. 3 (1995): 378-87.

An overview is provided of efforts to support adult learners enrolled in distance education courses. The technology used in distance education is altering the teaching/learning dynamic. The suggestion here is that colleges and universities should have as a priority assisting adult students to acquire the skills and resources needed to access this technology. E-mail is considered the most important technology available to students and instructors. With access to e-mail, the Internet, and an electronic library information system, much of the student's research can be done from home. M. Kascus.

364. Jones, Clifton H. "Library Support for Distance Learning and Rehabilitation Programs." *Journal of Rehabilitation Administration* 19, no. 4 (November 1995): 301-9. Comments by Terry Foster: 311-13.

Idaho State University (ISU) serves as an illustration of how one university with limited resources has been able to provide a wide range of library services to remote faculty and students by taking advantage of the Internet and the willing cooperation of other libraries. In describing ISU's approach, the current strengths and weaknesses of information technology in general are analyzed. The potential and limitations of the Internet are illustrated using the fields of rehabilitation and disabilities. The implication is that as the technology becomes more sophisticated, the user will need training to use it productively. The author stresses the importance of strong staff support and interlibrary cooperation to use technology to its fullest advantage. M. Kascus.

365. MacDougall, Alan. "The BIBDEL Demonstration Experiments: An Overview of Their Aims and Achievements." In *Proceedings of the First "Libraries Without Walls" Conference, Mytilene, Greece, 9-10 September 1995*, edited by Ann Irving and Geoff Butters. Preston, UK: Centre for Research in Library and Information Management, University of Central Lancashire, 1995, 23-32.

This overview of the BIBDEL demonstration experiments at Dublin City University, Ireland, University of the Aegean, Greece, and University of Central Lancashire, United Kingdom, describes three models of provision of library services with different solutions. The aims of these projects were to investigate and make recommendations on (1) delivery of information to remote users, (2) access to catalogues, (3) access to document ordering, (4) reference and inquiry services, and (5) delivery of materials. Also examined were the cost effectiveness of stock, buildings, issues of training, and staffing at all levels. M. Kascus.

366. MacDougall, Alan F. *Libraries Without Walls and Its European Implications: BIBDEL a European Research Project*. Paper distributed at the Seventh Off-Campus Library Services Conference, San Diego, California, October 25-27, 1995. 6 pp.

Developments and activities in the European BIBDEL (Libraries Without Walls) research project are reported in this paper. The objective of the project was to demonstrate the use of information technology in the provision of library services to remote users. The project involved three partner institutions, the University of Central Lancashire in the United Kingdom, Dublin City University in the Republic of Ireland, and University of the Aegean in Greece, each conducting its own demonstration experiment. Information is provided on the experiments of the three institutions and their initial findings. A. Slade.

367. McDuffee, Diana. "Information Connection: Information Technology, the Health Sciences Librarian, and the Community-Based Teaching Practice." *Medical Reference Services Quarterly* 14, no. 2 (Summer 1995): 69-74.

The increased placement of medical students in community primary care practices for clinical experience means that a large segment of the library's clientele will be located at a distance for a longer portion of their education. At the University of North Carolina at Chapel Hill, the Health Sciences Library has established the Information Connection Service (ICS) to coordinate support for community-based teaching sites. The goal is to have workstations linked to library-based information services at these usually rural community clinics. Librarians play a key role in selecting the equipment and resources considered to be most practical in a clinical setting. The information resources provided include (1) access to MEDLINE, GRATEFULMED, and other databases; (2) access to the Internet; (3) an electronic mail system; (4) full-text medical references; and (5) document delivery service via fax. On-site training and assistance is provided by outreach librarians. Students rotating to the clinical sites receive training in searching databases, library catalogues, electronic textbooks, and other databases as part of their curricula. Through ICS, reference service is successfully being extended to large numbers of individuals at scattered sites. M. Kascus.

368. McGreal, Rory. "A Heterogeneous Distributed Database System for Distance Education Networks." *American Journal of Distance Education* 9, no. 1 (1995): 27-43.

Distance education networks are expected to provide students, instructors, and administrators with timely information for many areas, including libraries. The heterogeneous distributed database system (HDDS) is considered an efficient and cost-effective database access system for distance education. Implementing a HDDS has great potential as an efficient way of managing the coordination of individual systems to provide access to library resources. The development of the Internet with its access to the World Wide Web has made a plethora of information available for everyone, and distance education networks need to facilitate efficient access. The library's database would include catalogues of the libraries in the region and around the world and should be supported by rapid electronic and physical delivery systems. Effective teaching and learning depend on access to library materials, and the credibility of distance education courses has been called into question when it is lacking. A list of distance education websites and their URLs is provided. M. Kascus.

369. Neuhaus, John. "The Regional Electronic Library Project at Southern Cross University." In *Access Through Open Learning: With a Major Focus on Networked Learning*, edited by Allan Ellis and Julie Burton. 2nd Edition. [Southern Cross University] Occasional Papers in Open Learning, vol. 5. Lismore, NSW: Norsearch, 1995, 119-23.

During 1994, Southern Cross University received two grants to establish a regional electronic network on the north coast of New South Wales. One grant was allocated for the development of the network infrastructure and staff training. The other grant was to create an electronic library service for the entire region to assist students in remote areas. The focus of this paper is on the electronic library service, including the background of the project, problems and opportunities, project objectives, technologies used, intended outcomes, and project implementation. Three main features of the service were a World Wide Web server, an electronic reserve collection using Adobe Acrobat Portable Document Format (PDF), and document transmission with Ariel software. The infrastructure project supported the development of the electronic library service and provided the opportunity to assess the convergence of electronic services within the university. For a related paper, see #351 above. A. Slade.

370. OFarrell, Jack. "Working Towards a Library Without Walls." *Library Association Record* 97, no. 3 (March 1995): 155-56.

   Dublin City University's participation in the European BIBDEL project is reported at the midpoint in the project's duration. The university's experiment involved a group of students in the Diploma in Information Technology program, each of whom had private access to an IBM-compatible computer loaded with remote access software. Students could dial-up the library's online catalogue and select items to be delivered to them by post. Electronic transmission of documents was tested in the early stages of the experiment but not offered due to copyright problems. At the time of writing, the experiment had demonstrated that it was possible for the library to provide services directly to off-campus students using relatively low-level technology. Some of the issues encountered in the project are discussed, including restrictions on provision of materials, access to CD-ROM networks, the role of public libraries, copyright issues, and the cost-effectiveness of technology. For a related article, see #359 above. A. Slade.

371. University of Central Lancashire. Centre for Research in Library and Information Management. *Access to Campus Library and Information Services by Distant Users: Final Report*. The final report from the BIBDEL Project (Libraries Without Walls: The Delivery of Library Services to Distant Users) funded by the Libraries Programme of the Commission of the European Communities. Preston, UK: Centre for Research in Library and Information Management, University of Central Lancashire, 1995. 23 pp.

   The European BIBDEL (Libraries Without Walls: The Delivery of Library Services to Distant Users) Project concluded in October 1995 after running for 21 months. The final report summarizes the scope and results of the project and offers a number of recommendations for further action. Included in the report are key findings from the demonstration experiments conducted by the University of Central Lancashire, Dublin City University, and University of the Aegean; overall conclusions drawn from the experiments; descriptions of the various activities to disseminate information about the project; and a list of ongoing activities. The report's recommendations identify a need for further work in the following areas: user interfaces in library/information systems, system design, inquiry services, collaboration with countries outside the European Union, collaboration within Europe, telecommunications equity for users in rural areas, cooperation between different types of libraries, economic aspects of service delivery to distant users, library staff development, and user training and instruction. For the other BIBDEL reports, see #284 and #285 in the second bibliography and #21, #254, #262, and #360 in this volume. A. Slade.

372. Van Borm, Julien. "Hyperlib: A Hypertext Interface to a Library Information System." In *Proceedings of the First "Libraries Without Walls" Conference, Mytilene, Greece, 9-10 September 1995*, edited by Ann Irving and Geoff Butters. Preston, UK: Centre for Research in Library and Information Management, University of Central Lancashire, 1995, 58-61.

   A progress report is provided on HYPERLIB, the European Commission funded project of Loughborough University, United Kingdom, and University of Antwerp, Belgium. The purpose of the project is to improve access to the services of the libraries of the University of Antwerp, making the services more cost-effective and user-friendly. An in-depth survey of users was conducted to assess cognitive characteristics, information retrieval skills, models of information use, and use of the system. Results of the survey indicated that gains in improvement of the OPAC would be achieved using new search facilities and modifying the interface. Electronic guides for library end-users were prepared as well as manuals for staff training. M. Kascus.

373.   Wynne, Peter M. "Libraries Without Walls: The Delivery of Library Services to Distant Users." In *One World, Many Voices: Quality in Open and Distance Learning: Selected Papers from the 17th World Conference of the International Council for Distance Education, Birmingham, United Kingdom, June, 1995: Volume 2*, edited by David Sewart. Milton Keynes, UK: The Open University in association with International Council for Distance Education, 1995, 304-7.

The author reports on the BIBDEL (Libraries Without Walls: The Delivery of Library Services to Distant Users) Project, which was underway at the time of writing. The issue of remote access to library services is discussed in a historical context and the demonstration experiments at the partner institutions (University of Central Lancashire, Dublin City University, University of the Aegean) are outlined. Characteristic of all three experiments is the intention to facilitate remote access at minimum cost. A. Slade.

Electronic Reference Services

For other works that discuss this topic, see the following headings in the Subject Index: "electronic mail," "electronic reference services," and "videoconferencing."

1999

---

374.   Haines, Annette and Alison Grodzinski. "Web Forms: Improving, Expanding, and Promoting Remote Reference Services." *College & Research Libraries News* 60, no. 4 (April 1999): 271-72, 291.

The authors propose that the use of Web forms can add value to reference services and improve upon the limitations of e-mail for providing assistance to remote users. The advantages of a Web form for reference service are identified as follows: provides access without the limitations of time and place, enhances approachability for users who are uncomfortable asking a question in-person, supplies a framework to help users structure their question, furnishes statistical feedback for staff, helps improve and expand librarians' skills, and promotes the visibility of the library. Other possibilities for using Web forms to expand library services are outlined and a number of sources for building a Web form are cited. A. Slade.

375. Tyckoson, David A. "What's Right with Reference." *American Libraries* 30, no. 5 (May 1999): 57-63.

In the context of an article about the failures and successes of reference reform, remote access to reference services is discussed as one of the reform measures that has not worked well. The author states that "in practice, e-mail reference service is far from adequate." Despite publicity and promotion, patrons tend not to use it. Lack of interactivity is identified as one of the major disadvantages of e-mail reference service. The author indicates that the telephone is a much more effective medium for providing remote reference services. A. Slade.

1998

376. Fishman, Diane L. "Managing the Virtual Reference Desk: How to Plan an Effective Reference E-Mail System." *Medical Reference Services Quarterly* 17, no. 1 (Spring 1998): 1-10.

The author discusses some of the management issues in providing reference services by electronic mail and examines use patterns in these services at the University of Maryland, Baltimore, and at other institutions as reported in the literature. The advantages of e-mail reference services include 24-hour access for users, reduced cultural and language barriers, and the option to build a database of questions and answers. Some of the challenges of e-mail reference services are questions taking longer to answer, lack of nonverbal cues, difficulties in sharing responsibilities with colleagues, and the risk of misinterpreting remarks. Other issues discussed in this article pertain to planning and organization, inclusion criteria, promoting the service, and time factors. Data collected by the Health Sciences Library at the University of Maryland at Baltimore during 1995–1996 and the findings at other institutions indicated that, at the time of writing, e-mail reference services were relatively underused. Future benefits of electronic reference services are considered and the popularity of reference e-mail is predicted to increase. A. Slade.

377. Frank, Ilene. "E-Mail Reference Service at the University of South Florida: A Well-Kept Secret." *Art Documentation* 17, no. 1 (1998): 8-9, 44.

E-mail reference services were introduced at the Tampa Campus Library of the University of South Florida in 1994 to improve remote access to collections and services as part of a general university promotion of technology use. The methods of advertising the service are listed and the responses received are described. With distance education courses "on the horizon," the author expects that the library will need to rethink its low-level service and provide more in-depth support for remote users. Due to the author's area of specialization, art and art history courses are emphasized in this context. A. Slade.

378. Lagace, Nettie and Michael McClennen. "Managing an Internet-Based Distributed Reference Service." *Computers in Libraries* 18, no. 2 (February 1998): 24-27.

Hosted by the University of Michigan School of Information, the Internet Public Library (IPL) has as its mission to provide library services to the global Internet community. This distributed reference service is virtually operated, serving patrons from all over the world while functioning as a laboratory for librarians and library students to advance their skills and the profession. The IPL Reference Center is a collaborative process involving volunteers who contribute time to answer questions submitted through e-mail. The questions are submitted to a local software system called QRC, which can be accessed by volunteers using their own Web browsers to select questions to answer. Work is underway to develop a searchable database of answered questions. A FARQ (Frequently Answered Reference Questions) list is available. There is a sidebar on QRC, which may be marketed to libraries in the future. M. Kascus.

379.   Schilling-Eccles, Katherine and Joseph J. Harzbecker, Jr. "The Use of Electronic Mail at the Reference Desk: Impact of a Computer-Mediated Communication Technology on Librarian-Client Interactions." *Medical Reference Services Quarterly* 17, no. 4 (Winter 1998): 17-27.

The Boston University Medical Center Library undertook a study to determine why its e-mail reference service, called e-reference, was not heavily used. The study involved analysis of e-reference messages, e-mail interviews with academic and health sciences librarians at other institutions, and a query posted to various listservers. Comments from other librarians combined with the analysis of e-reference transactions over a two-year time period indicated that relatively few clients choose to take advantage of e-mail reference services on a regular basis. Three potential barriers to use of these services are identified: limited computer access, inconvenience, and lack of personal contact. Topics discussed in relation to the findings of the study include use of computer-mediated communication (CMC) in libraries, the reference interview, the advantages and disadvantages of e-mail reference services, and considerations for service implementation and delivery. It is noted that e-reference is good for public relations because it demonstrates to patrons that the library is using "high-tech" means to make itself available in every way. A. Slade.

380.   Sloan, Bernie. "Electronic Reference Services: Some Suggested Guidelines." *Reference and User Services Quarterly* 38, no. 1 (Fall 1998): 77-81.

Pointing to similarities between electronic reference services and library support for distance learners, the author identifies a need for guidelines to assist libraries in planning and formalizing their electronic reference services. Specific issues to be addressed in such guidelines include administration, management, services, primary clientele, personnel, infrastructure/facilities, finances, and evaluation. Each of these issues is discussed in terms of library and user needs, situational variables, and key questions that the guidelines should answer. It is emphasized that the provision of electronic reference services has generally been conducted on an informal or ad hoc basis and guidelines are required to ensure the continuity of the service perspective in the digital library. A. Slade.

381.   Sloan, Bernie. "Service Perspectives for the Digital Library: Remote Reference Services." *Library Trends* 47, no. 1 (Summer 1998): 117-43. Also online. Available: http://alexia.lis.uiuc.edu/~b-sloan/e-ref.html (Accessed April 13, 2000).

This article explores the role of the librarian and of the service perspectives in the digital library environment. The author focuses on the concept of reference services in the digital library because reference librarians play a major instructional role, teaching users to efficiently and effectively navigate through a plethora of information resources. A number of experimental projects that have tested the extension of traditional reference services into the electronic environment are profiled. E-mail and video are the media of choice in extending reference services into the digital environment. The author proposes a reference services model for the digital library that combines video-based reference services with e-mail-based reference services. The suggestion is that such a combined service model is the best way to extend the human touch to remote users of reference service in the digital library. M. Kascus.

382. Staley, Laura. "E-Mail Reference: Experiences at City University." *PNLA Quarterly* 62, no. 4 (Summer 1998): 20-21.

The use of e-mail to provide reference services to City University's distance education students is the focus of this article. The advantages of e-mail reference services include constant availability, unlimited access for students in any time zone, rapid responses to remote students, cost-savings in comparison to fax and phone replies, and the ability to save e-mail messages to assist with future inquiries. The disadvantages include lack of non-verbal clues, the potential need for several transmissions to clarify and resolve a request, and the terse composition of an e-mail message. Based on two years of e-mail reference experience at City University, the following recommendations are offered: restate the student's original question and request explicit feedback in the first reply, include some information relevant to the request in a message seeking clarification about the question, use one central mail box to discourage students from corresponding with a particular librarian, include e-mail procedures and limits in advertisements, and include a reference questionnaire in all publicity to prompt users to consider search limits before submitting a request. A. Slade.

383. Summers, Robin. "Meeting Education Information Needs Through Digital Reference." *Art Documentation* 17, no. 1 (1998): 3-4, 68.

In a digital environment, reference librarians need to develop skills to utilize high-level technology for finding resources and communicating with patrons. The role of the librarian in this context is that of educator to empower patrons to locate appropriate resources, with the added responsibility of evaluating sources for the patrons. The primary means to communicate with patrons in this environment is e-mail. To illustrate the successful use of e-mail in providing electronic reference service, the AskERIC and KidsConnect services of the Educational Resources Information Center (ERIC) are described. Information is provided on the background, user community, workflow, types of questions received, and demand for each service. A. Slade.

384. Tinnin, Nathan, Jonathan Buckstead, and Kyle Richardson. "Remote Reference by Microcomputer: Setup and Installation." In *The Eighth Off-Campus Library Services Conference Proceedings: Providence, Rhode Island, April 22-24, 1998*, compiled by P. Steven Thomas and Maryhelen Jones. Mount Pleasant, MI: Central Michigan University, 1998, 299-12.

A system was installed at Austin Community College that uses networked computers for remote reference work. The project was intended to evaluate different approaches to real-time communications between the reference librarian and the remote distance learner. The project had these objectives: (1) to offer nursing students at the Fredericksburg site the benefits of asynchronous and synchronous reference service; (2) to test the usefulness of electronic network communications between reference librarians; and (3) to encourage wider use of software such as Microsoft's freeware, NetMeeting, and utilities like Microsoft Chat that allow routing of network processes over the Internet. An overview of the system is given, along with a description of the computer hardware. Student-initiated research via the World Wide Web or through direct or desktop access is described as well as reference librarian-mediated research using Microsoft Chat. The proposal for library support is included in the appendix. M. Kascus.

385.   Vine, Rita. "Cyberpulse: Software for Interactive Online Reference Service." *Bibliotheca Medica Canadiana* 20, no. 2 (Winter 1998): 83-84.

Electronic reference services provided by e-mail or through a website can be less than satisfactory due to delays in turnaround time and difficulties in question negotiation. Recent software offers the potential to help libraries deliver more appropriate and successful online reference service. Two generic types are "buddy software" and "call center software." Buddy software, such as ICQ, enables correspondents to send instant messages back and forth and offers a typewritten chat option. Call center software, such as LiveContact, uses a voice-enabled Web browser to permit a user to speak to an agent while browsing the Web, all over a single phone line. The author provides brief descriptions of the functions of the ICQ and LiveContact software and comments that several libraries in Canada are planning trials of the software. A. Slade.

1997

386.   Davenport, Elisabeth, Rob Procter, and Ana Goldenberg. "Distributed Expertise: Remote Reference Service on a Metropolitan Area Network." *The Electronic Library* 15, no. 4 (August 1997): 271-78.

As part of a research project to explore the potential of collaborative reference work, library reference services were linked at three higher education institutions in the United Kingdom: University of Edinburgh, Heriot Watt University, and Napier University. This support service was designed to provide assistance to remotely located users over computer networks. The emphasis in the project was on the experience of users in terms of the type of problems encountered and librarian responses across various media and methods of interaction. The methods used to interact were a FAQ (frequently asked questions) list to direct users to responses to previous inquiries, e-mail for specific requests, and conferences showing communication between user and librarian. The main objective was to determine the requirements for delivering an effective electronic reference service by examining the role of the different methods of interaction. The question raised here is the extent to which it is necessary to duplicate face-to-face interaction in designing an effective remote reference service. For a related paper, see #387 below. M. Kascus.

387. Davenport, Elisabeth R. and Rob N. Procter. "The Situated Intermediary: Remote Advice Giving in a Distributed Reference Environment." In *National Online Meeting Proceedings—1997: Proceedings of the 18th National Online Meeting, New York, May 13-15, 1997*, edited by Martha E. Williams. Medford, NJ: Information Today, 1997, 115-23.

A Scottish research project is investigating virtual reference work in academic libraries. The context of the project is a networked service that provides access to BIOSIS Abstracts on a consortial basis and connects reference services at the University of Edinburgh, Heriot Watt University, and Napier University. The project has a dual focus: creating a shared reference service that is available to searchers at any of the three participating universities, and exploring the role of different media in remote online reference work. The investigation has involved obtaining the views of the user population; observing and interviewing reference librarians; and constructing a design framework using insights from situated action research, work on genre systems, and empirical data from a pilot service on the World Wide Web. Initial analysis and observation of participating reference librarians revealed that their working day is highly fragmented, they multi-task continuously, they carry out reference work at a number of different locations, and their deployment as professional experts is not always optimal. While pointing to the potential benefits of a virtual reference service, the current nature of reference work presents significant challenges for the design and implementation of such a service. For a related paper, see #386 above. A. Slade.

388. Folger, Kathleen M. *The Virtual Librarian: Using Desktop Videoconferencing to Provide Interactive Reference Assistance*. Paper presented at the ACRL 8th National Conference: Choosing Our Futures: Nashville, Tennessee, April 11-14, 1997. Online. Available: http://www.ala.org/acrl/paperhtm/a09.html (Accessed April 13, 2000).

In a joint project at the University of Michigan, the Shapiro Undergraduate Library and the Residence Hall libraries collaborated to provide reference services to students using desktop videoconferencing. This paper provides an overview of desktop videoconferencing technology in libraries, discusses the University of Michigan project, and considers the future of this technology in libraries. Reaction to the project indicates that many students are curious about the technology but few have actually used the service to ask questions. Librarians' concerns relate to the quality of the audio and video and the lack of technical support on how to troubleshoot and solve problems from CU-SeeMe freeware. Other areas suggested for desktop videoconferencing include telecommuting, faculty outreach, and collaboration with colleagues at other institutions. M. Kascus.

389. Gleadhill, Daphne. "Electronic Enquiry Desk: Does the Nerd Have the Answer?" *Library Technology* 2, no. 2 (April 1997): 35-36.

The Newcastle University Library introduced in 1996 a networked inquiry service called The NERD (Newcastle Electronic Reference Desk). The NERD is available 24 hours a day on the World Wide Web and provides both an inquiry function and a database of questions and answers that can be searched by keyword or subject. The author describes the development of the service, the construction of the database, and the problems encountered with the software. It is anticipated that new improved software will enhance the service to the point where it can be publicized to the university community. A. Slade.

390.   Hahn, Karla. *An Investigation of an E-Mail-Based Help Service*. CLIS Technical Report No. 97-03. College Park, MD: College of Library and Information Services, University of Maryland, 1997. Online. Available: http://www.clis.umd.edu/research/reports/tr97/03/9703.html (Accessed April 13, 2000).

This research project used content analysis of e-mail transaction logs and interviews with staff and users to identify participants' models of successful exchanges and the impact of the communication medium on service provision. Findings of the study indicated that most e-mail exchanges are simple question/answer pairs and that users make explicit requests for instructions, explanations, specific answers, or staff action on behalf of the user. Interview results indicated a range of benefits and limitations in using e-mail as the communication medium. Benefits include increased service, access, convenience, and staff efficiency. Among the limitations are time lags and loss of communication richness. Incomplete information is a frequent occurrence, with users understating their information requests or omitting necessary information. As a result, staff often provide incomplete responses to queries. Included in the appendices are the content analysis code sheet, the consent form, interview questions for helpline staff, interview questions for helpline users, categories and examples of grouping of responses, and the chronology of data collection. M. Kascus.

391.   Lessick, Susan, Kathryn Kjaer, and Steve Clancy. *Interactive Reference Service (IRS) at UC Irvine: Expanding Reference Service Beyond the Reference Desk*. Paper presented at the ACRL 8th National Conference: Choosing Our Futures: Nashville, Tennessee, April 11-14, 1997. Online. Available: http://www.ala.org/acrl/paperhtm/a10.html (Accessed April 13, 2000).

Desktop videoconferencing technology is used at the University of California at Irvine to expand reference service to medical students at remote laboratories. The purpose of the project was to test the feasibility, costs, and benefits of implementing an ongoing service. Remote medical students are able to get point-of-need reference desk help with research papers, search strategy, and locating materials. The planning, implementation, and service considerations of this videoconferencing project are reported. Computer center staff collaborated with the library to co-host this Interactive Reference Service (IRS) project. To promote the use of IRS, library staff created a large banner and signage to publicize it at the remote laboratories. Another desktop videoconferencing program called Apple VideoPhone Kit is now used, providing color conferences and document-sharing capability. Feedback and suggestions for improving the service were obtained from volunteer students. Based on their experience and positive user reaction, the library concluded that desktop videoconferencing has potential for reference work when there is a need to deliver information to remote users. M. Kascus.

392.   Moss, Molly M. "Reference Services for Remote Users." *Katharine Sharp Review*, no. 5 (Summer 1997). Online. Available: http://edfu.lis.uiuc.edu/review/5/moss.html (Accessed April 13, 2000).

Libraries are responsible for providing off-campus students with the same services provided to on-campus students, although they might not be provided in the same way. While many services are needed, this paper focuses on the area of electronic reference services. The presentation of the discussion serves as a review of the literature related to reference services for remote users and looks at specific reference services offered by academic libraries. Among the methods being used to offer reference services are e-mail, postal services, telefacsimile, and Web forms. In concluding, there is a brief discussion of the challenges of providing reference services for remote use. Appendices include the Electronic Information Policy from Emory University and the Web form for the University of North Carolina at Chapel Hill. M. Kascus.

393. Philip, Brenda. *An Examination of the Past, Present and Future of Electronic Mail Reference Service*. Edmonton, AB: School of Library and Information Studies, University of Alberta, 1997. Online. Available: http://hollyhock.slis.ualberta.ca/598/brenda/emailref.htm (Accessed April 13, 2000).

This document explores the various social and technological issues a library needs to consider in providing an electronic mail reference service. In doing this, the author provides a brief history of the developments in the provision of e-mail reference and the applications of electronic reference services in four types of libraries: public, academic, corporate, and Internet. The Internet Public Library (IPL) is an example of a library designed solely to provide services through the Internet. The advantages and disadvantages are examined with a view to increasing the success of electronic mail reference systems. Among the advantages of e-mail reference service are unrestricted temporal and geographic access, anonymity, and provision of a printed copy of reference transactions. Among the disadvantages are security and confidentiality problems; difficulty of conducting an e-mail reference interview; limited access, in that not everyone has it; and software and inter-operability limitations. E-mail service at the University of Alberta Libraries is examined and described. What is stressed is that e-mail service is one of the options in addition to the established methods of in-person and telephone contact. By having a choice, the user can decide on the most effective, comfortable, and convenient way to get help. M. Kascus.

1996

394. Abels, Eileen G. "The E-Mail Reference Interview." *RQ* 35, no. 3 (Spring 1996): 345-58.

A three-phased project at the College of Library and Information Services at the University of Maryland was undertaken to explore the e-mail reference process. This paper focuses on the e-mail reference interview, discussing the differences between interviews conducted by e-mail and those conducted through other media. A taxonomy of approaches to e-mail reference interviews is presented. The importance of using a systematic approach to the e-mail reference interview is stressed and a model interview is introduced. The study results suggest that reference interviews can be conducted via e-mail for some complex questions. Further testing by experienced rather than student intermediaries is recommended. On the basis of the first phase of the project, the systematic approach was selected as the most effective and worthy of refinement. M. Kascus.

395.   Bushallow-Wilbur, Lara, Gemma DeVinney, and Fritz Whitcomb. "Electronic Mail Reference Service: A Study." *RQ* 35, no. 3 (Spring 1996): 359-71.

A survey was conducted at three units of the State University of New York at Buffalo to assess the use of electronic mail and reference service. Data were collected on user demographics, types of questions asked, and use patterns. Of the 174 surveys distributed, 114 were completed, for a 66% response rate. E-mail reference represented a small volume of use: 485 queries during an eighteen-month study period compared to 172,383 questions asked and answered in person. The e-mail reference activity is analyzed by user affiliation, academic department, age of users, preferred method of asking questions, day of the week, and time of day. The author stresses the importance of knowing more about the invisible user who asks questions, especially as we move closer to the virtual library. M. Kascus.

396.   Kelly, Julia and Kathryn Robbins. "Changing Roles for Reference Librarians." Co-published simultaneously in *Journal of Library Administration* 22, no. 2/3 (1996): 111-21, and *Managing Change in Academic Libraries*, edited by Joseph J. Branin. New York: Haworth Press, 1996, 111-21.

What library reference services will be like in the future and the role of the reference librarian are examined. Computers and computer networks have permanently altered the library landscape and changed reference service. It is projected that the Internet will play an even larger role in libraries of the future as the capacity to transmit multimedia materials increases. Internet use by reference departments includes the following: answering questions by e-mail, using Internet resources to answer questions, providing access to Internet public workstations, and mounting World Wide Web servers for patron use. Virtual libraries are defined as containing value-added services as well as connections to remote sites. The various ways in which rethinking reference has taken place are described. Also discussed are the importance of asking users about their needs, standards for information retrieval, and the application of artificial intelligence and expert systems to reference services. M. Kascus.

397.   Pagell, Ruth A. "The Virtual Reference Librarian: Using Desktop Videoconferencing for Distance Reference." *The Electronic Library* 14, no. 1 (February 1996): 21-26.

Videoconferencing is being used at academic institutions as a basis for distance learning. Emory University has beta tested AT&T's Vistium Desktop Video System as a means of delivering a distance reference service. This paper provides an overview of the technology, describes the beta test at Emory, and discusses evaluative factors necessary for success of desktop videoconferencing. Among the suggestions offered to those who are interested in using the technology are to make sure that the telecommunications staff know the requirements and are committed to the project and to test the product at the vendor's location first if the trial period is brief. Several applications for the technology are discussed, including ready reference, consultation, training, and sharing CD-ROM databases. It is suggested that the inability to market the technology systematically contributed to the users being less enthusiastic than anticipated. Some of the suggestions made in evaluating desktop videoconferencing are to identify desired applications and video characteristics needed for those applications, to investigate the organization's infrastructure and potential communications partner locations, and to talk to local desktop video providers. M. Kascus.

1995

398. Bristow, Ann and Mary Buechley. "Academic Reference Service Over E-Mail: An Update." *College & Research Libraries News* 56, no. 7 (July/August 1995): 459-62.

This article updates an earlier report on Indiana University's successful experience in offering an e-mail reference service (see #406 below). The update includes information on the increased use of the service, the type of questions asked, and the positive feedback from faculty and students using the service. With the success of the service, new questions are asked and challenges identified. Questions of particular concern are: "Where do we go from here?" and "Whom do we serve?" The importance of closely considering the campus networked information environment is stressed as well as the need to carefully define the institution's primary clientele for e-mail service, especially when moving to more open networked environments such as the World Wide Web. M. Kascus.

399. Johnston, Pat and Ann Grusin. "Personal Service in an Impersonal World: Throwing Life Preservers to Those Drowning in an Ocean of Information." *Georgia Librarian* 32, no. 2-4 (Summer, Fall, Winter 1995): 45-49.

An electronic reference service called "ASK a Librarian" was added to the Georgia Institute of Technology Electronic Library (GTEL) in 1994. The service is offered on GTEL's opening menu and messages are sent to an ASK e-mail address on the Library's main server. All GTEL users have to log on with an ID and password. Using this log-on information, the system automatically adds the user's name, department, phone number, and e-mail address to each question received at the ASK e-mail address. Several librarians take turns reading and responding to ASK questions. At the time of writing, approximately 30 to 40 requests were received each month. An online survey of ASK users was conducted in 1995 and responses were generally positive about the service. It is noted that ASK is the method of choice for remote users who do not like to use the phone, especially when they are already doing research on a computer. A recent development is that a button bar for ASK has been added to each GTEL web page and users now have a better opportunity to ask a question at the time and place where the question occurs. A. Slade.

400. Possin, Judith. "Remote Users: Providing Reference Assistance." In *Access Through Open Learning: With a Major Focus on Networked Learning*, edited by Allan Ellis and Julie Burton. 2nd Edition. [Southern Cross University] Occasional Papers in Open Learning, vol. 5. Lismore, NSW: Norsearch, 1995, 125.

This short conference paper attempts to identify, in point form, some of the issues associated with the provision of reference services to remote users. Brief comments are made under each of the following headings: (1) Electronic Library?, (2) Who are the remote users?, (3) What do they want?, (4) Should we provide assistance?, (5) Assistance options, (6) Staffing options, and (7) What do we know? A. Slade.

401.   Tibbo, Helen R. "Interviewing Techniques for Remote Reference: Electronic Versus Traditional Environments." *American Archivist* 58, no. 3 (Summer 1995): 294-310.

While directed towards archivists, the strategies discussed in this article for the provision of e-mail reference services are equally applicable to libraries. The author stresses that e-mail inquiries should be treated more like face-to-face reference interviews than like requests received by mail. Questions must be clarified and clients queried about the success of the reference process and product. Interviewing techniques for e-mail reference inquiries include setting the tone through prompt acknowledgement of the request, clarifying the request by use of open and neutral questions, summarizing for the client what has been said and requested in the online interview, determining the most effective way to deliver the requested information to the client, and assessing the success of the service by contacting clients after delivery of the information to determine if their needs have been met. It is recommended that a file be established for each client who submits an e-mail inquiry to facilitate follow-up service, if required, and to serve as a staff evaluation tool. A. Slade.

402.   Young, James B. "Providing Reference Service to Graduate Independent Study Students Worldwide." In *The Seventh Off-Campus Library Services Conference Proceedings: San Diego, California, October 25-27, 1995*, compiled by Carol J. Jacob. Mount Pleasant, MI: Central Michigan University, 1995, 399-402.

This is a report on Library Support, a department of the Embry-Riddle Aeronautical University's (ERAU) Extended Campus, with offices in Daytona Beach, Florida. The services available to graduate students include an *Independent Study Guide to Library Resources*; research assistance from a reference librarian available through CompuServe, the Internet, a toll-free number, or fax; and "Research Guides" tailored to the objectives and assignments of each course. Library Support uses technology whenever possible in assisting independent students. The CompuServe forum is used for reference services, enabling the librarian to virtually "sit in" on class discussions and to answer library-related questions in real-time. An illustration of the CompuServe forum is given in the appendix. The author suggests that interacting with students via the forum enables librarians to build long-term relationships with students. M. Kascus.

1994

403.   Abels, Eileen G. and Peter Liebscher. "A New Challenge for Intermediary-Client Communication: The Electronic Network." Co-published simultaneously in *The Reference Librarian*, nos. 41/42 (1994): 185-96, and *Librarians on the Internet: Impact on Reference Services*, edited by Robin Kinder. New York: Haworth Press, 1994, 185-96.

The library schools at the University of Maryland and Long Island University collaborated in a project to investigate the factors influencing the provision of remote electronic reference services. In this article, the authors present the background to the project, discussing the traditional reference process, the reference interview, follow-up interactions, and delivery of the final product. The following advantages of electronic reference services are noted: receiving a written request from the patron, being able to transmit the results to the patron electronically, and saving time by not having to meet patrons in person or contact them by telephone. The objectives of the joint project were to study the problems in delivering electronic reference services, suggest means to enhance the effectiveness of these services, and make recommendations to fully utilize the media for reference encounters. A. Slade.

404. Ross, Andrew M., Lorraine G. Miller, Emily L. Corse, and David N. Butterworth. "Electronic Access to Document Delivery and Reference Services." *Medical Reference Services Quarterly* 13, no. 4 (Winter 1994): 13-20.

This article describes a computer program allowing users to send interlibrary loan requests electronically to the University of Pennsylvania Biomedical Library. A module of the Electronic Document Delivery System (EDDS) was developed to process reference questions via e-mail. The technical aspects of the EDDS system and the user interface are described. The enhanced services offered electronically include submission of interlibrary loan requests, journal article photocopying, and transmission of reference questions. Several benefits of the system have been identified: user requests are received by staff quicker, information is legible and more complete, and paper forms have been eliminated. User reaction to the EDDS has been enthusiastic, as evidenced by the fact that, within a year of its implementation, 50% of all borrowing requests were sent electronically. The reference module of EDDS has two advantages: users can submit questions while staff are not there, and staff can reply by e-mail, telephone, or campus mail. The increased efficiency, staff benefits, and user benefits make this a model that other institutions may want to emulate. M. Kascus.

1993

405. Still, Julie and Frank Campbell. "Librarian in a Box: The Use of Electronic Mail for Reference." *Reference Services Review* 21, no. 1 (Spring 1993): 15-18.

The literature on the use of e-mail for the provision of reference services is reviewed up to 1993. It is noted that menu systems appear to be the most popular and easy to use for patrons. Document delivery seems to be the most common type of request. The staff time involved in maintaining the service should be weighed against potential low use. At the time of writing, few traditional reference queries were being submitted by e-mail. The author indicates that schools involved in distance learning may wish to investigate the use of e-mail to support their off-campus students. A. Slade.

1992

406. Bristow, Ann. "Academic Reference Service Over Electronic Mail." *College & Research Libraries News* 53, no. 10 (November 1992): 631-32, 637.

To get a better understanding of their experience in providing reference service via e-mail, library staff at Indiana University in Bloomington sent a four-question survey to e-mail users. This brief news item reports on that survey, providing helpful hints for offering reference service by e-mail. Some guiding principles for planning an e-mail service are as follows: make the service part of a larger electronic framework; provide a clear and succinct description of the service; describe the service parameters, giving examples of the kinds of questions for which the service was designed; and indicate the pick-up time for messages (daily, hourly, etc.). For an update to this article, see item #398 above. M. Kascus.

Networked Learner Support

For other works that discuss this topic, see the following heading in the Subject Index: "networked learner support."

1998

407.   Ashton, Sarah and Philippa Levy. "NetLinkS: Piloting Online Professional Development for Networked Learner Support." *Journal of Library Services for Distance Education* 1, no. 2 (June 1998). Online. Available: http://www.westga.edu/~library/jlsde/vol1/2/SAshton_PLevy.html (Accessed April 13, 2000).

In advancing the recommendations of the 1993 Follett Report in the United Kingdom, the Electronic Libraries (eLib) Programme addresses the issues in delivering quality information support online. NetLinkS is one of the eLib training and awareness projects intended to encourage the further development of networked learner support (NLS). The term NLS is used by the project to refer to the educational role of library and information staff in support of online learning, including user education; information skills training; and reference assistance using technologies such as electronic mail, the World Wide Web, computer conferencing, and videoconferencing. Focus groups were used to gather information for the project and to raise awareness about it. These groups confirmed the need for a flexible continuing professional development model for NLS. The focus here is on the piloting of a 16-week, Web-based distance learning course directed at an overview of the issues and trends in NLS. As part of the NetLinkS Project, the course is undergoing evaluation to assess the potential value of the model. M. Kascus.

408.   Heckart, Ronald J. "Machine Help and Human Help in the Emerging Digital Library." *College & Research Libraries* 59, no. 3 (May 1998): 250-59.

Sophisticated types of machine help are supplanting human help in the digital library. It is suggested that, in the future, patron interaction will occur via networked computers and help will be provided online. Library developments in online help parallel similar trends in the business world. Three specific trends promoting the rise of machine help are affecting library service: educational innovation in the area of distance learning, ongoing research efforts in the library and information science field to improve user interfaces, and the pattern of decline in academic library staffing levels over the last decade. These changes are viewed from the users' perspective, giving an imagined self-help scenario. It is suggested that human help may disappear altogether unless issues of machine help and human help are given explicit attention in the policy process. M. Kascus.

1997

409. Ashton, Sarah. "The 2nd International Symposium on Networked Learner Support." *Information Research: An Electronic Journal* 3, no. 1 (July 1997). Online. Available: http://www.shef.ac.uk/~is/publications/infres/paper23.html

This paper serves as both an introduction to and a review of the 2nd International Symposium on Networked Learner Support, held at the University of Sheffield in 1997. The symposium focused on partnerships for supporting online learning, the potential of computer-mediated communications and the World Wide Web for the provision of information support, and the organizational and professional development issues associated with the role of networked learner support. Details are provided on the 12 papers given at the symposium by presenters from the United Kingdom, Australia, the United States, Denmark, and Germany. For information on the individual papers, see entries #410, #412, #414-16, #419-21, and #423-26 below. A. Slade.

410. Banks, Bob. *Beyond the Online Library—The Learning Environment*. Paper presented at the 2nd International Symposium on Networked Learner Support, 23rd-24th June 1997, Sheffield, England: New Services, Roles and Partnerships for the On-line Learning Environment. Online. Available: http://netways.shef.ac.uk/rbase/papers/banks.htm (Accessed April 13, 2000).

To investigate ways to effectively support networked learners, 11 further education colleges in the United Kingdom formed the Learning Environment Club. Information is provided on the Club's activities and priorities, including the identification of key requirements for networked learner support (NLS), the development of a prototype online "Learning Environment" and information model to provide a structure for holistic NLS, the evaluation of prototype software and the architecture associated with the model, strategies for implementing NLS, typical uses of the Learning Environment, and key issues for the future. Effective support for networked learning is seen to involve three roles: a subject specialist, a tutor, and an information specialist or librarian. For a related paper, see #171 in this volume. A. Slade.

411. Fjällbrant, Nancy, Rose Marie Boström, Marie Ekman, John Fjällbrant, Ingrid Johansson, Mats Rohlin, and Gunilla Thomasson. *INTO INFO (EDUCATE) WWW Based Programs for Information Education, Training and Access*. Paper presented at the 63rd IFLA General Conference, Copenhagen, Denmark, August 31-September 5, 1997. Online. Available: http://ifla.inist.fr/IV/ifla63/63fjan.htm (Accessed April 13, 2000).

Libraries can play a role in education for information literacy and in the development of distance education programs. A tool that can be used in this connection is INTO INFO, produced by the EDUCATE (End-User Courses in

Information Access Through Communication Technology) Project of the European Union Telematics for Libraries Programme. EDUCATE was designed to help students, researchers, and practitioners develop information skills using a self-paced user education course in selecting and using information tools. INFO INTO programs have been created in four subject areas: chemistry, physics, energy, and electrical and electronic engineering. Pathfinders have been designed to provide structured networked learner support. INTO INFO can be used in several ways for teaching information retrieval, including in taught courses at colleges and universities, in distance learning, as a self-instruction tool, and in continuing education and professional development programs. M. Kascus.

412. Hammond, Michael. *Professional Learning and the Online Discussion*. Paper presented at the 2nd International Symposium on Networked Learner Support, 23rd-24th June 1997, Sheffield, England: New Services, Roles and Partnerships for the On-line Learning Environment. Online. Available: http://netways.shef. ac.uk/rbase/papers/hammond.htm (Accessed April 13, 2000).

In the context of a discussion of networked learning for professional development, the author looks at the opportunities offered by online debate and the complexities of structuring such debate. Included in the paper are comments on analyzing online discussions, information on the Just in Time Open Learning Project at the University of Sheffield, and an excerpt from a recent forum on telematics learning. A. Slade.

413. Hunter, Bob. "The Role of Learning Support in the Development and Implementation of a Key Skills Programme and an Intranet to Support It." *The Electronic Library* 15, no. 5 (October 1997): 357-62.

To provide training in information technology skills to first-year students, the University of Lincolnshire and Humberside (ULH) developed the Effective Language Programme (ELP) and an Intranet to support it. The intention was to make ELP available at all ULH campuses, supported by computer networks, open learning materials, and tutorials. The Department of Learning Support, consisting of library, computing, media, and language facilities, played a key role in the development of ELP. Its role included the development of IT skills materials, online diagnostic testing and profiling tools, and the Intranet that supports ELP. This article outlines the development phases of ELP and highlights the changing roles of Learning Support staff. One of these roles was that of Learning Advisor, which was created in partnership with the academic department to help students integrate IT skills into their areas of study. For a related paper, see #414 below. A. Slade.

414. Hunter, Bob. *Using a NLSI to deliver the Effective Learning Programme: Problems and Practicalities*. Paper presented at the 2nd International Symposium on Networked Learner Support, 23rd-24th June 1997, Sheffield, England: New Services, Roles and Partnerships for the On-line Learning Environment. Online. Available: http://netways.shef.ac.uk/rbase/papers/hunter.htm (Accessed April 13, 2000).

This paper describes the University of Lincolnshire and Humberside's use of the Networked Learner Support Intranet (NLSI) to support the delivery of its Effective Learning Programme (ELP). The primary objective of ELP is to promote independent lifelong learning. The first part of the paper discusses the organizational and strategic issues in developing the NLSI and linking it to centralized databases. The second part looks at the changes in staff roles necessary to develop, deliver, and support ELP and the NLSI. These changes included establishing closer working relationships with the central computing and information departments and working with faculty to develop open learning materials. For a related paper, see #415 above. A. Slade.

415. Langenbach, Christian and Freimut Bodendorf. *Learner Support in a Distributed Learning Environment: The Use of WWW-Based Teachware Packages*. Paper presented at the 2nd International Symposium on Networked Learner Support, 23rd-24th June 1997, Sheffield, England: New Services, Roles and Partnerships for the On-line Learning Environment. Online. Available: http://netways. shef.ac.uk/rbase/papers/clngnbch.htm (Accessed April 13, 2000).

A project to create a virtual campus at the University of Erlangen-Nuremberg in Germany is integrating networked learner support into the software for the online courses by means of navigational and orientation guides, with additional support provided by tutors who can be contacted through communications tools within the distributed environment. The discussion focuses on the design and implementation of the multimedia Web-based teachware packages and the flexible navigational and orientation guides included therein. An evaluation of the teachware packages will take place by giving 60 students in a business information systems course access to the packages. A. Slade.

416. Levy, Philippa. *Continuing Professional Development for Networked Learner Support: Progress Review of Research and Curriculum Design*. Paper presented at the 2nd International Symposium on Networked Learner Support, 23rd-24th June 1997, Sheffield, England: New Services, Roles and Partnerships for the On-line Learning Environment. Online. Available: http://netways. shef.ac.uk/rbase/papers/levy.htm (Accessed April 13, 2000).

One component of the NetLinkS Project in the United Kingdom is the design of an online professional development course on networked learner support (NLS). This paper discusses the rationale and curriculum model for the course and the training needs for NLS, identified through focus group sessions and interviews with various professionals in the information field. The need for institutions to establish a NLS coordinator position emerged as a theme in the focus group sessions. The skills needed for a NLS professional include IT expertise, specialization in the use and evaluation of networked information resources, awareness of the educational uses of networked technologies, ability to work in teams, and effective communication and interpersonal skills to liaise with faculty and academic staff. Through the NetLinkS Project and the Department of Information Studies at the University of Sheffield, two online distance learning courses are being planned to provide an overview of current practice and issues in NLS and to offer practical support for workplace activities in this field. A. Slade.

417. Levy, Philippa. "NetLinkS: Collaborative Professional Development for Networked Learner Support." *BUOPOLIS* (Bournemouth University Occasional Papers on Library and Information Services) 2 (1997): 51-59.

The author reviews the NetLinkS Project in the United Kingdom towards the end of its first year of funding. The focus of the project is on using networked delivery modes to provide learner support services, including library instruction, information literacy training, technical support, and reference assistance. This practice is labelled "networked learner support," or NLS. The project's primary goal is to facilitate local and national development of NLS by examining its potential and providing appropriate professional development activities and resources. With reference to the Follett and Fielden reports in the United Kingdom, the author summarizes the project's objectives and activities in 1995–1996. A significant information-collecting and awareness-raising activity involved focus group sessions with a cross-disciplinary mix of librarians, academics, information technology staff, and teaching and learning support staff. Various NLS services and initiatives were identified through these sessions and through reviews of the literature and information on the World Wide Web. The article concludes with a preview of NetLinkS objectives and activities planned for phase two of the project. A. Slade.

418. Levy, Phil, Nicholas Bowskill, Emma Worsfold, Sarah Ashton, and Tom Wilson. *NetLinkS Research Report.* April 1997. Online. Available: http://netways.shef. ac.uk/rbase/reports/contents.htm (Accessed April 13, 2000).

This report was prepared as part of the NetLinkS Project to describe the findings of a questionnaire and focus group survey, conducted in 1995–1996, of 19 higher education institutions in the United Kingdom on the topic of networked learner support (NLS). Using the information obtained from the survey, the report examines the following issues in networked learning and information support services: current practice, pedagogic models, perspectives on change and innovation, developing networked learning, stakeholder services and staff, and converging information and information technology (IT) support needs. Additional issues include the educational role of information support staff, developing networked approaches to information support, resourcing and organizing NLS, and staff development and training. Appendices include networked profiles of participating institutions and a review paper on networked learning. A. Slade.

419. McPherson, Madeleine. *Practising the Paradigm Shift: Real World Experience of On-Line Support.* Paper presented at the 2nd International Symposium on Networked Learner Support, 23rd-24th June, 1997, Sheffield, England. Online. Available: http://netways.shef.ac.uk/rbase/papers/mcphrsn.htm (Accessed April 13, 2000).

With a history of providing distance education, the University of Southern Queensland initiated a flexible delivery program to move some of its offerings into a networked environment. The first course to be delivered entirely via the Internet was the Graduate Certificate (Open and Distance Learning). The course was designed to have all instructional materials, administrative functions, assessments, and support services, including library services, provided on the World Wide Web. Library input occurred through librarians participating on the multidisciplinary course development team and involved compiling a resource base of websites relevant to the content of the course and providing online access to licensed electronic databases and full-text resources. The following issues arising from the library's experience with the Graduate Certificate are discussed in this paper: the quality of information provided on the World Wide Web, intellectual property issues, issues pertaining to the skills of librarians and students, cost issues, workforce issues, quality of education, and efficiency/convenience issues. A. Slade.

420. Mulvaney, Tracy K. *The TAPin Electronic Libraries Project and the Experience at the University of Birmingham*. Paper presented at the 2nd International Symposium on Networked Learner Support, 23rd-24th June 1997, Sheffield, England: New Services, Roles and Partnerships for the On-line Learning Environment. Online. Available: http://netways.shef.ac.uk/rbase/papers/mulvaney.htm (Accessed April 13, 2000).

The objectives of the Training and Awareness Programme in Networks (TAPin) Project at the University of Birmingham were to establish models for the effective transfer of skills for the utilization of networked resources, deliver training and support to enhance the expertise of academic staff in the use of information resources, and strengthen the internal support roles for both librarians and academic staff. Networked learner support (NLS) became an integral part of the TAPin model, using both old and new technologies to provide a hybrid approach. Following a discussion of information services at the University of Birmingham, this paper describes the TAPin Project in terms of equipment standards, access to the Library Information Network, orientation services through a library guide on the World Wide Web, and training and support for networked online and CD-ROM resources through work booklets and user guides. Additional topics include training and support for the Internet as a research tool through current awareness services on the Web, training and support for other IT applications, networked learner support for communication through an electronic enquiry service, and critical factors in the implementation of the project. A. Slade.

421. Pye, Jo. *Academic Partnership in NLS Resource Design: A European Case Study*. Paper presented at the 2nd International Symposium on Networked Learner Support, 23rd-24th June 1997, Sheffield, England: New Services, Roles and Partnerships for the On-line Learning Environment. Online. Available: http://netways.shef.ac.uk/rbase/papers/pye.htm (Accessed April 13, 2000).

The European Union's Telematics for Teacher Training (T3) Project, based at the University of Exeter, is a consortia effort to introduce educational technology into the teaching practice of teacher educators and students in European partner states. The project is unique in that it includes as one of its work packages provision for course development for librarians supporting teacher educators. Details are provided on the library work package, the results of a preliminary user needs analysis on networked learner support in the partner institutions, and the development of an online course for librarians. The paper concludes with a discussion of academic partnerships for professional development that stresses the role of librarians in providing networked learner support. A. Slade.

422. Rapple, Brendan A., with commentaries by Joanne R. Euster, Susan Perry, and Jim Schmidt. "The Electronic Library: New Roles for Librarians." *CAUSE/EFFECT* 20, no. 1 (Spring 1997): 45-51. Also online. Available: http://www.educause.edu/ir/library/html/cem971a.html (Accessed April 13, 2000).

This is a perspective on how librarians will function in the electronic library, with two commentaries on the ideas presented. According to the author, librarians will continue to refine their client-centered role as intermediaries and facilitators because there will be new and changing roles to play in an increasingly networked environment. Some of these new roles include fostering partnerships; collaborating with faculty, computer center staff, media specialists, and other campus professionals; communicating and partnering with the computer center; recognizing insularity as a weakness; and becoming more involved in campus technology planning groups. Other roles discussed are providing outreach to students, going to dormitories to deliver instruction, going to faculty offices and holding office hours in academic departments, teaching and facilitating information access by developing new pedagogical services in collaboration with faculty, developing web pages and designing information resources-based curricula, and teaching the campus community how to use the new information technology. M. Kascus.

423.   Salmon, Gilly, Ken Giles, and John Allan. *Large-scale Computer-Mediated Training for Management Teachers*. Paper presented at the 2nd International Symposium on Networked Learner Support, 23rd-24th June 1997, Sheffield, England: New Services, Roles and Partnerships for the On-line Learning Environment. Online. Available: http://netways.shef.ac.uk/rbase/papers/allan.htm (Accessed April 13, 2000).

This paper discusses and compares two online training programs in Computer Mediated Conferencing (CMC) for management education offered by the Open University Business School to its tutors. Information is provided about the background to the project, the testing of a five-stage model of CMC use, the tutors' evaluation of the software at the end of their online training, and changes and improvements made to the second training program based on experiences with the first. Results of the two programs showed that the model-based training was effective in enabling participants to progressively develop skills in the use of CMC. A. Slade.

424.   Schreiber, Trine and Camilla Moring. *The Communicative and Organisational Competencies of the Librarian in Networked Learning Support: A Comparative Analysis of the Roles of the Facilitator and the Librarian*. Paper presented at the 2nd International Symposium on Networked Learner Support, 23rd-24th June 1997, Sheffield, England: New Services, Roles and Partnerships for the On-line Learning Environment. Online. Available: http://netways.shef.ac.uk/rbase/papers/moring.htm (Accessed April 13, 2000).

The aim of this paper is to analyze the role of the facilitator in a networked learning environment and to compare that role with the role of the librarian. The authors address this objective by describing the role and functions of both a facilitator and an intermediary and by comparing and contrasting the two roles and functions. The role of facilitator is illustrated by a case study analysis of an online conference. In this analysis, the authors find a parallel between the role of the facilitator and the intermediary role of the librarian in terms of the identification, communication, and translation of a user's information needs. They conclude that, while there are clear distinctions between the two roles, the intermediary function could create a basis for the role of facilitator. Librarians need to develop characteristics of both the intermediary and the facilitator in networked learner support to successfully advance the understanding of the networked group. A. Slade.

425.   Williams, Helene and Anne Zald. *Redefining Roles: Librarians as Partners in Information Literacy Education*. Paper presented at the 2nd International Symposium on Networked Learner Support, 23rd-24th June 1997, Sheffield, England:

New Services, Roles and Partnerships for the On-line Learning Environment. On-line. Available: http://netways.shef.ac.uk/rbase/papers/zaldwill.htm (Accessed April 13, 2000).

The University of Washington (UW) has developed a campus-wide pro-gram called UWired to integrate both information technology (IT) and informa-tion literacy skills into teaching and learning. Librarians at UW are active partners in the UWired program, which involves faculty development, active student learning, and facilities redesign. Details are provided on several UWired initia-tives to illustrate the changing role of the librarian at UW, including the Freshman Interest Group Program, intercollegiate athletics, IT use in upper division classes, a computer-equipped teaching and learning facility called the Collaboratory, IT training and development for faculty, and outreach into the community. In these initiatives, librarians participate as partners with faculty, computing profession-als, and other campus personnel to bring information literacy and instruction about electronic resources into departmental curricula and other university activi-ties. A. Slade.

426. Wilson, Tina and Denise Whitelock. *Facilitation of Online Learning Environ-ments: What Works When Teaching Distance Learning Computer Science Stu-dents*. Paper presented at the 2nd International Symposium on Networked Learner Support, 23rd-24th June 1997, Sheffield, England: New Services, Roles and Partnerships for the On-line Learning Environment. Online. Available: http://netways.shef.ac.uk/rbase/papers/wils-abs.htm (Accessed April 13, 2000).

As part of the STILE (Students' and Teachers' Integrated Learning Envi-ronment) Project in the United Kingdom, the Open University integrated a pro-prietary conferencing system and online resources and support systems into its Fundamentals of Computing course. Using feedback from the tutors, this paper evaluates some of the support systems devised to facilitate online learning in the course and discusses the role of the Interactive Media Facilitator (IMF) in sup-porting tutors and students. Despite the advantages of online teaching, some tu-tors reported that they still saw a need for face-to-face teaching. The tutors indicated that they value the IMF's role in the online environment because this in-dividual can support ongoing changes to the technology, provide assistance to us-ers and respond to their feedback, make additional online resources available as required, and generally improve the quality of support to learners in a networked environment. A. Slade.

1996

427. Buckner, Kathy and Elisabeth Davenport. "Support Issues for Case-Based Learn-ing in an Undergraduate Human Factors Class." *Education for Information* 14, no. 4 (December 1996): 331-42.

The expanded area involving production and use of networked learning products is examined in this article. The main focus is on the management issues at the course, institutional, and national level. The article is based on the experi-ences gained by the authors in developing multimedia materials for an under-graduate course in human factors. The pilot learning package links five working areas: the case base, the theory base, the conference space, the query space, and the diary space. Specific issues discussed include cognitive issues, logistical procedures, support issues, ownership of materials, management of facilities, and organization of material. The implication here is that the involvement of librarians in networked course development issues could improve search mechanisms and procedures. The role of librarians in networked learner support is discussed, including the librarian as teacher of search skills for network-based information. Privacy and consent for the use of multimedia materials is a major issue. M. Kascus.

428. Carty, Joan, Isobel Stark, Robert van der Zwan, and Nicky Whitsed. "Towards a Strategy for Supporting Distance-Learning Students Through Networked Access to Information: Issues and Challenges in Preparing to Support the Doctorate in Education." *Education for Information* 14, no. 4 (December 1996): 305-16.

The Open University (OU) is the United Kingdom's largest university, but the OU Library has not historically supported the information needs of its students. A strategy of using networked access to information for supporting distance learners is presented. The focus in this article is on planned support for the anticipated Doctorate of Education, the importance of a collaborative approach to course delivery, and the specific issues to be addressed in the strategy for networked information provision. These issues include students' skills, tutorial and counselling staff, collaboration within the institution, choosing services for students, supporting services to students, conferencing, the World Wide Web, a help desk and instructional materials, and training of library staff. Support of distance learning through networked access to information will not be easy, but if the strategy is successful, the process will benefit both student and institution. M. Kascus.

429. Chamberlain, Ellen, and Miriam E. Mitchell. " 'BCK2SKOL': A Networked Learning Model Classroom." *Education for Information* 14, no. 4 (December 1996): 279-93.

The authors describe a collaborative professional development effort in the design and delivery of a course of instruction for librarians on the Internet's potential for research. Computer-mediated communication (CMC) technologies in a networked learning environment were used to design and deliver the course called "BCK2SKOL." The emphasis in this paper is on the importance of such collaborative efforts, the strengths and weaknesses of the current instructional design, the sharing of experiences as collaborators, and advice to those interested in emulating the networked learning model. At the close of registration for BCK2SKOL in September 1995, over 5,000 subscribers signed up from 62 countries. This networked learning model classroom is one example of a successful cross-campus and inter-departmental collaboration. M. Kascus.

430. Cochrane, Clive. "The Use of Videoconferencing to Support Learning: An Overview of Issues Relevant to the Library and Information Profession." *Education for Information* 14, no. 4 (December 1996): 317-30.

Among higher education institutions, there is a growing interest in the use of videoconferencing for the delivery of learning programs to support distance learners. Two universities in Northern Ireland, the University of Ulster (UU) and Queen's University of Belfast (QUB), are discussed to illustrate different uses of videoconferencing in higher education. Research undertaken at UU evaluated the use of videoconferencing in teaching and learning. A survey of all schools of librarianship and information science in the British Isles was conducted to determine the potential of videoconferencing for the library and information profession. Findings of the survey indicated a number of possible future uses of videoconferencing to support distance learning students and to demonstrate technology to students. M. Kascus.

431. Fjällbrant, Nancy. "EDUCATE—A Networked User Education Project in Europe." *IFLA Journal* 22, no. 1 (1996): 31-34.

The EDUCATE (End-User Courses in Information Access Through Communication Technology) Project in Europe was planned as a means to help libraries start courses on information handling in a networked environment and as a support tool for people engaged in individual learning. The original aim of the project was to produce self-paced user education courses on the selection and use of information resources and distribute these courses by means of the academic networks. The advent of the World Wide Web opened up new possibilities for the courses and a decision was made to use HTML to input the programs and to provide a structured interface to a wide variety of information sources. EDUCATE courses have been initially produced in two subject areas, physics and electrical and electronic engineering. Information is provided on the course design, production of the basic teaching material, and the choice of hardware and software for network applications. It is noted that EDUCATE will be ideal for distance learning and can be used by both librarians and academics in their education and training programs on information literacy. For a related paper, see #435 below. A. Slade.

432. Levy, Philippa, Susan P. Fowell, Nicholas Bowskill, and Emma Worsfold. "Net-LinkS: A National Professional Development Project for Networked Learner Support." *Education for Information* 14, no. 4 (December 1996): 261-78.

An overview is provided of NetLinkS, a professional development project for networked learner support (NLS). The project is funded by the UK Electronic Libraries Programme (eLib) and is aimed at encouraging the further development of NLS across the UK higher education sector. The overview includes the project's aims, objectives, and strategy; its achievements to date; a summary of findings of some research studies; and future plans. Twenty-three institutions participated in phase one of the project, which used focus groups as a means of gathering information and raising awareness at the local level. Phase two of the project was directed at facilitating the development of a networked learners' community, or "community of interest" for NLS. The following library-based NLS services were reported by participants: (1) electronic inquiry/reference work, (2) library orientation, (3) user education and information skills training, (4) support for distance learners, and (5) support for teaching and research. The focus group discussion guide is included in an appendix. M. Kascus.

433. Levy, Philippa, Sue Fowell, and Emma Worsfold. "Networked Learner Support." *Library Association Record* 98, no. 1 (January 1996): 34-35.

The emerging professional practice of networked learner support (NLS) and the NetLinkS Project in the United Kingdom are highlighted in a discussion of online user education and training. NetLinkS aims to support librarians in transferring user support into an electronic/networked environment. The need for NLS practice is outlined and the objectives and activities in phase one of the project are summarized. A sidebar provides a fictional glimpse into a day in the life of a NLS professional to illustrate some of the tasks that may be performed by a librarian in this role. A. Slade.

434. McClure, Charles R. "Libraries in the Global, National, and Local Networked Information Infrastructure." In *Marking a Milestone: The UTA Libraries' One Millionth Volume Celebration*, edited by Gerald D. Saxon. Arlington, TX: UTA Press, 1996, 1-17. ERIC ED 402 955.

This position paper assumes that the networked environment has altered the way in which people acquire and use information resources and services. The challenge to libraries is explored in terms of the need for new library missions, the need for collaboration among schools, equal access to information for all, virtual libraries made possible by telecommunications, and opportunities for distance education. Librarians are asked to rethink the kinds of services they will need to provide in a networked environment. They are also asked to develop strategies for obtaining new sources for funding. In addition, librarians are encouraged to remain current with the changing technology, develop new skills, and remain open-minded about the technology. Library administrators are asked to be sensitive to and supportive of the training needs of current staff. What is at stake in the networked environment is the extent to which the library will manage the use of information as opposed to being one of its many providers. M. Kascus.

435. Thomasson, Gunilla and Nancy Fjällbrant. "EDUCATE: The Design and Development of a Networked End-User Education Program." *Education for Information* 14, no. 4 (December 1996): 295-304.

This paper focuses on programs for the education of information users in the EDUCATE (End-User Courses in Information Access Through Communication Technology) Project. The aim is to produce a self-paced user education course in the selection and use of information sources and to provide a structured interface to relevant high-level, quality resources. EDUCATE is based on the World Wide Web with hyperlinks, and has been designed as multimedia programs that can be used in several ways: for self-instruction, as an instrument in formal courses and in distance learning, and as an access tool to information sources. EDUCATE programs have been developed in two subject areas: physics and electrical and electronic engineering. The aims and objectives of the EDUCATE programs are provided along with the development process. Evaluation is carried out during the development of a course to provide feedback about how different parts of the program function. User reactions to the programs were positive. A handbook on training for information literacy has been produced in connection with the EDUCATE Project. For a related paper, see #431 above. M. Kascus.

436. Walton, Graham, Joan Day, and Catherine Edwards. "Role Changes for the Academic Librarian to Support Effectively the Networked Learner: Implications of the IMPEL Project." *Education for Information* 14, no. 4 (December 1996): 343-50.

The University of Northumbria at Newcastle has been investigating the impact of the increasingly electronic environment of the United Kingdom's higher education system. The IMPEL Project (Impact on People of Electronic Libraries), conducted between December 1993 and December 1995, focused on three themes: (1) current and projected roles of academic librarians, (2) the changing role of the subject specialist, and (3) the potential for loss of control. Based on interview data, these themes are explored in depth. Subsequently, the IMPEL2 Project has adopted a broader perspective on the impact of electronic information provision, with concerns directed at academic staff and student users and the campus-wide implications of networked learner support in the teaching and learning experience throughout the United Kingdom. M. Kascus.

1995

437.   Fowell, S. P. and P. Levy. "Computer-Mediated Communication in the Information Curriculum: An Initiative in Computer-Supported Collaborative Learning." *Education for Information* 13 (1995): 193-210.

This paper describes a computer-mediated course at the University of Sheffield that uses collaborative learning techniques to introduce students to the elements of information management and communication in a networked environment. The course is intended to provide new skills to professionals, particularly those in the field of library and information studies. Details are provided about the course objectives, the curriculum model, and evaluation and refinement of the module. Key components in this pilot course include student group work and a group project; use of the Internet, the World Wide Web, e-mail, and newsgroup conferencing; access to networked information and library resources; and online tutor support. Feedback from the students indicated overall satisfaction with the course, and further development and refinements are planned. A. Slade.

438.   Fowell, S. and P. Levy. "Developing a New Professional Practice: A Model for Networked Learner Support in Higher Education." *Journal of Documentation* 51, no. 3 (September 1995): 271-80. Also online. Available: http://www.aslib.co.uk/jdoc/1995/sep/4.html (Accessed April 13, 2000).

The authors examine the emerging role of "networked learner support," defined as the delivery of learner support programs and services by means of computer-mediated communication. With reference to the Follett and Fielden reports in the United Kingdom, the authors discuss the nature of networked learning and resources and identify a new role for librarians as para-academics facilitating and supporting resource-based open learning. Networked learner support is seen to include support for curriculum development and delivery, user education and information/publishing skills training, reference inquiry services, and technical advisory work. The authors list a number of professional development criteria recommended for the practice of networked learner support and suggest that an electronically mediated program would be an appropriate means to convey the relevant information and training to professionals. A. Slade.

439.   Wagner, Gülten S. "The Networked Information Environment—New Roles for Information Professionals." *Education for Library and Information Services: Australia* 12, no. 2 (August 1995): 25-32.

The author advances the argument that the networked environment is creating chaos and information overload for users and that information professionals have a responsibility to provide some order by introducing search strategies, structured instructional packages, and tutorials. It is argued that a paradigm shift from traditional source orientation to process orientation is required of information professionals. In this context, process orientation refers primarily to search strategy development, and a hypermedia package is suggested as one means to undertake this development. A project at Edith Cowan University to create a hypertext-based index to essential readings in a first-year library science course is described to provide an example of using an electronic front-end to facilitate access to information. A. Slade.

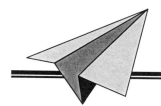

CHAPTER 6

Instruction Issues

This chapter includes works that focus on library instruction, information literacy, and Web-based instruction. Related terms subsumed under "library instruction" include "bibliographic instruction," "library orientation," "reader education" and "user education."

Library Instruction

The Subject Index provides further indexing under the heading "library instruction" for materials located in this and other chapters.

1999

440. Western Cooperative for Educational Telecommunications. "The Distance Learner's Library: The Indispensable Guide to Finding the Material." In *The Distance Learner's Guide*, edited by George P. Connick. Upper Saddle River, NJ: Prentice Hall, 1999, 69-87. Companion website: http://www.prenhall.com/dlguide (Accessed April 13, 2000).

This chapter is part of a guide designed to help potential distance learning students choose a distance education provider and to aid current students in improving their distance education performance. The library section provides general information and practical advice on the following topics: using library databases, downloading files, getting help, searching the online catalogue, requesting interlibrary loans, and using the Internet and World Wide Web. Included in the chapter are "questions to ask a distance education provider about library services" and "questions to ask a librarian about helpful databases." A website accompanies this guide to expand upon material in each chapter and to provide links to useful online resources. A. Slade.

1998

441. Barnes, Susan, Katherine Holmes, and Mem Stahley. "Library Instruction at a Distance: The High Tech/High Touch Mix: Three Case Studies." In *The Eighth Off-Campus Library Services Conference Proceedings: Providence, Rhode Island, April 22-24, 1998*, compiled by P. Steven Thomas and Maryhelen Jones. Mount Pleasant, MI: Central Michigan University, 1998, 183-95.

Extended campus librarians from three institutions, Lesley College, University of Central Florida-Brevard, and Linfield College, share insights on the challenges of delivering library instruction at a distance. Their approaches represent three different models of extended campus library services: (1) a librarian at the branch campus of a university library that serves students in the state university system; (2) a librarian at the main campus, with students scattered throughout the state; and (3) a librarian at the main campus, with students in 15 states without official branch campuses. All three librarians stress the fact that technology facilitates better communication with students but, by itself, it is not intrinsically a teaching tool. The approach at the University of Central Florida is described as a "high touch" information literacy program. The approach at Linfield College involves collaboration with faculty. The approach at Lesley College is "high tech," involving WebWhacker, PowerPoint, and a video. All three programs are committed to teaching students and offer several ways of connecting with the students so that they can better make use of library resources. M. Kascus.

442. Bean, Rick, "Lights ... Camera ... Instruction: Library Instruction Via Interactive Television." In *The Eighth Off-Campus Library Services Conference Proceedings: Providence, Rhode Island, April 22-24, 1998*, compiled by P. Steven Thomas and Maryhelen Jones. Mount Pleasant, MI: Central Michigan University, 1998, 29-34.

Library instruction via interactive television (ITV) is examined in this paper. The paper includes a review of the literature on the topic, a discussion of traditional library instruction components, and guidance on how to adapt them to ITV. The importance of planning an ITV presentation is stressed. Planning involves selecting appropriate activities and materials to be used during the presentation and ensuring interaction between the librarian and the students and faculty. Tips and suggestions for how to prepare for an ITV library instruction session are given. M. Kascus.

443. Kapoun, Jim. "Teaching Undergrads Web Evaluation: A Guide for Library Instruction." *College & Research Libraries News* 59, no. 7 (July/August 1998): 522-23.

An increase in expected student World Wide Web usage by faculty has prompted the need for librarians to include a teaching component on Web evaluation in undergraduate library instruction. When teaching the Web to students at Southwest State University, five criteria are used for Web evaluation: accuracy, authority, objectivity, currency, and coverage. These are the same criteria that are used for print evaluation. The sheet of criteria distributed to students is included in a chart that gives an outline of the five criteria for evaluating Web documents, how to interpret the basics, and how to put it all together. M. Kascus.

444. Kearley, Jamie P. "The Evolution of the Virtual Library and Its Impact on Bibliographic Instruction for Distance Learners." In *The Eighth Off-Campus Library Services Conference Proceedings: Providence, Rhode Island, April 22-24, 1998*, compiled by P. Steven Thomas and Maryhelen Jones. Mount Pleasant, MI: Central Michigan University, 1998, 207-12.

This paper discusses the evolution of the virtual library and its impact on bibliographic instruction for distance learners at the University of Wyoming. The steps toward the virtual library began in 1989, when the university libraries joined CARL (Colorado Alliance of Research Libraries). The second step was achieved with the addition of OCLC's FirstSearch service on CARL. The third step toward the virtual library came in 1997, with the replacement of CARL terminals with personal computers equipped with Netscape. The availability of a vast array of databases with different interfaces and the World Wide Web have created a greater need for bibliographic instruction than existed previously. The future development of bibliographic instruction will be guided and determined by ongoing advances in technology. M. Kascus.

445. Pival, Paul R. and Johanna Tuñón. "NetMeeting: A New and Inexpensive Alternative for Delivering Library Instruction to Distance Students." *College & Research Libraries News* 59, no. 10 (November 1998): 758-60.

Librarians at Nova Southeastern University (NSU) investigated use of Microsoft's NetMeeting software to reduce the need for face-to-face library instruction sessions at off-campus sites. The potential advantages of the software, which allows individuals and groups to interact via the Web, are outlined and the results of the preliminary trials are reported. Based on these results, the library team decided to limit transmission to a maximum of three to four sites at a time and to keep the initial sessions with off-campus classes simple. The NSU Library began delivering instruction to five Graduate Teacher Education Program sites in 1998. Evaluations from these sessions indicated that the students found NetMeeting to be a satisfactory method for delivering library instruction. The authors discuss problems encountered and lessons learned in the initial sessions and describe future plans. They conclude that while NetMeeting is not a perfect training solution, it does provide a new and inexpensive alternative for delivering library instruction to distance sites. A. Slade.

446. SchWeber, Claudine, Kimberly B. Kelley, and Gloria J. Orr. "Training, and Retaining, Faculty for Online Courses: Challenges and Strategies." In *Distance Learning '98: Proceedings of the 14th Annual Conference on Distance Teaching and Learning, August 5-7, 1998, Madison Wisconsin*. Madison, WI: University of Wisconsin-Madison, 1998, 347-51. Also available as ERIC ED 422 874.

The Graduate School of Management and Technology (GSMT) at University of Maryland University College (UMUC) takes a multi-faceted approach to training faculty to teach in an online environment. Instruction in the use of library resources is part of this training program so faculty can help students conduct research more effectively. Because most faculty are part-time and scattered throughout three continents, a series of Web-based workshops was developed to provide instruction in the use of full-text electronic resources and free Internet resources, as well as guidance on how to integrate online resources into course assignments. In addition to these voluntary workshops, an online library resources course has been developed for all new GSMT students and faculty. This required, non-credit course provides an in-depth introduction to conducting research online and using UMUC's electronic library for research purposes. A library staff member has been assigned to spend 40% of her time updating and maintaining the course. A. Slade.

447. Siegel, Dena and Susan Levendosky. "Teaching Library Users to Evaluate WWW Resources." In *Theory and Practice: Papers and Session Materials Presented at the Twenty-Fifth National LOEX Library Instruction Conference Held in Charleston, South Carolina, 8 to 10 May 1997*, edited by Linda Shirato and Elizabeth R. Bucciarelli. Library Orientation Series, no. 29. Ann Arbor, MI: Pierian Press, 1998, 83-89.

The need for librarians to teach students how to evaluate information found on the Internet is stressed in this paper. To this end, Ball State University has incorporated evaluation criteria into its library instruction sessions. The criteria established for the sessions are scope (subject matter); authority; currency; accuracy; purpose; intended audience; and organization, structure, and design. Included in the library instruction sessions are samples of Web resources that exemplify specific criteria and exercises to enable the students to practice application of the criteria. The evaluation sheet given to the students is reproduced in this paper along with a copy of the evaluation criteria handout. While the sessions described here are held on-campus, the criteria and exercises could also be incorporated into library instruction for distance learners. A. Slade.

1997

---

448. Beck, Susan E. and Brian Ormand. *Making the Leap to Hyperspace in Distributed Learning*. Paper presented at the 16th Annual Conference of the New Mexico Council for Higher Education Computing Communications Services, October 23, 1997, New Mexico Highland University, Las Vegas, New Mexico. 57 pp. ERIC ED 416 724.

In 1997, New Mexico State University offered a training program for faculty on using instructional technology to teach in a distributed learning environment. The aim of the program, called the Institute for Technology Assisted Learning (ITAL), was to enable faculty to develop a distance education course for the 1997/98 academic year. Training in the use of electronic library resources and services was included as part of ITAL. Two sessions held in the library gave an overview of library services and resources sources for distance education faculty and students and provided practice using electronic databases, remote library catalogues, document delivery resources, and the Internet. As a result of ITAL, the university library reformulated its service policies to take into account the needs of distance education students. In addition to discussing library services in the context of ITAL, this document includes the syllabus for the library training sessions in an appendix. A. Slade.

449. Boaz, Mary. "Preparing Students to Use an Electronic Library." *Distance Education Report* 1, no. 5 (September 1997): 6.

   This brief sidebar describes Murray State University's pre-class library instruction workshops offered to education graduate students at extended campus sites. The students receive class points for their participation in the workshops, in which a librarian on-campus utilizes compressed video to guide them through a series of hands-on exercises on using Internet search engines and the electronic resources of their local university library. The goals of the program are to bring the students up-to-date technologically, enable them to focus their research, and reduce the class dropout rate. A. Slade.

450. Butros, Amy. "Using Electronic Mail to Teach MELVYL MEDLINE." *Medical Reference Services Quarterly* 16, no. 1 (Spring 1997): 69-75.

   At the University of Southern California at San Diego (USCD), e-mail is used to teach MELVYL MEDLINE. A description is given of the course design, implementation process, and evaluation. The course provided a new format for instructional librarians to comply with the USCD Libraries' goal of a library without walls. The class was promoted through the library newsletter. Ninety-three participants registered for the first e-mail course, with faculty being the majority of the participants. Included in this article are the welcome e-mail message for the course, the electronic syllabus, and the questionnaire used for evaluation. M. Kascus.

451. Hamblin, Deb. "User Education for External Students." *DESIGnation*, nos. 11-12 (March 1997): 1-2.

   To help external students develop searching techniques, Murdoch University held a number of library sessions on campus during evenings and weekends. The weekend sessions proved popular with the students. The sessions introduced the students to library staff, the services available to them as external students, and the library's Innopac system. Subject-specific sessions covering access to and use of electronic resources were also held. A. Slade.

452. Henner, Terry A. "Invisible Users and Virtual Access: Bibliographic Instruction to Remote Users at the University of Nevada School of Medicine." *Bibliotheca Medica Canadiana* 18, no. 4 (Summer 1997): 141-43.

   The Savitt Library at the University of Nevada School of Medicine provides its remote users with a variety of ways to seek assistance and receive library instruction at a distance. Site visits promote use of the library and encourage students to communicate with library staff by telephone, e-mail, or fax. Library instruction is offered by videoconferencing and through tutorials, guides, and pathfinders mounted on the World Wide Web. The author notes that the greatest challenge in assisting remote users is helping them to understand and manage their computers and software. Initiatives to assist remote users have proved useful for supporting on-campus users as well. A. Slade.

453. Parker, Jo. "Information Handling Skills." *Assistant Librarian* 90, no. 10 (November/December 1997): 155-57.

   To assist its students with the use of information technology, the Open University in the United Kingdom has introduced a number of new library services with an emphasis on teaching transferable information handling skills. One new service is support of postgraduate students through help desk facilities using various media and instructional materials available via the FirstClass conferencing system and the World Wide Web. The web pages are used to publish information, train users, and guide access to Internet resources. To assist students in their use of databases, training materials in the form of simple HTML files sit alongside the links to the databases. Future plans include designing a suite of web pages dedicated to information handling skills training and using a computer-assisted learning package to deliver training to remote students. A. Slade.

454.   Vishwanatham, Rama, Walter Wilkins, and Thomas Jevec. "The Internet as a Medium for Online Instruction." *College & Research Libraries* 58, no. 5 (September 1997): 433-44.

The development of an introductory online course is described, focusing on how the Internet can be used as a medium of instruction especially suited for reaching remote users. The course content includes basic information, trouble shooting advice, and practice exercises. The 16-lesson course was distributed via listservs to students, faculty, and staff. The results of pre-tests and post-tests to assess prior knowledge and subsequent knowledge gain are discussed, as are the implications for the librarian's instructional role of using the Internet as an online instructional medium. The most important impact of this online course was the ability to reach a larger number of users than would have been possible in the traditional classroom setting while achieving a level of depth not possible in the typical one-hour, one-meeting instruction class. M. Kascus.

1996

455.   Burke, John J. "Using E-Mail to Teach: Expanding the Reach of BI." *Research Strategies* 14, no. 1 (Winter 1996): 36-43.

At Fairmont State College, librarians use e-mail and listservs to teach a 16-part Internet seminar. Computer-mediated communication (CMC) is the chosen delivery method for this instruction. The process of developing the seminar is discussed in detail. An evaluation form was distributed at the end of the seminar, but it received a very low rate of response. Advantages and disadvantages of using CMC-only instruction are indicated. Among the advantages are the ability to teach large groups and the ability to teach local and distance students simultaneously. The disadvantages are that students have to have e-mail accounts and know how to use them, they have to spend long periods in front of computer screens, and the delivery method lacks interactivity between student and instructor. The Internet seminar was successful in two ways: faculty and staff learned how to use the Internet, and librarians discovered that this method of teaching has other potential applications, including seminars on specific electronic library resources or conducting preliminary library instruction. M. Kascus.

456. Central Queensland University. Division of Library, Information and Media Services. *Virtual Residential School Project Report 1996*. Rockhampton, Queensland: Division of Library, Information and Media Services, Central Queensland University, 1996. Online. Available: http://www.library.cqu.edu.au/publish/report96.htm (Accessed April 13, 2000).

In 1996, Central Queensland University Library offered a second virtual residential school for students enrolled in the Scientific Information Sources course (see #468 in this chapter for the report on the first program). The virtual residential school provided the opportunity for students to participate in the program without having to be physically present on-campus. The school was conducted over two days with a class of ten students, five of whom were located on-campus and five off-campus. Computers were loaned to three students who did not have their own equipment. Two of the differences between the 1995 and 1996 programs were use of web pages as backup and use of Netscape Chat. Details are provided on the background of the project, objectives of the 1996 program, methodology, technologies selected, technology and communications links, staff preparation, teaching methods, backup procedures, the topics covered, student evaluations, evaluation of the hardware and software, and outcomes of the program. Experience with the delivery of the program demonstrated once again that it is possible to provide electronic instruction in information retrieval to off-campus students. It is noted, however, that the virtual residential school is best suited to reach small groups of postgraduate students living in remote areas and is not an appropriate vehicle to deliver programs to large groups of undergraduate students. A. Slade.

457. Fourie, Ina and Dorette Snyman. "Distance Teaching in Online Searching." In *Online Information 96: Proceedings of the 20th International Online Information Meeting, London, 3-5 December 1996*, edited by David I. Raitt and Ben Jeapes. Oxford: Learned Information Europe Ltd, 1996, 85-91.

To train the growing number of end-users, librarians will need to improve their online searching skills and their teaching skills. Practical problems arise in distance teaching of online searching. One solution used at the University of South Africa (Unisa) is to teach searching as a multimedia study package based on instructional design principles. The library provides an online training course for end-users. This collaborative effort of the Department of Information Science and the Library is intended to foster independent study. The author explains the application of instructional design principles to the study package and provides examples. The multimedia study package includes the use of printed media and videos, practical exercises, workbooks, computer-aided instruction, workshops, e-mail, and use of the Internet. M. Kascus.

458. Graziadei, William D. and Gillian M. McCombs. "The 21st Century Classroom-Scholarship Environment: What Will It Be Like?" *Journal of Educational Technology Systems* 24, no. 2 (1995-96): 97-112.

At the State University of New York (SUNY), Plattsburgh, the scientific process is used as an approach to teaching/learning through discovery. This paper describes the development of a teaching/learning module in biology that takes advantage of the Internet and other communications and computing media. The interactive learning module uses telephone, e-mail, CU-SeeMe, online catalogues,

FirstSearch, and Timbuktu to demonstrate a "real-time" need of a student in developing an undergraduate research paper on cancer treatment. The authors note that this module provides a glimpse of what the twenty-first century classroom will look like. Appendix III fully describes the equipment used to help others bring about the authors' vision of the classroom of the future. M. Kascus.

459. LaGuardia, Cheryl, Michael Blake, Laura Farwell, Caroline Kent, and Ed Tallent. "Teaching in Cyberspace: The Remote User, Libraries, and Distance Education." Chapter 13 in *Teaching the New Library; A How-To-Do-It Manual for Planning and Designing Instructional Programs*. How-To-Do-It Manuals for Librarians, no. 70. New York: Neal-Schuman, 1996, 139-54.

As part of a practical "how-to-do-it" manual on library instruction, the authors provide a chapter outlining how the various types of instruction can be adapted and implemented in an online or remote learning context. Recommended examples of each type of instruction are supplied together with the appropriate URLs. The chapter also provides definitions of various types of distance learning (e.g., audioconferencing, desktop videoconferencing, document sharing) and a discussion of general issues in distance and remote education pertaining to library instruction. The chapter concludes with a selected list of websites and other resources on distance learning of particular interest to librarians. A. Slade.

460. McAlpine, Iain. "A Combined Video and CAL Package on Advanced Level Library Skills for Open Learning Students." In *Learning Technologies: Prospects and Pathways: Selected Papers from EdTech '96 Biennial Conference of the Australian Society for Educational Technology, University of Melbourne, 7-10 July 1996*, edited by John G. Hedberg, James R. Steele, and Sue McNamara. Belconnen, ACT: AJET Publications, 1996, 82-86.

The University of Southern Queensland was commissioned by the Open Learning Library Information Service (OLLIS) of Open Learning Australia (OLA) to develop a combined video and computer-assisted learning (CAL) package to provide OLA students with instruction in library use. The package was developed for two levels, introductory and advanced. The basic skills package was completed and distributed to university libraries in 1996. At the time of writing, the video component of the advanced package was available and work on the CAL program was in the final stages of development. Both packages were developed by an instructional designer working as a team with three librarians and a project officer. The goal of the project was to enable OLA students to carry out searches for specific items or information on a topic using any library catalogue or CD-ROM index. This paper discusses the key elements in the instructional design of the two packages. For related papers, see #476 and #477 in this chapter. A. Slade.

461. Orr, Debbie, Trish Andrews, and Margaret Appleton. "The Creation and Delivery of a Residential School Program for Geographically Dispersed Students." *MC Journal: The Journal of Academic Media Librarianship* 4, no. 1 (Summer 1996): 85-105. Also online. Available: http://wings.buffalo.edu/publications/mcjrnl/v4n1/australia.html (Accessed April 13, 2000).

The virtual residential school offered by Central Queensland University (CQU) Library in 1995 is described in this paper. The intent of the program was to use technology to deliver library instruction to distance education students without making it compulsory for them to travel to the CQU campus. For further information on the virtual residential school, see #462, #468, and #500 in this chapter. A. Slade.

462.   Orr, Debbie and Judith Edwards. *The Creation and Delivery of a Virtual Residential Workshop at Central Queensland University Library*. Paper presented at the ASCILITE 1996 Conference, Adelaide, South Australia, 2-4 December, 1996. Online. Available: http://www.ascilite.org.au/conferences/adelaide96/papers/17.html (Accessed April 13, 2000).

Following a discussion of flexible delivery and information literacy, this paper describes the virtual residential school conducted by Central Queensland University (CQU) Library in 1995. The program was intended to trial the delivery of library instruction to off-campus students using current technologies. One of the main objectives was to create a program that used relatively inexpensive and readily available software and allowed students to participate from their homes. Details are provided on the planning, delivery, and evaluation of the program. It is noted that the knowledge gained through the project will assist librarians in preparing and delivering information literacy programs to all students remote from the CQU campus. For the full report on the 1995 virtual residential school, see #468 in this chapter. A. Slade.

1995

463.   Bean, Rick. "Two Heads Are Better Than One: DePaul University's Research Consultation Service." In *The Seventh Off-Campus Library Services Conference Proceedings: San Diego, California, October 25-27, 1995*, compiled by Carol J. Jacob. Mount Pleasant, MI: Central Michigan University, 1995, 5-15.

A research consultation service that allows a student or a faculty member the opportunity to request an individualized consultation session with a full-time suburban campus librarian has been implemented at DePaul University's Suburban Campus Libraries. A review of the literature on "research consultation" and "term paper counseling" is presented to address concerns about how these programs operate, how they are publicized, how effective they are, and how students have responded to them in relationship to DePaul's research consultation service. The appendices include Research Consultation Appointment Request, Procedures for Research Consultation, Evaluation of the Research Consultation Program, Librarian's Analysis of Research Consultation, and Research Consultation Evaluation. Findings from the evaluation forms indicate that the service has been beneficial for the patron who requests a consultation, but the total number of requests has been small and it was felt that more needs to be done to promote the service. M. Kascus.

464.   Black, Graham and Margaret Appleton. "The Development of Interactive Programs for Teaching Information Access Skills to Remote Students." In *Higher Education: Blending Tradition and Technology: Proceedings of the 1995 Annual Conference of the Higher Education and Research Development Society of Australasia (HERDSA)*, edited by A. C. Lynn Zelmer. Research and Development in Higher Education, vol. 18. Rockhampton, Queensland: Professional Education Centre, Faculty of Health Science, Central Queensland University, 1995, 124-27.

Central Queensland University Library developed two computer-assisted learning (CAL) programs to instruct distance learners in the use of online information sources. One program was designed to teach students how to use the online catalogue, while the other focused on teaching the skills required to search online databases. Details are provided on the design, software, and platforms used for the two programs. Following use of the first CAL program, a group of distance students was surveyed about its effectiveness. The majority of the students indicated that they appreciated the program and its self-paced style of learning. The second program, called RASCAL (Remote Access Searching Computer Assisted Learning), and the accompanying manual were due to be tested with a group of remote distance learners at the time of writing. A. Slade.

465. Blackwell, Cheryl. "Remote Access OPAC Searching." In *The Impact of Technology on Library Instruction: Papers and Session Materials Presented at the Twenty-First National LOEX Library Instruction Conference Held in Racine, Wisconsin, 14 to 15 May 1993*, edited by Linda Shirato. Library Orientation Series, no. 25. Ann Arbor, MI: Pierian Press for Learning Resources and Technologies, Eastern Michigan University, 1995, 159-64.

Remote access OPAC searching has been part of a library instruction assignment at Albion College. The assignment has three components requiring each student to (1) schedule a 90-minute block of time to perform searches on four OPAC systems, (2) present a 5-minute instruction session based on some aspect of OPAC searching, and (3) provide a summary review of the assignment. The OPACs used were NOTIS, GEAC, Dynix, and Innovative Interfaces. Almost all students commented favourably on how the OPAC searching assignment helped them apply what they had been learning in class in a hands-on environment. M. Kascus.

466. Blauer, Ann Taylor. "Librarian, Clone Thyself! Using a Video to Promote Your Library Service." In *The Seventh Off-Campus Library Services Conference Proceedings: San Diego, California, October 25-27, 1995*, compiled by Carol J. Jacob. Mount Pleasant, MI: Central Michigan University, 1995, 17-23.

A video was chosen as an inexpensive option to promote library services at the University of South Alabama at Baldwin County. The processes of casting, filming, and editing are fully outlined in this paper. Feedback from students was obtained using two methods of evaluation: questionnaires and focus groups. The questionnaire was designed to collect data regarding the students' pre-video knowledge of library services and to measure the knowledge gained post-video. The library video evaluation is included in the appendix. Results of the questionnaire indicate that the video served its intended purpose of disseminating information on the library services of the Baldwin County branch. Results of the focus group interviews indicate that the content of the video was very good. The value of a video for basic, repetitive presentations is stressed. M. Kascus.

467. Catania, Mem. "Uniform Quality and Convenient Access: Student-Centered Library Instruction Off Campus." In *The Seventh Off-Campus Library Services Conference Proceedings: San Diego, California, October 25-27, 1995*, compiled by Carol J. Jacob. Mount Pleasant, MI: Central Michigan University, 1995, 33-56.

Off-campus library instruction issues are described, emphasizing uniformity of academic quality and convenience of access at off-campus locations. The author advocates support for the academic research endeavours of off-campus students without burdening them with unnecessary travel or inconvenience in gaining access to needed information. This goal can be accomplished by providing a planned core of quality information resources and services. The results of a library instruction evaluation study conducted at a branch campus site are described. Findings indicate that, since the coursework demands library research skills, the students are interested in effective library use, electronic access to information, and effective library instruction. For comparative purposes, the library instruction evaluation forms are summarized in a table. M. Kascus.

468. Central Queensland University. Division of Library, Information and Media Services. *Virtual Residential School Project Report 1995*. Rockhampton, Queensland: Division of Library, Information and Media Services, Central Queensland University, 1995. Online. Available: http://www.library.cqu.edu.au/publish/vir_res.htm (Accessed April 13, 2000).

Special funds were made available to allow the Central Queensland University Library to offer a virtual residential school as a pilot project to study the value of this concept and its potential for delivering future programs. Students enrolled in the Scientific Information Sources course in 1995 were given the option of attending the residential school on campus or taking it off-campus in a virtual mode. The off-campus students were provided with use of a laptop computer preconfigured with appropriate software, a modem, a desktop camera, and a mobile phone. A mix of technologies was used to deliver the virtual residential school, including CU-SeeMe for desktop videoconferencing, teleconferencing, a Chat server, and Timbuktu Pro for connecting to remote computers. Details are provided on the planning of the residential school, the teaching methods, the technology selected for the project, instructional design issues, staff training, backup procedures, trial connections, communication problems, outcomes, and evaluations of the project and the technologies used. The students who participated in the virtual residential school reported that it was a stimulating and interesting experience. The project was successful in that it achieved its objectives and proved to have potential for delivering library instruction to off-campus students. For the report on the 1996 virtual residential school, see #456 in this chapter. A. Slade.

469. Craig, Monica Hines and Susan DuFord. "Off-Campus Faculty Perception of the Value of Library User Education." In *The Seventh Off-Campus Library Services Conference Proceedings: San Diego, California, October 25-27, 1995*, compiled by Carol J. Jacob. Mount Pleasant, MI: Central Michigan University, 1995, 69-73.

This study builds on an earlier study (see #433 in the second bibliography) in which a user evaluation survey was administered to Central Michigan University's (CMU) Detroit Metropolitan Area Extended Degree Program graduates who completed the Master of Science in Administration (MSA) program in the previous year. Findings from the survey indicate that students regarded the library instruction program as effective and useful to the completion of course assignments and their final project. To further build on the user instruction program, the authors surveyed the off-campus faculty's perception of the value of library instruction. The faculty survey consisted of 18 questions using the Likert Scale model. Of 278 surveys mailed to CMU faculty, 117 (42%) were returned. The overall results indicated that faculty appeared to be satisfied with the level, length, and frequency of the library presentations and the availability of library materials for their classes. M. Kascus.

470. Hall, Garry. "From Catalogues to Cyberspace: Collaborative Development of Library Skills Packages for Distance Learning." In *Distance Education: Crossing Frontiers: Papers for the 12th Biennial Forum of the Open and Distance Learning Association of Australia, Vanuatu: September 1995*, edited by Fons Nouwens. Rockhampton, Queensland: Division of Distance and Continuing Education, Central Queensland University, 1995, 124-28.

The development of library skills packages for training open and distance learning students is examined, with specific reference to two kits produced by the University of Southern Queensland (USQ) for the Open Learning Library and Information Service (OLLIS). Topics discussed in this paper include the trends affecting education and training in Australia, the shift towards flexible delivery of courses, the demands being placed on libraries by the expansion of the Internet, courseware development trends, future directions for library instruction, and the use of library skills packages. Three training packages are described: a computer-assisted learning (CAL) package for instructing postgraduate distance students at Central Queensland University, an in-house CD-ROM for teaching on-campus students at USQ, and a generic package consisting of two kits containing videos and CAL programs for Open Learning Australia students. In the latter package, the first kit is directed toward the novice open learning student, while the second kit is aimed at the more information literate student. It is noted that the development of a library skills package requires a considerable investment of time and energy by a team of high-level staff, and institutions should be prepared for some disruption of normal activities. A. Slade.

471. Jaggers, Karen Elizabeth. "Plugging Library Services Into Interactive Instructional Television (IITV) Classes." In *The Seventh Off-Campus Library Services Conference Proceedings: San Diego, California, October 25-27, 1995*, compiled by Carol J. Jacob. Mount Pleasant, MI: Central Michigan University, 1995, 197-203.

The focus in this paper is on the library concerns that need to be considered in the process of using Interactive Instructional Television (IITV) for instruction of students at the remote sites of Northern Arizona University. Using IITV, the librarian could instruct off-campus students in the use of the library online catalogue, electronic databases, and the Internet. This would be done in real-time, providing opportunities for practice. The need to adopt new technologies to provide the best access and delivery for the educational success of remote users is stressed. M. Kascus.

472. Jensen, Ann and Julie Sih. "Using E-Mail and the Internet to Teach Users at Their Desktops." *Online* 19, no. 5 (September/October 1995): 82-86.

Two University of California (UC) campuses, San Diego (UCSD) and Berkeley (UCB), share their successful experiences with e-mail as a delivery method for instruction modules. Librarians at UCSD designed and implemented an

INSPEC database tutorial using e-mail, which was adapted at UCB. Other UC campuses were invited to retrieve the lessons and adapt them for their needs. The INSPEC on MELVYL Electronic Workshop consists of a brief introduction and six short, self-paced tutorials delivered to users at their desktops. Users can then customize their own instruction. To solicit subscriptions to the workshop, electronic announcements and registration information are sent to the Internet accounts of all UCSD faculty and graduate students in the physical sciences. Promotion through library displays gave the workshop visibility beyond the physical sciences departments. Response to the tutorial has been very positive. The full text of each tutorial is available to anyone interested in adapting the modules for their own use. M. Kascus.

473. Kabel, Carole J., Rose P. Novil, and Jack Fritts. "The Electronic Library: Library Skills for Off-Campus Students, Program and Evaluation." In *The Impact of Technology on Library Instruction: Papers and Session Materials Presented at the Twenty-First National LOEX Library Instruction Conference Held in Racine, Wisconsin, 14 to 15 May 1993*, edited by Linda Shirato. Library Orientation Series, no. 25. Ann Arbor, MI: Pierian Press for Learning Resources and Technologies, Eastern Michigan University, 1995, 127-34.

In an effort to assess the impact of bibliographic instruction in the field-based model of education at National Louis University (NLU), a two-page survey was distributed to students who successfully completed NLU's Master's of Science in Management field program. A key component of each bibliographic instruction session is a hands-on segment intended to introduce students to available electronic resources. Results of the survey indicate that the library instruction is a relevant and necessary component in the field-based program. M. Kascus.

474. Lance, Kathleen and Susan Potter. "Integrating Library Instruction into Course Modules." In *The Seventh Off-Campus Library Services Conference Proceedings: San Diego, California, October 25-27, 1995*, compiled by Carol J. Jacob. Mount Pleasant, MI: Central Michigan University, 1995, 221-39.

After a 1993 survey indicated the need for a new approach to library instruction, Regis University integrated this instruction into the printed course modules. The full text of the library's component of one of the modules is included in the appendices, along with the 1993 survey. In 1995, a second set of surveys was distributed to 38 students, with a 100% response rate. The survey asked questions similar to those in the 1993 survey but included additional questions on the library instruction section of the course modules. Findings indicate that the module-integrated library instruction approach provides opportunities for librarians to reach a large number of students, to achieve overall long-term financial savings, and to foster continuing improvement in communication with faculty and administrators. M. Kascus.

475. Lockerby, Robin. "Teaching Library Skills to the Adult Student." In *The Seventh Off-Campus Library Services Conference Proceedings: San Diego, California, October 25-27, 1995*, compiled by Carol J. Jacob. Mount Pleasant, MI: Central Michigan University, 1995, 247-56.

This study examines the characteristics of adult learners, adult learning theory, and learning/teaching styles, and applies this knowledge to library instruction, identifying an andragogical model of learning as more appropriate for adults. The library instruction program of National University is mostly traditional in approach but operates on a more interactive, self-directing level. Three elements are included in the program: course-related instruction for research-based courses; course-integrated activities in the library, with brief focused sessions; and a term paper clinic based on a search strategy format. In addition, the library attempts to accommodate all learning styles by providing a variety of point-of-use aids, library guides, and self-paced exercises. Included in the appendices are a table listing "Four Orientations to Learning" and a selected annotated bibliography on "Teaching Library Skills to the Adult Learner." M. Kascus.

476. McAlpine, Iain. "Developing a Generic Library Skills Multimedia Package Using an Expert Strategy for Instruction." In *ASCILITE '95: Conference Proceedings, 4th-6th December, 1995: Learning with Technology*, edited by J. M. Pearce, A. Ellis, G. Hart, and C. McNaught. Parkville, Victoria: Science Multimedia Teaching Unit, Faculty of Science, University of Melbourne, 1995, 389-94.

To introduce Australian open learning students to library use, the Open Learning Library Information Service (OLLIS) commissioned the University of Southern Queensland to develop a combined video and computer-assisted instruction (CAI) package for distribution to libraries that participate in the open learning program. The key elements in the instructional analysis and design of the package are discussed in detail. It was decided that the video would cover the subject matter related to library research and the CAI program would provide hands-on practice in searching online catalogues and other library resources. An important requirement of the package was that it could be applied to any library or library system. For related papers, see #460 and #477 in this chapter. A. Slade.

477. McAlpine, Iain. "An Expert Strategy Approach to Instructional Design for a Generic Library Skills Video and Computer Aided Instruction Package." In *Access Through Open Learning: With a Major Focus on Networked Learning*, edited by Allan Ellis and Julie Burton. 2nd Edition. [Southern Cross University] Occasional Papers in Open Learning, vol. 5. Lismore, NSW: Norsearch, 1995, 127-32.

An expert strategy analysis was used in the instructional design of a combined video and computer-assisted instruction (CAI) package for open learning students in Australia. The intent of the package was to provide instruction and practice in the use of library catalogues and CD-ROM indexes. The author discusses the selection of media for the package, the instructional design process, the analysis of the strategies involved in library searching, and the approach used to teach these strategies. For further information on the library instruction package, see #460 and #476 in this chapter. A. Slade.

478. Orme, Bill. "A Library Instruction Course Via the Community Learning Network." In *The Impact of Technology on Library Instruction: Papers and Session Materials Presented at the Twenty-First National LOEX Library Instruction Conference Held in Racine, Wisconsin, 14 to 15 May 1993*, edited by Linda Shirato. Library Orientation Series, no. 25. Ann Arbor, MI: Pierian Press for Learning Resources and Technologies, Eastern Michigan University, 1995, 123-25.

As part of a proposal to the Annenberg/CPB Project "New Pathways to a Degree," Indiana University-Purdue University at Indianapolis (IUPUI) proposed the formation of a Community Learning Network to offer classes at community sites convenient for students and to provide support. An information literacy course, "Information Resources and Student Research," was developed, consisting of 15 videotaped fifty-minute lectures, a handbook of objectives, and a syllabus. This one-credit course was offered by the Indiana University School of Library and Information Science. The technology problems encountered in satisfying the distance education aspect of the effort are discussed. The potential educational impact on the community is seen as a by-product that may have long-term benefits. M. Kascus.

479. Pederson, Ann. "Teaching Over an Interactive Video Network." In *The Impact of Technology on Library Instruction: Papers and Session Materials Presented at the Twenty-First National LOEX Library Instruction Conference Held in Racine, Wisconsin, 14 to 15 May 1993*, edited by Linda Shirato. Library Orientation Series, no. 25. Ann Arbor, MI: Pierian Press for Learning Resources and Technologies, Eastern Michigan University, 1995, 187-91.

Library instruction is provided over an interactive video network (IVN) to acquaint students at remote sites with how to access, identify, and obtain library resources. The IVN supports coursework that is conducted live and involves two-way audio and video transmission between the instructor and the student during the actual class presentation. This paper provides an orientation to the interactive technology and the equipment to be used in the network and describes the coordination between the library and the IVN personnel. The focus here is on graphics, appearances, and camera etiquette, with the caveat that successful teaching on the IVN system requires even greater planning than for an on-campus classroom presentation by anyone using the system, either professor or librarian. As a follow-up to the instruction, the IVN coordinator and the librarian meet with each instructor for every course scheduled on the system. M. Kascus.

480. West, Sharon M. and Diane Ruess. "The Electronic Library: Teaching Students at a Distance." In *The Impact of Technology on Library Instruction: Papers and Session Materials Presented at the Twenty-First National LOEX Library Instruction Conference Held in Racine, Wisconsin, 14 to 15 May 1993*, edited by Linda Shirato. Library Orientation Series, no. 25. Ann Arbor, MI: Pierian Press for Learning Resources and Technologies, Eastern Michigan University, 1995, 135-40.

The development of a course, syllabus, and textbook for LS100, "Library and Information Strategies," is described. The course goal is to teach library research as a process that takes place outside the library, with access being solely electronic. The conceptual outline for the course includes seven major concepts: (1) information, (2) the library, (3) the library and its services, (4) the library and its resources, (5) types of information available in libraries, (6) electronic access to libraries, and (7) understanding the library research process. Findings from both objective evaluations and oral feedback indicate a uniformly high level of student satisfaction with the course as well as the skills learned in accessing the library's resources electronically. M. Kascus.

481. Whitehead, Anita and Maxine M. Long. "Providing Off-Campus Bibliographic Instruction: When Off-Campus Means Someone Else's Campus." Co-published simultaneously in *The Reference Librarian*, nos. 51/52 (1995): 171-80, and *Library Instruction Revisited: Bibliographic Instruction Comes of Age*, edited by Lynne M. Martin. New York: Haworth Press, 1995, 171-80.

Students at Genesee Community College receive their library instruction in the library of a nearby college, the State University of New York (SUNY) College at Geneseo. Librarians at both institutions cooperate to ensure that the off-campus library instruction provided is consistent with the instruction available on-campus. Faculty and librarians communicate to ensure that the instruction sessions directly relate to classroom assignments. The perceived benefit to the student is increased confidence and better library and information skills. A formal agreement between these institutions is recommended to continue the cooperative program of library instruction for off-campus students. M. Kascus.

482. Whyte, Susan Barnes. "Spanning the Distance: Using Computer Conferencing as Part of a Team-Taught Research/Writing Class." Co-published simultaneously in *The Reference Librarian*, nos. 51/52 (1995): 267-79, and *Library Instruction Revisited: Bibliographic Instruction Comes of Age*, edited by Lynne M. Martin. New York: Haworth Press, 1995, 267-79.

This paper describes a team-taught research/writing class for adults at Linfield College in Oregon. The course included a face-to-face classroom instruction component for one weekend, with the rest of the course conducted over a computer conferencing system. The strengths and weaknesses of computer conferencing are described in the context of the research/writing class. This is followed by a description of Linfield College's continuing education program for adults and an overview of the research/writing course. It is noted that the literature on how librarians interact with students in distance education programs focuses mostly on delivery systems and rarely mentions how librarians participate in the learning process. Librarians are urged to take advantage of computer conferencing technology to maintain a connection with students and their needs as learners. M. Kascus.

483. Witucke, Virginia. "Bibliographic Instruction in an Off-Campus Setting: The Evolution of a Class Presentation." In *The Seventh Off-Campus Library Services Conference Proceedings: San Diego, California, October 25-27, 1995*, compiled by Carol J. Jacob. Mount Pleasant, MI: Central Michigan University, 1995, 387-97.

A worksheet was used in planning bibliographic instruction modules for the required MSA Administrative Research & Report Methods course in the Extended Degree Program of Central Michigan University (CMU). The worksheet was designed in three parts: Part I focused on planning the search, including choosing a topic, determining the scope, and selecting the type of material to be used; Part II was the actual search, consisting of eight questions relating to resources; and Part III was optional, consisting of Boolean searches in an automated index. The library module ended with a debriefing of the entire class. The worksheet, which emphasizes the pattern of the search rather than specifics, is included in the appendix. M. Kascus.

1993

484. Rao, V. Chandrasekhar and G. Sujatha. "Designing User Education Programmes for Distance Learners." In *Academic Libraries: Role in the National Development: Festschrift Volume in Honour of Prof. N. B. Inamdar*, edited by Dorothy Isaac, A. A. N. Raju, and L. S. Ramaiah. Madras, India: T. R. Publications, 1993, 295-301.

Following a general examination of the facets and objectives of user education, this paper focuses on the provision of user education to distance learners in India. It is recommended that prior to designing user education programs for distance learners, five studies should be undertaken: (1) a study of the nature and characteristics of distance learners, (2) an assessment of user needs, (3) a survey of the library facilities available to the students, (4) an evaluation of the resources and services at these libraries, and (5) an assessment of the user's awareness of library facilities and services. Two types of user education programs are appropriate for distance learning: programs for faculty and resource personnel and programs for the students. User education for faculty can take place at the central library. Programs for the distance learners can include lectures and demonstrations at the various study centers, orientation sessions in local libraries, and audio-visual programs. The Travelling Workshop Experiment in the United Kingdom is suggested as a model for taking user education to the distance learners via a mobile van. A. Slade.

Information Literacy

For other works that discuss this topic, see the following heading in the Subject Index: "information literacy."

1999

485. Doherty, John J., Mary Anne Hansen, and Kathryn K. Kaya. "Teaching Information Skills in the Information Age: The Need for Critical Thinking." *Library Philosophy and Practice* 1, no. 2 (Spring 1999). Online. Available: http://www.uidaho.edu/~mbolin/doherty.htm (Accessed April 13, 2000).

Teaching information skills got a boost from the recent Boyer Commission report on undergraduate education, which points out that students are graduating without basic skills. The report challenges universities to rethink traditional instruction models and to encourage a model of inquiry-based learning that involves students in research. The role of libraries is discussed, focusing on the library instruction program at Montana State University (MSU). MSU revised its instruction program in 1994 and now concentrates on three areas: discipline-specific instruction, course-specific instruction, and library credit classes. In discipline-specific instruction, librarians approach various departments to cooperatively conduct library instruction sessions. Course-specific instruction offers faculty and students more advanced subject sessions. Both make use of the Internet and the World Wide Web. The third area of library instruction is an information literacy seminar emphasizing critical thinking and developing information skills. Formative evaluation is built into the instruction process, so students formulate their expectations for the course and determine if they were met. M. Kascus.

1998

486. Behrens, Shirley J. "Developing a Curriculum for an Information Literacy Course for Off-Campus Students: A Case Study at the University of South Africa." In *The Eighth Off-Campus Library Services Conference Proceedings: Providence, Rhode Island, April 22-24, 1998*, compiled by P. Steven Thomas and Maryhelen Jones. Mount Pleasant, MI: Central Michigan University, 1998, 35-45.

A curriculum for an information literacy course for off-campus students is being developed by an interdisciplinary course team at the University of South Africa (Unisa). The course is projected for implementation in the year 2000 and will provide links to user education programs presented by the Unisa Library. Information literacy is defined as "the ability of learners to access, use, and evaluate information from different sources, to enhance learning, solve problems, and generate new knowledge." The course curriculum is divided into two modules: (1) information-gathering skills, including theory of information science, library skills, Internet; and (2) broader information skills, including theory of information science, planning, retrieving, organizing, expository writing. User education programs of the Unisa library fit in with the curriculum content for the first module of the information literacy course. To be considered as information literacy, the user education or library skills offered by the library must include learning how to synthesize and evaluate information as related to a particular discipline. A typology of information handling skills and the contents of the textbook to be used are included in the appendices. M. Kascus.

487. Harvey, Kay. "Critical Literacy: A Librarian and an English Professor Collaborate." In *The Eighth Off-Campus Library Services Conference Proceedings: Providence, Rhode Island, April 22-24, 1998*, compiled by P. Steven Thomas and Maryhelen Jones. Mount Pleasant, MI: Central Michigan University, 1998, 175-82.

Critical thinking and evaluation skills are becoming important in the current learning environment as students turn their attention to the World Wide Web to satisfy their information needs. Librarians need to redefine their roles in the educational process by collaborating with teaching faculty to help students think critically and evaluate Internet information sources. The discussion in this paper focuses on critical literacy and its three significant components: knowledge base, critical thinking, and evaluation tools. Faculty/librarian collaboration at Penn State McKeesport resulted in redesigning an English course to integrate critical literacy instruction into the curriculum. An assessment tool was developed and incorporated to measure the effectiveness of the critical literacy module. The evaluation tool is described and the results discussed. Preliminary results indicate that students were more selective in their choice of information sources and improved their ability to cite Internet sources. M. Kascus.

488. Henning, J. C. and B. L. Oosthuizen. "Gedesentraliseerde Inligtinggebruik-eropleiding." [Decentralised Information User Education]. *South African Journal of Library and Information Science* 66, no. 2 (June 1998): 67-77. Summary in English.

The term "information user education" is used in this article to refer to all the components of the education process, both in and outside the library, that lead to information literacy. The need to develop decentralized information user education for distance education students at Technikon SA in South Africa prompted a review of the literature and a research study to determine what aspects of the training should be offered, who should provide the training, and what methods should be used. In the research study, 227 faculty and staff were surveyed by questionnaire for their views on information user education and their recommendations for implementing it. The recommendations included the following means for providing user education: written materials, lectures, video and slide programs, CD-ROM programs, and use of the Internet. The results of the study indicated that user education materials should be developed in conjunction with course materials and distributed with them. A. Slade.

489. Hinchliffe, Lisa Janicke and Tod Treat. "Teaching Information Literacy Skills in Online Courses." In *Distance Learning '98: Proceedings of the 14th Annual Conference on Distance Teaching and Learning, August 5-7, 1998, Madison Wisconsin*. Madison, WI: University of Wisconsin-Madison, 1998, 517-19.

This paper discusses the integration of information literacy skills into an online introductory chemistry course at Parkland College. One module of the online course was designed to support three information literacy objectives: developing an awareness of current scientific events, developing an ability to critically read articles on science issues, and developing an awareness of the relationship between scientific ideas and their impact on society. This paper was presented to an audience of mainly distance educators, and advice is given on the process of creating information literacy instruction for an online course, with emphasis on including a librarian or information professional in the development process. A. Slade.

490. Pourciau, Lester J. *Information Literacy, an Absolute Necessity for Chinese Higher Education in the 21st Century*. Paper presented at the International Conference on New Missions of Academic Libraries in the 21st Century, Beijing, China, October 25-28, 1998. Online. Available: http://www.lib.pku.edu.cn/98conf/proceedings.htm (Accessed April 13, 2000).

In his conference presentation, the author advances the argument that information literacy is essential to distance education and that educational institutions in China and elsewhere need to ensure that their graduates have acquired information literacy skills. The importance of information literacy in connection with electronic resources and the World Wide Web is stressed and the basic components of an information literacy program are outlined. The model of information literacy developed at Griffith University in Australia is discussed, with emphasis on the collaboration needed between faculty and library staff to make the program successful. A. Slade.

1997

491. Appleton, Margaret and Debbie Orr. "Achieving Change at a Distance by Access to Information." In *Processes of Community Change: Proceedings [of] a Colloquium Inspired by Professor John D. Smith, 31 October-1 November 1996*, edited by Shirley Gregor and Dave Oliver. Rockhampton, Queensland: Central Queensland University, 1997, 131-37.

Central Queensland University has a commitment to helping its distance students develop information literacy and lifelong learning skills. To this end, the library initiated a number of projects to enable the students to access, evaluate, use, and manage resources electronically, including (1) a residential school on-campus where information literacy skills were taught in a face-to-face setting; (2) a virtual residential school that used a combination of desktop videoconferencing and teleconferencing to teach students at a distance; (3) two computer-assisted learning (CAL) programs, one on searching the online catalogue and the other on accessing and searching electronic databases; and (4) a series of courses on the Web to teach selected professional groups how to use the Internet effectively. The library's future plans include incorporating the CAL programs into a coordinated information literacy package, creating a video to introduce the components in the package to the students, developing Web-based tutorials on specific topics, and modifying the virtual residential school concept to deliver information literacy programs to small groups of students. A. Slade.

492. Catts, Ralph, Margaret Appleton, and Debbie Orr. "Information Literacy and Lifelong Learning." In *Lifelong Learning: Reality, Rhetoric and Public Policy: Conference Proceedings, 4-6, 1997*, edited by John Holford, Colin Griffin, and Peter Jarvis. Guildford, UK: Department of Educational Studies, University of Surrey, 1997, 70-75.

The concept of information literacy is discussed with regard to definitions of the term, lifelong learning, undergraduate education at Central Queensland University (CQU), and the implications for distance education. It is argued that a collaborative approach between faculty and librarians is necessary to create the learning experiences through which information literacy can be developed. To provide opportunities for students to become information literate, a commitment from the university, staff, and students is required. CQU has recognized the importance of information literacy as a component of lifelong learning and requires that strategies promoting information literacy be incorporated into all courses offered by the University. CQU librarians work with faculty and lecturers to fulfil this objective. It is noted that, because of the increase in the amount of information in electronic format that can be accessed from remote locations, it is especially important for distance education students to develop information literacy skills. A. Slade.

493. Dewald, Nancy H. and Gloriana S. St. Clair. "Active and Collaborative Learning in Online Courses: Penn State's Project Vision." In *Libraries and Other Academic Support Services for Distance Learning*, edited by Carolyn A. Snyder and James W. Fox. Foundations in Library and Information Science, vol. 39. Greenwich, CT: JAI Press, 1997, 41-55.

At Pennsylvania State University, Project Vision was developed to explore how using technology could enhance the learning experience, facilitate collaborative learning, and help undergraduate students to develop information and critical thinking skills. Project Vision empowered students to learn to communicate in several modes, including e-mail, computer conferencing, and videoconferencing. Students developed and enhanced their information skills using online catalogues, electronic journals, and the World Wide Web. A library studies course was collaboratively taught by several faculty, a librarian, and a technical person. The costs and rewards of collaborative learning are discussed as well as future directions. The authors conclude by discussing three barriers to the implementation of the digital library: (1) the discomfort of reading from computer screens, (2) costs, and (3) ownership and intellectual property. M. Kascus.

494. Harvey, Kay and Nancy Dewald. *Collaborating with Faculty in Preparing Students for the Asynchronous Classroom*. Paper presented at the ACRL 8th National Conference: Choosing Our Futures: Nashville, Tennessee, April 11-14, 1997. Online. Available: http://www.ala.org/acrl/paperhtm/d33.html (Accessed April 13, 2000).

Academic libraries need to pursue opportunities for collaboration with teaching faculty and technical support personnel to prepare students to be part of the student-centered asynchronous classroom. Librarians need to incorporate critical thinking, evaluation of resources, and computer searching skills into their instruction sessions. In doing this, they can partner with teaching faculty to give students what they will need to succeed in this new educational environment. Penn State University's Project Vision Library Studies Course is the model used here. Asynchronous learning is facilitated by computer-mediated communication, the World Wide Web, and remote access to online catalogues and databases. Various ways in which collaboration can take place are discussed, including librarians at different campuses working together, faculty from different disciplines developing course modules, and pairing of courses that lend themselves to collaboration. The stages in the process of effective collaboration are described as well as five types of collaboration. M. Kascus.

495. Mishra, Sanjaya. "Teaching Information Literacy to Distance Learners." *University News* (New Delhi) 35, no. 20 (May 19, 1997): 3-6.

With reference to the literature on information-based education, self-directed learning, and distance education, the concept of information literacy is examined in relation to distance learners. Examples from the literature illustrate how some international institutions are providing instruction in information literacy skills for distance learners. With the proliferation of information technology and electronic access to information, the author stresses the need for a course at the undergraduate level on information literacy to be offered through distance delivery mode. To this end, a proposed syllabus for a four-credit course on information literacy is provided in an appendix to this article. While this syllabus is directed primarily towards Indian universities, it has broad applicability to any institution with distance learners. A. Slade.

496. Moore, Penny, Sandra Mann, David Clover, June Stratton, and Ken Marshall. "Information Literacy: What Does It Imply in Distance Education?" In *The New Learning Environment: A Global Perspective: Papers Written for the 18th ICDE World Conference, June 2-6, 1997, The Pennsylvania State University, University Park, Pennsylvania*. University Park, PA : Pennsylvania State University, 1997. [CD-ROM].

The Open Polytechnic of New Zealand initiated a study to explore and describe the implications of information literacy for staff involved in providing distance education. The objectives of the study were to (1) raise awareness and understanding of information literacy concepts through discussion among a broad range of staff at the Polytechnic, (2) describe the implications of information literacy for work practice for people in different roles in the Polytechnic, and (3) identify factors critical to the development of a team approach to integrating information literacy into Polytechnic courses. The discussion that resulted from a Delphi exercise with staff demonstrated the importance of the availability of appropriate information access and training for students in both distance and contact settings. While technology may assist with this, there was a strong emphasis on the need to provide expertise from librarians, teaching staff, and the course materials. Factors emerging from the Delphi exercise were a need for staff to develop a greater understanding of what information literacy means and a need to clarify the role of the library in integrating information literacy into Polytechnic courses. A. Slade.

497. Orr, Debbie, Margaret Appleton, and Garry Hall. "The Impact of Technology Upon the Delivery of Information Services to Distance Education Students." In *Distance Education: Past, Present and Future: Reflecting on the Past, Learning from the Present and Preparing for the Future: National Open and Distance Education Student Network Inc (NODES Net) 7th Annual Conference, 6-9 July 1998, Rockhampton Campus, Central Queensland University*, edited and compiled by Bryan Cranston. Rockhampton, Queensland: Central Queensland University Publishing Unit, 1997, 154-62.

The information literacy initiatives of Central Queensland University (CQU) and the University of Southern Queensland (USQ) are highlighted in this paper. The focus of the initiatives is on the use of current technology to provide information literacy training to distance learners who access electronic resources from remote locations. At CQU, library staff have produced two computer-assisted learning programs to assist off-campus students, conducted a virtual residential school on the use of electronic information sources for both on- and off-campus students, and are developing a series of courses on the Web aimed at professional groups. At USQ, a multidisciplinary team produced an information skills package for open learning students and developed web pages for a graduate course taught via the Internet. Details of these various projects are provided in the paper, together with information on the evaluation of the computer-assisted learning programs from the two institutions and CQU's virtual residential program. A. Slade.

498. Sexty, Suzanne. "Information Access for Students: Value Added for Today and the Future." *Communiqué* (Canadian Association for Distance Education) 13, no. 2 (December 1997): 3-5. Also online. Available: http://itesm.cstudies.ubc. ca/561g/mexico/resources/sexty.html (Accessed April 13, 2000).

In an article directed primarily toward distance educators, the author examines the role of information literacy in an electronic environment. The issues considered include librarian/faculty partnerships to enhance teaching and learning, the library as a concept versus the library as a space, the design and use of library websites, and teaching information literacy skills to remote users. The argument is advanced that educators and librarians need to work together to ensure that learners know why they need information, how to find and evaluate that information, and how to transform the information into knowledge for future use. A number of library websites are listed to provide examples of Canadian sites that meet three criteria for effectiveness: visibility (easily located), user compatibility (not dependent on the latest equipment or software), and value-added resources (useful for distance learners). A. Slade.

499. Ward, Michelle. "Information Literacy and the Geographically Challenged: Central Queensland University Initiatives." *DESIGnation*, nos. 11-12 (March 1997): 2-4.

Central Queensland University Library is developing strategies for teaching information literacy skills to distance education students. These strategies include two computer-assisted learning packages, a generic multimedia and modularised information skills package, integration of information literacy into the distance education course curriculum, a virtual residential school, and a subject search checklist. The aim of these projects is to make students aware of the resources available to them and to provide instruction on how to access and evaluate information in those resources. A. Slade.

1996

500. Orr, Debbie, Margaret Appleton, and Trish Andrews. "Teaching Information Literacy Skills to Remote Students Through an Interactive Workshop." *Research Strategies* 14, no. 4 (Fall 1996): 224-33.

With a focus on teaching information literacy skills, the authors describe the virtual residential school offered to both on- and off-campus students at Central Queensland University in 1995. Three conditions were determined to be essential in this learning environment: (1) each participant felt comfortable with the technology, (2) the technology was as transparent as possible, and (3) all participants were able to communicate easily with the instructor and the rest of the class. The following aspects of the program are discussed in this paper: the planning phase, staff training, equipment, the workbook, software, program objectives, and evaluation. For the full report on the 1995 virtual residential school, see #468 in this volume. A. Slade.

1995

501. Cheek, Julianne, Irene Doskatsch, Pauline Hill, and Lynn Walsh. "Meeting a Need: The Development of an Information Literacy Package." In *One World, Many Voices: Quality in Open and Distance Learning: Selected Papers from*

the 17th World Conference of the International Council for Distance Education, Birmingham, United Kingdom, June, 1995: Volume 2, edited by David Sewart. Milton Keynes, UK: The Open University in association with International Council for Distance Education, 1995, 62-65. Reprinted with minor changes in *The Learning Link: Information Literacy in Practice*, edited by Di Booker. Adelaide, SA: Auslib Press, 1995, 157-62.

Because open learning students in Australia were not being exposed to information literacy skills in their course work, Open Learning Australia (OLA) decided to develop a print-based package to assist its students in acquiring these skills. Under contract to OLA, staff from the University of South Australia produced a package with two sections. The first part defined and identified information literacy skills and related them to the students' needs, while the second part contained instructions on how to use the package and a number of leaflets on specific topics. An important aspect in the development of the package was an ongoing evaluation process built into all phases of the project, including consultations with students and tutors. These consultations and the collaboration between academic staff and the library contributed to the success of the package. A. Slade.

502. Espinal, Jack and Sharon Geiger. "Information Literacy: Boole to the Internet and Beyond." In *The Seventh Off-Campus Library Services Conference Proceedings: San Diego, California, October 25-27, 1995*, compiled by Carol J. Jacob. Mount Pleasant, MI: Central Michigan University, 1995, 75-100.

A description is given of the development of the course "Computer/Information Literacy," which links library information access skills with management information skills, using the Internet as the focal point. Information literacy is defined as "the ability to effectively access and evaluate information for problem solving and decision making," as taken from the American Library Association. The course outline and the course syllabi are included in the appendices. A course assessment was conducted to identify both the strengths and problem areas within the course. Among the problem areas, two were identified and addressed: (1) the wide range of student computer skills made the course more difficult to teach and (2) some of the class projects were too difficult to accomplish for students with limited basic computer skills. Librarians and faculty members are using the course evaluations and the evolving information needs perceived by faculty and students to include computer literacy and information literacy as core competencies within the Bachelor of Science in Management program. M. Kascus.

503. George, Rigmore and Rosemary Luke. *The Critical Place of Information Literacy in the Trend Towards Flexible Delivery in Higher Education Contexts*. Paper delivered at the Learning for Life Conference, Adelaide, 30 November–1 December 1995. Online. Available: http://www.lgu.ac.uk/deliberations/flex. learning/rigmor_fr.html (Accessed April 13, 2000).

The Australian higher education system is in the process of dramatic change due to the emerging information age and is moving towards a learner-centered approach known as "flexible delivery." Flexible delivery is discussed in terms of its definition, characteristics, and relationship to information literacy and lifelong learning. It is argued that information literacy is pivotal in flexible teaching and learning because it enables individuals to engage in a variety of learning situations and opportunities in optimal ways. The focus on meta-skills in the flexible delivery mode presents a challenge to institutional structures and traditional ways of teaching and learning. To meet this challenge, collaboration between faculty and librarians is necessary to provide the learners with appropriate information literacy skills. A. Slade.

504. George, Rigmore and Adela Love. "The Culture of the Library in Open and Distance Education Contexts." *Australian Academic and Research Libraries* 26, no. 2 (June 1995): 129-36. Previously published as "The Culture of the Library in Open and Distance Education Contexts: The Case for Flexibility." In *Access Through Open Learning: With a Major Focus on Achieving Flexibility*, edited by Allan Ellis and Jean Lowe. [Southern Cross University] Occasional Papers in Open Learning, vol. 4. Lismore, NSW: Norsearch, 1994, 199-205.

Distance learners are disadvantaged in terms of learning the process of library research and understanding the "culture" of the library. In distance learning, the emphasis tends to be on the product or end result rather than on the process of locating information. Librarians should encourage distance students to become involved in the process of information gathering so that these students can assume more control over their learning and research skills. To facilitate this involvement, librarians can introduce distance learners to library culture by defining library language and jargon; explaining the nature of information databases and networks; demonstrating how materials are organized, identified, and retrieved in their field of study; and discussing the relationships between libraries and other information providers. The authors advocate the need for flexibility in providing library support for distance learners to take into account the student's understanding of information systems, the particular characteristics of the student's field of study, and the requirements of course assignments and assessment criteria. A. Slade.

505. Lowe, Susan S. "Collaboration with Faculty: Integrating Information Literacy into the Curriculum." In *The Seventh Off-Campus Library Services Conference Proceedings: San Diego, California, October 25-27, 1995*, compiled by Carol J. Jacob. Mount Pleasant, MI: Central Michigan University, 1995, 257-60.

This paper focuses on library instruction as information literacy and on the role of the librarian in identifying ways to integrate research skills into the curriculum to enhance coursework. At the Education Network of Maine, basic training targets three groups: students, staff and local cooperating librarians, and faculty. Staff training includes five major components: a video, a general description of the state-wide online public access catalogue, a point-of-use guide, a flip chart with local log-in instructions, and a staff manual. Student training begins with an orientation over the interactive television network. Librarians also participate in nine classroom hours of the Introduction to College Experience Curriculum. Library workshops provide faculty with opportunities to receive training in the use of library technologies, learn about new information resources, understand the need to include critical thinking skills in the curriculum, and generate ideas for incorporating these skills into library assignments. M. Kascus.

506. Ruess, Diane E. and Sharon M. West. "Library and Information Literacy for Distance Education Students." *Journal of Distance Education* 10, no. 2 (Fall 1995): 73-85.

The core undergraduate curriculum at the University of Alaska-Fairbanks (UAF) includes library and information literacy as an essential component.

Technological advances have improved access to information, providing distance education students with new opportunities for conducting research. This article reviews the literature on library services and instruction for distance learners, describes the development of the core course, and discusses the implementation process. While remote access to electronic resources and services brings distance education students closer to equity, the challenge is providing them with ways of achieving information literacy. The UAF library developed the core course, LS 100, and built it around e-mail, document delivery, reference programs, use of local resources, and remote searching of electronic resources. A textbook with 11 units was written for the course, which has been taught by two faculty. Standardized Student Opinion Instruments (SOI) were administered to the students, but response was low. Those that did respond indicated that they had gained a basic understanding of library research concepts and increased skill in remotely accessing resources and services. M. Kascus.

1994

507. Wilson, Vicky. "Developing the Adult Independent Learner: Information Literacy and the Remote External Student." *Distance Education* 15, no. 2 (1994): 254-78.

With reference to adult learning theory and independent learning, this article examines the development of information literacy skills among adult students in general and external students in particular. A review of the literature on library services for distance learning is used to outline various issues affecting information literacy development in external students, including the quality of distance education, guidelines and standards for library services, user education services, reciprocal borrowing arrangements with other libraries, difficulties experienced by isolated students in accessing library resources, and use of new technologies. To assist isolated students, the author emphasizes that it is essential for information skills training to be integrated into distance education study packages during the design stage. Also, anything done to improve access to collections and document delivery for isolated students will have a significant effect on the provision of information skills training. It is noted that new technologies offer opportunities to improve library access for external students and to integrate information literacy training into educational materials in efficient and cost-effective ways. A. Slade.

1992

508. Harrison, Chris. "Open and Flexible Learning: Information Literacy as a Key Competency." In *Information Literacy: The Australian Agenda: Proceedings of a Conference Conducted by the University of South Australia Library*, edited by Di Booker. Adelaide: University of South Australia Library, 1992, 110-12.

The activities at a workshop on information literacy are outlined in this paper. The objectives of the workshop were to promote understanding of open and flexible learning, identify the skills needed to participate in this type of education, and identify the key competencies associated with information literacy. Through the workshop activities, participants were able to discuss ways to effectively support learners in a flexible learning environment. The following recommendations are offered at the end of the paper: (1) information literacy competencies should be described in terms of learning outcomes, assessment, and performance in curriculum documents; (2) support structures should be established and maintained for flexible learning programs; (3) library staff, lecturers, and course writers should receive some training on information literacy; and (4) information literacy competencies should be incorporated into flexible learning courses. A. Slade.

Web-Based Instruction—General Works

For other works that discuss this topic, see the following heading in the Subject Index: "Web-based instruction—general works."

1999

509. Burns, Elizabeth. *The Classroom vs. the Web: Comparing Two Ways to Teach Web-based Resources*. Paper presented at the ACRL 9th National Conference: Racing Toward Tomorrow: Detroit, Michigan, April 8-11, 1999. Online. Available: http://www.ala.org/acrl/pdfpapers99.html (in pdf format) (Accessed April 13, 2000).

This paper describes research-in-progress at Ohio State University to compare two methods of teaching competency with Web-based resources. Students in a "for credit" library instruction course divided themselves into two groups. One group attended a weekly one-hour class with instructors, while the other group used a Web-based instructional program. Each group was given identical content and projects. The author describes some of the variables and changes that have affected delivery of the course and the results of the study. She acknowledges that she does not have any conclusions to report at this time and indicates that the project will be continued for two more quarters. A. Slade.

510. Dewald, Nancy H. "Transporting Good Library Instruction Practices into the Web Environment: An Analysis of Online Tutorials." *Journal of Academic Librarianship* 25, no. 1 (January 1999): 26-31.

Following an examination of what constitutes good library instruction, the author applies those principles to Web tutorials. To investigate whether online tutorials exhibit the best practices of traditional library instruction, a study was conducted using 20 Web-based tutorials previously selected by the Research Committee of the Library Instruction Round Table of the American Library Association. The findings are discussed in terms of course-related instruction, active learning, collaborative learning, media, objectives, concepts versus mechanics, and help available from librarians. Among the conclusions are that Web-based library tutorials are best used in connection with academic classes rather than in isolation, some form of active and collaborative learning should be included in the tutorials, instructional materials should include graphics as well as text, Web-based instruction should include clear objectives for the students, concepts should be taught as well as the mechanics of searching, and Web-based tutorials should not substitute completely for librarian interaction with students. A. Slade.

511. Dewald, Nancy H. "Web-Based Library Instruction: What Is Good Pedagogy?" *Information Technology and Libraries* 18, no. 1 (March 1999): 26-31.

The application of pedagogical principles to Web-based library instruction is the focus of this paper. In the context of the discussion, Web-based instruction is limited to sites that are interactive and require thoughtful action or feedback by the learner. Following a review of behavioural and cognitive models of learning and their application in a Web environment, pedagogical guidelines for Web-based instruction are examined in terms of learner motivation, organization of library modules, and interactivity for learning and assessment. Web-based library instruction is most effective when students can engage in active learning to create their own understanding of the subject matter. Web elements that can enable librarians to integrate interactivity into instruction include hypertext; frames; CGI-scripting; and newer technologies like Macromedia's Authorware, which allows users to move and manipulate objects on the screen. Examples of best practices in Web-based library instruction are provided in the discussion, and the addresses of these exemplary sites are listed at the end of the paper. A. Slade.

512. Hubble, Ann and Deborah A. Murphy. *The UCSC NetTrail: Web-based Instruction for Online Literacy*. Paper presented at the ACRL 9th National Conference: Racing Toward Tomorrow: Detroit, Michigan, April 8-11, 1999. Online. Available: http://www.ala.org/acrl/pdfpapers99.html (in pdf format) (Accessed April 13, 2000).

At the University of California, Santa Crusz (UCSC), a coalition of librarians, computer center staff, and faculty developed an online literacy course called "The UCSC NetTrail." The objective of the course was to establish a basic level of computer literacy whereby faculty could presume that students are able to make use of online resources without further instruction. A set of four self-paced modules provides students with an introduction to browsing the World Wide Web, using e-mail, connecting with online library resources, using newsgroups, and understanding Web etiquette. NetTrail, which is available as a website, is aimed at users who are new to the online environment or those with differing starting points in terms of initial computer skills and interests. This paper provides information on the usage, evaluation, and continuing development of NetTrail. It is noted that the library module has consistently received the best reviews from users, with even experienced users commenting on its usefulness. A. Slade.

513. O'Hanlon, Nancy and Fred Roecker. *How Students Use Web-based Tutorials and Library Assignments: Case Studies from Ohio State University Libraries*. Paper presented at the ACRL 9th National Conference: Racing Toward Tomorrow: Detroit, Michigan, April 8-11, 1999. Online. Available: http://www.ala.org/acrl/pdfpapers99.html (in pdf format) (Accessed April 13, 2000).

Two online instructional projects have been developed and implemented by Ohio State University (OSU) Libraries. The first, *net.TUTOR*, provides Web-based tutorials on using the Internet for research purposes. Ten interactive lessons focus on basic skills, Internet tools, searching and research skills. A growing number of OSU faculty are using *net.TUTOR* in their courses. The second project delivers a Web-based library assignment to approximately 10,000 first-year students. Hands-on lessons focus on the evaluation of Web resources and on practicing the search skills needed to effectively use online encyclopedias, full-text periodical indexes, and the online catalogue. This paper describes the two instructional projects and reports on data collected from several studies of user behaviour and perceptions of Web-based instruction at OSU. Evaluations from users indicate that both the tutorial program and the online library assignment have proved to be successful. A. Slade.

1998

514. Latta, Gail F., Tracy Bicknell-Holmes, and Sara Martin. "Improving Academic Rigor Through Curriculum Redesign." In *Distance Learning '98: Proceedings of the 14th Annual Conference on Distance Teaching and Learning, August 5-7, 1998, Madison Wisconsin*. Madison, WI: University of Wisconsin-Madison, 1998, 209-16. Also available as ERIC ED 422 861.

A team approach was used at the University of Nebraska-Lincoln to redesign the curriculum of the introductory credit course on library research skills. The course was to be migrated from a self-paced, paper manual to a Web-based multimedia platform. To increase the academic rigor of the course, faculty development was identified as a key component in the redesign process, the aim being to foster the acquisition of multimedia instructional design skills by faculty involved in the project. Information is provided on the goals of curriculum redesign, the steps in the redesign process, and the outcomes of the project. A structured interview with members of the redevelopment team at the end of the project showed that the faculty development goals had, for the most part, been met and the team approach to curriculum redesign had proved effective. A. Slade.

515. Legge, Tiffany and Bruce Reid. "User Education on the Web." *Library Association Record* 100, no. 8 (August 1998): 413-14.

The focus of this article is on sharing user education materials on the Internet. With examples from the EDUCATE Project in Europe, the advantages and constraints of using Web-based library instruction materials are examined. To assess the potential of the Internet for sharing user education materials, an investigation was conducted to determine what materials were currently available on it. From the assessment of the sites found in the study, it was concluded that many of them failed to exploit the full potential of the Internet. Five methods of sharing user education materials on the Internet are identified: (1) providing access to complete courses; (2) creating a website consisting of links to selected resources at other sites; (3) creating a website that provides advice, lesson plans, etc., to help information professionals set up their own user education program; (4) copying selected materials, with permission, and mounting them on a separate site; and (5) using examples of user education on the Internet as models for creating one's own Web-based materials. The advantages and disadvantages of each of these methods are presented in a table at the end of the article. A. Slade.

516. Lombardo, Nancy. "The Internet Navigator: Collaborative Development and Delivery of an Electronic College Course." *PNLA Quarterly* 63, no. 1 (Fall 1998): 12-14.

A one-credit course called "Internet Navigator" was collaboratively developed for delivery via the World Wide Web by a team of librarians from 13 academic libraries in Utah. The course has been offered continuously at eight Utah institutions since 1996. The goals of the project were to implement a model for an electronically delivered course using Internet technology, train students in the use of the Internet, create an interactive learning environment without the restrictions of time and place, and initiate a state-wide electronic reference tool. This paper outlines the forming of the course development team, the curriculum development process, the implementation of "Internet Navigator," and the results achieved. While the course has proved popular with students, many issues remain unresolved, including a mechanism for continuing funding. For a related article, see #530 in this chapter. A. Slade.

517. Nipp, Deanna. "Innovative Use of the Home Page for Library Instruction." *Research Strategies* 16, no. 2 (1998): 93-102.

The process of creating innovative web pages for library instruction is the focus of this article. Competency in the following four areas is required for the effective design of any computer-assisted instruction: content, instructional design, programming, and evaluation. The nine steps in creating automated interactive instruction are (1) reviewing other instructional sites on the Web, (2) providing for the four competencies, (3) writing instructional goals and objectives, (4) determining organizational design, (5) writing the script and developing graphic support for each objective, (6) creating the HTML text and graphic files, (7) evaluating, (8) revising, and (9) re-evaluating. Examples of innovative instruction on the Web and and links to instructional resources are listed, with URLs, in tables within the text of the article. A. Slade.

518. Orr, Debbie, Cathy Duncum, and Margie Wallin. "CHEMPAGE: A Model for Exploring the Internet for Professional Development." *Australian Library Journal* 47, no. 2 (May 1998): 183-89.

A professional development course for chemists, called "CHEMPAGE," has been developed by Central Queensland University (CQU) for delivery via the World Wide Web. The course is intended to be the first of several targeted towards professional groups, and much of the content can be easily adapted to the needs of other disciplines. The aim of "CHEMPAGE" is to teach users how to access, evaluate, and manage electronic resources. Several hands-on activities are incorporated into the course so participants can practice searching for their own sources on the Web. To complement the course, each participant receives a video on information access and two computer-assisted learning (CAL) programs, one on using the CQU catalogue and the other on searching electronic databases. It is hoped that future programs will permit interaction between participants as well as interaction between the student and the tutor. A. Slade.

519. Ragains, Patrick. "Constructing Web Pages for Course-Related Library Instruction: A Business and Government Information Perspective." In *Theory and Practice: Papers and Session Materials Presented at the Twenty-Fifth National*

LOEX Library Instruction Conference Held in Charleston, South Carolina, 8 to 10 May 1997, edited by Linda Shirato and Elizabeth R. Bucciarelli. Library Orientation Series, no. 29. Ann Arbor, MI: Pierian Press, 1998, 73-81.

The focus of this paper is on integrating Web-based information sources into library instruction for business and government information at the University of Nevada, Reno. The advantages of instructional web pages are outlined and their effect on the author's library instruction sessions is described. The need to teach students how to evaluate information found on the World Wide Web is identified as an important component of Web-based library instruction. Several examples of the author's instructional web pages are reproduced in this paper. A. Slade.

520. Sabol, Laurie. "The Value of Student Evaluation of a Website." *Research Strategies* 16, no. 1 (1998): 79-84.

To integrate library instruction into a biology class, librarians at Tufts University, in partnership with the course instructor, created a website to serve as the delivery method for both the instruction and the library assignment. Evaluation was stressed during the second year of the partnership. Details of the evaluation process and anecdotal comments from the students are provided in this article. Over 50% of the students responded to the evaluation form and the majority of comments received were very positive about the Web-based instruction. Negative comments and suggestions for improvement led to some changes in the website in the third year of the partnership. A forthcoming change for the fourth year will be the addition of a more advanced version of the website aimed at high-level biology students. A. Slade.

521. Watson, Bradley C. "OCLC Office of Research Explores Distance Learning." *OCLC Newsletter*, no. 231 (January/February 1998): 22-23.

In 1997, the OCLC Office of Research initiated a project in distance learning, DISLEAP, to learn what roles OCLC might play in supporting libraries in their distance learning functions. DISLEAP has concentrated on Web-based training (WBT) as a means for providing user training capabilities. WBT is defined as training delivered over the Internet using the nonproprietary World Wide Web server and client (Web browser) technology. This report discusses the what, the why, and the how of Web-based training in a general sense, focusing on the advantages of WBT over other means of user training. A. Slade.

1997

522. Andrew, Paige G. and Linda R. Musser. "Collaborative Design of World Wide Web Pages: A Case Study." *Information Technology and Libraries* 16, no. 1 (March 1997): 34-43.

This article details the experiences of two librarians at Pennsylvania State University in redesigning a web page created by a faculty member. The steps in the process involved clarifying the objectives of the web page, determining its target audience, grouping websites by theme, weeding out inactive or inappropriate sites, recommending where annotations would be useful, and improving the aesthetic design of the web page. The authors point out that it is appropriate for librarians to be involved in web page design because they work with websites on a regular basis and have experience in packaging information for their clients. A. Slade.

523. Au, Ka-Neng and Roberta L. Tipton. "Webpages as Courseware: Bibliographic Instruction on the Internet." In *National Online Meeting Proceedings—1997: Proceedings of the 18th National Online Meeting, New York, May 13-15, 1997*, edited by Martha E. Williams. Medford, NJ: Information Today, 1997, 21-25.

Librarians in the John Cotton Dana Library at Rutgers University collaborate with faculty to develop web pages that provide research guidance to students. The web pages are based on course syllabi, teaching notes, and traditional library pathfinders. They serve three functions: teaching outlines for information literacy classes; handouts for students; and access guides to print, online, and Internet resources for specific research needs. At the time of writing, the web pages were used to supplement classroom teaching and to facilitate the reference process after the instruction had been completed. A. Slade.

524. Brandt, D. Scott. "The Multiple Personalities of Delivering Training Via the Web." *Computers in Libraries* 17, no. 8 (September 1997): 51-53.

Delivering training via the World Wide Web is discussed in terms of training resources and tutorials on the Web. Delivering training on the Web has a variety of faces, including non-interactive, lists and resources, interactive tutorials, listservs, e-mail, concepts, and skills. What is suggested here is that educators have been developing ways of delivering education over the Web and that the delivery of training could be developed in the same way. One strategy recommended is to use Web-based course development software packages. What is important is not the variety of personalities that Web training can take, but whether it benefits the learner to use the Web for delivery. M. Kascus.

525. Cameron, Lynn and Lorraine Evans. *Go for the Gold: A Web-Based Instruction Program*. Paper presented at the ACRL 8th National Conference: Choosing Our Futures: Nashville, Tennessee, April 11-14, 1997. Online. Available: http://www. ala.org/acrl/paperhtm/d34.html (Accessed April 13, 2000).

A Web-based instruction program was developed at James Madison University (JMU) to teach information-seeking skills to beginning students. The program comprises 17 instructional modules based on objectives that are part of a competency-based general education curriculum. "Go for the Gold" replaces the self-instruction workbook that had been used by JMU for a decade. While the Web-based program has several advantages over the workbook, evaluations of the program indicate the need for more faculty training in technology skills and assistance in integrating modules into their curricula. M. Kascus.

526. Clay, Sariya, Sallie Harlan, and Judy Swanson. *The Launching Pad: Delivering Information Competence Through the Web*. Paper presented at "The Universe at Your Fingertips: Continuing Web Education" Conference, Santa Barbara, CA, April 25, 1997. 11 pp. ERIC ED 412 907. Also online. Available: http://www. library.ucsb.edu/universe/clay.html (Accessed April 13, 2000).

A multi-campus project was undertaken at California State University (CSU) to develop interactive instructional materials to facilitate the teaching and learning of information competence. The project objectives were to create an information competence course, develop a self-paced course on the World Wide Web, develop classroom presentations using Macromedia Director, identify discipline-specific information competencies, and integrate the course into discipline-related instructional modules. The steps in the process of developing Web-based modules were to (1) determine a list of core competencies to be covered, (2) determine the content of each competency tutorial, (3) develop tutorials as a word processing "storyboard" document, and (4) mount the tutorials on the Web. Also discussed are the maintenance of the tutorial on the Web, the hardware and software used to develop the tutorial, and problems encountered and lessons learned. M. Kascus.

527. Cooper, Eric A. "Library Guides on the Web: Traditional Tenets and Internal Issues." *Computers in Libraries* 17, no. 9 (October 1997): 52-56.

The need for thoughtful preparation of Web-based guides is stressed. The discussion focuses on basic design principles for electronic library guides as well as specific issues these guides present for internal policy making. The same design principles apply to an electronic library guide as for effective access to print guides. However, the guide's content must also anticipate the equipment and knowledge differences inherent in diverse audiences. It may be necessary to prepare more than one version of the guide for different types of audiences. Several helpful HTML websites are identified for guidance on using HTML code in Web documents. An example is given of the HTML code necessary for following the design guidelines as well as an example of how the text would appear on the World Wide Web given these tags. Uniform Resource Locators (URLs) are provided for selected websites helpful in determining color and background design. The policy issues discussed are whether to provide access to the library's online catalogue via the website, solidification of circulation policies, implications for reference service, and responsibilities for Web-based guides. M. Kascus.

528. Cox, Andrew. "Using the World Wide Web for Library User Education: A Review Article." *Journal of Librarianship and Information Science* 29, no. 1 (March 1997): 39-43.

This review article explores the potential of the World Wide Web for library user education and training, focusing on websites produced in the United States. By way of introduction, the author discusses the hypertext protocol underlying the Web and its application to the creation of computer-assisted learning (CAL) packages. The websites for library user education reviewed are the Research Center (Houston Community College System), Library Research at Cornell: a hypertext guide (Cornell University), Virtual Library Tutor (University of Delaware), and the Information Literacy Program (University of Wisconsin-Parkside). Full URLs are given for all websites and products. There is also a list of URLs for those who want to keep current with CAL applications in libraries. M. Kascus.

529. Graff, Rebecca, Pam Proctor, Yu-Chin Chang, and Kay Schwartz. *Library User Instruction on the World Wide Web*. 1997. Online. Available: http://www-personal. umich.edu/~kschwart/ed601/library.htm (Accessed April 13, 2000).

This website contains a paper titled "Bibliographic Instruction (BI): Yesterday and Today" and an analysis of two Web-based instructional resources. The paper examines library instruction in terms of its history, current issues, why it should be offered, the advantages and disadvantages of Web-based instruction, and its relationship to information literacy. The two Web-based resources reviewed are the University of Wisconsin-Parkside Information Literacy Program and Ohio State University's Gateway to Information. A list of information literacy standards is provided in an appendix. These standards are based on criteria from the American Association of School Librarians (AASL), the Association for Educational Communications and Technology (AECT), and the Association of College and Research Libraries (ACRL), as well as input from individual bibliographic instruction librarians. A. Slade.

530.   Hansen, Carol and Nancy Lombardo. "Toward the Virtual University: Collaborative Development of a Web-Based Course." *Research Strategies* 15, no. 2 (Spring 1997): 68-79.

A Web-based credit course on Internet use was developed as a collaborative project of ten colleges and universities in Utah. The course emphasizes information literacy skills and the critical evaluation of Web resources rather than the mechanics of Internet use. The self-paced, independent study course consists of five modules and one optional module. A final project requires students to produce a web page representing the five best resources located on their individual topic. The course has been offered simultaneously at all ten institutions since 1996. Details are provided on the course development process, the purpose of the course and its content, student/faculty interaction, the collaborative model, bureaucratic and political issues affecting the course, and future prospects for Web-based courses. For a related article, see #516 in this chapter. A. Slade.

531.   Jayne, Elaine and Patricia Vander Meer. "The Library's Role in Academic Instructional Use of the World Wide Web." *Research Strategies* 15, no. 3 (1997): 123-50.

Following discussions on the benefits of the World Wide Web for students and faculty, the authors suggest a new service role for librarians that involves collaborating with computing center personnel to teach faculty about instructional uses of the Web. The rationale for collaboration between libraries and computing centers is examined and suggestions are offered for a collaborative instructional program. The suggestions for a successful program include obtaining political support and identifying the relevant stakeholders in the planning process, knowing one's audience, scheduling activities in accordance with faculty needs, selecting appropriate content for the sessions, and developing a mechanism for evaluation and feedback. A checklist of criteria is provided to assist librarians in choosing sites for demonstration to faculty and to help faculty plan the construction of their own web pages. An appendix lists a sample of websites useful for demonstrating university instructional applications. Examples of interactive assignments are also included. A. Slade.

532.   Khan, Badrul H. *Web-Based Instruction*. Englewood Cliffs, NJ: Educational Technology Publications, 1997. 463 pp. ISBN 0-87778-296-2.

The topic of Web-based instruction is examined from a variety of educational and instructional perspectives. The book's 59 chapters are divided into five sections: (1) "Introduction to Web-Based Instruction," (2) "Web-Based Learning

Environments and Critical Issues," (3) "Designing Web-Based Instruction," (4) "Delivering Web-Based Instruction," and (5) "Case Studies of Web-Based Courses." Distance learning is the focus of four chapters. While there is no significant discussion of the role of libraries in Web-based instruction, some of the information in this book will be relevant for librarians who are involved in designing or delivering instruction via the World Wide Web. A. Slade.

533. Martin, Lyn Elizabeth M., ed. *The Challenge of Internet Literacy: The Instruction-Web Convergence*. New York: Haworth Press, 1997. 254 pp. ISBN 0-7890-0346-5.

Eighteen papers about bibliographic instruction and the Internet are contained in this compilation. The topics covered include Web-based instruction, information literacy in the context of the Web, online research strategies, and teaching conceptual frameworks to users. Web addresses are provided and a selected bibliography of resources for Internet trainers is included. A. Slade.

534. Still, Julie M., ed. *The Library Web*. Medford, NJ: Information Today, 1997. 221 pp. ISBN 1-57387-034-X.

The focus of this monograph is on designing, creating, and maintaining library web pages. Nineteen case studies are divided into three sections: (1) "Academic Library Websites"; (2) "Special and Public Library Websites"; and (3) "Instructional Materials, Unique Resources, and Commercial Design." The first two sections provide examples of web pages at specific institutions and libraries, including University of Saskatchewan, Christopher Newport University, University College London, University of Southern Mississippi, Stanford University Medical Library, and Western Illinois University. The third section covers topics such as instructional materials and handouts on the Web, development of a library research tutorial, and subject-oriented library web pages. A. Slade.

1996

535. Scholz, Ann Margaret, Richard Cary Kerr, and Samuel Keith Brown. "PLUTO: Interactive Instruction on the Web." *College & Research Libraries News* 57, no. 6 (June 1996): 346-49.

Purdue University has developed an online orientation program called PLUTO (Purdue Libraries Undergraduate Tutorial Online). This is an interactive, learner-centered World Wide Web information literacy model. In planning for PLUTO, several learning objectives were established: to define and formulate keyword searching in a given topic, to retrieve information on a given topic from the online catalogue, and to locate information from the online catalogue within the Purdue Libraries system. Program requirements were identified after these objectives were established. The PLUTO program comprises a tutorial and two quizzes. Future plans are to revise and refine the program for a wider audience and to add other instructional modules. M. Kascus.

536. Sloan, Steve. "The Virtual Pathfinder: A World Wide Web Guide to Library Research." *Computers in Libraries* 16, no. 4 (April 1996): 53-54.

The University of New Brunswick (UNB) is relying more on information technologies to disseminate information. To this end, librarians have designed a Web-based Virtual Pathfinder as a guide to library research. This article discusses the process of designing for the World Wide Web, noting that a well-designed pathfinder should be automatically updated, contain hypertext links to additional resources, and link to information available on the Internet. The resources needed for building virtual pathfinders are the Z39.50 gateway and the pathfinder Perl program. URLs are given for these resources. Three enhancements were made to the original Virtual Pathfinder: to allow some pathfinders to display the choice of retrieving more pathfinders, to have the program search for "non-virtual" Web documents before constructing a pathfinder, and to allow users to construct their own pathfinder. The Virtual Pathfinder has been well received by librarians, and transaction logs show that students are using it. Some strengths and weaknesses of virtual pathfinders are indicated. M. Kascus.

537. Tate, Marsha and Jan Alexander. "Teaching Critical Evaluation Skills for World Wide Web Resources." *Computers in Libraries* 16, no. 10 (November/December 1996): 49-55.

One of the problems associated with the World Wide Web as a research tool is the need to determine the quality of the information found. A three-part lesson plan is given to teach students critical evaluation skills for using Web resources. Part One presents background information needed to evaluate sources, including examples that illustrate how to evaluate both print and Web-based sources. Five criteria traditionally used to evaluate print resources (accuracy, authority, objectivity, currency, coverage) are given and discussed as they relate to web page evaluation. Seven evaluation challenges unique to the Web, with no equivalent in the print world, are discussed: (1) marketing-oriented web pages; (2) pages blending entertainment, information, and advertising; (3) hypertext links; (4) software requirements; (5) search engine retrieval; (6) instability of websites; and (7) susceptibility to alteration. Part Two introduces a practical approach to evaluating Web resources based on the concept of page-specific checklists using the five criteria traditionally used to evaluate print materials. Part Three requires students to practice evaluating web pages using these checklists. M. Kascus.

538. Turner, Diane J. "Incorporating the WWW into Instruction: Some Considerations." *Colorado Libraries* 22, no. 4 (Winter 1996): 42-43.

The author discusses some of her concerns about incorporating the World Wide Web into library instruction. A library home page that provides links to valuable resources is recommended as a good teaching tool. One of the more difficult challenges in teaching students about the World Wide Web is that it lacks bibliographic control. Two problems that make Internet instruction difficult are site instability and availability during the day. One suggestion is that faculty need to be encouraged to relinquish class time for an instruction session dedicated to Internet resources. The author recommends using one of the many useful guides to the Internet rather than recreating the wheel. M. Kascus.

539. Whitley, Katherine M. *Instruction on the Web: Authoring Tutorials in HTML*. Paper presented at Untangling The Web, the University Center, University of California, Santa Barbara, April 26, 1996. Online. Available: http://www.library. ucsb.edu/untangle/whitley.html (Accessed April 13, 2000).

Librarians at the University of California, San Diego, have taken advantage of the instructional possibilities of the World Wide Web to reach users at their own workstations. Two tutorials authored in HTML have been developed. One tutorial is an introduction to Netscape for beginners that covers strategies for finding information on the Web. The other tutorial is an in-depth guide to the Compendex online database. Design concerns and helpful hints are provided from the authoring experience. A view is given of technology advances anticipated in the future. M. Kascus.

540. Wilson, Katie, Heather Cooper, and Dianne Southwell. "World Wide Web Walkabout: A Subject-Oriented Program for Teaching and Learning the Internet." In *AusWeb 96: Landscaping the Web: Proceedings of AusWeb 96, the Second Australian World Wide Web Conference, Gold Coast, Queensland, 7-9 July 1996*, edited by Roger Debreceny and Allan Ellis. Lismore, NSW: Southern Cross University Press, 1996, 215-18.

Macquarie University Library in Australia has developed an Internet training program called World Wide Web Walkabout, which can be used on an independent basis or as part of classroom instruction. This Web-based program offers two approaches to teaching and learning the Internet: by subject and by Internet tool or protocol. The program is modular and uses live hypertext links in a range of subject areas. One of the main advantages of World Wide Web Walkabout is its accessibility to off-campus users and open learning students. Information is provided on the background of the program, the development process, design considerations, applications and uses, evaluation and feedback, and maintenance and support. Relevant URLs are listed at the end of the paper. A. Slade.

1995

541. Alberico, Ralph and Elizabeth A. Dupuis. *The World Wide Web as an Instructional Medium*. A paper originally presented at the 1995 LOEX Conference. Online. Available: http://staff.lib.utexas.edu/~beth/LOEX/ (Accessed April 13, 2000).

This paper explores the use of the World Wide Web as an instructional medium. At the University of Texas at Austin (UTA), the World Wide Web is being used for course-integrated sessions and general workshops. For course-integrated sessions, web pages are used to organize electronic resources in a given subject area and to provide an outline for the class. The approach to teaching networked resources is described in detail, as are the advantages and disadvantages of using web pages for instruction. Among the ways in which UTA is using web pages for instruction are tutorials on the Internet, pathfinders created for specific classes, and personal research pages designed by the students themselves to help them with their research. The conclusion is that web pages have a definite role to play in library instruction and information literacy. M. Kascus.

Web-Based Instruction for Distance Learners

For other works that discuss this topic, see the following heading in the Subject Index: "Web-based instruction—for distance learners."

1998

542. Adams, Chris. "A Web Handbook for Library Research." In *The Eighth Off-Campus Library Services Conference Proceedings: Providence, Rhode Island, April 22-24, 1998*, compiled by P. Steven Thomas and Maryhelen Jones. Mount Pleasant, MI: Central Michigan University, 1998, 1-16.

This paper reports on a multimedia project for providing library research skills to students via the Internet at the University of Saskatchewan Libraries. The project, which resulted in the online *U-Study Virtual Library Handbook*, required preparation of about 50 web pages of material, the creation of five audio-visual video clips, and the use of computer-mediated conferencing software. A description of the design parameters for the project is included. The "Main Contents" or "Informational Page" gives users the noteworthy features, including planning course work or research, how to search, applying critical thinking, how to request material, and planning and writing. A "Table of Contents" frame redirects users to the key topics contained in the main "Contents" or "Informational" pages. An index frame works similarly to a back-of-the-book index. The project budget and costs are provided in the appendices. M. Kascus.

543. Grealy, Deborah S. "Web-Based Learning: Electronic Library Resources and Instruction." In *Distance Learning '98: Proceedings of the 14th Annual Conference on Distance Teaching and Learning, August 5-7, 1998, Madison Wisconsin*. Madison, WI: University of Wisconsin-Madison, 1998, 133-37. Also available as ERIC ED 422 851.

To train remote users how to effectively use electronic library materials, the University of Denver Library received a grant to create Web-based instructional materials. The immediate objective of the project was to provide instructional support to the faculty and staff involved in a first-year course that teaches basic library and research skills. The longer-term goal was to prepare curricular and research support tools to help students critically evaluate paper and electronic information resources and to mount these materials on the library's home page so they can be accessed on demand from any location. The project has benefited the university's off-campus students, who are now able to access online bibliographic assistance at any time of the day or night. The web pages include instructions on the use of the online catalogue and specific databases, information on how to evaluate search results, a list of frequently asked questions, a glossary, annotated guides to discipline-specific research literature, and links to system and vendor-based help pages. Various evaluation methods are being used to measure and report on the effectiveness of the Web-based training project. A. Slade.

544. Jayne, Elaine Anderson, Judith M. Arnold, and Patricia Fravel Vander Meer. "Casting a Broad Net: The Use of Web-Based Tutorials for Library Instruction." In *The Eighth Off-Campus Library Services Conference Proceedings: Providence, Rhode Island, April 22-24, 1998*, compiled by P. Steven Thomas and Maryhelen Jones. Mount Pleasant, MI: Central Michigan University, 1998, 197-205.

This case study focuses on Western Michigan University's experience in planning, creating, and testing two Web-mounted tutorials for library instruction. The tutorials chosen were a basic tutorial whose primary audience is non-traditional adult students and a subject-specific tutorial for upper division majors. The basic tutorial demonstrates how to find books and articles. The subject-specific tutorial evolved out of the need for advanced instruction in the discipline of criminology and is the model for future discipline-based tutorials. Both tutorials are discussed in detail. Also discussed are the following aspects of creating a Web-based tutorial: planning, development, implementation, and evaluation. According to the authors, the experience gained in developing the original tutorial greatly facilitated the process of planning for additional tutorials. M. Kascus.

545. Loven, Bridget, Kevin Morgan, Julia Shaw-Kokot, and Lynn Eades. "Information Skills for Distance Learning." *Medical Reference Services Quarterly* 17, no. 3 (Fall 1998): 71-75.

In 1997, the University of North Carolina at Chapel Hill, Health Sciences Library developed six Web-based tutorials designed to teach information skills to students on campus and in distance education programs. The modules covered (1) searching bibliographic databases, (2) selecting bibliographic formatting software, (3) using the Internet as a research tool, (4) researching health legislation, (5) finding health statistics, and (6) guidelines for writing academic papers. The designers of the modules decided to go beyond HTML and utilize the multimedia capabilities of the World Wide Web. The software used included Director, a CD-ROM authoring package, and Shockwave, its Web browser plug-in. The article describes the implementation of the project, the problems with the Director package, the users' experiences with the modules, and the lessons learned in creating a virtual learning module. A. Slade.

546. Parise, Pierina. "Information Power Goes Online: Teaching Information Literacy to Distance Learners." *Reference Services Review* 26, nos. 3-4 (1998): 51-52, 60.

Marylhurst University converted its three-credit course, "Information Power: Accessing, Assessing, and Acting on Information in an Era of Overload," into an online format for distance learners, using WebCT course management software. The author describes the features of the WebCT software, the specific components of the class, and the measurement of the learning outcomes. The challenges encountered by the author include formulating class and lecture notes into web pages, designing assignments to enable students to practice the skills learned, and determining how assignments could be transmitted in a way that they can be evaluated. Based on her experience with this online class, the author discusses the advantages and disadvantages of Web-based instruction. On the positive side, students can work at their own pace and take responsibility for their education. On the negative side, the class can be time-consuming for the instructor and the mechanics of the course can detract from the content, especially at the beginning. A. Slade.

547.   Prestamo, Anne Tubbs. "Development of Web-Based Tutorials for Online Data-
       bases." In *National Online Meeting Proceedings—1998: Proceedings of the
       19th National Online Meeting, New York, May 12-14, 1998*, edited by Martha E.
       Williams. Medford, NJ: Information Today, 1998, 275-87. Abridged version in
       Issues in Science and Technology Librarianship, no. 17 (Winter 1998). Online.
       Available: http://www.library.ucsb.edu/istl/98-winter/article3.html (Accessed April
       13, 2000).

       To provide bibliographic instruction to remote users of the ProQuest Direct
       database, Oklahoma State University Library developed an interactive, Web-
       based tutorial. A need for remotely accessible bibliographic instruction materials
       covering a variety of electronic databases had already been identified, and Pro-
       Quest Direct was selected as a prototype for future development due to its high
       use and Web-based interface. The instructional design of the tutorial is described,
       outlining use of the Jones/Li/Merrill ID_2 Model, local implementation of the
       model, and the formative evaluation conducted during the design process. A.
       Slade.

548.   Sedam, Rebecca E. and Jerilyn Marshall. "Course-Specific World Wide Web
       Pages: Evolution of an Extended Campus Library Instruction Service." In *The
       Eighth Off-Campus Library Services Conference Proceedings: Providence,
       Rhode Island, April 22-24, 1998*, compiled by P. Steven Thomas and Maryhelen
       Jones. Mount Pleasant, MI: Central Michigan University, 1998, 251-58.

       This paper describes the Class and Academic Web Pages Project, developed
       as part of a course-integrated user instruction program for adult evening students
       at Northwestern University. The project was intended to enhance students' ability
       to conduct effective research from remote sites as well as in the extended campus
       library. Course-specific web pages link to library services and sources, syllabi,
       class projects, and relevant resource collections. Elements considered important
       to the success of the project are standardization of web page templates, develop-
       ment of guidelines for Internet resource selection, and collaboration with faculty.
       Marketing and publicizing the service have been part of the outreach effort. The
       library has collaborated with the University College Faculty Development Coor-
       dinator to create a faculty service to generate interest in the integration of elec-
       tronic technology such as the World Wide Web into this course. The authors note
       that the Class and Academic Web Pages are not a substitute for personal contact
       between student and librarian. M. Kascus.

1997

---

549.   Barton, Mary Ann. "Collaboration: Teaching Faculty and Librarians." *College &
       Research Libraries News* 58, no. 6 (June 1997): 390.

       This brief report from ACRL's 8th National Conference in Nashville de-
       scribes collaboration between teaching faculty and librarians at Lesley College in
       creating a library research workshop for a required graduate level course. Web
       pages were developed for presentation of this library research workshop to pre-
       pare students for computerized research. M. Kascus.

550. Bing, JoAnn, Susanne Flannelly, Jessica Goodwin, and Michael T. Hutton. *An Analysis of Web-Based Bibliographic Instruction*. A paper presented to the Ed.D. Program in Instructional Technology and Distance Education in partial fulfillment of the Requirements for the Degree of Doctor of Education, Nova Southeastern University, August 1997. Online. Available: http://www.fcae.nova.edu/~huttonm/isd3.html (Accessed April 13, 2000).

Findings from curricula analysis of Web-based bibliographic instruction at Valdosta State University, University of Delaware, Emerson College, Virginia Tech University, and Houston Community College System are presented. The analysis team consisted of four distance education graduate students who rated the websites according to the following criteria: goals and objectives, learning environment, access, content, technological media, and feedback. In assessing the effectiveness of program design at their first choice, Houston Community College System, the measurement criteria used were usage of the course elements and student satisfaction. The instructional design process emphasizes the variety of learner characteristics as a priority in creating learning opportunities for distance learners. M. Kascus.

551. Warner, Elizabeth R., Michael D. Hamlin, Anthony Frisby, Christopher Braster, and Sharon Lezotte. "World Wide Web Tutorials for Teaching Online Searching in Distance and Individual-Learning Environments." In *National Online Meeting Proceedings—1997: Proceedings of the 18th National Online Meeting, New York, May 13-15, 1997*, edited by Martha E. Williams. Medford, NJ: Information Today, 1997, 357-68.

At Thomas Jefferson University in Philadelphia, a team approach is used to develop case-based multimedia learning materials for teaching knowledge management strategies and online searching techniques to students. The program is based on learning principles derived from research in cognitive psychology. The team typically includes librarians, instructional designers, database and Web programmers, and media designers. These collaborators combine multimedia, World Wide Web, and database technology to produce online courses. The courses consist of pre- and post-tests to determine students' baseline skills, a case study of an academic topic, self-assessment quizzes followed by tutorials on the various databases, and interfacing to Oracle databases for record keeping. As part of each course, students are asked to evaluate aspects of the program using online forms. A. Slade.

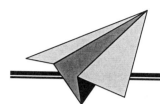

CHAPTER 7

Interlibrary Cooperation

This chapter includes works that focus on cooperation between libraries generally and cooperation between different types of libraries. For access to other works that pertain to interlibrary cooperation, see the following headings in the Subject Index: "agreements (formal) between libraries," "collection development—cooperation," "collections, shared," "consortia," "extended campuses—cooperation," "interlibrary loans," "reciprocal borrowing," "resource sharing," and "unaffiliated libraries."

General

For other general works that discuss this topic, see the following heading in the Subject Index: "interlibrary cooperation."

1998

552. Burdick, Tracey. "One State's Approach: The Florida Distance Learning Library Initiative." *Journal of Library Services for Distance Education* 1, no. 2 (June 1998). Online. Available: http://www.westga.edu/~library/jlsde/vol1/2/TBurdick. html (Accessed April 13, 2000).

The Florida Distance Learning Library Initiative (FDLLI) is a cooperative effort of the Community College System, the State University System, and the State Library of Florida. The main purpose of the initiative is to provide cost-effective expanded access to library services, building on existing strengths and cooperation of Florida's libraries. Five components have been funded: access to electronic resources, reference and referral services, library user training, borrowing privileges, and document delivery. Two additional components to be added later are electronic reserve materials and access to equipment. The most active and visible of the components is access to electronic resources, including OCLC's FirstSearch service. The importance of ongoing assessment and revision of services is stressed in meeting the changing needs of distance learning programs. M. Kascus.

553. Madaus, J. Richard. "The Florida Distance Learning Library Initiative: Realizing That Technology is Only Part of the Answer." In *Distance Education in a Print and Electronic World: Emerging Roles for Libraries: Proceedings of the OCLC Symposium, ALA Midwinter Conference 1998, New Orleans, LA, January 9, 1998*. Dublin, OH: OCLC Online Computer Library Center, Inc., 1998, 6-10. Also online. Available: http://purl.oclc.org/oclc/distance-1998 (Accessed April 13, 2000).

The author first points out that the expanding print and digital information economies complicate the issues in supporting distance learning. He then discusses Florida's working model, which attempts to address these issues in a comprehensive way. In the Florida Distance Learning Library Initiative, public libraries and academic libraries are partners. Five service modules make up this initiative: reference and referral services, library user training, document delivery, borrowing privileges, and electronic resources. Each component in this comprehensive model is discussed in detail. Electronic resources are the most costly of the five modules, but this cooperative effort is still cost-effective in maximizing statewide resource sharing with reduced duplication of effort. The distance learner benefits by ease of access to a standard set of electronic resources available at the nearest library. The five-year projected funding plan is discussed. Several websites are listed for additional information concerning both the library distance education activities and the general distance education climate in Florida. For a related paper, see item #554 below. M. Kascus.

554. Madaus, J. Richard and Lawrence Webster. "Opening the Door to Distance Learning." *Computers in Libraries* 18, no. 5 (May 1998): 51-55.

In Florida, the library community has assumed full responsibility in the development of public postsecondary distance learning and has provided a solution to making print and electronic resources and services available to the distance learner. Florida's history of statewide library cooperation and resource sharing through six regional multitype library cooperatives has facilitated ongoing collaboration and communication among libraries of all types. The Florida Distance Learning Library Initiative is a comprehensive model of library support that began in 1997. This initiative has five components: (1) reference and referral services, (2) library user training, (3) document delivery, (4) expanded borrowing privileges, and (5) electronic resources. The author stresses the need "to solidify the perception of the library as a provider of unique services in an age of technology in which people believe everything the distance learner might need is free and online." For a related paper, see item #553 above. M. Kascus.

1997

555. Dugan, Robert E. "Distance Education: Provider and Victim Libraries." *Journal of Academic Librarianship* 23, no. 4 (July 1997): 315-18.

In this opinion piece, the author discusses distance education from the perspective of its challenge to academic libraries and their management. The academic library whose institution is responsible for the distance education program is referred to as the "provider" library, while the non-affiliated library is referred to as the "victim" library. The two issues discussed are (1) the logistics of providing library service at the extended campus, including responding to student requests; and (2) meeting the distance education student's need for library instruction. Some libraries have contracted with other libraries to provide library services to their distance education students, and compensation is provided through a formal written agreement. The position here is that because some "provider" libraries are not adequately servicing their distance education students as expected in the ACRL Guidelines, "victim" libraries need to develop a written information policy. Such a policy would specify if and to what extent the library would directly provide assistance and material to unaffiliated students in distance education programs. M. Kascus.

1996

556. Jagannathan, Neela. "Library and Information Services for Distance Learners." *Resource Sharing and Information Networks* 11, nos. 1/2 (1996): 159-70.

The topic of library services for distance learners is considered in relation to the development of distance education in India and the structure of Indian open universities. Three needs of distance learners are identified: materials and facilities, information services, and user services. The provision of library services to distance learners is briefly examined in an international perspective and then discussed in the context of the problems encountered by Indian open universities. It is advocated that libraries of all types focus on supporting distance learners through use of information technologies, networking, and resource sharing in areas such as collections, personnel, finances, infrastructure facilities, and equipment. A. Slade.

1995

557. Brophy, Peter and Alan Macdougall. "A Seamless Service: Libraries, Learners, Materials and Users: Co-operative Tactics and Planning the Future of Library Service Delivery in Europe." In *Proceedings of the First "Libraries Without Walls" Conference, Mytilene, Greece, 9-10 September 1995*, edited by Ann Irving and Geoff Butters. Preston, UK: Centre for Research in Library and Information Management, University of Central Lancashire, 1995, 71-72.

Those attending the first "Libraries Without Walls" conference stressed the need for partnerships and other collaborative actions to help develop better library services for distant library users. The kinds of cooperative activities discussed include sharing experiences, identifying good practice, discussing problems, exchanging information on technology standards, transfer abilities, cooperative projects across Europe, and cooperation with the rest of the world. Among the practical actions delegates to the conference were urged to consider were regular conferences, e-mail communication, a website, acting as partners, and establishing an association. The conference supported a proposal for an Association for the Delivery of Library Services in Europe (ADELISE). M. Kascus.

558.   Clark, Linda M. and Phil Tullar. *Three Government Entities Collaborate to Build a Satellite Community College Campus in Northern Arizona: Working Together to Create a "One-Stop Learning Center."* Flagstaff, AZ: Coconino Community College, 1995. 25 pp. ERIC ED 395 618.

Coconino Community College (CCC), Northern Arizona University (NAU), and the city of Page are cooperating to provide library services to a remote community in northern Arizona. In this collaborative effort, the city donated the land to create a CCC satellite campus in Page, NAU is installing its computerized database, and CCC is constructing the library building. These three government entities are working together to provide "a one-stop learning center." A report of the educational specifications for the campus and the intergovernmental agreement between the CCC district and the city of Page are included in the appendices. M. Kascus.

559.   Salvesen, Helge. "Co-operation in Library Services for Distance and Decentralised Education in Norway." In *Proceedings of the First "Libraries Without Walls" Conference, Mytilene, Greece, 9-10 September 1995*, edited by Ann Irving and Geoff Butters. Preston, UK: Centre for Research in Library and Information Management, University of Central Lancashire, 1995, 62-66.

This paper reports on the role of libraries in open learning in Norway. An effort to improve access and services for distance students began with the establishment of a committee of representatives from public libraries, academic libraries, and their national planning, research, and policy making institutions. One of the objectives was to assess the need for decentralized library services and evaluate the alternative approaches to satisfying the literature needs of the distance students. M. Kascus.

560.   Schafer, Steven A. "Northern Alberta Library and Information Network (NORALINK): Challenges and Highlights of a Collaborative Initiative." In *The Seventh Off-Campus Library Services Conference Proceedings: San Diego, California, October 25-27, 1995*, compiled by Carol J. Jacob. Mount Pleasant, MI: Central Michigan University, 1995, 335-40.

NORALINK, the Northern Alberta Library and Information Network, is described. Participating libraries included Keyano College, Grande Prairie Regional College, Grande Prairie Public Library, Lakeland College, Alberta Vocational College, University of Alberta (U of A), and Athabasca University (AU). The agreement focused on reference assistance, reciprocal borrowing privileges, and individual service for all students. For staffing purposes, each NORALINK library other than Athabasca University participated using existing staff. The service was promoted via a letter to the students outlining the service and the location of the NORALINK office. The services provided by the NORALINK Office included online access to the AU library collections, online access to journal indexes, instruction in the use of CD-ROM databases, and shared use of U of A institutional borrower's cards. Comments from a sampling of students using the service were generally positive. After the pilot project was completed, the office was closed because of the small number of students using the service. However, the spirit of cooperation remains. M. Kascus.

| **1990** |
---

561. Binder, Michael, Harley Brooks, and James Hyatt. "Service to Off-Campus Students Using Telefacsimile." In *Convergence: Proceedings of the Second National Conference of the Library and Information Technology Association, October 2-6, 1988, Boston*, edited by Michael Gorman. Chicago: American Library Association, 1990, 202-4.

As a result of an administrative request, the director of the libraries at Western Kentucky University (WKU) was asked to develop a plan to provide more effective library services to off-campus students. The task force appointed in 1987 proposed various elements: cooperation with the public library; use of the high school library after hours; and the use of courier, mail, and telefacsimile for document delivery. A central part of the plan for the full-service program offered at Glasgow and Owensboro has been fax. Fax use was heavy during the first semester, with 40% of all article delivery done by fax. The knowledge and experience gained from the university's success in applying fax to meet the needs of its off-campus students enabled WKU to take the lead in the development of a telefacsimile library network for the eight state universities of Kentucky. M. Kascus.

Cooperation Among Academic Libraries

For other works that discuss this topic, see the following heading in the Subject Index: "interlibrary cooperation—among academic libraries."

| **1999** |
---

562. Davis, Mary Ellen. "News from the Field: Statewide Reciprocal Borrowing and Document Delivery Come to Florida." *College & Research Libraries News* 60, no. 3 (March 1999): 157.

As part of Florida's Distance Learning Library Initiative (DLLI), a reciprocal borrowing agreement has been endorsed by 28 community colleges and 10 public universities in the state. The agreement, which went into effect in December 1998, enables students to freely borrow materials from the libraries of any of the participating colleges or universities. The DLLI, in its second year of operation, has provided several statewide initiatives to enhance library services for distance education, including coordination of the acquisition of electronic resources such as Britannica Online and 60 OCLC FirstSearch databases, coordination of a courier service, and support of a reference and referral center for distance learners. A. Slade.

1998

563.   Barsun, Rita. "Walden University and Indiana University: Unlikely Partners Providing Services to Off-Campus Students." In *The Eighth Off-Campus Library Services Conference Proceedings: Providence, Rhode Island, April 22-24, 1998*, compiled by P. Steven Thomas and Maryhelen Jones. Mount Pleasant, MI: Central Michigan University, 1998, 17-28.

A formal agreement between Walden University and Indiana University—Bloomington provides library services for Walden students. A history of the relationship between these institutions is given along with the provisions of their written contract. The services offered by Walden University are year-round and include (1) reference assistance; (2) computer-based bibliographic and information services; (3) access to institutional and other networks, including the Internet; (4) consultation services; (5) a program of library user instruction; (6) assistance with non-print media and equipment; (7) reciprocal or contract borrowing; (8) document delivery service; (9) access to reserve materials; (10) adequate service hours; and (11) promotion of library services. The costs and benefits to both institutions are explained. M. Kascus.

564.   Duesing, Ann. "Outreach Information Services Partnership: An Academic Health Science Center and a Rural Satellite Campus." In *The Eighth Off-Campus Library Services Conference Proceedings: Providence, Rhode Island, April 22-24, 1998*, compiled by P. Steven Thomas and Maryhelen Jones. Mount Pleasant, MI: Central Michigan University, 1998, 139-45.

An outreach information service partnership between the University of Virginia (UVA) and Clinch Valley College (CVC) in Southwest Virginia is described in this paper. The authors discuss the design of the outreach program, the contributions of both institutions, and the implementation process. The outreach model has been developed along four fronts: (1) working with information services already available in the communities, including hospital, academic, and public; (2) promoting and enhancing information resources, services, and training for UVA preceptors and other allied health professionals in Southwest Virginia; (3) working with the Southwest Virginia Area Health Education Center (AHEC); and (4) developing regional network relations to support health care information and services for people of Southwest Virginia. The success of the UVA and CVC partnership has resulted in a strong outreach program, as measured by continued relationships, positive evaluations, and increased demand for information services. M. Kascus.

565.   Gilmer, Lois C. "Writing Formal Documents for Program Planning and Development." In *The Eighth Off-Campus Library Services Conference Proceedings: Providence, Rhode Island, April 22-24, 1998*, compiled by P. Steven Thomas and Maryhelen Jones. Mount Pleasant, MI: Central Michigan University, 1998, 159-63.

This is a case study of the process used to complete a formal memorandum of understanding between the University of West Florida at Walton Beach and Okaloosa-Walton Junior College. This cooperative endeavor includes a reciprocal borrowing agreement, an agreement for interchanging library cards, and the memorandum of understanding. In all instances, policies and procedures are clearly delineated. The memorandum of understanding has a provision for amending the document and/or terminating the partnership. If the partnership ceases to exist, the collections, equipment, and furnishings placed in the joint use library will be reclaimed by the supplying institution. Written agreements are an important means to avoid misunderstanding when policies or procedures change due to circumstances or change in personnel. M. Kascus.

566. Scepanski, Jordan M. and Barbara von Wahlde. "Megasystem Collaboration: Cross-Continent Consortial Cooperation." *Information Technology and Libraries* 17, no. 1 (March 1998): 30-35.

The Consortium for Electronic Technology for University Systems (CETUS) includes three major universities: California State University (CSU), City University of New York (CUNY), and State University of New York (SUNY). This article outlines the formation, current issues, and future of CETUS. The consortium established four working groups to investigate specific issues: the changing roles of library staff, copyright, acquisition of scholarly and instructional materials, and library services for distance learning. The aim of the latter group was to determine institutional standards for supporting distance education. The group began its activity by identifying existing library programs in California and New York and selected several of them, along with some in other states, for further analysis. This project resulted in a report that suggested means for developing and endorsing standards and guidelines for library services to distance learners. The twelve principles of library services delineated by the working group are listed in this article. For the full report from CETUS, see #240 in this volume. A. Slade.

1996

567. Association of Atlantic Universities Librarians Council. *Library Support for Distant Learners: A Report to the Association of Atlantic Universities Librarians Council, July 18, 1996*. Online. Available: http://libmain.stfx.ca/rita/aaulc.htm (Accessed April 13, 2000).

Each of the four Atlantic provinces in Canada has cooperative ventures in distance education. This report, prepared by the Distance Education Committee of the Association of Atlantic Universities Librarians Council (AAULC), recommends strategies for improving library services to distance learners in New Brunswick, Nova Scotia, Prince Edward Island, and Newfoundland. The Canadian Guidelines for Library Support of Distance Learning in Canada form the basis for the recommendations in this report, which include strategies for identifying course requirements, library resources, student skills, and communication issues. Strategies for cooperative library support involve the sharing of databases and electronic resources, use of a Web-based information system called ALIS (Atlantic Provinces Information Services), research initiatives for grant funding, and a fee-based reciprocal borrowing/electronic access scheme. The report concludes by recommending the formation of working groups to coordinate efforts for achieving the goals identified by the Committee in the areas of standards, services, resources, ALIS development, and funding. A. Slade.

568. Brophy, Peter. "Resourcing the Learning Experience." In *Further and Higher Education Partnerships: The Future for Collaboration*, edited by Mike Abramson, John Bird, and Anne Stennett. Buckingham, UK: Society for Research into Higher Education and Open University Press, 1996, 46-57.

Issues having an impact on the provision of library services in partnerships between further and higher education institutions in the United Kingdom are reviewed in this book chapter. Using examples from the University of Central Lancashire's experience with franchised courses, the following topics are addressed: the library's involvement with course development and validation, standards and guidelines for library services, the differences between the libraries of colleges and universities in the provision of books and periodicals, copyright issues, availability and use of information technology and non-traditional learning resources such as CD-ROMs, collaboration with computing services, information literacy, and staff development. Cooperation between learning resource services is a primary means to ensure that off-campus students have equitable access to library resources and is considered vital to the success of partnership arrangements. A. Slade.

569. Watson, Linda A., Gretchen N. Arnold, Elaine May Banner, Judith G. Robinson, and Phyllis C. Self. "Library Outreach Across the Commonwealth: Pathways to Improved Health." *Virginia Medical Quarterly* 123, no. 3 (Summer 1996): 172-75.

Library outreach services for health professionals in the Commonwealth of Virginia are the focus of this article. The academic health sciences libraries at the Eastern Virginia Medical School, the University of Virginia, and Virginia Commonwealth University/Medical College of Virginia work collaboratively to provide outreach services to remote clients. These services include reference assistance, computerized searches of databases, document delivery, training in searching electronic resources, and consultative services. A particular emphasis of the University of Virginia Health Sciences Library is information support for community preceptors of medical and nursing students. A. Slade.

1995

570. Barsun, Rita and Sherrill L. Weaver. "Veritable and Virtual Library Support for Graduate Distance Education in America's New Public University." *Indiana Libraries* 14, no. 3 (Winter 1995): 3-17.

Since lifelong learning is a goal supported by all Indiana libraries, a program of library services to support distance education has been under development there. Through an inter-institution agreement between Indiana University Bloomington (IUB) Libraries and Walden University, library services are provided to graduate students at a distance. Walden University compensates IUB Libraries for services rendered. "Best Practice" is the basis for the existing agreement between these two institutions, with primary emphasis on the process of achieving competitive quality. The ACRL *Guidelines for Extended Campus Library Services* serve as a point of reference in describing areas of activity involved in planning the extended campus library. M. Kascus.

571. Bilyeu, David. "Developing Distance Education." *OLA Quarterly* (Oregon Library Association) 1, no. 2 (Summer 1995). Online. Available: http://www. olaweb.org/quarterly/quar1-2/bilyeu.shtml (Accessed April 13, 2000).

A plan for developing distance education exists in Oregon. This inter-institution technology project is funded through "The New Pathways to a Degree" project and includes Oregon State University, Eastern Oregon State College, Oregon Health Sciences University, and Central Oregon Community College. Various councils and committees within the Oregon State System of Higher Education (OSSHE) are writing policy drafts for decisions. One policy statement comments on the importance of the following: (1) library involvement early in the planning phases; (2) budget support for staff, materials, and technology; and (3) providing students with access to library services. The policy statement also recommends using the ACRL *Guidelines for Extended Campus Library Services* as a guide for planning library support and that issues be addressed from a state-wide perspective. M. Kascus.

572. deBruijn, Deb. "The British Columbia Electronic Library Network—Affordable Innovation." *Feliciter* 41, no. 11/12 (November/December 1995): 32-36.

The Electronic Library Network (ELN) was established in 1989 as a project of the Open Learning Agency in British Columbia. Two of its main objectives are to extend the collective resources of academic libraries in the province and to facilitate resource sharing among those libraries through the use of technology. ELN's projects and services at the time of writing included union databases for serials and media, a union catalogue of the holdings of college and selected public libraries in British Columbia, consortium access to reference databases, an end-user journal article requesting and delivery service, training manuals for library staff, and various resource sharing initiatives. In addition to describing these projects and services, the article looks at the administration, funding, and future of ELN. A. Slade.

573. Morrison, Rob, Kathleen M. McCloskey, Julianne P. Hinz, Michele Zandi, Peggy Grimm Pierce, K. C. Benedict, and Amy Brunvand. "Developing Off-Campus Services in Utah: A Cooperative Experience." In *The Seventh Off-Campus Library Services Conference Proceedings: San Diego, California, October 25-27, 1995*, compiled by Carol J. Jacob. Mount Pleasant, MI: Central Michigan University, 1995, 261-68.

A description of Utah's statewide technology initiative, the Utah Education Network, and the Utah Academic Library Consortium (UALC) is given. The UALC has developed cooperative programs that provide the infrastructure for delivering library services to distance learners. This study reports on the survey conducted by the UALC ad hoc Task Force on Off-Campus Programs to determine the library services available to distance learners. Of 38 surveys distributed in 1994, 37 were returned. Survey results revealed a lack of full-time library staff assigned to distance learners and inadequate funding. The authors emphasize the benefits of cooperation and the progress that has taken place at Utah Valley State College, Weber State University, University of Utah Health Sciences Library, and College of Eastern Utah, San Juan Campus, since the survey. M. Kascus.

574. Ruddy, Sister Margaret. "Resource Sharing: The SWITCH Experience." In *The Seventh Off-Campus Library Services Conference Proceedings: San Diego, California, October 25-27, 1995*, compiled by Carol J. Jacob. Mount Pleasant, MI: Central Michigan University, 1995, 329-34.

This study describes resource sharing through institutional cooperation, focusing on the Southeastern Wisconsin Information Technology Exchange (SWITCH). The following four institutions in Wisconsin agreed to fund the implementation costs of the joint library system and formed the current SWITCH Consortium in 1991: Alverno College, Cardinal Stritch College, Concordia University (WI), and Wisconsin Lutheran College. The agreement provides mutual borrowing privileges and reference services to anyone with a valid SWITCH identification. Common circulation policies regarding length of loan, overdue fines, and number of renewals are used throughout the consortia. This cooperative effort is considered successful to the extent that the combined resources meet the needs of patrons better than do the resources of any single institution. M. Kascus.

575. Weaver, Sherrill L. and Harold A. Shaffer. "Contracting to Provide Library Service for a Distance Graduate Education Program." *The Bottom Line: Managing Library Finances* 8, no. 3 (1995): 20-27.

An inter-institutional agreement exists between Walden University (WU), a private distance education university, and Indiana University (IU) at Bloomington, a public research institution, to provide library services by contract. For WU's students, the main advantage of this arrangement is that it provides a uniform program of access and delivery to a diverse and geographically dispersed population. For IU, this agreement is serving as a pilot program to test a model of library support for its distance education programs in the future. The library services included by contract are access to library materials, photocopying services, circulation privileges, reference services, reserve services, and library instruction. Among the stipulations established by the IU administration are that (1) the partnership has to be accredited by the North Central Association of Colleges and Schools (NCA), (2) IU must not be misrepresented through misuse of its logo or other official insignia, and (3) IU must be compensated for both its direct and indirect costs. M. Kascus.

576. Weaver, Sherrill L. "Using the Academic Institution-Building Model (AIBM) to Assess the Institutional Performance of Off-Campus Library Services Offered Through an Inter-Institutional Agreement to Distance Education Graduate Students." In *The Seventh Off-Campus Library Services Conference Proceedings: San Diego, California, October 25-27, 1995*, compiled by Carol J. Jacob. Mount Pleasant, MI: Central Michigan University, 1995, 375-80.

This case study assesses the institutional performance of a program of library services provided to graduate students through an inter-institutional agreement between Walden University, a private distance graduate education institution, and Indiana University, Bloomington, a large research institution. The Academic Institution-Building Model (AIBM), a self-study process to determine level of satisfaction and to describe the value of the exchange of resources for services between institutions as perceived by the constituent group, was used to evaluate the library services provided. By measuring the institutional performance of a program of library service, the approach offers an assessment that identifies the strategic value of the program in furthering the institution's goal for higher education. M. Kascus.

Public Library Cooperation with Academic Libraries

For other works that discuss this topic, see the following heading in the Subject Index: "interlibrary cooperation—public library cooperation with academic libraries."

1999

577. Humphreys, Judy and Malcolm Cooper. *A Joint Academic/Public Library: Bringing the Mountain to Mohammed*. OECD Experts Meeting on Libraries and Resource Centres for Tertiary Education by the Programme on Educational Building and the Programme for Institutional Management in Higher Education, Paris, 9-10 March 1998: Case Studies. Online. Available: http://www.oecd.org//els/edu/peb/casestud.htm (in pdf format) (Accessed April 13, 2000).

The University of Southern Queensland (USQ) established a joint-use academic/public library at its Wide Bay Campus in partnership with Hervey Bay City Council. The joint library supports the flexible delivery of education and lifelong learning for students studying on-campus, by distance education, and through the enhanced delivery mode. Students taking courses through the Wide Bay Campus have access to the World Wide Web, electronic indexes and full-text databases, and the resources of the main campus library in Toowoomba via a student Intranet. This case study describes the background to the establishment of the joint library, flexible delivery and distance education at USQ, the role of the university library in flexible delivery, access to electronic resources, the impact of information technology and communications on library design and facility management, and the current situation of the joint library. The benefits of a joint-use library and the structure of the model are discussed in terms of a number of issues. The paper concludes with a list of lessons learned from the Hervey Bay experience and recommendations for institutions considering a joint-use library venture. The authors note that the Hervey Bay Library is the first joint-use academic/public library in Australia and one of the few in the world. Its success hinges on its ability to clearly meet the requirements of all its various stakeholders. A. Slade.

578. Morrison, Rob. "Academic Resources Available to Help Public Libraries Serve Distance Learners." *Directions for Utah Libraries* 11, no. 5 (January 1999): 4-5. Also online. Available: http://www.state.lib.ut.us/dful0199.htm (Accessed April 13, 2000).

As part of a series on the impact of distance learners on Utah public libraries, the author looks at the proliferation of distance learning opportunities in the state and the role of the Utah Academic Library Consortium (UALC) in providing library services to distance learners. A new service called UTAD (Utah Article Delivery) will provide fast delivery of journal articles held in the collections of Utah libraries. Students can use UTAD's website to order articles at no cost for fax delivery within two working days. The author indicates that UALC is prepared to work with public libraries to assist them in supporting the information needs of distance learners. For a related article, see #579 below. A. Slade.

1998

579.   Hinz, Juli and Margaret Landesman. "All Libraries for All People." *Directions for Utah Libraries* 11, no. 2 (September 1998): 1-3.

This article examines the use of Utah libraries by members of the public and provides an overview of academic library support for off-campus students in the state. The authors attempt to reassure public libraries that academic libraries recognize their responsibility to off-campus students and much is being done to support these students through the Utah Academic Library Consortium (UALC). Through the UTAD (Utah Article Delivery) service, higher education students can request fax delivery of articles from any UALC library. Plans are underway to contract for commercial delivery of books and other materials throughout the state. Students can presently access many library services via the Web, including instruction, interlibrary loans, book renewals, hold and recall requests, and reference assistance. Proxy servers at several institutions allow students to access databases from home. Due to limited funding and increasing demands from many different types of library users, the authors advocate the highest level of cooperation between public and academic libraries to provide better access to collections and services for all Utah library patrons. For a related article, see #578 above. A. Slade.

1996

580.   Salvesen, Helge. "Library Services for Distance and Decentralized Education in Norway." *Scandinavian Public Library Quarterly* 19, no. 3 (1996): 11-14.

To improve library services for distance education students in Norway, the Ministry of Culture, through the Norwegian Directorate for Public Libraries, has appointed a committee to determine the current state of affairs, identify and evaluate alternative ways of providing services, and advise the Ministry on future directions. Part of the strategy chosen by the committee is that any distance education project must have three participants: the institution offering the program, university or research libraries that can support the program, and a network of public libraries that can function as local resource centers. The committee's action plan includes a survey of 1,200 students from Lillehammer College to determine how distance learners meet their library needs and a project at four public libraries to examine the effects of different approaches to providing library services. At the time of writing, the committee was in the process of designing the different investigations and collecting data. The potential role that Norwegian public libraries can play in supporting distance education is stressed in this report on the committee's progress. A. Slade.

1995

581. Kühne, Brigitte. "The IT Project at the County Library in Kalmar." In *Proceedings of the First "Libraries Without Walls" Conference, Mytilene, Greece, 9-10 September 1995*, edited by Ann Irving and Geoff Butters. Preston, UK: Centre for Research in Library and Information Management, University of Central Lancashire, 1995, 55-57.

The Swedish project "IT education from a distance" is described. This cooperative project involved 12 head libraries in Kalmar County and the University of Kalmar. Kalmar County is a very poor area in Sweden, with a low average level of education among the 250,000 residents. Training was planned for library staff in database access, Internet, and multimedia. E-mail was used for communication. Plans for the future include extending this kind of cooperation to other Nordic countries, that is, Denmark, Finland, and Norway. The goal of the participating institutions is to become leaders in Scandinavia regarding IT in rural areas and give "ordinary" people access to information sources in databases. M. Kascus.

582. Schmidt, Ted. "Extended Campus Library Services: A Loveland Perspective." *Colorado Libraries* 21, no. 1 (Spring 1995): 20-21.

From the perspective of Loveland Public Library, a mutually beneficial cooperative relationship exists between Loveland and Regis College (now Regis University). The relationship was clarified in a memorandum of agreement that provides for full borrowing privileges for Loveland card holders and Regis students. The contract also provides many useful reference resources for Loveland as well as ongoing access to the CARL system through Regis. The relationship has strengthened over time as public library staff meet regularly with library staff from the parent campuses as well as with faculty and students from the Loveland campus. M. Kascus.

583. Watkin, Alan. "Distant Providers, Distant Learning: Provider Experiences." In *Proceedings of the First "Libraries Without Walls" Conference, Mytilene, Greece, 9-10 September 1995*, edited by Ann Irving and Geoff Butters. Preston, UK: Centre for Research in Library and Information Management, University of Central Lancashire, 1995, 43-46.

This paper illustrates the opportunities for public libraries to respond to the educational needs and training needs of society. PLAIL (Public Libraries and Adult Independent Learners) is a European Commission Telematics Programme funded project in cooperation with partners in Wales, Portugal, Spain, and Scotland. The aims of PLAIL were to identify customer needs of open learners, determine what services the library should provide, explore the implications for librarians' skills, and agree on a plan to develop those skills. The partnership also explored the development of criteria for assessing the level of service a library provides for adult learners. The final outcome of PLAIL is intended to be a multimedia distance learning training pack to introduce staff to this area. M. Kascus.

1993

584. Menadue, Pam. *Supporting Open Learning Students Utilising Community Resources*. Port Pirie, SA: Goyder College of TAFE, 1993. 14 pp. + 4 appendices.

Goyder College of TAFE in South Australia initiated a project to support the public and community/school libraries used by the college's open learning students. Libraries in the region were surveyed by means of a questionnaire, correspondence, and personal contact. The responses highlighted the general need for TAFE information and support. As a first step in addressing this need, a newsletter providing information about TAFE courses and the library services available to open learning students will be produced and sent to the libraries on a regular basis. It is noted that each library in the region will require a different level of support from TAFE depending on the number of students using the library and the nature of the courses offered. The project has so far been successful in that dialogue has been established between TAFE and libraries in the region. The next step is to inform the students about the type of support they can expect to receive from local libraries. A newsletter and information inserted into course packages are suggested as ways to communicate with the students. A. Slade.

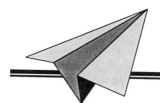

CHAPTER 8

Library Surveys

International

For other works that describe international surveys, see the following heading in the Subject Index: "surveys of libraries—international."

1998

585. Casey, Anne Marie and Marissa Cachero, eds. *Off-Campus Library Services Directory*. 3rd Edition. Mount Pleasant, MI: Off-Campus Library Services, Central Michigan University, 1998. 217 pp.

The third edition of this directory lists 161 colleges and universities in the United States and Canada that provide off-campus library services. The information is based on responses to questionnaires distributed to participants at the Seventh and Eighth Off-Campus Library Services Conferences, institutions represented in the second edition of the *Directory*, and respondents to messages posted on several electronic lists. This edition is divided into two sections. Section I contains the main entries, grouped geographically, for each of the institutions represented. Section II comprises various indexes, covering topics such as organizational structure of the library unit that supports off-campus users, funding and budgeting, access to computers, OPAC interfaces, library instruction, reference services, document delivery methods, reserve materials and electronic reserves, and program sites. For information on the first two editions of the *Directory*, see #394 in the first bibliography and #373 in the second bibliography. A. Slade.

United Kingdom

For other works that describe library surveys in the United Kingdom, see the following heading in the Subject Index: "surveys of libraries—United Kingdom."

1997

586. Allred, John. *Open Learning in Public Libraries: Third Baseline Survey*. Research Report No. 19. London: Department for Education and Employment, 1997. 26 pp. ISBN 0-85522-611-0.

The aim of the Open for Learning Project, which ran in England from 1992 to 1995, was for 90% of all public libraries authorities to have open and flexible learning centers. Baseline surveys were conducted in 1992 and 1994 to evaluate the project and monitor changes (see #385 in the second bibliography and #589 in this chapter). A third survey was conducted in 1996 and found that 83% of library authorities in the United Kingdom now provide an open and flexible learning service. Among the other findings were that the average public library has more stock of open learning materials than in 1994 and a better selection of titles, the number of suppliers of open learning materials has increased since the last survey, there has been a slight drop in the proportion of libraries charging for service, nearly every library has the necessary equipment and hardware for supporting open learning, and a third of the libraries have CD-ROM multimedia materials and Internet access. In addition, most of the libraries have trained staff, over one-quarter have formal service standards, and the extent of formal liaison with other organizations has remained fairly stable since 1994. A. Slade.

587. Bilby, Linda. *Distance Learning in Higher Education: Impact of Information Technology and Implications for Libraries and Information Services*. B.A. (Hons) diss., Leeds Metropolitan University, 1997. 101 pp.

The objectives of this research project were to examine the extent to which UK universities are providing library services to their distance learners and to determine the impact of information technologies on such services. Information and data were collected by means of a questionnaire distributed to and interviews with a small group of distance learning students from selected institutions; a journal article on library services at the Open University; and interviews with library staff at the University of Sheffield, Sheffield Hallam University, Leeds Metropolitan University, and the University of Leeds. Among the findings were that the five university libraries are all at different stages with regard to services for distance learners, Sheffield Hallam University is the only institution offering extensive library services to distance learners, none of the five universities provides remote access to networked library resources due to licensing restrictions, and use of information technologies is not seen by any of the universities as currently providing the major impetus for service provision. The results from the student questionnaires and interviews showed a low awareness of library services, especially in relation to remote access via computer and modem. The implications of the findings for the provision of library services to distance learners in the United Kingdom are discussed and evaluated. A. Slade.

1996

588.   Allred, John. *Improving Access to Open and Flexible Learning: Open Learning in Public Libraries: The Evaluation Report*. Education and Training Technologies OL241. Sheffield, UK: Department for Education and Employment, 1996. 62 pp.

This report was produced under contract for the U.K. Employment Department to evaluate the Open for Learning Project, which concluded in 1995. The project was designed to make open and flexible learning available to adult learners through public libraries in England. The methods of data collection included statistics provided by participating libraries, library visits, interviews with learners, and two baseline surveys (see #385 in the second bibliography and #589 in this chapter). Based on the information collected, the report measures how well the project's five target goals were met and describes the open learning centers, the learners, the liaison between libraries and other agencies, and the quality of services. Among the findings were that 90% of all English public libraries provide at least one open leaning center with trained staff and support services; networks for tutorial support had been established with local colleges, educational guidance agencies, and training councils; and the library centers were cost effective compared to other open learning services, with £16 being the cost of an average loan. In addition, approximately 13 new users register at the typical library each month, 97% of the users interviewed indicated that they had benefited in some way from the open learning services, and 64% of the respondents used the services to improve their employment or career prospects. A. Slade.

1995

589.   Allred, John. *Open for Learning: Open and Flexible Learning in Public Libraries: The Second Baseline Survey: Changes Between 1992 and 1994*. Boston Spa, UK: Information for Learning, 1995. 21 pp. ISBN 0-9525462-0-5.

The Open for Learning Project, funded by the Employment Department (U.K.) for the period 1992 to 1995, was designed to make open and flexible learning widely available to adult learners through public libraries in England. To monitor changes during the project, baseline data were collected in 1992 using a postal questionnaire sent to all public library authorities in the United Kingdom (see #385 in the second bibliography). A second survey was conducted in 1994 to determine the changes during the first two years of the project. The same questionnaire was sent to 174 public library authorities and 139 responses were received. Among the findings: (1) 53% of public library authorities stocked open learning materials, compared to 23% in the first survey; (2) training and publicity for open learning showed a small increase; (3) there was an increase in the provision of open learning packs in Scotland and Wales; (4) over one-third of library authorities charge for open learning services, a slight increase from 1992; (5) nearly every library has supporting equipment such as computers, and most have trained staff; (6) there was little change in formal liaison with related organizations but a small decline in liaison with higher education organizations; and (7)

49% of the public library authorities received external funding from sources other than the Employment Department. For related works, see #586 and #588 above. A. Slade.

590. Library Association. "Learning Opens Up." *Library Association Record* 97, no. 2 (February 1995): 76.

    This brief news item reports on the Open for Learning Second Baseline Survey, conducted in 1995 to determine changes in the provision of open and flexible leaning materials and services in UK public libraries between 1992 and 1994. For the full report on the survey, see #589 above. A. Slade.

United States

For other works that describe library surveys in the United States, see the following heading in the Subject Index: "surveys of libraries—United States."

1999

---

591. Jones, Debbie. "Management Planning for Extended Library Services." *Christian Librarian* 42, no. 2 (April 1999): 36-39, 45.

    In preparation for the introduction of a distance learning program at Florida Christian College, a study was conducted to investigate a management plan for extended library services. A select group of privately funded Bible colleges was surveyed to determine the extent to which they follow criteria in the ACRL *Guidelines for Extended Campus Library Services.* Five out of 34 institutions contacted returned questionnaires. Among the findings were that only one of the five institutions provided additional funds for distance education library services; all respondents indicated that the extension site is responsible for the facility, equipment, and resources; and three of the five respondents reported that they provide some sort of reference and document delivery services to their distance students. There was little evidence of support for computer services. Based on the results of the survey, it was concluded that there are no common methods for delivering library services to distance education students at Bible colleges and that the ACRL Guidelines are not followed with much consistency. Generally speaking, extended library services seem to be lacking in Bible colleges. For a related article, see #729 in this volume. A. Slade.

1997

---

592. National Center for Education Statistics. *Statistical Analysis Report: Distance Education in Higher Education Institutions.* (NCES 98-062). October 1997. Online. Available: http://nces.ed.gov/pubs98/distance/index.html (Accessed April 13, 2000).

This survey requested by the National Institute on Postsecondary Education, Libraries, and Lifelong Learning (U.S. Department of Education) was intended to provide the first nationally representative data about distance education course offerings in higher education. Data collection took place in the fall of 1995. Among the highlights of the survey are the following: one-third of higher education institutions offered distance education courses, an estimated 27,500 distance education courses were offered, courses were delivered by two-way interactive video at 57% of the institutions, there were an estimated 753,640 students enrolled, and about 25% of the institutions offered degrees that students could complete by taking distance education courses. Access to library resources varied depending on the type of library resource. Access to an electronic link with the home institution's library was available for some or all courses at 56% of the institutions, and cooperative agreements for students to use other libraries were available at 62% of the institutions. Library staff were assigned to assist distance education students at 45% of the institutions, while library deposit collections were available at remote sites at 39% of the institutions. The survey form is appended to the report. M. Kascus.

593. Snyder, Carolyn A., Susan Logue, and Barbara G. Preece. *Expanding the Role of the Library in Teaching and Learning: Distance Learning Initiatives*. 1997. Paper presented at the ACRL 8th National Conference: Choosing Our Futures: Nashville, Tennessee, April 11-14, 1997. Online. Available: http://www.ala.org/acrl/paperhtm/d28.html (Accessed April 13, 2000).

A summary is provided of a survey on the extent and the type of involvement ARL libraries play in distance learning. Results indicate that of the 76 (64%) respondents, 46 (62%) reported that their institution participated in distance learning programs. However, only seven libraries reported that they administered the distance education program. In terms of library support, the libraries are providing a variety of services. Half of the respondents provide instructional design, multimedia development, and institutional evaluation. Other service areas include reserve collections, library instruction, and information literacy. All respondents indicated that catalogues are online and 74% circulate materials. Patrons use interlibrary loan either through e-mail or the World Wide Web. Another library service to distance learners is reference service using telephone, e-mail, or the Web. One library indicated using electronic reserves. Libraries offer the same type of services to remote users that are available on-campus and at the same time they play an important role in instructional design and World Wide Web development for distance learners. For further information on the survey, see #596 below. M. Kascus.

1996

---

594. Butler, John T., comp. *Minnesota Off-Campus Library Services Directory, 1995-96,* [1996]. 123 pp. ERIC ED 396 756.

The University of Minnesota-Twin Cities conducted a survey of Minnesota higher education institutions to collect data for this state-wide directory of library services that support off-campus academic programs. Both institutional information and information on library services to distance learners is provided for each contributing college or university. For those institutions providing library services, additional information is included on reference and information service, collection access and document delivery, information access, and administration. The purpose of the directory is to provide baseline data on library support for distance learners in the state of Minnesota. The hope is that it will be seen as a means of identifying opportunities for inter-institutional cooperation in serving distance faculty and learners in the future. M. Kascus.

595. Lahmon, Jo Ann. *An Examination of the Level of Library Service Provided for Off Campus Programs According to the Association of College and Research Libraries Guidelines for Extended Campus Library Service*. Ph.D. diss., Florida State University, 1996. 147 pp. UMI Number 9712151.

This doctoral dissertation examines the level of library support provided by academic libraries for their off-campus programs in relation to the 1990 ACRL *Guidelines for Extended Campus Library Services*. The population for the study included higher education institutions in the United States listed in the 1993 *Off-Campus Library Services Directory* (see #373 in the second bibliography). A mail questionnaire was sent to 137 individuals listed as the contact person for off-campus library services at those institutions. The questionnaire was divided into six broad categories corresponding to each section in the guidelines: management, finance, personnel, facilities, resources, and services. A section was included on demographics. Findings from the study indicated that over half of the respondents consulted the 1990 ACRL Guidelines when developing off-campus library services. Of those responding, 85% reported that some consideration was given to the extended campus in budget allocations. While funding was provided, it was not adequate, and seemed to be the most critical issue in providing library support. Among other findings: 80% of the respondents indicated that librarians plan, implement, and evaluate library resources and services; 76% provided access through agreements with libraries not affiliated with the parent institution; and 76% of the respondents offered reference services at extended sites, but 24% did not. Among the recommendations coming from the study is the need for a training course for distance librarianship. M. Kascus.

596. Snyder, Carolyn A., Susan Logue, and Barbara G. Preece. *Role of Libraries in Distance Education*. SPEC Kit #216. Washington, DC: Office of Management Services, Association of Research Libraries, 1996. 145 pp. Summary online. Available: http://www.arl.org/spec/216fly.html (Accessed April 13, 2000).

A survey of 119 ARL (Association of Research Libraries) libraries was undertaken for three reasons: (1) to identify libraries involved in distance education and the extent of their involvement, (2) to determine library services delivered to remote patrons, and (3) to assess the management and support provided by libraries for distance learners. The response rate was 62% (74/119). In the findings, 23 libraries provided instructional support assistance to faculty for the development of distance education courses. Library services that support distance learning courses were offered by all but three of the libraries responding, with remote access to the online catalogue provided. Thirty-two libraries permitted circulation to distance education students at remote sites. Among the services provided to distance learners were interlibrary loan, reserve, and reciprocal borrowing. Only six libraries reported having a permanent budget for distance education. M. Kascus.

1995

597. Colbert, Gretchen. "Extended Campus Programs and Four Year Institutions."
      Colorado Libraries 21, no. 1 (Spring 1995): 12-14.

      A survey was conducted at 13 four-year institutions in Colorado to deter-
      mine the programs offered and the library services provided to off-campus stu-
      dents. Findings indicated that the library services vary by institution but generally
      include reference and referral services, search assistance, online searching, inter-
      library loans, document delivery, and user instruction. Telephone and fax are the
      usual means of request. Two institutions, Regis College and Mesa State Univer-
      sity, have contractual agreements with local libraries to provide services to their
      students. Six of the institutions surveyed belong to the Colorado Consortium for
      Independent Study (CCIS), a state-wide coordinated program of off-campus in-
      struction operating under the policies of the Colorado Commission of Higher
      Education. M. Kascus.

598. Corrigan, Andy. "A National Study of Coordination Between External Degree
      Programs and Libraries." In *The Seventh Off-Campus Library Services Confer-
      ence Proceedings: San Diego, California, October 25-27, 1995,* compiled by
      Carol J. Jacob. Mount Pleasant, MI: Central Michigan University, 1995, 61-68.

      This study, conducted in 1993, examined coordination mechanisms be-
      tween external degree programs and libraries as perceived by external program
      deans and directors at colleges and universities throughout the United States. To
      make generalizations about the extent and the types of coordination that the study
      found to be present, the author used Henry Mintzberg's typology of coordination
      types that generally occur in an organization, as well as concepts related to loose
      and tight coupling in organizations. The methodology utilized four types of coor-
      dination defined in relation to library services: (1) mutual adjustment; (2) direct
      supervision; (3) standardization of work processes; and (4) standardization of
      skills, knowledge, and values. A "Library Assessment Survey" was designed to
      collect data. The population for the study included 104 colleges and universities
      in the United States. Findings of the study suggest that external degree program
      administrators should be more proactive in seeking knowledge about library serv-
      ices, and librarians, administrators and faculty should assess the degree to which
      program needs are met by specific types of library services. For the original study,
      see #388 in the second bibliography. M. Kascus.

599. Davis, Mary Ellen. "News from the Field: ECLSS Seeks Researchers." *College &
      Research Libraries News* 56, no. 6 (June 1995): 381, 383.

      This brief item is about the efforts of the ACRL Extended Campus Library
      Services Section to stimulate interest in conducting original research by identify-
      ing key research topics. The survey of extended campus librarians across the
      United States and Canada itemized three dozen potential research topics. The
      leading five topics were (1) bibliographic instruction, (2) use of new technologies
      to enhance library support for distance learners, (3) perceptions of campus admin-
      istrators regarding the value of extended campus library services, (4) funding ex-
      tended campus library services, and (5) providing library services to independent

learners not able to use an academic library in person. Other topics included copyright issues and how library schools are preparing future librarians to serve remote users in an electronic environment. M. Kascus.

600. Newsome, Jim and Vicki Rosen. "Isolation or Affiliation: How Distance Education Librarians Stay Connected." In *The Seventh Off-Campus Library Services Conference Proceedings: San Diego, California, October 25-27, 1995,* compiled by Carol J. Jacob. Mount Pleasant, MI: Central Michigan University, 1995, 317-28.

A survey was conducted to assess the extent of distance librarians' feelings of isolation, the factors contributing to it, and its positive and negative aspects. The 27-item instrument included multi-dimensional and open-ended questions. The questionnaire was sent to 95 individuals in April 1995 and 57 responses were received, for a return rate of 60%. Results of the survey indicated that 70.2% of the respondents reported feelings of professional isolation. Working alone was the factor most often identified as contributing to a sense of isolation and lack of learning. Respondents indicated that the lack of contact with other librarians was the single most negative aspect of the job. Most of the respondents indicated that their central site colleagues did not have an accurate perception of off-campus library services. Most respondents were very positive about the independence that their distance librarian position afforded them. The respondents identified the following general strategies to use to maintain or enhance connectedness: communications, personnel management, feedback, training, administrative or organizational support, and professional growth and development. M. Kascus.

601. Peterman, Thomas W. and G. Ann Schultis. "Customer Service at Off-Campus Locations: Measuring Quality." In *The Seventh Off-Campus Library Services Conference Proceedings: San Diego, California, October 25-27, 1995,* compiled by Carol J. Jacob. Mount Pleasant, MI: Central Michigan University, 1995, 277-301.

This study reviews Park College Library's support of off-campus sites through the provision of books, periodicals, audio-visual materials, and a variety of CD-ROM products. Two areas of particular interest are how these services are provided and how quality customer service is measured at the off-campus sites served by the college. In assessing the perceived quality of library service, five similar questionnaires were developed to survey the population at the extended campus learning sites. Surveys were administered to the Resident Center Administrator, the Academic Director, the Installation Librarian, and a random sample of faculty and students. The results of the survey were used to identify trends across sites as well as specific concerns with the site providing decision support for program modification. The questionnaire is included in the appendices. M. Kascus.

602. Potter, Susan. "Out of State, Out of Mind?" *Colorado Libraries* 21, no. 1 (Spring 1995): 28-31.

A survey was conducted to determine if the academic institutions located outside Colorado offering courses to Colorado residents are providing library services and resources to support their coursework. Eight institutions were included in the survey: Chapman University (Orange, CA); Columbia College (Columbia, MO); Emporia State University (Emporia, KS); Lesley College

(Cambridge, MA); National College (Rapid City, SD); Parks Junior College (Gulfport, MI); University of Phoenix (Phoenix, AZ); and Webster University (St. Louis, MO). Data from the survey are presented in six tables, labelled General Institutional Information, Subject Areas Taught, Library Services, Branch Library Information, Library Services from "Main" Campus, and Cooperative Library Agreements. Findings indicate that of the eight institutions, five have branch libraries, six provide some kind of library services from the "main" campus, and four have either written or verbal agreements with local libraries in Colorado to provide a range of services to the students. M. Kascus.

603.   Wilson, Mareth and Melinda Stasch. "Off-Campus Librarianship: The View from the Reference Desk." In *The Seventh Off-Campus Library Services Conference Proceedings: San Diego, California, October 25-27, 1995*, compiled by Carol J. Jacob. Mount Pleasant, MI: Central Michigan University, 1995, 381-85.

This is a report on a survey conducted to identify patterns of awareness, mutual concerns, and satisfaction among reference librarians serving off-campus students. Of the 250 surveys distributed, 124 were returned. In addition, reference librarians serving off-campus students were interviewed and asked a series of open-ended questions. Findings of the study indicated that 42% of the responding institutions had included the needs of off-campus students in the library mission statement, 20% had a written profile of the research needs of these students, and 58% reported participation with administration in planning for off-campus library services. Statements resulting in the largest number of responses in the dissatisfied/very dissatisfied range focused on budget, financing, and the allocation of support staff. Statements resulting in the highest levels of librarian satisfaction related to systems in place by which students can contact them and the professional nature of the work. M. Kascus.

1994

604.   Hammer, Kevin G. *Off-Campus Library Services and the Impact of NCA Accreditation*. M.L.S. research paper, Kent State University, 1994. 38 pp. ERIC ED 376 849.

Members of the North Central Association of Colleges and Schools were surveyed to determine the library services considered essential to quality in distance education. The issue of accreditation was raised as a way of enforcing compliance with standards of library service to extended campus education programs. The response rate was 46% (106/217). Of those responding, 72.6% indicated that they assess the needs of their extended campuses for library resources, services, and facilities. However, few of the respondents (10.6%) have a written profile of these needs. In most institutions (68.9%), a librarian is not assigned responsibilities for planning library services to the extended campus. Respondents indicated the availability of the following services: collections at distant sites (55.2%); audio-visual equipment and services (65.7%); mail, telephone, and e-mail reference assistance (78.6%); database searches (67.3%); and interlibrary loan service (91.4%). Funding is not related to need, and in 57.7% of the libraries, funding for the extended campus program is not identified in the library budget. The survey cover letter and questionnaire are included in the appendices. M. Kascus.

1990

605. Abbott, John P. and Jinnie Y. Davis. "Extending Service Beyond the Library Walls: The Effect of Remote Access to Online Catalogs in Large Academic Libraries." In *Convergence: Proceedings of the Second National Conference of the Library and Information Technology Association, October 2-6, 1988, Boston,* edited by Michael Gorman. Chicago: American Library Association, 1990, 94-98.

This paper is based on a survey conducted while planning to implement remote access at North Carolina State University. Major points and anecdotal comments from the survey and follow-up telephone interviews are included. An attempt is made to provide a profile of remote access in ARL libraries. The questions most frequently asked about remote access include funding, ports, baud rate, parity, passwords, and hours of operation. User issues include training, e-mail, remote access, user's time online, and user evaluation of the remote access system. Management issues include policy statements (only 8% report having one), keeping statistics (only 25% report collecting them), personnel assignments to remote access (considered the weakest link), and the effect on other library units (thought to be too soon to tell). The author concludes by suggesting that libraries build flexible management structures, then concentrate on details. The following suggestions are made for implementing remote access: (1) ensure management support, (2) coordinate with other campus user units, (3) select technical features or options, (4) allocate adequate staff, (5) prepare to help remote users, and (6) build in evaluation. For further information on the survey, see item #275 in the second bibliography. M. Kascus.

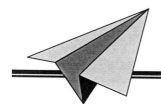

CHAPTER 9

User Studies

 Africa

For other works that describe user studies in Africa, see the following headings in the Subject Index: "user studies—Nigeria," "user studies—South Africa."

1999

606. Benza, Timothy E. S., Ruben Chitsika, Farai S. Mvere, Darlington Nyakupinda, and Julius G. Mugadzaweta. *A Critical Assessment of Learner Support Services Provided by the Zimbabwe Open University*. Paper presented at the Pan-Commonwealth Forum on Open Learning, Brunei Darussalam, 1-5 March 1999: Empowerment through Knowledge and Technology. Online. Available: http://www.col.org/forum/casestudies.htm (in pdf format) (Accessed April 13, 2000).

A study was conducted in three regions of Zimbabwe to critically assess the learner support services provided by the Zimbabwe Open University. Thirty tutors and 510 students engaged in second- and third-year courses through distance education were interviewed and/or asked to complete survey questionnaires. The findings indicated that distance education students and tutors encounter a wide array of problems, which include high travelling costs, long distances to the regional study centers, lack of adequate reference books, and limited access to library facilities. In the results, 67% of the students and 56% of the tutors were unhappy with the provision of library and reference material services by regional centers. To compensate for the inadequate library services, some tutors provide library books to students during their visits to the centers. The authors suggest that the answer to this problem is to fully stock the study centers with relevant reference materials. A. Slade.

1997

607. Mlotshwa, Peter. *The Practice of Distance Librarianship in Zimbabwe*. Paper presented at the Commonwealth Library Association Workshop on Library Services to Distance Learners, Harare, Zimbabwe, August 6, 1997. Available from: Learning Resource Centre, University of the West Indies, Cave Hill Campus, Bridgetown, Barbados.

In the context of this paper, the term "distance librarianship" pertains primarily to the provision of postal lending services to distance learners. Since distance librarianship had become an important area of library practice in Zimbabwe, the author conducted a study to investigate its current status in that country. Of 19 libraries contacted, approximately half were practising distance librarianship. Of 18 library users consulted, 50% indicated that they had benefited from the services of distance librarianship. A number of problems with the postal system were identified in the study, including cost of postage, registration of parcels, delivery delays, damage, payment for lost or damaged books, reliability of delivery in rural versus urban areas, and overdue materials. Pointing to the expansion of distance education in Zimbabwe, the author delineates a critical need for increases in library resources and personnel to support the practice of distance librarianship. If both of these resources can be provided by the appropriate authorities, the author predicts that the future of distance librarianship in Zimbabwe will be bright. A. Slade.

1995

608. Kamau, Judith. "Distance Learners' Perceptions of the Quality of Course Materials and Student Support in Distance Learning Programmes in Kenya." In *One World, Many Voices: Quality in Open and Distance Learning: Selected Papers From the 17th World Conference of the International Council for Distance Education, Birmingham, United Kingdom, June, 1995: Volume 2*, edited by David Sewart. Milton Keynes, UK: The Open University in association with International Council for Distance Education, 1995, 262-65.

This paper examines learner perceptions of the quality of study materials and support services provided by distance teaching institutions in Kenya, with particular attention to the External Degree Programme of the University of Nairobi. Few distance learners in Kenya reside in areas well served by public libraries. A study of external degree students at the University of Nairobi found that approximately 50% of the students live over 20 kilometers away from the nearest public library. The author points out that these students may be forced to depend solely on their course materials. To counter this problem, there is a need to place copies of recommended readings in the various study centers. A. Slade.

Australia

For other works that describe user studies in Australia, see the following heading in the Subject Index: "user studies—Australia."

1997

609. Brogan, Martyn. "Off-Campus and Off-Line? Access to the Internet of Post-graduate TESOL Students at Deakin University." In *Research in Distance Education 4: Revised Papers from the Fourth Research in Distance Education Conference, Deakin University, 1996*, edited by Terry Evans, Viktor Jakupec, and Diane Thompson. Geelong, Victoria: Deakin University Press, 1997, 115-27.

This paper outlines a project by TESOL (Teaching English to Speakers of Other Languages) staff at Deakin University to introduce computer-mediated communication to off-campus students enrolled in TESOL programs. As part of the project, a questionnaire was sent to 207 TESOL students in 1996 to investigate, among other things, their need for training in computer systems. Of the 158 respondents, 54% were off-campus students. From this group, 70% of the master's students and 84% of the certificate and diploma students indicated a need for training in the use of the Internet. An interesting finding was that, of the 22 students who had access to computers with modems and who were already using the Internet, only one indicated no need for training, implying that those students currently online felt uncertain about their skills in using the tools of the Internet. Among strategies identified to provide training to these students, printed materials were to be sent to off-campus students who could not visit Deakin's campus and on-campus workshops were to be offered to students who could come to Deakin. A. Slade.

610. Cavanagh, Tony. "Electronic Access to Library Catalogues—How Much Do Off Campus Students Use It?" *DESIGnation*, no. 13-14 (September 1997): 3-5.

A study was conducted in 1996 to provide information on the electronic usage patterns of Deakin University's off-campus students and to compare this information with similar data collected in 1995. All requests received by e-mail or dial-in to the online catalogue during May 1996 were logged. In 1995, approximately 10% of requests to the off-campus library service were received electronically. In the 1996 data, this number had increased to 15%. Among the other findings of the study were that students preferred using the electronic ordering feature on Deakin's INNOPAC library system over free-text e-mail, the average student accessed the library electronically once a month, the number of female users increased from 44% to 52% in 1996, and there was a 50% increase in electronic ordering between May 1995 and May 1996. The author notes that the results can be used as guidelines to possible expected usage for other libraries contemplating providing electronic access to their off-campus students. For related articles, see #617 and #622 in this chapter. A. Slade.

611. Macauley, Peter. "Distance Education Research Students and Their Library Use." *Australian Academic and Research Libraries* 28, no. 3 (September 1997): 188-97.

The results of the author's research study on the information needs of postgraduate distance education students are reported in this article. The study involved a survey of 276 Australian-domiciled higher degree by research students. The basic objective was to determine if the students needed to use the home institution library. In the findings, many students received little guidance from their supervisors on how to conduct a research project, students did make extensive use of libraries, other libraries were used for convenience and browsing, usage of public libraries was lower than reported in other studies, and some students did not take advantage of available electronic databases. Overall, it was determined that the home institution library is needed by postgraduate distance students, but they can get by without it on many occasions. The author notes that research students need to shift their attitude and willingness to use electronic services if they are to benefit from the resources available through the Internet. For more information on the study, see #619 in this chapter. A. Slade.

612. Macauley, Peter. "The Information Needs of Higher Degree by Research Distance Learners." In *Open, Flexible and Distance Learning: Education and Training in the 21st Century: Selected Papers from the 13th Biennial Forum of the Open and Distance Learning Association of Australia, University of Tasmania, Launceston, 29 September-3 October 1997*, edited by Jo Osborne, David Roberts, and Judi Walker. Launceston, Tasmania: University of Tasmania, 1997, 276-80.

The results of the author's research study on the information needs of postgraduate distance learners at Deakin University are reported in this paper. For more information on the findings of the study, see #619 in this chapter. A. Slade.

613. Macauley, Peter. "Information Needs of Students." *inCite* (Australian Library and Information Association) 18, no. 3 (March 1997): 10.

The findings of a study on the information needs of higher degree by research students at Deakin University are summarized in this article. All students were studying by distance education at the time of the survey. The findings indicated that postgraduate distance learners have specialized information needs and require services that are different from those provided to undergraduates. A broader role for librarians is implied in this context due to a lack of support from the students' supervisors. For more information on the research study, see #619 in this chapter. A. Slade.

614. Macauley, Peter. *Library Services for Postgraduates: What You Asked For and What You Get!* Paper presented to the Deakin University Postgraduate Association Conference, June 1997 at the Woolstores Campus. Available from the author, Woolstores Campus, Deakin University Library, Geelong, Victoria, Australia, 3217.

Three themes are addressed in this paper: the results of a study on the information needs of postgraduate distance learners at Deakin University, the library services available to these students, and advice for higher degree by research students based on the author's experiences. The tips for postgraduate students include starting one's literature review right away, making better use of supervisors, introducing oneself to the liaison librarian, reading the library guide for off-campus students, being careful of jargon when designing questionnaires, doing a thorough pilot study, and recording all bibliographic details the first time one consults a reference. These tips are supported by the findings of the author's research study. For more information on the study, see #619 in this chapter. A. Slade.

615. Monash University. Gippsland Research and Information Bank. "Computer Access Survey of Distance Education Students." In *Libraries and Other Academic Support Services for Distance Learning*, edited by Carolyn A. Snyder and James W. Fox. Foundations in Library and Information Science, vol. 39. Greenwich, CT: JAI Press, 1997, 185-205.

Distance education students' computer access was surveyed at Monash University Gippsland Campus. The 1996 survey was conducted across nine schools involving 5,978 graduate and undergraduate students. The response rate was 40%. In terms of access to computers for study purposes, 86% (2,047) indicated that they had access at either home or work. About 33% of the respondents reported that they accessed the Internet and the World Wide Web, with most accessing via a private provider. A profile of the respondents is given, showing a representative sample was achieved across various demographic characteristics of school, gender, age, and geographic area. Students responded favorably to the idea of a "drop-in" center to make use of a campus videoconference or other facility, and were flexible in terms of the hours of service of such a study center. M. Kascus.

616. Vautier, Lynne. *Library and Information Service Support for Undergraduate Distance Education Students at Curtin University of Technology: Current Research and Some Responses by the Curtin Business School*. Paper presented to the Australian Library and Information Association Distance Education Special Interest Group National Conference: Shifting Sands, Charles Sturt University, Wagga Wagga, December 5-6, 1997. Available from: Christine Cother, Editor DESIGnation, University of South Australia Library, Holbrooks Road, Underdale, South Australia 5032.

With reference to the growth of distance education at Curtin University of Technology, the author discusses her research project to explore issues pertaining to library support for undergraduate distance learners. Students and academic staff were interviewed to determine the need for library materials in distance education courses and the students' level of access to electronic resources. Among the preliminary findings were that the need for library materials varies from course to course and that there is a difference between having remote access to electronic resources and using that access. While 40% of the surveyed students had use of a computer with remote access capabilities, only 26% had actually used this access. Using anecdotal comments from the respondents, the author looks at the intentions and impediments of students without access, the attitudes of academics to the use of computers with remote access capabilities, and the responses to the distance education environment by the Library and the Curtin Business School. The research project indicates that students are underusing library services currently in place and points to the need for more library instruction, publicity, and effective marketing of existing library services. A. Slade.

1996

617.   Cavanagh, Tony. "Electronic Ordering of Library Materials: Why Aren't Off Campus Students Using It?" *DESIGnation*, no. 10 (May 1996): 5-7.

Since only 10% of Deakin University's off-campus students were using the library's electronic ordering system in 1995, the author conducted a survey to determine some of the reasons for the low usage. A survey form was sent to 105 students who were known to be regular users of the off-campus library service and 75 responses were returned. While the majority of the respondents (84%) indicated they knew about remote access to the library system, only 28% owned or had access to a computer and modem. Of this group, only 19% claimed to be electronic library users. The rest either did not know how to use the system or were content with their current means of obtaining library material. Among the non-owners of computers and/or modems, 61% stated that they could not afford the necessary equipment and 38% indicated they were happy using non-electronic methods of ordering library material. From the total number of respondents, 76% indicated that they did not intend to use electronic access in 1996. The author expresses concern that the students' comfort with conventional means of ordering library items will pose problems for libraries in their library instruction programs. For related articles, see #610 and #622 in this chapter. A. Slade.

618.   Macauley, Peter D. and Anthony K. Cavanagh. "Information Needs of Distance Education Higher Degree by Research Students." In *Reading the Future: Proceedings of the Biennial Conference of the Australian Library and Information Association, World Congress Centre, Melbourne, Australia, 6 October-11 October 1996*. Canberra, ACT: Australian Library and Information Association, 1996, 109-18.

A survey was conducted in Australia to determine whether the information needs of Deakin University distance education higher degree by research students were being met by libraries other than Deakin University Library. This paper examines the perceived needs of off-campus research students, electronic access to library resources, the characteristics of the off-campus research student, and the findings of the survey. Overall, the findings showed that the home institution library is needed but some postgraduate students get by without it. The majority of the students surveyed used both the home institution library and other libraries to satisfy their information needs. The main reasons students use other libraries are convenience, access to material not held by Deakin, and to browse. For more information on the survey, see #619 below. A. Slade.

619.   Macauley, Peter. *Is the Home Institution Library Needed? The Information Needs of Deakin University Distance Education Higher Degree by Research Students: A User-Centered Approach*. M.A.S. (Information Studies) diss., Charles Sturt University–Riverina, 1996. 127 pp.

For his master's thesis, the author conducted a study on the information needs and information-gathering behaviour of Australian postgraduate students seeking a degree by research. The methodology involved using a questionnaire to survey 276 Ph.D. and master's by research students from Deakin University who were studying off-campus within Australia in 1995. To supplement the information received from the questionnaire, statistical data on library use were obtained from Deakin University. Among the findings were that 84% of the respondents had used Deakin University Library at least once during their graduate program; 86% indicated that they had used other libraries for their thesis research; and 64% had received some library instruction from Deakin's library staff, but only 26% had been given any guidance from their supervisor on how to carry out a research project in an off-campus setting. The most important services expected from the library were online and CD-ROM searches. The implications of the findings for the provision of library services to off-campus postgraduate students are discussed and areas requiring further research are identified. A. Slade.

620. Phelps, Renata. "Information Resources and the Off-Campus Student: Are We Expecting Students to Use Them?" In *Access Through Open Learning: Sharing Learning Resources: Opportunities for Universities, TAFE and Other Education Providers*, edited by Allan Ellis. [Southern Cross University] Occasional Papers in Open Learning, vol. 6. Lismore, NSW: Norsearch, 1996, 20-28.

The author discusses the results of her research study on the attitudes and perceptions of teaching staff at Southern Cross University toward the information needs of their distance education students. The study involved in-depth interviews with distance educators to determine their understanding of information skills, their values regarding information literacy, and the influence of these factors on their approach to distance education courses. The interviews revealed that many distance educators had confused and poorly formulated approaches to information skill development in their courses. While distance educators expected their students to access information resources, they did not necessarily expect the students to use library-based information. The author concludes that these approaches and expectations may be hindering the students' development of information literacy skills. It is emphasized that self-directed learning and information literacy are strongly connected and that teaching staff, librarians, and instructional designers have a major role in promoting these skills. For the full report on the author's research, see #621 below. A. Slade.

621. Phelps, Renata. *Information Skills and the Distance Education Student: An Exploratory Study into the Approaches of Southern Cross University Distance Educators to the Information Needs of External Students*. M.D.Ed. thesis, Deakin University, 1996. 120 pp.

As part of her Master of Distance Education degree, the author undertook a research study to examine the attitudes, values, and perceptions of the teaching staff at Southern Cross University (SCU) regarding their external students' information needs and use of libraries. One of the primary aims of the investigation was to determine how librarians can cooperate with faculty members to promote self-directed learning and information literacy. The research was conducted through in-depth interviews with ten SCU distance educators. Among the findings were that the distance educators placed little practical emphasis on the use of libraries to satisfy the information needs of their external students but rather stressed a broad range of other sources, including life skills and experience, media and news sources, the workplace, local organizations, and the private collections of professionals in their community. In terms of information skill development and self-directed approaches to learning, the teaching staff generally had facilitatory methods in place for their on-campus students but had not fully considered how to translate these methods into a distance education context. The author discusses the implications of the findings for distance education provision, SCU structure and function, and further research, and offers a number of recommendations for each of these areas. A. Slade.

1995

622. Cavanagh, Tony. "Electronic Access to Library Catalogues—What Use Do Students Make of It?" *DESIGnation*, no. 7 (April 1995): 10-12.

To investigate the use of electronic ordering of library materials by off-campus students at Deakin University in 1995, data were obtained from the book ordering facility of Deakin's INNOPAC system and from e-mail requests sent to the library. It was found that 7% of all requests received from off-campus students in March 1995 were submitted electronically. In a similar study conducted in 1993, approximately 3% of the requests were received by e-mail or direct ordering through the catalogue. The author notes that in 18 months the number of requests received electronically had more than doubled and observes that electronic access to library services will become increasingly important to off-campus students. For more recent information on electronic ordering at Deakin University, see #309, #610, and #617 in this volume. A. Slade.

623. Wilson, Vicky. "Learning to Learn: The Acquisition of Information Literacy by Isolated Students of Edith Cowan University." *Education for Library and Information Services: Australia* 12, no. 1 (May 1995): 19-31.

Following a discussion of adult learning theory and the concept of information literacy, this paper reports on a study undertaken at Edith Cowan University to determine isolated students' acquisition of information literacy skills and levels of information literacy. In general, the findings suggested that the academic content of the course and the attitude of the lecturers affected information skills acquisition. Among the specific findings were that external students felt disadvantaged by their mode of study; direction from lecturers was not perceived as a major motivational factor for library use; timely delivery of library materials from campus seemed to be more important for external students than the ability to search for information themselves; students who had been away from study for a considerable period of time were much less confident in using electronic resources than students who had taken courses recently; and female students were more confident than males in using basic library services, but less confident in their ability to handle electronic resources. For a related paper, see #625 below. A. Slade.

1994

624. Bowser, Donald R. *Critical Elements of a Student Preferred Distance Support System: A Study of Distance Education Students at an Australian Education Institution*. M.Ed. thesis, University of South Australia, 1994. 113 pp.

The intention of this study was to identify, from a student perspective, critical support services and preferred support practices in distance education. A questionnaire and interviews were used to collect data from distance education students at an unidentified university. Library services, including access to library databases, were identified as a major component of the distance education support system. Among the findings in the survey was that 81% of the students reported using library services. All students felt the university should provide access to adequate stocks of relevant library materials. Students residing in areas with minimal library resources relied heavily on the institution at which they were enrolled. Students with access to good local library resources were less reliant on the university. In the conclusions, direct access to course-related information resources such as library materials is considered to be one of the critical elements of a student preferred support system in distance education. A. Slade.

625. Wilson, Vicky. "Information Literacy and Remote External Students: Exploring the Possibilities Offered by New Communications Technologies." *Australian Academic and Research Libraries* 25, no. 4 (December 1994): 247-52.

A study was undertaken at Edith Cowan University (ECU) to investigate the use of new communications technologies for providing information literacy training to remote external students. Adult learning theory and CPPT (Cooperative Planning, Programming and Teaching) concepts form the basis of a discussion of the study. The findings indicated that external students felt disadvantaged by their mode of study, they made little use of the library services available to them, and their resistance to purchasing new technology was high. Those students who had been away from formal study for a considerable period of time were less confident in their information-seeking abilities than those who had studied recently. Use of new technologies and ECU's Virtual Campus project offer opportunities to develop effective information skills training programs for isolated external students. A major barrier, however, is the attitudes of the academic staff, who need to be convinced of the importance of building information literacy and critical thinking skills into their course materials. The educational role of librarians is stressed in this context and the author advocates that academic librarians need to become more assertive in promoting their services to academic staff. For a related paper, see #623 above. A. Slade.

1993

626. University of New England. Armidale Students' Association. *On the Outside Looking In: External Student Opinion on Distance Education at the University of New England—Armidale, 1992*. Armidale, NSW: Armidale Students' Association, University of New England, 1993. 152 pp.

The Armidale Students' Association of the University of New England conducted a questionnaire survey of 8,760 external students to determine their views on distance education course materials, access to resources and assistance, and residential schools. The survey produced 2,159 responses, representing approximately 26% of the external student population. The questions in the survey concerning libraries and resources were specifically designed to determine the students' satisfaction with the opening hours of the various libraries at the University of New England and whether external students had adequate access to library resources. In the report on the results of the survey, the information on libraries is analyzed by faculty, age, and sex, and is presented under each of the three categories. In the sum total of respondents, the majority found that access to resources other than distance education course materials was adequate and students were generally satisfied with the opening hours of the four campus libraries. Satisfaction rates varied between 67% and 93%. A. Slade.

627.   Wilson, Victoria Jillian. *Information Skills for Isolated Students: New Possibilities*. M. App. Sci. thesis, Curtin University of Technology, 1993. 215 pp.

A study was conducted to investigate the information seeking skills of remote external students of Edith Cowan University and the opportunities for providing information literacy instruction to these students. The methodology involved discussions with faculty librarians at the university, a questionnaire sent to 415 students considered to be geographically isolated, and interviews with the academic staff who taught the courses. Three main areas were investigated in the student questionnaire: attitudes to external study and library use, attitudes and access to technology, and confidence levels in information-seeking tasks. In the findings, students' use of existing library delivery services was low, resistance to technology was high, and students who had been away from formal study for a considerable period of time were consistently less confident in their abilities than those who had studied recently. It was found, however, that isolated external students displayed sophistication in their acquisition of affective information-seeking skills and that lack of confidence was not an obstacle in their information-seeking behaviour. The interviews with academic staff revealed a lack of understanding on their part of the importance of information-seeking skills, and the author concludes that the attitudes of faculty constitute a major barrier to the development of any program of instruction in information literacy. For related papers, see #623 and #625 above. A. Slade.

 **Canada**

For other works that describe user studies in Canada, see the following heading in the Subject Index: "user studies—Canada."

1998

628.   Schafer, Steve. "Student Satisfaction with Library Services: Results of Evaluation Using Focus Groups." In *The Eighth Off-Campus Library Services Conference Proceedings: Providence, Rhode Island, April 22-24, 1998*, compiled by P.

Steven Thomas and Maryhelen Jones. Mount Pleasant, MI: Central Michigan University, 1998, 245-50.

The findings of a focus group survey of student satisfaction with library services at Athabasca University are presented in this paper. The process of selecting participants for inclusion in the focus groups is also outlined. Students who participated in the sessions reported an overall high level of satisfaction with current library services and recommended the need for more publicity about the services and resources available. Students also indicated the need for instruction on how to access library services and how to access information in electronic format. Focus groups were found to be helpful in identifying areas in which the library is effective in its provision to students while at the same time identifying areas of weakness. M. Kascus.

India

For other works that describe user studies in India, see the following heading in the Subject Index: "user studies—India."

1996

---

629. Mishra, Kalpana. "Students' Definition of Support Services." In *Innovations in Distance and Open Learning: Proceedings of the 10th Annual Conference of the Asian Association of Open Universities, November 14-16, 1996, Tehran.* Tehran, Iran: Payame Noor University, 1996, 226-34.

Since there was a lack of research-based information on the effectiveness of student support services at open universities in India, Indira Gandhi National Open University conducted a study to determine how its distance learners perceive the support services available to them and to find ways to change or improve these services. The methodology involved in-depth interviews with a random sample of 50 students and a questionnaire survey of another 100 students. The response rate was 80%. Use of the study center libraries was one of the areas investigated. It was found that most students felt that the library facilities were not well designed or convenient. Problems reported included a shortage of reference books and study materials, limited open hours, and a lack of trained staff to assist the students. Enhanced use of technology and networking was recommended by the students as one way to address some of the problems with the support services. A. Slade.

New Zealand

For other works that describe user studies in New Zealand, see the following heading in the Subject Index: "user studies—New Zealand."

1997

630.   Field, Guy Warwick Wallace. *Your Request Is in the Mail: An Investigation into Client Preferences for the Provision of Distance Library Service.* M.L.I.S. research paper, Victoria University of Wellington, 1997. 80 pp.

   The author investigated the client perspective on distance library services by surveying Open Learning Students enrolled in the Masters of Library and Information Studies program at Victoria University of Wellington. The objectives of the study were to (1) develop and test an instrument for collecting data on user reaction to off-campus library services; (2) investigate the effectiveness of off-campus library services being provided by measuring usage and user satisfaction; and (3) assess the library needs of distance students in relation to advances in educational, communication, and information technologies. A questionnaire, posted to all 75 students, received a 71% response rate. Findings included significant use of other university libraries, high levels of Internet access among students, general satisfaction with services from the campus library, and greater use of catalogue and database access and article supply as opposed to book supply and reference services. Concerns expressed by students focused on rapid delivery of requested material, the ability to place requests by e-mail, the need for user-friendly access to the online catalogue and databases, and access to reserve materials. A. Slade.

United Kingdom

   For other works that describe user studies in the United Kingdom, see the following heading in the Subject Index: "user studies—United Kingdom."

1999

631.   Stephens, Kate. "Notes From the Margins: Library Experiences of Postgraduate Distance Learning Students." In *The Convergence of Distance and Conventional Education: Patterns of Flexibility for the Individual Learner*, edited by Alan Tait and Roger Mills. London: Routledge, 1999, 124-40.

   The findings of a 12-month diary study on the use of libraries by postgraduate distance learning students in the United Kingdom are discussed in relation to the concept of convergence. This concept is considered in two senses: convergence of conventional and distance education and convergence of traditional library services and new information technologies. In relation to the first aspect, the author questions whose responsibility it is to provide a library service for distance learning students and suggests that interlibrary cooperation may be an appropriate guiding principle in this context. With regard to the second sense of convergence, the author points out that visions of the electronic library seem to have little reality for the students who participated in the diary study and electronic resources may actually restrict access to library materials rather than extend it. For a related paper, see #636 below. For further information on the diary study and research project of which it is a part, see #637 in this chapter. A. Slade.

1998

632. Bolton, Neil, Lorna Unwin, and Kate Stephens. "The Use of Libraries by Postgraduate Distance Learning Students; Whose Responsibility?" *Open Learning* 13, no. 1 (February 1998): 3-8.

Selected findings are presented from the national study in the United Kingdom on the library use of postgraduate distance learning students. A qualitative analysis of the open-ended questions in the survey is used to investigate the issue of whose responsibility it is to meet the library needs of distance learners. The questions inquired about the extent of the students' need for libraries, library instruction, problems of distance and time, costs and charges for services, and the library services required by distance students. While the responses indicated a generally positive attitude towards the use of libraries, concerns were expressed about the lack of instruction in the use of libraries, the lack of cooperative arrangements between university libraries, and the charges levied by other academic libraries for borrowing privileges. The responses point toward the need for wider shared responsibility across institutional boundaries for the support of distance learners. For the full report on the survey, see #637 in this chapter. A. Slade.

633. Farmer, Jane, Amanda Richardson, and Sally Lawton. "Library Access: Campaigning for Better Information. Net Profit." *Nursing Standard* 12, no. 17 (January 14, 1998): 28-31.

The findings of the research project on the information needs of nursing staff in remote areas of Scotland are summarized and discussed. For the full report on the project, see #640 in this chapter. A. Slade.

634. Lock, Debbie and Jennifer Nordon. "Designing DiLIS: A Distance Learners' Information Service." *Journal of Library and Information Science* 30, no. 4 (December 1998): 241-48.

As part of the "Library Support for Distance Learners" initiative at the University of Surrey, a questionnaire survey was undertaken to identify the information needs and resource requirements of the university's distance learners. Undergraduate and postgraduate students were included in the survey. Among the findings were that all the respondents had used more than one library or information service for their studies; 62% of the respondents had purchased books and articles; 67% had Internet access; and 53% had not used the university's George Edward Library, either physically or electronically. Based on the needs identified by the distance learners, a Distance Learner's Information Service (DiLIS) was introduced with the following features: a written policy on students' borrowing privileges, a Web-based information gateway, a postal loan and document delivery service, a staffed telephone helpline, remote literature search facilities, a mediation service for arranging access to other libraries, and a user education program. A. Slade.

635.   Mulvaney, Tracy K. and Elaine Lewis. "Analysis of Library Services for Distance Learning Students at the University of Birmingham." *Education Libraries Journal* 41, no. 1 (Spring 1998): 29-34.

Convergence of information services at the University of Birmingham resulted in an enhanced infrastructure for providing library support to distance learners. To determine the use of current library services and the need for improvements, a questionnaire survey was conducted in 1997 of UK-based students registered in distance education programs of the School of Education. With a 32% response rate, the survey yielded the following information: lack of reciprocal borrowing privileges from other university libraries was the most common problem, more library training was required, there was little awareness among the students of the range of electronic resources available to them, and there was a lack of awareness of the guides written for users of the Education Library. When asked to rank potential new services, the respondents identified postal loans, telephone reservations, ability to make more than two telephone renewals for items, and creation of an e-mail box to which general inquiries can be sent. Following the survey, a number of service upgrades were planned, including a library training period integrated into residential weekends, an increase from two to five in the number of renewals permitted on borrowed items, an extension of literature search services to include a wider range of databases, the creation of an Education Library e-mail box, postal loans, and telephone reservations. These new services will be introduced on a pilot basis. A. Slade.

636.   Stephens, Kate. "The Library Experiences of Postgraduate Distance Learning Students or *Alice's Other Story*." In *Libraries Without Walls 2: The Delivery of Library Services to Distant Users*, edited by Peter Brophy, Shelagh Fisher, and Zoë Clarke. London: Library Association Publishing, 1998, 122-42.

A research project on the library experiences of postgraduate distance learning students in the United Kingdom was undertaken at the University of Sheffield from 1994 to 1996 (for the full report on the project, see #637 below). Forty-seven students kept records of their library use in 1995 for periods ranging between three months and a year. The first part of this paper presents a fictional account, based on empirical research, of a distance student going about the process of locating library material for her course. The second part of the paper discusses the findings of the diary study and illustrates some of the typical problems faced by distance students with regard to library access in the United Kingdom. The results of the study indicate that students prefer using libraries in person rather than by remote access. In order of frequency, the libraries most often used are those of other universities, professional and workplace libraries, and public libraries. The most common problems for the students were restricted access to university libraries, inconvenient opening times, commuting distances, and time pressures. A notable finding from the study was that use of other libraries is a clandestine activity for some distance students due to time limitations for site visits and the restrictive policies of many university libraries. For a related paper, see #631 in this chapter. A. Slade.

637.   Unwin, Lorna, Kate Stephens, and Neil Bolton. *The Role of the Library in Distance Learning: A Study of Postgraduate Students, Course-Providers and Librarians in the UK*. London: Bowker Saur, 1998. 256 pp. ISBN 1-85739-221-3.

The authors undertook a large-scale research project through the University of Sheffield in 1994 to investigate the use of libraries by postgraduate distance learning students in the United Kingdom. The project, which lasted until 1996, consisted of five related studies: (1) a questionnaire study of approximately 1,000 postgraduate distance learning students, (2) a diary study involving 47 of the students who completed the questionnaire, (3) interviews with 11 course providers concerning their perceptions of library support for their students, (4) a questionnaire study of 116 university librarians to collect information on services offered to distance learners and on staff attitudes about the role of university libraries in supporting distance learning, and (5) a questionnaire survey of 134 public libraries to determine their role in distance learning. In the findings, 72% of the students who completed the questionnaire reported using a library for course purposes. The students identified many obstacles to library access, reported using public libraries more frequently than other types of libraries, and stated a clear preference for better access to university libraries. The interviews with course providers revealed that these bodies do not give much thought to the integration of library use into student learning experiences and tend not to involve librarians in the planning and delivery of distance learning courses. The survey of academic librarians demonstrated that staffing and resource problems limited the services available to distance learners. While some services are offered on an ad hoc basis, very few examples were found of libraries providing publicized postal services to distance learners. The results from the questionnaire to public libraries showed that the staff regard support of lifelong learning to be one of their primary functions and, in this context, do not distinguish distance learners from other adult independent learners. In addition to presenting a full report on the research project, the authors include in this monograph an extensive review of the literature on distance learning library services from the United Kingdom, North America, and Australia. A. Slade.

1997

---

638. Brophy, Peter and Deborah Goodall. "The Role of the Library in Franchised Higher Education Courses." *Library & Information Briefings*, no. 72 (July 1997): 1-11.

Library services are one of the key elements in the provision of franchised university courses at further education colleges in the United Kingdom. Research conducted at the University of Central Lancashire between 1993 and 1995 examined library support for franchised courses from the points of view of students, tutors, and librarians in both colleges and universities. This report on the research project looks at the growth of franchising in the United Kingdom, library responses to franchised courses, the experiences of librarians in franchising and franchisee institutions, and the student experience of franchising. Sample comments from the various respondents are included in this "briefing" paper. For the full report on the research project, see #642 below. A. Slade.

639.   Farmer, Jane and Amanda Richardson. "Access to Information for Nursing Staff in Remote Areas: Does the Internet Have the Answer?" *Libraries for Nursing Bulletin* 17, no. 1 (1997): 4-7.

The results of the research project on the information needs of nursing staff in remote areas of Scotland are summarized. For the full report on the project, see #640 below. A. Slade.

640.   Farmer, Jane, Amanda Richardson, Sally Lawton, Patricia Morrison, and Rebecca Higgins. *Improving Access to Information for Nursing Staff in Remote Areas: The Potential of the Internet and Other Networked Resources*. Aberdeen, UK: School of Information and Media, Robert Gordon University, 1997. 105 pp.

This is the final report on a research project conducted by the School of Information and Media at Robert Gordon University and funded by the Scottish Library and Information Council and the National Board for Nursing Midwifery and Health Visiting Scotland. A multi-disciplinary team explored the information needs of nurses in the Western Isles of Scotland and the ways in which the provision of information services could be developed or improved. The project methodology included a survey of nursing staff in the Western Isles, an audit of Internet sites that might be useful for nursing staff, a series of workshops to test the value of the Internet in assisting nurses to locate information, and interviews with senior health care managers. The findings identified the following difficulties for nursing staff: remoteness from the hospital library, lack of local information sources, uncertainty about what information is available, and lack of knowledge about how to assess the relevance and quality of information. The research team suggests three models to improve information access for nurses in remote locations: training in information skills, networking the local health sciences library catalogue, and providing access to the Internet and resources on the World Wide Web. For related articles, see #633, #639, and #641 in this chapter. A. Slade.

641.   Farmer, Jane and Amanda Richardson. "Information for Trained Nurses in Remote Areas: Do Electronically Networked Resources Provide an Answer?" *Health Libraries Review* 14, no. 2 (June 1997): 97-103.

A research project on the information needs of nursing staff in remote areas of Scotland examined the potential of the Internet and other networked resources to improve access to information. This paper reviews the literature in the field, describes the research methodology of the project, summarizes the findings, and discusses the implications of these findings. The project revealed that there are gaps in the nursing information available on the Internet and there is a need for more information, originating in the United Kingdom, which is oriented towards the nurse practitioner working in the community. For the full report on the project, see #640 above. A. Slade.

642.   Goodall, Deborah and Peter Brophy. *A Comparable Experience? Library Support for Franchised Courses in Higher Education*. British Library Research and Innovation Report 33. Preston, UK: Centre for Research in Library and Information Management, University of Central Lancashire, 1997. 233 pp. ISBN 090-6694-655.

An extensive research study funded by the British Library between 1993 and 1995 sought to determine how library services were provided to franchised courses in the United Kingdom, what improvements could be made to these services, and how students taking franchised courses obtained needed library materials. The project examined library support from four points of view: the students, their tutors, the college librarians, and the university librarians. The student perspective was obtained through a diary study, interviews, and focus group sessions. A sample of 45 off-campus students and 46 on-campus students was selected from a range of subject disciplines. The perspective of tutors came from interviews and liaison between librarians and tutors about student assignments. The points of view of college and university librarians were obtained through a series of interviews and two major questionnaire surveys. The report provides an extensive literature review, a discussion of the two surveys, details and anecdotal evidence from the student diary study, examples of good practice, and recommendations for developing good practice from the perspectives of the four stakeholders. For related articles, see #162, #382-84, and #424 in the second bibliography and #638, #644, and #649 in this chapter. A. Slade.

643. Stephens, Kate, Lorna Unwin, and Neil Bolton. "The Use of Libraries by Postgraduate Distance Learning Students: A Mismatch of Expectations." *Open Learning* 12, no. 3 (November 1997): 25-33.

This paper reports selected findings from a survey on library use by postgraduate distance learning students in the United Kingdom. Among the key findings are that the expectations of the course providers influence library use; students perceive that course providers frequently underestimate the need for library use in their respective courses; libraries other than those of the host institution are affected by the expansion of distance learning activities; and students make considerable use of public libraries, despite criticism about their adequacy. The authors emphasize that these findings have significant implications for the funding of university courses and the planning of services at both university and public libraries. Consultations among the various stakeholders are urged to ensure adequate library support for distance learning students. For the full report on the survey, see #637 in this chapter. A. Slade.

1996

644. Goodall, Deborah. "Academic Franchising: Some Pointers for Improving Practice." *Library Management* 17, no. 4 (1996): 4-9.

The focus in this article is on the library experiences of students enrolled in franchised courses in the United Kingdom. The information is based on the findings of the British Library funded project "Library Support for Franchised Courses in Higher Education," carried out by the Centre for Research in Library and Information Management at the University of Central Lancashire (see #642 in this chapter for the full report on the project). Students participating in the project kept diaries to record their everyday experiences in using libraries and provided verbal feedback to the researcher in focus group sessions. This article reports some of the weaknesses that students found with college and university libraries, the students' coping strategies to deal with the weaknesses, their assumptions about library use, and their suggestions for improving practice. Based on the students' experiences, the author offers suggestions for improving library services for franchised courses in both the college and the university. A. Slade.

645. Myhill, Martin and Sue Jennings. "The Electronic Library and Distance Resourcing: The Exeter Experience." *Program: Automated Library and Information Systems* 30, no. 2 (April 1996): 111-20.

The University of Exeter investigated the use of information technology by Postgraduate Certificate in Education (PGCE) secondary course students to provide access to library and e-mail facilities. The focus is on the potential offered by the electronic library, other alternative strategies, and the results of a survey questionnaire of library lending patterns of the PGCE group over a two-year period. While dial-up use of the electronic library was reported to be minimal, the results of the survey indicate that electronic access to information services is feasible and an option for supporting distance learning in combination with postal services and an understanding of individual student needs. According to the data collected, personal motivation rather than distance was the single most important factor influencing visits to the university, while proximity to the university influenced library borrowing patterns. The university planned to continue to encourage electronic access by hands-on training, using a portable laptop, lending modems, encouraging remote dial-up, and promoting the World Wide Web. M. Kascus.

646. Owen, Gareth Wyn. *Library Provision for Distance Education at Leicester University*. M.A. diss., Loughborough University, 1996. 74 pp.

A study of library support for distance education at Leicester University involved a questionnaire survey of distance students enrolled at the Education Library and interviews with faculty and library staff. The questionnaire was sent to 219 domestic and overseas students and had a response rate of 43%. The findings compared information from the home and overseas students. Among these findings were that 63% of the home students and 44% of the overseas students had used the information and delivery services of the Education Library; 68% of the home students had access to other libraries, while only 41% of the overseas students had such access; home students relied more on book loans, while overseas students depended more on photocopying; and 35% of the home students had access to information technology, while 52% of the overseas students had such access. The interviews with faculty and library staff confirmed that library provision had not been a consideration in planning distance education programs, including TESOL programs, and that no formal communication procedure was in place between the faculty and the library. In the conclusions, the author proposes that the role of the library be a central consideration in distance education course design and development, and goes on to recommend the creation of a library policy statement on provision for distance education and the inclusion of research methodology and information skills in the distance education courses at Leicester University. A. Slade.

1995

647. Brophy, Peter. "From Understanding Off-Campus Learners to the Virtual Library." In *The Seventh Off-Campus Library Services Conference Proceedings: San Diego, California, October 25-27, 1995*, compiled by Carol J. Jacob. Mount Pleasant, MI: Central Michigan University, 1995, 25-32.

The focus in this paper is on the student experience, based on the belief that better services can only be provided by understanding how students act and why they work in the ways they do. The discussion is based on the "Library Support for Franchised Courses in Higher Education" project, one phase of which involved detailed studies of the student experience. These studies included interviews with instructors and diary and focus group studies of students that compared on- and off-campus students. The paper reports on the provisions of the VALNOW (Virtual Academic Library of the North-West) project, which is intended to bring all the academic libraries in the region together as a single resource for the use of all students. What is stressed here is that continued research into user behaviour and ongoing development of information technology will result in a future in which library services to off-campus students are as comprehensive as those available on-campus. For further information on the "Library Support for Franchised Courses in Higher Education" project, see #642 in this chapter. M. Kascus.

648. Goodall, Deborah. "Distant Students, Distant Libraries: The Student Experience." In *Proceedings of the First "Libraries Without Walls" Conference, Mytilene, Greece, 9-10 September 1995*, edited by Ann Irving and Geoff Butters. Preston, UK: Centre for Research in Library and Information Management, University of Central Lancashire, 1995, 34-42.

The Centre for Research in Library and Information Management (CERLIM) has investigated how library services for franchised courses are being and will be provided. The project examined library support from four perspectives: students, tutors, university libraries, and universities. A sample of 45 students, with a control group of 46 students, was selected from the following academic disciplines: business, engineering, English, health, and leisure. Diaries were kept by the students to record their experiences using libraries to complete class assignments. Focus interviews were used as follow-up with students. Interviews were conducted with college and university libraries to reflect on student experiences. Among the problems encountered by distance students were time, the reserve system, study environment, access to books and journals, and access to staff. Coping strategies are included and suggestions are made for developing better practices. For the full report on the project, see #642 in this chapter. M. Kascus.

649. Goodall, Deborah. "Just in Time, Just in Case, or Just Do Without: The Student Experience of Library and Information Services for Franchised Courses." *CoFHE Bulletin* (The Library Association: Colleges of Further and Higher Education Group), no. 76 (Autumn 1995): 2-7.

From the findings of the research project on library support for franchised courses in the United Kingdom, the author reports on the student experience of library services. The topics covered in this article include how franchised students use libraries, the influence of the tutor on library use, the problems encountered in library use, the students' coping strategies to compensate for these problems, and suggestions for better practice. For a related article, see #644 in this chapter. A. Slade.

1994

650. Library Association. "Franchise Study." *Library Association Record* 96, no. 2 (February 1994): 77.

This brief item reports on the research study being conducted by the Centre for Research in Library and Information Management at the University of Central Lancashire to determine how library services are provided to franchised courses in the United Kingdom. For the full report on the study, see #642 in this volume. A. Slade.

1993

651. Library Association. "Equal Support for Franchise Students." *Library Association Record* 95, no. 10 (October 1993): 551.

This news report announces that a research study funded by the British Library is being conducted by the Centre for Research in Library and Information Management at the University of Central Lancashire to investigate library services for franchise course students in the United Kingdom. For the full report on the study, see #642 in this volume. A. Slade.

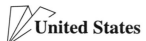# United States

For other works that describe user studies in the United States, see the following heading in the Subject Index: "user studies—United States."

1998

652. Abate, Anne K. *The Role of the Einstein Library of Nova Southeastern University in Meeting the Needs of Distance Education Students*. Ph.D. diss., Nova Southeastern University, 1998. 177 pp. UMI Number 9914576.

The objectives of this study were to investigate the library needs of distance learning graduate students at Nova Southeastern University (NSU) and to propose a new model of service for the Einstein Library based on implementation of current and emerging technologies. To accomplish these objectives, several survey instruments were prepared and distributed by e-mail to students and faculty in selected NSU distance education programs. A variation of the Quality Function

Deployment methodology was used to analyze the results. Among the findings was that many of the students have difficulty locating the information they require and are turning to the Internet as a primary information resource. Based on the results of the surveys, a new model of library service for distance education is proposed, emphasizing a balance between traditional library resources and electronic resources. In this model, students need to develop new skills to acquire and evaluate information. To assist students in developing these skills, librarians will have a role as filtering agents, scanning the entire spectrum of information and selecting resources that will be useful for the students. Ways to accomplish this include authoring guides and user aids, creating web pages, and working with faculty to create links to information resources within online course materials. A. Slade.

653. Burich, Nancy J., Harvey R. Gover, and Kathleen A. Schwanz. "Index Utilization Patterns in University Branch Campus Libraries Which Provide FirstSearch as a Virtual Indexing Tool." In *The Eighth Off-Campus Library Services Conference Proceedings: Providence, Rhode Island, April 22-24, 1998*, compiled by P. Steven Thomas and Maryhelen Jones. Mount Pleasant, MI: Central Michigan University, 1998, 63-110.

Three university branch campus libraries—University of Kansas Regents Center, Washington State University at Tri-Cities, and Washington State University at Spokane—participated in a course-integrated user instruction program for adult evening students to enhance student ability in conducting effective research from remote sites. Analysis is provided on student use patterns of OCLC's FirstSearch across campuses. Among the elements examined are (1) the five most heavily used databases for each site, (2) the relationships found between the average length of a search in these top five databases and the number of uses reported, (3) the possible relationship between program enrollment and the use of databases as a predictor of future use, and (4) trends and changes in FirstSearch use patterns during the four-year study period. For all branch campus libraries, the use of FirstSearch has increased significantly since its introduction in 1992. The study results will inform libraries as to what factors might help to predict future use. M. Kascus.

654. Cassner, Mary and Kate Adams. "Instructional Support to a Rural Graduate Population: An Assessment of Library Services." In *The Eighth Off-Campus Library Services Conference Proceedings: Providence, Rhode Island, April 22-24, 1998*, compiled by P. Steven Thomas and Maryhelen Jones. Mount Pleasant, MI: Central Michigan University, 1998, 117-31.

A survey was conducted to assess instructional support provided by the University of Nebraska-Lincoln (UNL) Libraries to rural graduate students. Faculty who had taught extended education courses were also surveyed as to the use of library services in support of course delivery to students. The population for the study included 184 students who completed one or more courses in the College of Human Resources and Family Sciences (HRFS) extended education program. Responses were received from 110 students (61%). The survey questions are included along with the corresponding results. Findings of both the student and faculty surveys indicate that UNL library services and resources are underutilized. Many students indicated a preference for using other academic and community college libraries in completing their course work. Findings from the study will be used as decision support for improving library services. M. Kascus.

655. Chavez, Todd, Anna Perrault, Stephanie Race, and Rhonda Smith. "The Florida Distance Learning Reference and Referral Center: A Study of User Satisfaction and Some Provider Reflections." In *Internet Librarian '98: Proceedings of the Second Internet Librarian Conference, Monterey, CA, November 1-5, 1998*, compiled by Carol Nixon, M. Heide Dengler, and Mare L. McHenry. Medford, NJ: Information Today, 1998, 67-76.

The final report of the Library Subcommittee of the Florida Institute on Public Postsecondary Distance Learning (see #241 in this bibliography) recommended establishment of a Reference and Referral Center (RRC) to provide assistance to distance learners throughout the state. This center became operational in late 1997 and a preliminary assessment of user satisfaction was conducted in the spring of 1998. All 58 users of the RRC's services were surveyed by questionnaire, with a 65.5% response rate. Among the findings were that 84% of respondents were "extremely satisfied" with RRC services, graduate students used the services more than undergraduates, 69% of respondents were affiliated with Florida's publicly funded universities, and 72% had little or no previous experience with distance education. Following a discussion of the survey results and current RRC operations, future challenges for the Reference and Referral Center are considered. These include increased promotion of direct services and building relationships with distance faculty. A. Slade.

656. Ruddy, Sister Margaret. "Using Citation Analysis to Identify and Monitor Journal Usage by Off-Campus Graduate Students." In *The Eighth Off-Campus Library Services Conference Proceedings: Providence, Rhode Island, April 22-24, 1998*, compiled by P. Steven Thomas and Maryhelen Jones. Mount Pleasant, MI: Central Michigan University, 1998, 239-43.

Citation analysis is used to monitor journal usage by off-campus graduate students. An analysis of citations from master's theses at Cardinal Stritch University was used to determine the type of materials used by students for graduate research, the currency of the material, and the pattern of usage. Included in the study were the theses submitted by students from four master's degree programs: Master of Science in Management, Master of Business Administration, Master of Business Administration-International, and Master of Science in Health Service Administration. The study reinforces the importance of assisting students with their research needs on an individual basis. M. Kascus.

1997

657. Hesser, Lois Ann and George Kontos. "Distance Education: Applications in a Masters and Doctoral Program." *Journal of Educational Technology Systems* 25, no.3 (1996-97): 249-71.

A survey was conducted in 1995 to assess the influence of technology on the ability of doctoral distance education students at Nova Southeastern University to complete their course of study. One question in the survey asked students to rate their use of online research capabilities. More than half of the students in the "cluster" that ran from 1991 to 1994 relied heavily on traditional library facilities for research, while 70% of the students in the 1992–1995 cluster used Nova

Southeastern's online library access for research. The authors attribute part of this difference to the fact that the library's online capabilities were limited in the first two years of the 1991–1994 program. A. Slade.

658. MacFarland, Thomas W. *Students of Nova Southeastern University Evaluate the University's Library and Library Services*. Report 97-12. Fort Lauderdale, FL: Research and Planning, Nova Southeastern University, 1997. 62 pp. ERIC ED 417 738.

Nova Southeastern University (NSU) conducted a survey in 1997 of 941 students, including both on-campus and distance education students, to determine the level of use of the university's libraries and the level of satisfaction with the libraries and library services. The response rate was approximately 17%, but there was ample evidence that the responding sample was representative of the population. Approximately 30% of the respondents indicated no use of the university's libraries or library services and over 40% reported no use of other libraries during a typical term. Respondents indicated general satisfaction with the university's libraries and library services. Despite the fact that NSU has an Electronic Library to meet the needs of distance education students, none of the questions in the survey specifically targeted these students or use of the Electronic Library. As a result, the only information about the use of libraries and library services by distance students is found in the anecdotal comments of the respondents reported at the end of the survey data. A. Slade.

659. Paneitz, Becky. *Community College Students' Perceptions of Student Services Provided When Enrolled in Telecourses*. Ph.D. diss., Colorado State University, 1997. 128 pp. UMI Number 9735008.

A doctoral research study sought to determine whether the type of delivery system used to provide advising, counseling, and library/media services to distance education students at two-year colleges affected the utilization of and satisfaction with such services. The types of delivery systems examined in the study were categorized as "no technology," "low technology," and "high technology." The methodology involved the use of two questionnaires, one sent to 59 community colleges to inquire about services provided and the other sent to a sample of distance students at 10 institutions selected from the responses to the first questionnaire. The findings showed that the type of delivery system used to provide services did not significantly affect the utilization by students nor, for the most part, their satisfaction with the services. Of the three services, advising was found to be the most essential to distance education students. Access to library/media services was found to be second and counseling services was rated third. A. Slade.

660. Rozum, Betty and Kevin Brewer. "Identifying, Developing, and Marketing Library Services to Cooperative Extension Personnel." *Reference & User Services Quarterly* 37, no. 2 (Winter 1997): 161-65.

Since Utah State University (USU) Library had no specific services in place to assist Cooperative Extension personnel, many of whom are in remote areas of the state, a survey was conducted to determine the information needs of this group. The objective was to identify, develop, and market library services that would help extension personnel fulfil their role of disseminating information about university-based research to the people of Utah. The survey had a 65%

response rate and the results indicated the type of information used by extension personnel, where they go to obtain that information, their familiarity with technology, and the time constraints under which they work. Using the survey results, USU librarians selected two services to offer to extension personnel: a web page providing links to relevant resources and an e-mail reference service. A brochure was created to market these services. The authors report that, at the time of writing, initial response to the new services has been minimal. Remote access to full-text databases offers the potential of enhancing support for extension personnel, and USU librarians are planning to promote use of selected databases to this group. A. Slade.

1996

661. Johnson, William. "The Library Component of Distance Learning: Extended Campus Services—The Junction Experience." *Texas Library Journal* 72, no. 4 (Winter 1996): 182-87. Also online. Available: http://www.txla.org/pubs/tlj-4q96/johnson.html (Accessed April 13, 2000).

Texas Tech University, through the Texas Tech Center, provides extended campus services to the rural community of Junction. In this paper, the library use patterns are analyzed to determine the level of interest in updating services. Phase one consisted of an evaluation of the collection and phase two consisted of a survey of faculty who have conducted workshops at Junction. One result of this effort was a decision to provide training for local staff in the use of the library catalogue, periodical indexes, and the Internet. Remote access was facilitated using two modems and two Macintosh computers. The survey response rate was 61% (25/41). The survey explored how the information needs of students were being met by faculty and assessed faculty interest in expanding services. According to the survey, most faculty met the information needs of their Junction students with personal or departmental collections. It was determined that there is sufficient interest to justify upgrading the electronic information services at Junction Center. M. Kascus.

662. Swigger, Kathleen M. and Ken Hartness. "Cooperation and Online Searching via a Computer-Supported Problem Solving Environment." *Journal of the American Society for Information Science* 47, no. 5 (May 1996): 370-79.

This article examines the way we teach librarians to work, noting that both technical and cooperative skills are needed in the workplace. Librarians need to be educated to work in a collaborative environment that promotes clients' needs. A Computer-Supported Cooperative Training (CSCT) problem-solving environment was designed to help librarians and remote users work together in conducting online searching. After developing different online tools, a list of specific performance indicators was created. The CSCT fosters cooperative work yet monitors both individual and group performances. An overview of the CSCT system is given that includes physical components, software, and effective group problem-solving skills. The population for the study was composed of 48 graduate students enrolled at the University of North Texas. Results of the analysis indicated that the groups using the CSCT interface demonstrated more effective skills than the groups that performed the same task face-to-face. M. Kascus.

1995

663. Kabel, Carole J., Carol M. Moulden, and Jack Fritts. "Assessment of Faculty Awareness and Attitudes Regarding Library Services to Off-Campus Students." In *The Seventh Off-Campus Library Services Conference Proceedings: San Diego, California, October 25-27, 1995*, compiled by Carol J. Jacob. Mount Pleasant, MI: Central Michigan University, 1995, 205-12.

This is a report on the results of a survey of faculty awareness of library services and level of satisfaction with those services at National-Louis University (NLU). Of 35 questionnaires distributed to faculty, 24 were returned, for a 69% response rate. When asked whether their assignments required library use, 23 of the respondents (96%) said "yes." The same number indicated that they believed their students had used NLU services in completing library assignments. Three of the questions dealt with library instruction sessions. When asked if they had attended a library instruction session, 23 of the respondents (96%) indicated that they had. A high level of satisfaction with library services was reported and attributed, in part, to using the bibliographic instruction sessions in publicizing library resources and services. M. Kascus.

664. Lauber, Jeanne. *Adult Returning Students and Their Library Needs*. M.S.L.S. thesis, University of North Carolina at Chapel Hill, 1995. 31 pp.

This master's paper is based on a sample of 20 adult returning students obtained from four institutions: University of North Carolina at Chapel Hill, North Carolina Central University, North Carolina State University, and Alamance Community College. Personal interviews were conducted using a set of 13 written questions. An additional open-ended question was added during the data collection process. Findings of the study indicated that adult returning students do have needs different from those of traditional students, especially in the area of computer technology. Several respondents indicated that librarians need to have patience with adult returning students while at the same time they need to be sensitive to their need not to feel inadequate. A majority of the respondents indicated that they would have liked to have received one-to-one assistance, supporting the idea that personal attention is important to this group. These students also indicated a strong desire for a workshop or course on using the library. The importance of libraries evaluating and re-evaluating services for adult returning students is stressed. M. Kascus.

665. Miller, Greg. "Off-Campus Study in Agriculture: Challenges and Opportunities." *Journal of Agricultural Education* 36, no. 2 (1995): 1-7.

In this research study, the experiences of former agricultural distance learners at Iowa State University are reported and their perceptions regarding obstacles to off-campus study are described. The population for the study was all bachelor's (7) and master's (46) of agriculture students graduating from Iowa State University through the fall of 1993. The instrument used was a six-point Likert-type scale ranging from significant to insignificant. Data collection was by mail questionnaire. Survey results indicated that 62.5% of those responding identified "access to library facilities" as one of the most significant obstacles to off-campus study. The research will help program managers to assess the needs of agriculture distance learners as decision support for planning services. M. Kascus.

666. O'Neal, Willie Mae. "Faculty and Liaison for the Off-Campus Library Services Conference." In *The Seventh Off-Campus Library Services Conference Proceedings: San Diego, California, October 25-27, 1995*, compiled by Carol J. Jacob. Mount Pleasant, MI: Central Michigan University, 1995, 269-76.

A survey was conducted to investigate the perceptions of faculty concerning library services at Western Michigan University's five regional centers. Of 274 faculty surveyed, responses were received from 119. The findings indicated that 24% of the respondents used the service and 18% were unaware of the service. On rating library services, 48% rated the availability of these services at the regional centers as excellent. The results suggest the need for faculty and librarians to have a closer working relationship through improved communication and more frequent contact. A copy of the survey instrument is included in this paper. M. Kascus.

667. Schwellenbach, Sue. "Student Perspectives on Extended Campus Programs and Library Services." *Colorado Libraries* 21, no. 1 (Spring 1995): 25-27.

Examples of the variety of students taking courses in Colorado's higher education institutions via distance education are provided along with insights into student attitudes toward extended campus programs and the library services that support them. The conversations resulting from an informal survey of students taking distance learning courses at Colorado State University, University of Northern Colorado, and Regis University are described here. The results from this survey are compared with the findings from surveys on student characteristics and perceptions conducted at other institutions. The findings from this survey indicate that flexibility is the single most important reason for choosing distance education over traditional on-campus education, and the overall perception of students about library services is positive. M. Kascus.

668. Shouse, Daniel L. "Library Needs of Rural Distance Education Students." In *The Seventh Off-Campus Library Services Conference Proceedings: San Diego, California, October 25-27, 1995*, compiled by Carol J. Jacob. Mount Pleasant, MI: Central Michigan University, 1995, 355-62.

This paper reports on a survey of rural distance education students at East Carolina University to determine their library and information needs. Previous research on distance education students is reviewed, the methodology of the present study is described, and the results of the survey and its implications for library services are summarized. The survey collected demographic data as well as data on which library students used to complete their course work, the performance of the library, and an open-ended question on what services students would like to see the library provide. Survey results indicated that most of the respondents were graduate students (83%) over the age of 25 (82%). In general, the students reported using mostly local libraries and they were fairly satisfied with the resources and services of those libraries. Only 27% of the students responded to the open-ended question with requests for access to the online catalogue, longer hours, longer check out time for books, and more librarians for bibliographic instruction. M. Kascus.

1992

669. Dillon, Connie L., Charlotte N. Gunawardena, and Robert Parker. "Learner Support: The Critical Link in Distance Education." *Distance Education* 13, no. 1 (1992): 29-45.

The Oklahoma Televised Instruction System was evaluated through an analysis of the learner support services. The study examined student attitudes in three areas: (1) the resources available, (2) the coordination of services among the on-campus and distance sites, and (3) the mechanical and electronic transfer of information to the learner. A comparison was made of the attitudes and performance of the participating on-campus and distance students toward the teaching-learning experience. Findings from the study indicated that library services are a prime concern of the distance students and that telecommunications technology helps to bridge the gap between the on-campus library and the distance learner. The authors note that, contrary to prevailing opinion, distance students are not adversely affected relative to course performance. This article is an expanded version of #434 in the second bibliography. M. Kascus.

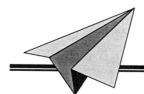

CHAPTER 10

Library Case Studies

Asia

1999

670. Saroja, G. and G. Sujatha. *Application of Total Quality Management to Library and Information Services in Indian Open Universities*. Paper presented at the Pan-Commonwealth Forum on Open Learning, Brunei Darussalam, 1-5 March 1999: Empowerment through Knowledge and Technology. Online. Available: http://www.col.org/forum/casestudies.htm (in pdf format) (Accessed April 13, 2000).

      The concept of total quality management (TQM) is examined and applied to Indian distance education institutions and their library services. The experiences of Dr. B. R. Ambedkar Open University in providing quality information services are outlined, with reference to surveys conducted on the use of resources at the study center libraries. A proposal is offered for a TQM framework for the distance education libraries, emphasizing policies, resources, processes, and user satisfaction. Suggestions for implementing quality in distance education libraries include integration of library quality assurance with the university's TQM project, development of standards for assessing quality of information services, development of methodologies for improvement of services, allocation of specific funding for studying quality of information services, and training library staff in providing quality services. A. Slade.

1998

671. Ali, Muhammad Saadat. *The "State-of-the-Art" of Information Management in the Bangladesh Open University Library*. Paper presented at the AAOU Asian Librarians' Roundtable, November 1-2, 1998, The Open University of Hong Kong. Online. Available: http://www.ouhk.edu.hk/~AAOUNet/round/round.htm (in pdf format) (Accessed April 13, 2000).

The current operations of the Bangladesh Open University Library are described and future plans are outlined. The central library in Gazipur provides reference services and reading materials for teachers, research students, and staff members. The 12 Regional Resource Centres have library facilities for listening to audiotapes, viewing videotapes, reading books, and consulting reference materials. In the near future, the library will be fully computerized and a multimedia network, including networked CD-ROMs, will provide access to library and information resources for students at the regional and local centers and other locations in Bangladesh. A. Slade.

672. Ding, Xingfu. *The Library System and Its Services in China's Radio and TV Universities*. Paper presented at the AAOU Asian Librarians' Roundtable, November 1-2, 1998, The Open University of Hong Kong. Online. Available: http://www.ouhk.edu.hk/~AAOUNet/round/round.htm (in pdf format) (Accessed April 13, 2000).

China's national distance teaching system consists of Radio and TV Universities (RTVUs), including a central RTVU, 44 provincial-level RTVUs, 831 city-level branch schools, and more than 1,600 county-level working stations. The library in the central RTVU provides services to academics and professional staff. The libraries in the provincial-level RTVUs serve both academics and students. The libraries in the branch schools and workstations serve mainly local students who participate in group-based learning. Since 1995, a growing number of students are studying on an independent basis. To solve the access problems for these students, the RTVUs are planning to develop an electronic library system with outreach services by first connecting libraries to local campus networks, then establishing a distributed study center network, and finally developing means for home-based personal computers to be connected to the various networks. The author notes that China has a long way to go to reach this destination. A. Slade.

673. Ismail, Abd. Akla Wan. *The Role of Electronic Library Service Supporting Distance Education Students, and Current Trends in Library Related Information Technology*. Paper presented at the AAOU Asian Librarians' Roundtable, November 1-2, 1998, The Open University of Hong Kong. Online. Available: http://www.ouhk.edu.hk/~AAOUNet/round/round.htm (in pdf format) (Accessed April 13, 2000).

Library services for the distance students of Universiti Sains Malaysia include formal agreements with other libraries in the country, postal services for book loans and provision of photocopies, library instruction, Internet access to the online catalogue and five virtual subject libraries, online reference services, and home page access to course materials. Future plans involve enhanced relationships with other libraries in Malaysia, linking regional center libraries to the main library through the cooperative network, development of in-house databases with content relevant to distance education, and a patron-initiated electronic inquiry service. A. Slade.

674. Jagannathan, Neela. *Library System and Information Services at the Indira Gandhi National Open University*. Paper presented at the AAOU Asian Librarians' Roundtable, November 1-2, 1998, The Open University of Hong Kong. Online. Available: http://www.ouhk.edu.hk/~AAOUNet/round/round.htm (in pdf format) (Accessed April 13, 2000).

Indira Gandhi National Open University (IGNOU), with over 400,000 distance students in India, has a three-tier library system, consisting of a central library at its headquarters and branch libraries at its 21 regional centers and 342 study centers. The central library serves primarily the academic, professional, and administrative staff of the university. The libraries at the regional and study centers serve IGNOU distance students as well as counsellors and academic and support staff posted at the centers. Details are provided on services available through the central library, collection development practices, and computerization and digitalization in the IGNOU library system. Future plans include CD-ROM networking, CD-ROM publishing, online access to commercial databases, Internet services, participation in external library networks, development of a local area network (LAN), and involvement in a wide area network (WAN) of distance teaching institutions. A. Slade.

675. Kwak, Duk-Hoon. *The Establishment of Digital Library System for Audio/Video Materials*. Paper presented at the AAOU Asian Librarians' Roundtable, November 1-2, 1998, The Open University of Hong Kong. Online. Available: http://www.ouhk.edu.hk/~AAOUNet/round/round.htm (in pdf format) (Accessed April 13, 2000).

The digitization of audio and video materials for distance students at the Korea National Open University is described in this brief paper. The advantages of this initiative include utilization of computer networks to provide education on demand, reductions in space for storing broadcasting material, elimination of the need to convert data for broadcasting, access to study materials outside the limits of broadcasting time, and facilitation of the development of a virtual education system in Korea. A. Slade.

676. Payawal, Eleanor S. *UPOU Library Plans*. Paper presented at the AAOU Asian Librarians' Roundtable, November 1-2, 1998, The Open University of Hong Kong. Online. Available: http://www.ouhk.edu.hk/~AAOUNet/round/round.htm (in pdf format) (Accessed April 13, 2000).

At present, the University of the Philippines Open University (UPOU) supplies its distance students with "readers" containing copies of information resources and readings needed for distance education courses. Some supplementary and reference materials are also made available at the various UPOU learning centers. The university intends to maintain its own library at the central administration site and to send materials from there to its distance learners. Other plans involve computerization of the library, resource sharing through membership in a consortium of libraries in the Philippines, and arrangements with local libraries to enable students to use those facilities. A. Slade.

677. Prudtikul, Somsuang. *Library Services at Sukhothai Thammathirat Open University*. Paper presented at the AAOU Asian Librarians' Roundtable, November 1-2, 1998, The Open University of Hong Kong. Online. Available: http://www.ouhk.edu.hk/~AAOUNet/round/round.htm (in pdf format) (Accessed April 13, 2000).

Sukhothai Thammathirat Open University (STOU) in Thailand provides library services through its Office of Documentation and Information (ODI). ODI's central library serves staff members, researchers, members of the public, and students who attend activities on campus. Library services are also available at the university's regional Academic Development Service Centers and Graduate Educational Resource Centers. Each center acts as a repository for current library materials and offers reference and information services to students and staff. Provincial services are offered at STOU Corners, located in 75 public libraries in Thailand. ODI currently uses information technology to provide access to a number of library functions, including the online catalogue, commercial online and CD-ROM databases, the Internet, and locally developed databases on specific subjects. Future plans for ODI involve linking the Academic Development Service Centers to the library network. A. Slade.

678. Shewale, Madhukar N. *Networking of Indian Open Universities: A Proposal*. Paper presented at the AAOU Asian Librarians' Roundtable, November 1-2, 1998, The Open University of Hong Kong. Online. Available: http://www.ouhk.edu.hk/~AAOUNet/round/round.htm (in pdf format) (Accessed April 13, 2000).

Following a brief discussion of the structure of Yashwantrao Chavan Maharashtra Open University and the role of its Library and Resource Centre, the author presents a proposal to network all the open universities in India. The advantages of this proposal are described in terms of online access to university programs, study materials, projects and assignments, students and tutors, and a database of alumni. A. Slade.

679. Sujatha, G. *Brief Note on the Services Provided and Future Plans of Dr.. B. R. Ambedkar Open University Library, Hyderabad*. Paper presented at the AAOU Asian Librarians' Roundtable, November 1-2, 1998, The Open University of Hong Kong. Online. Available: http://www.ouhk.edu.hk/~AAOUNet/round/round.htm (in pdf format) (Accessed April 13, 2000).

Dr. B. R. Ambedkar Open University in India has a central library at its headquarters and small libraries at its various study centers and postgraduate centers. Brief information is provided on the library collections, staff, finance and budget, technical processes, library services, clientele, and computerization. Computerization of library operations is expected to be completed in 1999, followed by development of a local area network (LAN) and a dial-up facility to link the study centers to the central library. Future plans include providing Internet services at the central library, giving distance students access to the Internet and the resources of the central library through the proposed network, establishing a multimedia unit, and extending home-lending of books to students through the study centers. A. Slade.

680. Sulaiman, Wahid. *Tun Abdul Razak Library, Institut Teknology Mara Shah Alam, Selangor Darul Ehsan*. Paper presented at the AAOU Asian Librarians' Roundtable, November 1-2, 1998, The Open University of Hong Kong. Online. Available: http://www.ouhk.edu.hk/~AAOUNet/round/round.htm (in pdf format) (Accessed April 13, 2000).

The library system of the Institut Teknology Mara in Malaysia consists of five libraries at the main campus and 11 libraries at branch campuses located throughout the country. While computerization of the libraries is under development, electronic access is currently provided to the library catalogue, networked CD-ROMs, and commercial database services. Future plans of the library include migration to a new integrated application system, purchase of a document imaging system, development of a local area network (LAN), and introduction of a smart card system and a self-charge system. A. Slade.

681. Sahyono, Effendi and M. Hum. *A Plan for the Development of the Library of Indonesia Open Learning University*. Paper presented at the AAOU Asian Librarians' Roundtable, November 1-2, 1998, The Open University of Hong Kong. Online. Available: http://www.ouhk.edu.hk/~AAOUNet/round/round.htm (in pdf format) (Accessed April 13, 2000).

The library collection of the Indonesian Open Learning University, Universitas Terbuka, supports the institution's academic staff but not its 400,000 distance students. Agreements with selected libraries, including the Indonesian National Library, provide access for students who live near those libraries. However, many students who live in remote areas cannot benefit from these arrangements. The author argues that developing electronic library systems can overcome this disadvantage. Progress in this regard is noted. The main obstacle to providing electronic resources to students is the cost of computer equipment and network access. To address this challenge, the University Library plans to establish cooperative working arrangements with other university libraries to extend services to remote students. State postal offices in Indonesia provide a point of access to computer networks and the Internet. One of the significant problems associated with this plan is the lack of trained staff to manage electronic resources. A. Slade.

682. Wong, Wai-man. *Library Services for Distance Learners in the Open University of Hong Kong*. Paper presented at the AAOU Asian Librarians' Roundtable, November 1-2, 1998, The Open University of Hong Kong. Online. Available: http://www.ouhk.edu.hk/~AAOUNet/round/round.htm (in pdf format) (Accessed April 13, 2000).

The Open University of Hong Kong (OUHK) has developed an electronic library to provide its distance students with round-the-clock remote access, through a Web-based common user interface, to the online catalogue, bibliographic databases, reserve materials, and full-text products. In addition, a video server has been established to supply on-demand instructional videos over the Internet to teach students how to use the electronic library services. Other services of the OUHK Library include a Voice Response System for telephone renewals, classroom instruction sessions on campus at the beginning of each semester, a CD-ROM on the use of the electronic library and the campus library, and an agreement with the public library system in Hong Kong to deposit course materials and set books at selected public libraries and to provide a link to the OUHK electronic library on the public libraries' web pages. Future plans call for more information literacy programs to promote the use of the electronic library and application of the latest information technology to allow full remote access to the electronic library services without compromising security controls. A. Slade.

1997

---

683. Wong, Wai-man. "Library Resources: Going Electronic to Provide Quality Support for Learners." In *Quality Assurance in Distance and Open Learning: Papers Prepared for the 11th Annual Conference of the Asian Association of Open Universities (AAOU), Kuala Lumpur, Malaysia, November 11-14, 1997*, edited by C. P. Chooi, et al. Selangor, Malaysia: Institut Teknologi MARA. 1997, 261-73.

The Open University of Hong Kong (OUHK) has found that approximately 90% of its distance students have easy access to personal computers. This access and the shortage of space in Hong Kong have prompted OUHK to develop an electronic library that can be used at off-campus locations, including students' homes and local public libraries. Through a common user Web interface, students can search over 1,000 full-text and bibliographic databases as well as OUHK's online catalogue and other catalogues available on the Internet. They can also place online reservations for material, renew borrowed items, and access course reference materials that have been digitized and mounted on the system. Statistics on usage of resources can be easily collected and monitored through an electronic logging system. Space on the system is not a problem and there is ample room for future expansion of the electronic library to respond to increases in student population and course provision by the university. For a more recent paper on OUHK's electronic library, see #682 above. A. Slade.

1996

---

684. Korale, S. R. "Library Services for Distance Education: The Sri Lankan Experience and Vision." *Information Development* 12, no. 2 (June 1996): 113-16.

With reference to the development of distance education in Sri Lanka, the challenges of providing library services to the students of the Open University of Sri Lanka (OUSL) are examined from both a historical and a future perspective. The OUSL central library was intended to serve primarily the academic and administrative staff. Early attempts to provide library services to students through public libraries proved to be unsuccessful. Since then, limited amounts of library materials have been deposited at OUSL's regional and study centers for student use. The introduction of information technologies and an online catalogue holds great promise for enhancing services to students. The university''s immediate aim is to link regional and study centers to the main campus. The ideal future at OUSL will provide distance learners with access to library services equal to those available to on-campus users. The problems to be overcome include cost control and training end-users in accessing databases. A. Slade.

1995

685. Chandraiah, I. "Library in Distance Education—A Case Study." *Herald of Library Science* 34, nos. 1-2 (January-April 1995): 14-20.

    Details are provided on the library services of Dr. B. R. Ambedkar Open University in India. The primary purpose of the central library at headquarters is to support the university's teaching staff and course writers. The libraries of the study centers assist students and counsellors at the centers. Topics covered in this article include collection development, technical services, information services, reprography services, users and library use, budget, and facilities. Two problems facing the library at the time of writing were space issues and staff development. A. Slade.

686. Kanjilal, Uma and S. M. Tripathi. "Collection Development: Planning for IGNOU Library System." *Library Acquisitions: Practice and Theory* 19, no. 1 (Spring 1995): 83-95.

    The library collections at the regional and study centers of Indira Gandhi National Open University (IGNOU) generally contain books recommended for the various distance education courses, self-instructional course materials, audio-visual materials, and some reference resources. Faculty recommendations are the basis for the selection of resources for the centers. Acquisition and processing of books take place at the headquarters library to avoid unnecessary duplication. Since the budget to acquire materials for the regional and study centers cannot match the increases in student enrollments and the library resources at the centers cannot meet the needs of all IGNOU distance students, it is necessary for some students to use local public and academic libraries. The authors point to the need for a well-planned collection development program for IGNOU and identify potential strategies to meet future requirements, including formal agreements with other libraries, development of a multimedia resource center, and use of fax transmission to send copies of articles and book chapters to the regional and study centers. A. Slade.

1994

687. Chandhok, Seema. "Computer Applications at IGNOU Library." *Library Science with a Slant to Documentation* 31, no. 2 (June 1994): 66-86.

    Indira Gandhi National Open University (IGNOU) in India provides mass education at a distance. At the time of writing, the university was in the process of automating its central library and establishing local and wide area networks to provide information and reference assistance to IGNOU's regional and study centers. This article discusses the various databases created by the library as well as their structures and worksheets. It also highlights some of the unique features required by the library for an automated system and outlines IGNOU's short- and long-term plans for the computerization of library operations. A. Slade.

Australia

For other works that describe the services of specific institutions in Australia, see the following heading in the Geographic Index: "Australia—case studies."

1999

688.   Peacock, Judith and Michael Middleton. "Mixed Mode Education: Implications for Library User Services." *New Library World* 100, no. 1146 (1999): 11-19.

Although the Queensland University of Technology (QUT) does not offer any of its courses by distance education, it has introduced electronic means for students to complete some of their coursework off-site. The QUT Library has supported these developments by providing access to electronic reference services, online and CD-ROM databases on existing networks, the Electronic Reserve Collection, and an electronic document delivery service called REDD (Regional Document Delivery Project). In addition to supplying details about these library initiatives, the paper discusses support services for faculty and the changing role of the library and librarians in the context of information technologies. A. Slade.

1998

689.   Clark, Judith and Ron Store. "Flexible Learning and the Library: The Challenge." *Journal of Library Services for Distance Education* 1, no. 2 (June 1998). Online. Available: http://www.westga.edu/~library/jlsde/vol1/2/JClark_RStore.html (Accessed April 13, 2000).

Flexible learning and flexible delivery pose challenges for librarians in Australian higher education. Flexible delivery is defined as "the provision of learning and assessment opportunities in modes which serve to increase the degree of student control over when, how, and at what pace they learn." The focus in this paper is on James Cook University in Queensland, which recently re-examined the library's role in relationship to flexible delivery. The library's changing role is discussed based on the model of course development teams in which libraries can make the following contributions: identifying appropriate literature, networking resources to support course preparation, and providing an information literacy component. The need for flexible learning students to develop information literacy skills is stressed. Because the flexible learning environment is an interactive one, librarians will need to develop new ways of interacting with students to ensure that their needs are met. M. Kascus.

690.   Grigg, Trevor and Allison Brown. "Creating a Centre of Excellence in Flexible Teaching and Learning." *HERDSA News* 20, no. 3 (November 1998): 6-7.

Pointing to the expansion of flexible learning in Australian university programs, this paper describes the University of Queensland's new campus in Ipswich. The campus has been built specifically for the purpose of flexible delivery, with hi-tech facilities, state-of-the-art computer rooms that accommodate a high ratio of computers to students, and library facilities to support online teaching, learning, and research. A. Slade.

691. McKnight, Sue. "Library Services to Off-Campus Students: An Australian Perspective." In *Libraries Without Walls 2: The Delivery of Library Services to Distant Users*, edited by Peter Brophy, Shelagh Fisher, and Zoë Clarke. London: Library Association Publishing, 1998, 52-62. Also online. Available: http://www.deakin.edu.au/library/lww6.html (Accessed April 13, 2000).

> Deakin University has earned a reputation for providing high-quality library services to its off-campus students. Deakin's services are described with reference to the Australian context of higher education, the characteristics of its off-campus student body, the guiding philosophies of the library, information service statistics, and performance standards. Three broad types of services support Deakin's distance education programs: collection development, information services, and interlibrary loans. These services are complemented by the electronic resources available through remote access, a reciprocal borrowing scheme in the state of Victoria, and a guide developed especially for off-campus students. Management of the service, research studies conducted by Deakin staff, and future directions in library services constitute the remaining topics discussed in this overview. A. Slade.

1997

---

692. Cavanagh, Tony. "Flexible Learning—Where Does the Library Fit in?" In *Flexible Learning in Action: Case Studies in Higher Education*, edited by Rachel Hudson, Sian Maslin-Prothero, and Lyn Oates. London: Kogan Page, 1997, 153-59.

> The philosophy of library service for distance learners at Deakin University is that these students have the same rights to a quality library service as do on-campus students. In practice, the library has accepted responsibility for supplying books, audio-visual items, and photocopies to off-campus students. It also provides a reference service, interlibrary loans for eligible students, and letters of introduction to other libraries. This case study describes Deakin's off-campus library service in terms of the library collection, requesting material, delivery of material, reference assistance, the future role of electronic access, and minimum standards for library services. The keys to the success of the service are identified as a willingness by the institution to support and fund the service, publicity and ease of access for students, a reliable method of delivering material, and an acceptable satisfaction rate for requests. A. Slade.

693. Lim, Edward and Marie Thérèse Van Dyk. "Library Support Models for Distance Education: The Australian Experience." In *Libraries and Other Academic Support Services for Distance Learning*, edited by Carolyn A. Snyder and James W. Fox. Foundations in Library and Information Science, vol. 39. Greenwich, CT: JAI Press, 1997, 57-91.

Following a brief history of distance learning in Australia, three broad educational models are described. The first model, created by the University of Queensland, has parity of access as its major principle. The second model, which has equity of access and cooperation as its major principles, is exemplified by the University of New England, Macquarie University, and Monash University. This model has a wide range of support materials, including study guides, videos, CD-ROM, computer-assisted learning (CAL) packages, and supplementary collections. The third model is open learning, characterized by flexible, innovative, self-paced learning. There is discussion of the impact of technology and the range of networking technology used to deliver education to remote students. This technology includes voice processing systems, public telecommunications networks, cable television networks, cellular networks, local area networks, mobile computing, telecenters, and the Community Information Network (CIN). Several library support models are discussed: Monash University, Gippsland; OLLIS (Open Learning Library and Information Service); and Monash University, Berwick. The authors conclude with a discussion of the virtual campus concept and virtual library services. M. Kascus.

694. Parnell, Stephen. *A Distance Education Library Management Project at Charles Sturt University*. Paper presented to the Australian Library and Information Association Distance Education Special Interest Group National Conference: Shifting Sands, Charles Sturt University, Wagga Wagga, December 5-6, 1997. Available from: Christine Cother, Editor DESIGnation, University of South Australia Library, Holbrooks Road, Underdale, South Australia 5032.

Charles Sturt University Library has initiated a project to improve services to distance education students with the following objectives: to develop and implement an effective management system to even out workload and turnaround time, to identify high-demand items for inclusion in a reserve collection and possible digitization, and to provide a profile of use and users of the Distance Education Library Service. This project is part of an overall proposal to shift emphasis from document delivery of hardcopy items to student-initiated electronic article delivery. Details are provided about the major components of the proposal, its rationale, anticipated benefits, progress, costs, and evaluation. Progress to date includes establishment of a database of requests received from distance students and an analysis of the database to determine the need to purchase multiple copies of books and set up a collection of high-demand material. A. Slade.

695. Steel, Kay. *Service Enhancement Via Restructuring*. Paper presented to the Australian Library and Information Association Distance Education Special Interest Group National Conference: Shifting Sands, Charles Sturt University, Wagga Wagga, December 5-6, 1997. Available from: Christine Cother, Editor DESIGnation, University of South Australia Library, Holbrooks Road, Underdale, South Australia 5032.

The following major changes at Monash University have resulted in improved library services for distance education students: reorganization of the Gippsland campus library, a move of the distance education operation into the university's main library service, and a survey of Monash University distance education students. In the library reorganization, off-campus services changed from being a centralized unit to a decentralized unit called External Services, with document delivery functions added to the work of the unit. This has resulted in faster turnaround time as more staff are available to perform the work. While the findings of the survey of distance education students indicated that most students were satisfied with the services currently provided, feedback prompted the library to make material held at other campus libraries available to the distance students and to improve publicity about off-campus library services. A. Slade.

1996

696.   Cother, Christine. "A Change Is as Good as a Holiday!" *DESIGnation*, no. 10 (May 1996): 7-8.

The Flexible Delivery Service at the University of South Australia was formed by bringing together Interlibrary Loans, the Distance Education Library Service, and the National Periodical Service for Schools. There have been several advantages for staff, including better access to phones and personal computers. It is noted that the consolidation has been achieved in a way that has been almost invisible to users of the Distance Education Library Service. Its collection and service will remain separate within the larger unit, continuing to provide excellent delivery and reference services to the university's distance, flexible, and open learning students and staff. A. Slade.

697.   Lim, Edward. "The Virtual Library Meets the Virtual Campus: Strategies for the 21st Century." In *Electronic Dream? Virtual Nightmare: The Reality for Libraries: Conference Proceedings: 1996 VALA Biennial Conference and Exhibition, 30 January to 1 February 1996, World Congress Centre, Melbourne*. Melbourne, Victoria: Victorian Association for Library Automation Inc., 1996, 21-37.

With reference to the development of online teaching in Australian universities, the author describes the virtual campus and virtual library model at Monash University's Berwick Campus. From the beginning of the campus in 1991, the university decided to use networked communications technologies to deliver many of the courses based at Berwick. To support these courses, Monash developed a virtual library service. The model is based on an alliance with the Casey Institute of TAFE, which is located opposite the Berwick Campus. Books and other print resources needed for the courses are housed at the Casey Institute Library. The Berwick Campus has allocated a small area, called the "electronic library," where students can access various online services and resources, including an electronic reserve collection. Discussion is provided on the technical, legal, financial, training, and social/cultural problems and issues associated with the electronic library. A. Slade.

698.   Parnell, Stephen. "Literature Searches and Distance Education: Whose Problem?" [Charles Sturt University. Open Learning Institute] *Occasional Papers in Open and Distance Learning*, no. 20 (November 1996): 7-14. Also online. Available: http://www.csu.edu.au/division/oli/oli-rd/occpap20/parnell.htm (Accessed April 13, 2000).

With particular reference to Charles Sturt University (CSU), the challenges in providing literature search services for distance education students are examined. Three difficulties are identified in this context: (1) conducting a reference interview with a distant user, (2) balancing requests from off-campus students with requests from on-campus library users, and (3) resolving ethical issues regarding the provision of information to students who are expected to develop the skills of information retrieval. This latter difficulty pertains especially to library school students studying at a distance. Issues concerning information literacy and the library's role in lifelong learning are discussed in relation to CSU's services to distance learners. The question is posed as to who should take responsibility for the intellectual content of literature searches. CSU's policy in this regard is to offer differential service based on the nature and level of the course and the degree of isolation of the student. A. Slade.

1995

699. Dowling, Sue and Pim McCready. "Visions at Murdoch University." *DESIGnation*, no. 9 (October 1995): 2.

As part of the "Visions" campaign to mark the 20th anniversary of Murdoch University, a library link was added to the university's web page. The External Services Section of the Library used this link as an opportunity to widen students' access to information and expand their means to contact library staff. Through online forms, external students can submit requests for books, articles, and subject requests. These trial services have been positively received by Murdoch's distance learners. A. Slade.

700. Kis-Rigo, John. "From the North." *DESIGnation*, no. 9 (October 1995): 1-2.

The challenges in providing library services to distance learners living in remote areas are illustrated by a report on the Library at Batchelor College in the Northern Territory of Australia. Many of the students live in the "bush," where the seasonal wet weather can disrupt transportation and communication systems. Instances of downed telephone lines and closure of roads and airstrips add complications to the delivery of library materials to isolated areas. In spite of these problems, the Batchelor College Library still manages to provide users "with the resources they want when they want them." A. Slade.

701. Redding, Jennifer. "External Students at the University of Southern Queensland." *DESIGnation*, no. 7 (April 1995): 2-3.

Details are provided on the Off-Campus Library Service unit at the University of Southern Queensland. Library staff participate in regional orientation sessions for the distance students. The Off-Campus Library Service unit, which is part of Lending Services, has a full-time librarian, two library assistants, and two administrative assistants. Services provided include a toll-free telephone number, an e-mail address, reference services, and book and article delivery. It is noted that, despite the toll-free telephone number and e-mail address, about 70% of requests from off-campus students are received by fax. A. Slade.

702. Wilson, Vicky. "The Virtual Campus: Encouraging the Acquisition of Information Seeking Skills with Distance Education Students." In *The Learning Link: Information Literacy in Practice*, edited by Di Booker. Adelaide, SA: Auslib Press, 1995, 163-68.

   This case study describes the use of Edith Cowan University's Virtual Campus, an electronic bulletin board service, to promote information literacy skills among distance education students enrolled with the Department of Library and Information Science. Details are provided on students' reactions to services available through the Virtual Campus, including bulletin board features, access to online databases, chat facilities, and e-mail. It is noted that traditional bibliographic instruction programs tend to ignore the affective domain of feelings and attitudes, and Edith Cowan University's experiments in using the Virtual Campus to promote study and information-seeking skills have proved effective in addressing the affective needs of its external students. A. Slade.

# Canada

For other works that describe the services of specific institutions in Canada, see the following heading in the Geographic Index: "Canada—case studies."

1997

703. Copeland, Lynn, Elaine Fairey, and Todd M. Mundle. "Libraries and Online Teaching and Learning." *Journal of Distance Education* 12, no. 1/2 (1997): 289-93.

   The electronic library services available to Simon Fraser University's distance education students are described. These Web services, known as the KIOSK, provide comparable support for both on- and off-campus students. The KIOSK enables users to access subject resource pages, online library catalogues, bibliographic and full-text databases, library guides, electronic reference services, and online document delivery services. Future options being explored include increased use of library subject pages to support course and research interests; interactive reference assistance through chat facilities; interactive tutorials with self-pacing quizzes; further integration of online indexes/abstracts, library holdings, requesting, and full-text services; and increased online full text. A. Slade.

704. Seaborne, Kate. "Quality Assurance in the Provision of Library Services in British Columbia." In *Perspectives on Distance Education: Quality Assurance in Higher Education: Selected Case Studies*, edited by Alan Tait. Vancouver, BC: Commonwealth of Learning, 1997, 77-88.

   A case study is presented to apply the principles of quality assurance to the INFOLINE library service for distance education students at the University of Victoria. Even though INFOLINE does not have a formal quality assurance system in place, it demonstrates in practice many of the key elements that such a system comprises, including a service policy and plan, standards for service, procedures for service delivery, documentation of procedures, monitoring of service quality, and involvement of users. INFOLINE's strategic plan, procedures manual, use of student evaluation forms, student surveys, and dedication of its staff contribute to the provision of quality services. It is pointed out that introduction of a more formal quality assurance system would have cost implications and would require a significant reorganization of the staff's roles and responsibilities to incorporate monitoring tasks. A. Slade.

1996

705.   Appavoo, Patricia J. "Distance Education, Interlending, and Document Delivery—A Re-interpretation." In *Interlending and Document Supply: Proceedings of the Fourth International Conference: Papers from the Conference Held in Calgary, June 1995*, edited by Judy Watkins. Boston Spa, West Yorkshire: Programme for Universal Availability of Publications and Office for International Lending, International Federation of Library Associations and Institutions, 1996, 125-30.

Based on her experience as director of two Canadian academic libraries, the author discusses the provision of interlibrary loan (ILL) and document delivery services to distance students and describes arrangements in place at the University of Northern British Columbia (UNBC). Part of the planning for the new UNBC Library centered around the concept of access rather than ownership. To this end, the library established cooperative arrangements with college libraries in northern British Columbia to provide support to UNBC distance students, including ILL services. Concern about ILL turnaround time led to the introduction of an unmediated document delivery service whereby UNBC students could send on-line requests for material directly to the University of British Columbia Libraries in Vancouver. The author stresses that user-initiated ILL requests using current technologies have the potential to improve the traditional ILL system. A. Slade.

1995

706.   Wilson, Alane. "Education from a Distance." *PNLA Quarterly* 59, nos. 2/3 (Winter/Spring 1995): 22.

This short article describes a service called Library Connection at the University of Calgary. Library Connection allows students to make requests for known items using the phone, fax, e-mail, or postal services. The author points out that there is a gap between the mission statement for the University of Calgary's Distance Education Library Service and reality due to insufficient funds and staffing. Library Connection provides a framework for building the type of equivalent library services, called for in the mission statement, that the library staff would like to provide. M. Kascus.

New Zealand

1997

707. Mann, Sandra. *Undergraduate Library Use: Is it Required by the Curriculum? A Distance Education Case Study*. M.A. (Applied) thesis, Victoria University of Wellington, 1997. 149 pp.

   The general focus of the author's thesis is the low use of academic libraries by undergraduate students, with a specific emphasis on the extent of library use by students in a distance education degree program of the Open Polytechnic of New Zealand. The aim of the study was to establish a quantitative and qualitative measure of the integration of library use into course material, based on an analysis of course syllabi. The first part of the study involved the development and application of a library use scale to analyze course material and assignments in specific subject areas. The second part involved a focus group interview with librarians who provide services to distance learners at the Open Polytechnic. The purpose of the interview was to discover the librarians' experience of student behaviour in relation to library use for particular courses and to cross-check course analysis findings. Among the findings from both parts of the study were that essays were the only assignment type requiring sophisticated library use; the quantity of readings supplied with the course materials undermined the need for students to independently access other sources of information; support tools for students, such as generic information on essay and report writing, were not integrated into the courses; and students did not recognize the importance of library and information skills for fulfilment of the degree. The thesis concludes with a number of recommendations for the Open Polytechnic, including the need to clarify the role of library use in the information literacy continuum, to involve librarians in the curriculum development process, and to provide opportunities for students to develop information literacy skills. A. Slade.

South Africa

1998

708. "Advancing Distance Education: The Unisa Library and Innovation." *INN Touch* 12, no. 1 (January 1998): 4-5.

   This short article in the newsletter of Innovative Interfaces, Inc., highlights the University of South Africa's selection of the INNOPAC integrated library system to enhance library services for its 130,000+ distance education students. The University's library services are briefly described and some of the functionality of the INNOPAC system is discussed in relation to specific services. A. Slade.

709. Grobler, Lorraine and Marieta Snyman. "The 'Electronic MBL': Providing South African Business Students with Remote Access to Information." *Mousaion* 16, no. 1 (1998): 59-73.

In conjunction with Athabasca University in Canada, the Graduate School of Business Leadership at the University of South Africa (Unisa) initiated a project to deliver its Master of Business Leadership (MBL) program electronically using Lotus Notes. An electronic document delivery system was developed to provide library support to students in the program. Articles are scanned at the main library and mailed electronically to the students using Lotus Notes. Book requests are received electronically and the books are mailed to students in the conventional way. The topics discussed in this article include the background of the project, the operation of the electronic MBL program, the requirements to run Lotus Notes, the integration of the electronic delivery system into the library's information technology infrastructure, the Lotus Notes library database, a comparison of Lotus Notes and the Internet for electronic delivery, and future directions of the system. It is noted that this program provides a major opportunity for the Unisa Library to refine its role in information management and to work collaboratively with faculty in the overall learning process. A. Slade.

710. Grobler, Lorraine. "Towards the Virtual Library: Meeting Remote Business Students' Library and Information Needs." In *The Eighth Off-Campus Library Services Conference Proceedings: Providence, Rhode Island, April 22-24, 1998*, compiled by P. Steven Thomas and Maryhelen Jones. Mount Pleasant, MI: Central Michigan University, 1998, 165-73.

This paper describes a pilot project in computer-based distance education using Lotus Notes at the University of South Africa (Unisa). The pilot project resulted in the reconceptualization of existing library and information support for the virtual library. The transition from print-based services required a closer collaboration between librarians and faculty and a more focused approach to copyright issues, current awareness, value-added services, and staff and end-user training. An overview is provided of each of these issues. Value-added services of the virtual library include reducing the constraints of time and place; providing new, more dynamic integrated formats; supporting new forms of collaboration; and customization and personalization. M. Kascus.

711. Hartzer, Sandra, Brian Paterson, Dorette Snyman, Lisa Thompson, Louise van Heerden, Marza Vorster, and Ansie Watkins. "Web Information Services at the University of South Africa Library: A Work in Progress." *Library Trends* 47, no. 1 (Summer 1998): 91-116.

The process undertaken at the University of South Africa (Unisa) Library to develop online support to its remote users is described in this paper. In 1997, Unisa made two decisions that influenced this development: (1) approval of the Students on Line (SOL) experimental project and (2) a contract with Cyber Connections to provide networked computers to students free-of-charge. A Web Information Services (WIS) Team was formed. WIS had as its goals to deliver, directly to the users' desktop via the World Wide Web, training programs, current awareness services, and full-text databases to support research and learning. A Research Information Skills course was developed in response to a request from the Chemistry Department. In terms of marketing, all available channels of communication were used, including bulletins, newspapers, flyers, and brochures. The authors note that the most urgent problem to solve is the system of user authentication and authorization to be used. M. Kascus.

1996

712. Raubenheimer, J. "Ariel for Windows: Enhancing Electronic Document Delivery at Unisa." *South African Journal of Library and Information Science* 64, no. 4 (1996): 194-98.

The University of South Africa (Unisa), a distance teaching university, investigated the use of Ariel software to improve its document delivery services. The findings from a literature search and a test conducted by the Unisa Library indicated that the features of Ariel offered many advantages to improve the delivery of journal articles and copied materials. A. Slade.

1995

713. Grobler, Lorraine M. "Information Support to Distance Postgraduate Business Students at the Graduate School of Business Leadership, University of South Africa." In *The Seventh Off-Campus Library Services Conference Proceedings: San Diego, California, October 25-27, 1995*, compiled by Carol J. Jacob. Mount Pleasant, MI: Central Michigan University, 1995, 163-74.

Library and information support to distance graduate business students at the University of South Africa (Unisa) is described. The study includes background information on Unisa, a profile of its students, a description of the library infrastructure, and an assessment of student needs in a changing South African environment. The information support is affected by three trends: (1) the open-learning approach, (2) the need for locally relevant information, and (3) the enhanced information technologies available. Several factors are identified that will influence the future information support scene: the development of individual information literacy skills, the shift from print-based library services to remote delivery, and ownership versus access. Information literacy development skills are critical to the future and will be a prominent part of the re-engineering of the traditional functions of information support to South African distance graduate students in the direction of electronic libraries and remote access. M. Kascus.

714. Raubenheimer, J. "Rapid Document Delivery—the Unisa Experience." *South African Journal of Library and Information Science* 63, no. 1 (1995): 30-34.

The University of South Africa conducted two experiments to improve its document delivery services. One experiment involved using overseas databases such as CARL Uncover to establish how quickly documents could be delivered. It was found that these suppliers surpassed local services for speed of delivery. In the second experiment, a scan and fax procedure was introduced to deal with requests for journal articles from local libraries. The results indicated that this procedure had several advantages, especially with regard to cost and speed of delivery. A. Slade.

715.   Snyman, Dorette. "CDROM Networking in an Academic Library: The UNISA Library Experience." *The Electronic Library* 13, no. 4 (August 1995): 363-69.

The University of South Africa (Unisa) Library installed a CD-ROM network in 1994 to enable teaching staff and distance education students to conduct their own literature searches. Details are provided in this article on the background of the project, planning and installation of the network, marketing the network, training issues, and the operational phase. With the introduction of the network, the role of library staff shifted from that of intermediary between information and the user to one of training and advising users. It is noted that the training component of the library staff workload has increased tremendously and there is a need to develop a structured training package to reach a large number of users in the shortest possible time. One of the benefits of the network is that users now have a greater appreciation of the extent of available information and the work previously done on their behalf by Unisa subject librarians. A. Slade.

716.   Suttie, Mary-Lynn. "Designing for Democracy: Academic Librarians and Postgraduates in Distance Education in South Africa After Apartheid." In *One World, Many Voices: Quality in Open and Distance Learning: Selected Papers from the 17th World Conference of the International Council for Distance Education, Birmingham, United Kingdom, June, 1995: Volume 1*, edited by David Sewart. Milton Keynes, UK: The Open University in association with International Council for Distance Education, 1995, 170-74.

Written not long after the 1994 democratic elections in South Africa, this paper takes a critical look at post-apartheid education at the University of South Africa (Unisa). The focus of the paper is on black postgraduate students and the links between these students and the subject librarians at Unisa. Because many of the black postgraduate students entering Unisa to study by distance education are not as information literate as their counterparts at residential universities, the subject librarians need to assume more of a teaching role in research methodology and assist the students in developing analytical and writing skills. Contact seminars and a short library internship for all postgraduate students during the preparation of their research proposals are recommended as ways to make the Unisa Library more accessible to distance students. In addition, the author advocates that subject librarians be appointed to an academic advisory panel to supervise dissertations so that postgraduate students can be directed into viable fields of investigation and are able to utilize the expertise of librarians. The teaching function of subject librarians should also be made available to undergraduate students at Unisa to provide them with some information literacy skills before they reach the postgraduate level. Use of technology may help in this regard, especially if computing centers can be developed at Unisa's main and branch campuses. A. Slade.

United Kingdom

For other works that describe the services of specific institutions in the United Kingdom, see the following heading in the Geographic Index: "United Kingdom—case studies."

1998

717. Blackmore, Paul. "The Learning Web: A Learning Environment for Remote and Campus-Based Distance Learners." In *Libraries Without Walls 2: The Delivery of Library Services to Distant Users*, edited by Peter Brophy, Shelagh Fisher, and Zoë Clarke. London: Library Association Publishing, 1998, 33-46.

A vision of Wirral Metropolitan College (UK) is to provide its remote learners with "access to learning resources and support 24 hours a day, regardless of time and the individual's location." The Learning Web, a multimedia system utilizing the World Wide Web, the College's Intranet, and CD-ROM technologies, was developed as a means to actualize this vision. The user, technical, and administrative issues of the system are outlined and the benefits of the Learning Web are identified. Aspects of the Learning Web are discussed in relation to a theoretical learning framework, the economical delivery of learning materials, and the future impact of communications technologies on the learning environment. A. Slade.

718. Hall, Lorraine. "Supporting Distance Learning: Experience and Initiatives in Sunderland, UK." In *Libraries Without Walls 2: The Delivery of Library Services to Distant Users*, edited by Peter Brophy, Shelagh Fisher, and Zoë Clarke. London: Library Association Publishing, 1998, 63-71.

A number of library initiatives have been introduced at the University of Sunderland to respond to an increased emphasis on distance learning. The Library now provides access to its electronic resources via the Web, postal and fax delivery of library materials, and telephone and e-mail helplines. Future directions include a resource bank of digitized text available over the Web, a mediated inquiry service, and an information skills package using Internet conferencing technologies. Four current issues requiring attention are access to services for distance learners, improved communication with the distance learner, improved training in information skills and new technologies, and the librarian's role as mediator. Other topics discussed in this chapter include the services provided to various off-campus user groups, the relationships with other libraries, and the barriers to service development. A. Slade.

719. Hunt, Mary. "The Open University Library—Towards Electronic Delivery of Services to Students." *SCONUL Newsletter* (Standing Conference of National and University Libraries), no. 13 (Spring 1998): 13-14.

Recent developments at the Open University (OU) Library are highlighted in this short article. A new mandate for the library is to provide electronic services for OU students. OU subject specialists and library staff are researching appropriate databases and producing helpsheets to assist students in using these resources. A part-time help desk is available through the FirstClass conferencing system, e-mail, and telephone. The library is involved in two electronic projects: the ROUTES (Resources for Open University Teachers and Students) Project to identify and classify relevant information on the Internet for students and the Edbank Project to investigate the development of a full-text database of digitized teaching materials for use by remote teacher training students. Other developments and initiatives include a guide for students on accessing other academic libraries in the United Kingdom; the Interactive Open Learning Centre, containing printed and multimedia materials; a project to create an online digital video library; extended access to the OU Library for local students; a Collection Management Policy to guide development of collections over the next ten years; and plans to expand the existing library building. A. Slade.

720.   Jolly, Jean. "Library Support for Distance Learning: A Personal View of the Northern College Perspective." *Education Libraries Journal* 41, no. 1 (Spring 1998): 21-28.

The author offers her views on the success of the library services provided to distance education students of Northern College in Scotland. Key factors in the success are recognizing the problems facing distance learners and making a commitment to solving them. In the author's opinion, commitment is needed from four areas: the college, the library, the student's employer, and the student. Problems facing distance learners include isolation, time factors, lack of confidence, lack of a sense of belonging, and finance. Institutional commitment should be to empowering the student to become an independent learner, making prompt responses to student needs, using a specific member of the library staff as a central contact person, having effective mechanisms to communicate with the students, encouraging collaboration between library staff and faculty, and being responsive to change. Areas identified as requiring more attention are budget and costing of services, the reasons why some distance students do not use library services, service to off-campus students and "in-between" students who are not currently registered in distance education courses, and reciprocal arrangements with other libraries. A. Slade.

721.   Lock, Debbie. "DiLIS Shrinks the Globe." *Ariadne: The Web Version,* no. 18 (December 1998). Online. Available: http://www.ariadne.ac.uk/issue18/dilis/ (Accessed April 13, 2000).

As a result of a user study conducted in 1997–1998, the University of Surrey introduced a new library service called Distance Learners Information Service (DiLIS). Through DiLIS, distance students have access to postal loans, document delivery services, a helpline, literature search services, a Web-based information gateway, and a mediation service to facilitate use of other libraries. Distance students will also participate in a trial of a full-text electronic journal service. To improve services to non-UK-based distance learners, the library plans to develop links with other academic institutions through a system of agents. It is noted that DiLIS is the library's first step towards redressing the imbalance between services for on- and off-campus students and provides a foundation for building flexible, client-oriented services for all users. A. Slade.

1997

722.   Van der Zwan, Robert and Nicky Whitsed. "Innovation in the Open University Library: The Interactive Open Learning Centre and Media Archive." *VINE*, no. 107 (1997): 25-29.

A number of recent changes have taken place at the Open University (OU) Library. Its mandate has been extended to include development of a strategy for supporting distance students through networked access to information. At the time of writing, a student services project was underway to investigate student information and library support needs and to determine how the library can meet those needs. In addition, an Information Technology Development Group has been established to promote and support technological innovation and conduct research on all relevant aspects of an electronic library. A third recent initiative is creation of the Interactive Open Learning Centre and Media Archive (IOLCMA) to collect all OU-produced audio-visual and printed course materials as well as externally produced materials and staff training resources. This article focuses on the projects and digital archiving strategy of IOLCMA. It is noted that IOLCMA is becoming a hybrid library by providing a mixture of traditional resources in a physical location and digital resources available via online access. A. Slade.

723.   Whitsed, Nicky. "Focus Interview: A Look at the Open University Library." *The Electronic Library* 15, no. 5 (October 1997): 369-70.

An interview with the Director of Library Services at the Open University (OU) addresses the following issues: OU's electronic strategy to serve its distance students, the library's input into course planning, the current role of librarians, the impact of technology on library services, collaboration between the OU Library and other academic units, and future plans. In terms of electronic library services, a number of new librarians will have responsibilities for learner support, working with the subject librarians to provide help desk support, training materials, information management skills, and access to databases. Subject librarians at the OU participate on course development teams and assist with course planning in a variety of ways. The OU Library works closely with other areas such as academic computing, and the director sees that trend continuing. Future plans for the library include having a central role in archiving British television footage and making it available for use in contemporary materials. A. Slade.

724.   Wynne, Peter M., Geoff Butters, and Peter Brophy. "Delivering the Library to its Users: From the BIBDEL Project to the Virtual Library of the North-West." *Interlending & Document Supply* 25, no. 4 (1997): 166-74.

As a result of the demonstration experiments conducted during the BIBDEL (Libraries Without Walls: The Delivery of Library Services to Distant Users) Project, which ran in 1994–1995, operational library services were being put into place at the partner institutions. This paper describes the introduction of the Virtual Academic Library of the North-West (VALNOW) service at the University of Central Lancashire and examines a number of library management issues that arose during the BIBDEL Project. Although based on Central Lancashire's BIBDEL experiment, VALNOW is wider in scope, using an IT link to extend services to all the associate colleges. VALNOW services to remote users include catalogue access, book loan, periodical article supply, reference inquiries, and access to external information sources. The establishment of VALNOW as an ongoing service necessitated changes to some of the measures used in the BIBDEL experiment, including communications links with the colleges, patron type on the circulation system, loan period, and interlibrary loan services. For a related paper, see #236 in this volume. A. Slade.

1996

725.   Bye, Dan J. "Library Services for Distance Learners at Sheffield Hallam University." *SCONUL Newsletter* (Standing Conference of National and University Libraries), no. 8 (Summer/Autumn 1996): 3-4.

With reference to the Follett Report in the United Kingdom, the author describes the development of library services for distance learners at Sheffield Hallam University. As distance learning expanded at the university, the need for a distinct, marketable library service became apparent. The current model of service delivery came into effect in 1994 when two staff members were appointed full-time to Distance Learner Support. The main components of the service are access through post, telephone, fax, or e-mail; postal book loans; postal supply of articles; interlibrary loans; mediated database searches; and access to other libraries by payment of membership fees. Evaluations of the service have shown that students are satisfied with the support received. Among the issues facing the service are copyright concerns, loans to overseas students, and service to part-time students. Future developments include dial-in access to the library catalogue and development of two in-house databases, one containing information on student usage patterns and the other consisting of the external access policies of other academic libraries. A. Slade.

726.   Whitsed, Nicky and Philip Adams. "Focus Interview: Libraries and Learning." *The Electronic Library* 14, no. 5 (October 1996): 424-26.

In this interview, the Director of Library Services at the Open University (OU) and the Senior Assistant Librarian at De Montfort University discuss their views on distance learning, developments in learning technologies, OU library services, and staff training. The OU has undertaken a project to provide electronic library services to its distance students. The services to be offered will include access to online bibliographic databases, access to electronic texts, and electronic ordering of print materials. Support mechanisms will include training in database and Internet search skills and a help desk facility. The World Wide Web, the FirstClass conferencing system, and interactive learning packages have been proposed as means to provide training support to distance students. The interviewees note that librarians are becoming more engaged in a teaching role, and staff training at the OU is supporting this role. A. Slade.

United States

For other works that describe the services of specific institutions in the United States, see the following heading in the Geographic Index: "United States—case studies."

1999

727.   Cutler, Kay A., Beth Blanton-Kent, and Judy Jordan. "Going the Distance: Instructional and Reference Services in Distance Learning." *Virginia Libraries* 45, no. 1 (January-March 1999): 6-8.

Library staff at the University of Virginia are being proactive about participating in distance learning initiatives. Library involvement in the following teaching methods is described: one-to-many instruction, the case method of instruction, and collaborative instruction. Support is mostly in the form of instructional and reference services, but document delivery, full-text electronic resources, and a website are also offered. The authors state that the inclusion of library staff in the university's distance learning programs increases the visibility of the library and its services to the university community. A. Slade.

728.   Heller-Ross, Holly. "Library Support for Distance Learning Programs: A Distributed Model." *Journal of Library Services for Distance Education* 2, no. 1 (July 1999). Online. Available: http://www.westga.edu/~library/jlsde/vol2/1/HHeller-Ross. html (Accessed April 13, 2000).

This paper describes the distributed model used by the Feinberg Library at Plattsburgh State University of New York to deliver library services to distance learning students. The intention in designing the service was to integrate support for distance students into on-campus library activities, not to create a library unit with separate staff. This integration would ensure that emerging technologies and learning applications could be simultaneously studied and incorporated into both on- and off-campus environments. Application of the model at Plattsburgh is discussed in relation to the University's Telenursing Education Program and the role of the Outreach Librarian. Library support for the program involves three key service areas: (1) access to electronic and print resources, (2) information literacy and assistance, and (3) course curriculum enrichment through collaboration between library staff and telenursing faculty. It is noted that the distributed model of distance learning library service has several advantages for on-campus services, including solutions to remote access issues and expansion of the electronic reserves and interlibrary loan "direct from the lender" projects. A. Slade.

729.   Jones, Debbie. "Florida Christian College Conducts Study to Help Institution Plan for Needs of New Distance Education Program." *Journal of Library Services for Distance Education* 2, no. 1 (July 1999). Online. Available: http://www.westga.edu/~library/jlsde/vol2/1/reports/DJones.html   (Accessed April 13, 2000).

In this "Report from the Field," the author briefly describes a study conducted at Florida Christian College (FCC) to help the library prepare a management plan, based on ACRL Guidelines, for serving distance education students. The libraries of selected Bible colleges were contacted to determine what services were available to their off-campus students. The findings revealed that library services for distance education students seemed to be lacking at those institutions. Following the survey, a number of services were introduced at FCC, including enhanced collections at site libraries; reciprocal borrowing privileges at a local library; a library website with links to online resources; e-mail, fax, and telephone reference services; and a brochure that is distributed to all extension and correspondence students. For more information on the survey, see #591 in this volume. A. Slade.

730.   Lee, Angela. "Delivering Library Services at a Distance: A Case Study at the University of Washington." *Journal of Library Services for Distance Education* 2, no. 1 (July 1999). Online. Available: http://www.westga.edu/~library/jlsde/vol2/1/ALee.html (Accessed April 13, 2000).

In this case study, the author describes the planning and implementation of library support for a social work distance learning program at the University of Washington. Four services were identified as critical for the program: establishing an on-site collection of materials, providing document delivery services to the students, offering on-site library instruction, and answering reference and information questions. Following delivery of the pilot courses in the program, library services were evaluated by means of user surveys and focus group interviews. Among the findings was that students were pleased with access to library resources and impressed with the quick response time for document delivery but had difficulties with network connections, slow computers, and the techniques of searching online databases. The paper concludes with a summary of problems and successes and a list of lessons learned in delivering services to distance students. A. Slade.

1998

731.   Adams, Kate, Tracy Bicknell-Holmes, and Gail F. Latta. "Supporting Distance Learners and Academic Faculty Teaching at a Distance." In *Distance Learning '98: Proceedings of the 14th Annual Conference on Distance Teaching and Learning, August 5-7, 1998, Madison Wisconsin*. Madison, WI: University of Wisconsin-Madison, 1998, 3-8. Also available as ERIC ED 422 836.

In the first part of this paper, the authors discuss the need for academic institutions to provide opportunities for distance students to engage in independent learning activities using scholarly resources and the challenges that the institutions must address in this regard. Following this discussion, the authors describe the library services provided by the University of Nebraska-Lincoln to its distance learners. A coordinator facilitates three primary aspects of library operations for distance learners: remote access to electronic resources, instructional support through subject liaison librarians, and document delivery services by mail or fax. Services are publicized through class handouts and a web page. Future directions include working with publishers to resolve copyright and intellectual property issues, providing multimedia instruction via the World Wide Web, developing creative approaches to liaison services, and investigating the potential of digitizing print resources for delivery through the Internet. A. Slade.

732. Alley, Lisa. "Conrad Library Moves into Virtual Age." *Army Communicator* 23, no. 1 (Winter 1998): 32.

This article reports that the Conrad Library at U.S. Army's Signal Center is becoming a virtual library. Its objective is to support the Signal Corps's distance learning program by providing access to online sources of information. The resources available through the website are listed and future directions for the library are outlined. Future issues include password protection for the library's collection and the addition of a multimedia lab for developing Web-based distance learning materials. A. Slade.

733. Brown-Woodson, Ina A. "Online Services to AT&T Employees." *Library Trends* 47, no. 1 (Summer 1998): 172-79.

This article describes AT&T's transformation from mainframe to client-server open architecture, focusing on how end-users participated in the process. The computing change expanded the online services available to library and information service customers, especially AT&T employees. The topics covered include moving from traditional to electronic services, assessing users' needs and expectations, library staff as team participants, developing vendor partnerships for outsourced services, and evaluating service quality. While more customers did use online services, a major finding was the ongoing need to market the full range of products and services available to employees. AT&T continues to use customer satisfaction as its primary focus for measuring service quality. M. Kascus.

734. Burkhardt, Joanna M. "Distance Education at the University of Rhode Island—Providence Center: Picture-Tel, E-mail and Library Support." In *The Eighth Off-Campus Library Services Conference Proceedings: Providence, Rhode Island, April 22-24, 1998*, compiled by P. Steven Thomas and Maryhelen Jones. Mount Pleasant, MI: Central Michigan University, 1998, 111-16.

At the University of Rhode Island (URI) Providence campus, e-mail and Picture-Tel are used to provide courses for distance learners. Library support for distance learners is in the fledgling stage, but growing and improving. URI belongs to a consortium of six academic libraries that share an electronic catalogue. A reciprocal borrowing agreement exists among the members. Reserve materials are available in the library but not electronically. Access is provided to online full-text journals and electronic indexes. CARL UnCover SUMO (subsidized ordering) is available for document delivery. Other databases and reference works are available through the World Wide Web. Reference service is provided in the traditional manner, and library instruction is available to distance learners. M. Kascus.

735. Coder, Ann. "Service Challenges of a Virtual Library Clientele." In *The Eighth Off-Campus Library Services Conference Proceedings: Providence, Rhode Island, April 22-24, 1998*, compiled by P. Steven Thomas and Maryhelen Jones. Mount Pleasant, MI: Central Michigan University, 1998, 133-37.

This paper describes library services for George Washington University's graduate campus in Virginia, where students are primarily executives who commute in from around the country for weekend programs. The need for a comprehensive program of research support to match the characteristics of the students and the campus is stressed. Among the services considered essential are rapid document delivery; Web-based research technique instruction; delivery technology, including e-mail, fax, and telephone; and a highly personalized, client-centered service. The emphasis here is on convenient library services. M. Kascus.

736.   Edge, Sharon M. and Denzil Edge. "Building Library Support for Distance Learning Through Collaboration." In *Libraries Without Walls 2: The Delivery of Library Services to Distant Users*, edited by Peter Brophy, Shelagh Fisher, and Zoë Clarke. London: Library Association Publishing, 1998, 14-32.

The University of Louisville's program of library support for distance learning began as a collaborative partnership between the University Libraries and the Department of Special Education. The program has expanded in recent years as distance learning initiatives have been introduced in other disciplines. The development and collaborative aspects of the program are described with reference to university standards and the philosophy and rationale for providing library services to distance learners. The emphasis in the library support program is on access to electronic resources and "empowerment of students to access information and to perform their own research on a self-service basis." Three types of services are offered by the Libraries: information literacy, reference services, and document delivery. Each type of service is described and the resources required to provide these services are outlined. The paper concludes with a discussion of the fees charged to students and the assessment of library services. A. Slade.

737.   Hobbs, Janet L. and David P. Bunnell. "The Emergence of Distance Education and the Challenge to Academic Library Service." *Georgia Library Quarterly* 35, no. 4 (Winter 1998): 6-11.

Distance education programs generally share four challenges with regard to library services: (1) accessing sufficient books and journals to support the curricula, (2) providing student reference resources, (3) having enough skilled reference personnel available to help with student questions, and (4) providing library research instruction services. Some of the solutions to these challenges at Mercer University in Georgia are described. Library services at Mercer's extended campuses include access to GALILEO (Georgia Library Learning Online) databases and other electronic resources available from the main library, delivery of books and articles by courier, interlibrary loan services, a librarian who rotates among the four extended campus libraries, and library instruction sessions held on-site at the extended campuses. Future challenges to library services are outlined and use of information and communications technologies to address these challenges is discussed. Topics considered in this context include electronic reserves; Web-based request and inquiry forms; document delivery by Ariel; electronic journals; full-text electronic materials; course-specific websites for distance learners; on-line research guides; and Web-based instruction using compressed video, streaming audio narration, and interactive websites. A. Slade.

738.   Maze, Susan and Joni Blake. "The Academic Library's Role in Distance Learning Support Services: What Your Library Can Do for You." In *Distance Learning '98: Proceedings of the 14th Annual Conference on Distance Teaching and Learning, August 5-7, 1998, Madison Wisconsin*. Madison, WI: University of Wisconsin-Madison, 1998, 239-42.

To support its off-campus students and faculty, William Woods University Library provides access to research databases, reference assistance, interlibrary loan services, and adjunct-faculty course materials. The library has developed a web page designed specifically for cohort students and has mounted on it a variety of databases and collections of Web-based resources. One of the major obstacles to providing access to electronic resources is the legal restrictions placed on database use by the various vendors. Options to address this issue include negotiating with vendors for password access, modem dial-up via an 800 number, and use of a proxy server. Other services provided to the university's off-campus students include packets of printed bibliographic instruction materials, online assistance with databases via the web page, and a delivery service for books and articles. A. Slade.

739. Milstead, Jeri A. and Ramona Nelson. "Preparation for an Online Asynchronous University Doctoral Course: Lessons Learned." *Computers in Nursing* 16, no. 5 (September/October 1998): 247-58.

This article describes the planning, implementation, and evaluation of the first course in an online doctoral program in nursing offered by Duquesne University. In the section "University Issues in Planning," library services are discussed in relation to the traditional university library, the online and virtual library, and other library arrangements. Services to be provided from the traditional library to the distance education students include more flexible loan periods, fax delivery of journal articles, and a library orientation web page specifically for learners in the online course. The discussion of the online and virtual library is more theoretical, focusing on a comparison of full-text and bibliographic databases and licensing issues pertaining to online library services. Under "Other Library Arrangements," an example is provided of a database vendor working with distance education students to give them access to legal materials. There is also brief discussion of the students' access to unaffiliated libraries. A. Slade.

740. Pettingill, Ann. "Off Campus Library Resources: Collection Development for Distance Education and Its Impact on Overall Library Collection Goals." In *The Eighth Off-Campus Library Services Conference Proceedings: Providence, Rhode Island, April 22-24, 1998*, compiled by P. Steven Thomas and Maryhelen Jones. Mount Pleasant, MI: Central Michigan University, 1998, 221-29.

Collection development is a significant issue for distance education programs. Library collection development for the Distance Education Program at Old Dominion University provides a case study of the issues. The history of the program and the specific principles established by the Committee for Collections for distance education are listed and current changes described. Remote access to full-text journals and indexes/abstracts is a current concern. Institutional goals for digital collection building are outlined. The importance of identifying priorities is stressed. The conclusion from this study is that distance education needs will permanently alter the entire landscape of the library's collections and the use of its collections in the future. M. Kascus.

741.   Rose, Robert F. and Barbara Ripp Safford. "Iowa iIs Our Campus: Expanding Library Resources and Services to Distant Education Students in a Rural State." In *The Eighth Off-Campus Library Services Conference Proceedings: Providence, Rhode Island, April 22-24, 1998*, compiled by P. Steven Thomas and Maryhelen Jones. Mount Pleasant, MI: Central Michigan University, 1998, 231-37.

This paper reports on the process of expanding access to library resources and services to rural students of the University of Northern Iowa (UNI). This was accomplished with the aid of the fiber optic Iowa Communications Network (ICN). A needs assessment of off-campus students and faculty indicated seven services or collections necessary for successful completion of course assignments. There was a fair degree of congruence between the two groups in terms of the ranking. The seven services or collections identified were home delivery of library materials, an 800 telephone number, remote access to the CD-ROM network, guides to research in subject areas, bibliographies of source materials, remote access to the library catalogue, and library instruction. A view is presented of both the library and faculty perspectives on the evolution of library services for ICN students, including successes, problems, and future directions. M. Kascus.

742.   Stewart, Henry R. "Zip Drive into Distance Education." In *Distance Education in a Print and Electronic World: Emerging Roles for Libraries: Proceedings of the OCLC Symposium, ALA Midwinter Conference 1998, New Orleans, LA, January 9, 1998*. Dublin, OH: OCLC Online Computer Library Center, Inc., 1998, 15-18. Also online. Available: http://purl.oclc.org/oclc/distance-1998 (Accessed April 13, 2000).

A historical perspective is given on what Troy State University has done in the area of distance education and how library services have been provided. Three models of service have been used at the various sites throughout the six regions served: a centralized model, a site-specific model, and an emerging virtual model. Traditional services for all students are described because these define the types of services considered essential to distance education students. These services include online full-text periodical databases, interlibrary loan, and reference services via e-mail and telephone. Site-specific services are provided through professional, part-time staff who can be contacted by e-mail or fax. To supplement library services, the regional librarian may contract with a local library to provide services. This is accomplished via a Memorandum of Agreement (MOA). MOAs exist in Florida, with six base libraries, two community college libraries, four university libraries, and one public library. Within the developmental stage of a course, the department proposing the course has to demonstrate how students will receive access to library materials, including web pages, online or distributed reserve readings, library databases, the Internet, and online catalogues. The checklist for course development includes five items relating to libraries for course approval. M. Kascus.

1997

743. Adams, Kate and Carla Rosenquist-Buhler. *Libraries as Partners in Distance Education*. Lincoln: University of Nebraska-Lincoln, 1997. 16 pp. ERIC ED 410 975.

The University of Nebraska at Lincoln has combined administrative planning and recent technological advances to improve access to education for students at a distance. The focal point of this paper is on the role of the library in providing database access, online searching instruction, reference assistance, and document delivery to Teachers College students enrolled in distance education graduate programs. Both current and future electronic resources for remote students are discussed. M. Kascus.

744. Butler, John. "From the Margins to the Mainstream: Developing Library Support for Distance Learning." *LibraryLine* 8, no. 4 (May 1997). Online. Available: http://www.lib.umn.edu/pubs/LibLine/LLvol8no4.html (Accessed April 13, 2000).

The University of Minnesota used a three-year grant from the Bush Foundation to develop a comprehensive program of library services for distance learners. The findings of a 1995 needs assessment survey of distance learners and faculty revealed limited access affecting choices and quality, an awareness gap about available library services, weak library-faculty interaction, and access to technology strong but minimally used. The Library Plan emphasized four major areas of development: (1) faculty liaison and communications, (2) expanded access to information resources, (3) reference and consultative services, and (4) instruction in the use of information resources. To advance these efforts, the library developed a basic library and network instruction curriculum and materials and collaborated with the digital media center on its "Learn Online" initiative. The issues requiring faculty involvement were integrating library and information instruction into curricula and courses and making tough decisions about supporting both print and electronic-based systems at full levels. M. Kascus.

745. D'Andraia, Frank. "The Politics and Economics of Distance Education." In *Libraries and Other Academic Support Services for Distance Learning*, edited by Carolyn A. Snyder and James W. Fox. Foundations in Library and Information Science, vol. 39. Greenwich, CT: JAI Press, 1997, 31-39.

The University of North Dakota is the lead campus in the North Dakota Interactive Video Network (ND IVN). The primary mission of this cooperative is to use technology to expand the delivery of distance education programs. ODIN, the Online Dakota Information Network, was an early effort that resulted in library automation. The primary focus is on the politics and economics of distance education and why it is important for academic libraries to follow the lead of their academic institutions in developing new marketing strategies for their services. What is of importance to librarians in this context is how to remain relevant in a business climate that threatens to overshadow it. Cooperation is key to survival in terms of shared economies, reduced costs, and expanded services. M. Kascus.

746. Dickason, John. "Serving Remote Students: A Librarian's Response." In *Summary of Proceedings of the Fiftieth Annual Conference of the American Theological Association, Iliff School of Theology, Denver, Colorado, June 21-24, 1996*, edited by Melody S. Chartier. Evanston, IL: American Theological Association, 1997, 54-56.

Library services to off-campus students at the Fuller Theological Seminary are outlined. These services include (1) access to campus collections, (2) core collections at some remote sites, (3) contracted access to nearby collections, (4) reference and library instruction, (5) mediated CD-ROM and database searches, and (6) document delivery through interlibrary loan and direct mail. To provide the services, staffing levels were increased and schedules staggered. Future plans include a website to facilitate extended library services. M. Kascus.

747. Jones, Maryhelen and Thomas J. Moore. "Providing Library Support for Extended Learning Programs: A Partnership Model." In *Libraries and Other Academic Support Services for Distance Learning*, edited by Carolyn A. Snyder and James W. Fox. Foundations in Library and Information Science, vol. 39. Greenwich, CT: JAI Press, 1997, 1-15.

A partnership model between Central Michigan University (CMU) Libraries and the College of Extended Learning (CEL) is based on three premises: both units are linked through library services, library services are considered vital to the success of the college, and technology is enabling "virtually-based" platforms to deliver instruction and services. The administrative structure involves a significant level of integration between the two units that includes regularized budgeting and planning for library services to off-campus faculty and students within the overall college budgeting process. The model is unique to CMU, but has relevance to other institutions in terms of the importance of structured communication and cooperation between extended learning and libraries. M. Kascus.

748. Rodgers, Judith E. "Supporting Distributed Learning at the University of Alabama: A Teacher's Perspective." In *Libraries and Other Academic Support Services for Distance Learning*, edited by Carolyn A. Snyder and James W. Fox. Foundations in Library and Information Science, vol. 39. Greenwich, CT: JAI Press, 1997, 123-32.

Examples are given of various distributed learning projects at the University of Alabama, followed by a discussion of the inter-campus interactive telecommunications system and library support. Library support includes the following: 26 collection development librarians working with academic departments to build collections for the distance learning programs, electronic reserve materials, telephone information and request services, electronic journals, library instruction, improvements in technology connections and support, online catalogue access, and full Internet access. Library support is expanded through increased cooperation with other information services, allowing sharing of resources, facilities, and equipment at remote sites. Additional support comes from faculty/library and computer center/library collaboration. M. Kascus.

749. Starratt, Jay and Jerry C. Hostetler. "Distance Learning and Library Affairs: Technology Development and Management at Southern Illinois University at Carbondale." In *Libraries and Other Academic Support Services for Distance Learning*, edited by Carolyn A. Snyder and James W. Fox. Foundations in Library and Information Science, vol. 39. Greenwich, CT: JAI Press, 1997, 17-30.

An overview is provided of the Illinois Distance Learning Initiative at Southern Illinois University at Carbondale. Through membership in two of the state's telecommunications consortia, the Southwestern Illinois Higher Education Consortium (SIHEC) and the Southern Illinois Collegiate Common Market (SICCM), the library has sole responsibility for the technical, instructional development, and administrative aspects of delivering SIUC's distance learning initiative. Also discussed is the Regional Center for Distance Learning and Multimedia Development. The regional center provides training for faculty in developing multimedia-based instructional programs. The Southern Illinois Learning Resources Cooperative (SILRC) provides for staff development, resource sharing, and interlibrary loan. What is stressed is the importance of academic libraries assuming primary responsibility for technology initiatives through collaboration with teaching faculty and computing centers. M. Kascus.

750. Tuñón, Johanna and Paul R. Pival. "Library Services to Distance Students: Nova Southeastern University's Experience." *Florida Libraries* 40, no. 6 (September/October 1997): 109, 118.

The development of library services for distance learning at Nova Southeastern University (NSU) is outlined and the paradigm shift caused by the availability of online resources is discussed. Teaching research skills to field-based students was a challenge, and NSU responded by initiating a multi-faceted approach to library instruction. Initiatives included hands-on training sessions when distance students came to campus, site visits by librarians, a video and booklet about distance learning services, and slide presentations on online searching. Currently, librarians are developing Web-based library instruction materials and exploring the use of collaborative resources such as Microsoft's NetMeeting. The future direction for NSU is to devise methods for delivering library instruction that do not depend on face-to-face or synchronous interactions. For a related article, see #445 in this volume. A. Slade.

751. Wang, Jun. *Statewide Collaboration in Adult Continuing Education: A Case Study of Distance Education in Maine*. Ed.D. diss., Northern Illinois University, 1997. 212 pp. UMI Number 9807799.

This case study assesses Maine's state-wide collaboration for the provision of distance education through the Education Network of Maine. Support services are among the areas assessed and particular attention is paid to off-campus library services. Information is provided on the background to these services in Maine, the partnerships developed in the state, and the services available to off-campus students. The author used a time-series analysis of student requests for the period 1990–1996 and a survey of 248 distance education students to assess Maine's off-campus library services. Findings indicated that requests for books and articles have increased significantly over the years and the majority of the students are satisfied with the off-campus library services. Ensuing discussions focus on the value of off-campus library services, the benefit of collaborative efforts, contracts and agreements with other institutions, the use of online information technologies, and remote access to electronic resources. A. Slade.

752.   Welty, Ellen. "The Contribution of Electronic Libraries to Distance Education and the Contribution of Distance Education to Electronic Libraries." In *Competition, Connection, Collaboration: Proceedings of the 13th Annual Conference on Distance Teaching and Learning, August 6-8, 1997, Madison Wisconsin*. Madison, WI: University of Wisconsin-Madison, 1997, 355-59.

When Arizona State University established a branch campus called ASU East, library staff decided to substitute services for printed resources at the campus. Among the services provided were document delivery, interlibrary loans, a listserv for faculty and staff at ASU East, a web page, and access to a full-text database. Future services will include class aids pages, electronic reserves, computer conferencing software to enable librarians to provide synchronous assistance to distance learners, and document delivery software to enable scanned documents to be delivered to a patron's e-mail account as an image file. A. Slade.

1996

---

753.   Adams, Kate. *Library Support for UNL Distant Learners*. Lincoln: University of Nebraska-Lincoln, 1996. 19 pp. ERIC ED 399 962.

The library services available to distance learners enrolled in graduate programs at the University of Nebraska-Lincoln (UNL) are described. There are three components of the University Libraries distance education program: (1) remote access to electronic resources; (2) a liaison librarian for reference assistance and instruction; and (3) document delivery, mainly through interlibrary loan. The role of the libraries in the university's planning process for distance education is outlined. A collaborative effort with the Division of Continuing Studies is described, including joint outreach activities. The appendices include two flyers on library services to UNL distance education students and a list of handouts distributed to students for the 1996 summer session. M. Kascus.

754.   Goodson, Carol. "A Continuing Challenge for Librarians: Meeting the Needs of Distance Education Students." *MC Journal: The Journal of Academic Media Librarianship* 4, no. 1 (Summer 1996): 1-9. Also online. Available: http://wings. buffalo.edu/publications/mcjrnl/v4n1/goodson.html (Accessed April 13, 2000).

This guest editorial discusses the challenge of meeting the needs of distance education students, focusing on the full-service model in place at the State University of West Georgia. In this model, all the library needs of off-campus students are met from the home institution's resources. Instructors teaching satellite courses receive a packet of materials that includes information on services available to students, a form for reserve materials, a form for joint borrowers' cards, request forms for library services, and an e-mail account application for each student. A toll-free number is available for telephone information and request services. Survey findings indicate that the majority of West Georgia's students do not use off-campus library services or come to the library. The implication is that students are using libraries other than the home library for their information needs. M. Kascus.

755.   Heller-Ross, Holly. "Librarian and Faculty Partnerships for Distance Education." *MC Journal: The Journal of Academic Media Librarianship* 4, no. 1 (Summer 1996): 57-68. Also online. Available: http://wings.buffalo.edu/publications/ mcjrnl/v4n1/platt.html (Accessed April 13, 2000).

At the State University of New York (SUNY), Plattsburgh, a library services component was included for its Telenursing Distance Education Program in a successful five-year, million-dollar grant proposal. Funding was included in the proposal for a part-time outreach librarian to establish connections with the librarians at each distant site. Library support to distance education students is distributed throughout the library, with primary coordination and service responsibilities remaining with the outreach librarian. Strategies used at SUNY Plattsburgh for curricular enrichment are meeting with faculty to discuss their courses and library involvement, reading copies of course syllabi and offering ideas, attending classes to get a sense of the courses, and consulting with faculty for input on library acquisitions. Librarians also identify Internet resources for faculty as part of Internet teaching sessions and have created web pages with links to important websites. In this two-way partnership, librarians consult with faculty to get input on making library instruction more relevant to students. For a related paper, see #728 in this chapter. M. Kascus.

756.   Silveria, Janie Barnard and Barbara G. Leonard. "The Balancing Act: Collection Development in Support of Remote Users in an Extended Campus Setting." Co-published simultaneously in *Collection Management* 21, nos. 3/4 (1996): 139-51, and *Collection Development: Past and Future*, edited by Maureen Pastine. New York: Haworth Press, 1996, 139-51.

University library collections developed to serve off-campus users require the same level of planning as those collections developed for on-campus use. Collection development policies and procedures for remote users should parallel those on-campus. In this article, an approach to developing and maintaining collections for remote users is discussed based on the experiences of San Jose State University (SJSU). The collection development process began with a two-part needs assessment for remote users: the needs prior to the opening of the off-campus library and the needs that developed over time. After the core collection was developed, ongoing needs assessment was accomplished through faculty surveys, consultation by telephone and in person, and evaluation of course content against the core collection. A separate budget from the main campus was provided for supporting off-campus collection needs. Some of the issues and problems encountered at SJSU are discussed, including faculty-liaisons, maintaining awareness of new sources, ownership versus access, and the virtual library. What is recommended is the need for striking a balance between print and electronic resources and for remaining flexible to meet off-campus needs. M. Kascus.

1995

757.   Baird, Constance Mulligan and Sarah Connelly Vaughn. "Dialogue for Distance Learning: Ensuring Excellence in Distance Learning Library Services." In *The Seventh Off-Campus Library Services Conference Proceedings: San Diego,*

California, October 25-27, 1995, compiled by Carol J. Jacob. Mount Pleasant, MI: Central Michigan University, 1995, 1-4.

Innovative telecommunications networks and the successful programming delivered over them are the result of a team approach to distance learning at the University of Kentucky. This includes ensuring that all library and academic support services available on the main campus are replicated through distance learning. The Director of Distance Learning Library Services (DLLS) and the Director of Distance Learning Programs (DLP) work closely together and with library and administrative support personnel throughout the state to achieve that goal. Specific library services to students include individualized bibliographic searches, reference requests, provision of copies of journal articles and books, instruction and orientation in library use, local reserve material, and access to electronic information. Access methods include traditional mail requests, toll-free telephone lines, electronic mail, and telefacsimile. Ongoing evaluation and dialogue about DLLS make it possible to respond, with the appropriate resources, to changing student needs, programmatic concerns, budgeting requests, and accreditation visits. M. Kascus.

758. Colbert, Gretchen. "Interactive Access: Rocky Mountain Peak MBA." In *The Seventh Off-Campus Library Services Conference Proceedings: San Diego, California, October 25-27, 1995*, compiled by Carol J. Jacob. Mount Pleasant, MI: Central Michigan University, 1995, 57-60.

The informational needs of students in the University of Denver's remote MBA program in Vail, Colorado, are described. The decision to develop a formal program of library services for both remote MBA programs, Vail and Summit County, is discussed. This program includes an orientation for new students, handouts describing services available, and forms for requesting materials. The ongoing library services provided include access to NEXIS. Two lessons were learned during the planning and implementation of the program: first, the importance of contacting the libraries in the remote areas to explain the program, and second, the importance of informing both faculty and administrators of what services the library can provide to their students. M. Kascus.

759. Edge, Sharon M. "Library Support for Distance Learning: The University of Louisville's Experience." *Kentucky Libraries* 59, no. 4 (Autumn 1995): 8-14.

Library support for distance learners at the University of Louisville has been very positively received. Feedback from students indicates that the ease with which they can accomplish required library assignments is a significant factor contributing to the success of the courses. Four goals were developed for the library support program: (1) immediacy of access to information resources, (2) centralization of access to diverse resources, (3) empowerment of students to access information, and (4) rapid turnaround time for remote delivery. Library services include reference, document delivery, and information literacy instruction. In addition to phone, mail, and fax access, the use of electronic methods has evolved. Also included is information on technology used, staffing, and budget. M. Kascus.

760. Grudzien, Pamela and Maryhelen Jones. "Internal Partnerships for External Sourcing: Interlibrary Loan as Supplier-Provider for Off-Campus Students." In *The Seventh Off-Campus Library Services Conference Proceedings: San Diego, California, October 25-27, 1995,* compiled by Carol J. Jacob. Mount Pleasant, MI: Central Michigan University, 1995, 175-86.

This case study examines two supply/delivery projects for off-campus students. The first involved obtaining journal articles through the CARL UnCover document delivery service. The second involved borrowing books through standard interlibrary loan procedures. The study took place at Central Michigan University (CMU) and involved divisional units within the CMU organization. The areas examined include cross-unit dynamics, staff training needs, staff attitudes, and technology. These projects contributed to a stronger sense of service commonalities and capabilities in the two units, Document Access and Off-campus Library Services. Working on these projects provided staff in each unit with a common ground for understanding the other, and the service benefit to the student was clearly demonstrated. M. Kascus.

761. Holmes, Katherine E. "ERIC on CD-ROM as a Multicultural Research Tool for Off-Campus Students." In *The Seventh Off-Campus Library Services Conference Proceedings: San Diego, California, October 25-27, 1995,* compiled by Carol J. Jacob. Mount Pleasant, MI: Central Michigan University, 1995, 187-96. Also available as ERIC ED 401 164.

The ERIC database was evaluated to assess its coverage of multicultural and diversity topics, which are of concern to Lesley College graduate courses in education. The topic areas studied were African-American studies, American Indian studies, women's studies, and multicultural research. ERIC's breadth of coverage, depth of coverage, journal title list, and thesaurus were examined in the above four topic areas. The ERIC information system was found to provide a broad range of material on multicultural education and is a rich and comprehensive research tool. Multicultural issues are well covered, but more coverage will be needed to broaden and deepen access to ethnic and cultural information. M. Kascus.

762. Sagan, Edgar L., Robert W. Johnson, and Andy Spears. "Video and Computer Technologies for Extended-Campus Programming." In *Association of Small Computer Users in Education: Proceedings of the 1995 ASCUE Summer Conference: 28th Annual Conference, June 18-22, 1995, Myrtle Beach, South Carolina,* edited by Donald Armel. n.p.: Association of Small Computer Users in Education, 1995, 150-56. ERIC ED 387 107.

This paper discusses the use of interactive video and computer technologies for extended campus programs. The presentation is divided into four sections. The first section is an overview of the distance education programs at the University of Kentucky (UK), focusing on improved access to graduate programs, technology advances, funding, staff, and library assistance. The second section describes the UK's comprehensive video system and programs with the following partners to improve access to health services in rural areas: the University of Kentucky Interactive Television Network, the Kentucky TeleLinking Network (KTLN), the KTLN Star Schools project, and the Telemedicine Network. The third section focuses on distance learning initiatives by Owensboro Community

College and the Community Networking Cooperative to provide community e-mail to all citizens of Owensboro. The fourth section describes the services of the University Libraries, and the fifth section discusses the initiatives of small colleges. M. Kascus.

763.   Woods, Julia A. "The Impact of Extended Campus Programs on the Mesa State College Library." *Colorado Libraries* 21, no. 1 (Spring 1995): 18-19.

The impact of extended campus graduate programs in Colorado on Mesa State College (MSC) Library is described. The main impact is on the public service areas of the library, including library instruction. Increased workloads have been experienced by circulation, reference, and media departments. Funding for additional resources and staffing has been a basic concern, especially since the contracts developed between the MSC Continuing Education Department and the institution delivering the course have not earmarked specific funds for library support. The need to secure funding for resources that support library services and materials for students in these programs is emphasized. M. Kascus.

1994

764.   Pettingill, Ann. "Library Services for Distance Education at Old Dominion University." *Virginia Librarian* 40, no. 1 (January/February/March 1994): 10-13.

Old Dominion University is extending the university's program state-wide through Teletechnet, a technology-based program that brings faculty, students, and library together through telecommunications. The library's involvement in distance education at extended campus sites began with document delivery, interlibrary loan, and online catalogue access. Providing instruction and support services has been the challenge. The library has developed a multilevel, systematic approach to instructional support through a four-step process: (1) information gathering, including a needs assessment survey; (2) collection building involving duplicate sets of core collections at four extended campus sites; (3) instructional sessions to nursing classes that include either general orientation or subject-specific sessions; and (4) extending document delivery service to community college sites. The needs assessment survey has been redesigned for use in ongoing evaluation of services. M. Kascus.

Author Index

Geographic Index

Numbers in this index refer to entry numbers rather than pages. Entry numbers in italic and followed by (1) are located in the first bibliography: *Library Services for Off-Campus and Distance Education: An Annotated Bibliography* (Ottawa, ON: Canadian Library Association, 1991). Entry numbers in italic and followed by (2) appear in the second bibliography: *Library Services for Off-Campus and Distance Education: The Second Annotated Bibliography* (Englewood, CO: Libraries Unlimited, 1996). All other entry numbers are for items in this volume.

Each entry in this index contains some reference to the corresponding country regardless of whether the name of the country appears in the abstract for that work.

Aegean area. *See* Greece
Africa, *43(2)*, 35, 130, 159. *See also* names of countries
Alabama, *353(1), 373(1), 394(1), 403-04(1), 495(1), 217(2), 248(2), 309(2), 373(2), 505(2), 511(2)*, 163, 357, 466, 585, 742, 748
Alaska, *394(1), 403-04(1), 501(1), 514(1), 168(2), 292(2), 301(2), 317(2), 337(2), 373(2), 452(2), 504(2), 513(2)*, 82, 328, 333, 480, 506
Alberta, *5(1), 201(1), 204(1), 209(1), 219(1), 268-69(1), 282(1), 334(1), 347(1), 388-91(1), 394(1), 404(1), 425-26(1), 469(1), 142(2), 243(2), 373(2), 379(2), 414-15(2), 452-53(2)*, 97, 186, 393, 560, 585, 628, 706
Antigua, *417-18(2)*
Arizona, *394(1), 403-04(1), 196(2), 212(2), 243(2), 311(2), 373(2), 397(2), 437(2), 484(2)*, 82, 163, 275, 471, 558, 585, 752
Arkansas, *403-04(1), 397(2)*
Asia, 12, 209
Australia, *7-9(1), 14(1), 20-21(1), 39(1), 61(1), 81(1), 85(1), 88(1), 90-91(1), 167(1), 184(1), 186(1), 211(1), 216(1), 225-26(1), 228(1), 230(1), 239(1), 242(1), 250(1), 259(1), 273(1), 275-76(1), 286(1), 289(1), 294(1), 310(1), 360(1), 362(1), 364-65(1), 371(1), 13(2), 30(2), 41-42(2), 48(2), 53-54(2), 70(2), 72-75(2), 83(2), 85-86(2), 95(2), 97(2), 100(2), 105-06(2), 109-10(2), 149(2), 156-57(2), 159(2), 164(2), 202(2), 204(2), 209(2), 213(2), 225(2), 266(2), 280(2), 282(2), 290-91(2), 293(2), 298(2), 303(2), 308(2), 315(2), 323-24(2), 327-29(2), 354(2), 356(2), 367(2), 369(2)*, 4, 11, 39, 44, 54, 65, 73, 101, 105, 119-21, 127, 139, 150, 156, 161-62, 166, 174-75, 209, 215, 217-18, 220, 232, 280, 312, 332, 354, 400, 419, 439, 451, 456, 460-62, 464, 468, 470, 476-77, 490-92, 497, 499-501, 503-04, 507-08, 518, 540, 577, 584, 637

case studies, *455-67(1), 81(2), 203(2), 220(2), 224(2), 442-51(2)*, 117, 123, 261, 263, 309, 321, 345, 351, 369, 688-702
surveys of libraries, *98(1), 172(1), 215(1), 366(1), 369(1), 381-86(1), 40(2), 346-47(2), 370(2), 375-77(2), 403(2), 405(2)*, 119, 174-75, 232, 584
user studies, *247(1), 409-24(1), 40(2), 81(2), 84(2), 87(2), 186(2), 198(2), 203(2), 219(2), 242(2), 254(2), 279(2), 286(2), 288(2), 304(2), 334(2), 346-47(2), 368(2), 371(2), 398-411(2)*, 4, 39, 105, 119, 139, 156, 174-75, 186, 309, 321, 345, 501, 609-27, 695.
See also names of states
Austria, 190-91

Bangladesh, 671
Belgium, 302, 372
Botswana, 130, 159
Britain. *See* England; United Kingdom
British Columbia, *48(1), 224(1), 237(1), 262(1), 374(1), 388-91(1), 394(1), 404(1), 468(1), 19(2), 53(2), 86(2), 166(2), 255(2), 373(2), 412-13(2)*, 34, 56, 97, 572, 585, 703-05
British Virgin Islands, *417-18(2)*

California, *266(1), 270(1), 323(1), 332(1), 349(1), 394(1), 402-04(1), 450(1), 496(1), 518-19(1), 31(2), 142(2), 151(2), 168(2), 214(2), 229(2), 243(2), 245(2), 250(2), 252(2), 275(2), 297(2), 343(2), 345(2), 349(2), 362(2), 373(2)*, 163, 240, 275, 287, 322, 391, 450, 472, 475, 511-12, 526, 534, 539, 566, 585, 746, 756
Canada, *1(1), 5(1), 34(1), 48(1), 121(1), 136(1), 29(2), 35(2), 41(2), 53(2), 82(2), 86(2), 141-43(2), 145(2), 147(2), 166(2), 211(2), 255(2)*, 11, 39, 42, 55, 104, 118, 125, 161-62, 232, 300, 385, 393, 498, 534, 536, 542, 560, 567, 572, 637
case studies, *468-71(1), 19(2), 166(2), 174(2), 316(2), 319(2), 321(2), 341(2), 452-55(2)*, 56, 703-06

301

Kenya, *26(1), 45(2), 463(2)*, 608
Kerala, India, *56(2), 59(2), 132(2), 134(2)*
Korea, 675

Lagos, *432(1)*
Louisiana, *95(1), 373(1), 394(1), 403-04(1), 373(2)*, 163, 585
Luxembourg, 296

Maine, *394(1), 403-04(1), 168(2), 217(2), 318(2), 373(2), 477(2)*, 41, 91, 163, 272, 277, 505, 585, 751
Malaysia, *380(1)*, 673, 680
Manitoba, *238(1), 380(1), 388-91(1), 243(2), 295(2), 373(2), 379(2), 412-13(2)*, 585
Maryland, *113(1), 179(1), 328(1), 353(1), 355(1), 394(1), 403-04(1), 531(1), 243(2), 373(2)*, 26, 74, 163, 272, 277, 285, 347, 349, 376, 390, 394, 403, 446, 585
Massachusetts, *403-04(1), 243(2), 264-65(2), 273(2), 373(2)*, 379, 441, 520, 549-50, 585, 761
Michigan, *17(1), 19(1), 53(1), 83(1), 87(1), 165(1), 222(1), 236(1), 243(1), 257(1), 260(1), 272(1), 303(1), 327(1), 394(1), 403-05(1), 444(1), 494(1), 500(1), 502(1), 520(1), 522-26(1), 534(1), 144(2), 194(2), 210(2), 215-18(2), 275(2), 302(2), 320(2), 366(2), 373(2), 390(2), 397(2), 433(2), 439(2), 512(2), 516(2)*, 26, 79, 81, 89, 163, 378, 388, 465, 469, 483, 544, 585, 666, 747, 760
Minnesota, *355(1), 361(1), 378(1), 394(1), 403-04(1), 497(1), 44(2), 294(2), 361(2), 373(2), 397(2)*, 163, 282, 443, 585, 594, 744
Mississippi, *353(1), 373(1), 394(1), 403-04(1), 507(1), 296(2), 373(2)*, 534
Missouri, *179(1), 265(1), 394(1), 403-04(1), 510(1), 517(1), 191(2), 217(2), 373(2), 397(2)*, 71, 163, 249, 348, 585, 601, 738
Montana, *55(1), 333(1), 404(1)*, 82, 485

Nebraska, *404(1), 168(2), 173(2), 231(2), 373(2), 397(2), 510(2)*, 82, 163, 319, 514, 585, 596, 654, 659, 731, 743, 753
Netherlands, *15(1), 108(1), 110-11(1), 118(1), 129(1), 299(1), 342(1), 136(2)*, 212-13, 296, 326, 421
Nevada, *403-04(1)*, 82, 452, 519
New Brunswick, *389-91(1), 373(2), 379(2)*, 536, 567
New Hampshire, *404(1), 275(2)*, 585
New Jersey, *351(1), 359(1), 403-04(1)*, 50, 163, 293, 523, 659
New Mexico, *404(1), 243(2), 373(2), 397(2)*, 82-83, 448, 585
New South Wales, *81(1), 230(1), 242(1), 259(1), 273(1), 276(1), 365(1), 381(1), 383(1), 459-60(1), 463(1), 109-10(2), 198(2), 213(2), 220(2), 224-25(2), 242(2), 254(2), 266(2), 280(2), 282(2), 290-91(2), 323(2), 329(2), 334(2), 354(2), 356(2), 368-69(2), 398(2), 405-07(2), 411(2), 442(2), 446-47(2), 449(2)*, 312, 345, 351, 354, 369, 540, 620-21, 626, 693-94, 698

New York, *127(1), 142(1), 280(1), 311(1), 350(1), 353(1), 401(1), 403-04(1), 452(1), 454(1), 527(1), 243-44(2), 253(2), 275(2), 373(2)*, 26, 163, 231, 238, 240, 285, 299, 308, 342, 352-53, 395, 403, 458, 481, 528, 566, 585, 596, 728, 755
New Zealand, *380(1), 430-31(1), 475(1), 46(2), 158(2), 167(2), 464-66(2)*, 39, 232, 239, 246, 496, 630, 707
Newfoundland, *389-91(1), 373(2), 379(2)*, 567
Nigeria, *86(1), 214(1), 338(1), 432(1), 93(2)*, 129
North Carolina, *55(1), 353(1), 373(1), 394(1), 403-04(1), 528(1), 243(2), 275(2), 348(2), 373(2), 430(2)*, 311, 367, 392, 545, 585, 605, 664, 668
North Dakota, *403-04(1), 373(2), 397(2)*, 82, 163, 479, 585, 745
Northern Ireland, *47(1), 114(1), 251(1)*, 430, 586
Northern Territory, Australia, *259(1), 381(1), 383(1)*, 700
Norway, *66-67(1), 123(1), 128(1), 380(1)*, 135, 143, 296, 559, 580
Nova Scotia, *389-91(1), 373(2), 379(2)*, 567, 585

Ohio, *100(1), 179(1), 243(1), 248(1), 394(1), 397(1), 403-04(1), 511(1), 520(1), 243(2), 275(2), 373(2), 397(2)*, 163, 285, 342, 509, 513, 529, 596, 659
Oklahoma, *71(1), 99(1), 394(1), 403-04(1), 296(2), 310(2), 373(2), 397(2), 434(2)*, 547, 585, 659, 669
Ontario, *57-59(1), 136(1), 138(1), 160(1), 183(1), 207(1), 235(1), 267(1), 354(1), 387-91(1), 394(1), 428-29(1), 470-71(1), 142(2), 172(2), 174(2), 243(2), 275(2), 373(2), 379(2), 416(2), 455(2)*, 585, 596
Oregon, *263(1), 403-04(1), 240(2), 243(2), 287(2), 299(2), 313(2), 373(2)*, 82, 89, 145, 258, 441, 482, 546, 571, 585, 659

Pacific region. *See* South Pacific region
Pakistan, *217(1), 476(1)*
Papua New Guinea, *380(1)*
Pennsylvania, *81(1), 194(1), 329(1), 341(1), 353(1), 355(1), 380(1), 403-04(1), 532(1), 230(2), 262(2), 275-76(2)*, 72, 158, 180, 342, 404, 487, 493-94, 522, 551, 585, 659, 739
Philippines, 676
Portugal, 214, 421, 583
Prince Edward Island, *389-91(1), 379(2)*, 567
Puerto Rico, *403-04(1)*

Quebec, *126(1), 183(1), 389-91(1), 404(1), 373(2), 379(2)*, 300
Queensland, *20(1), 215(1), 226(1), 250(1), 259(1), 365(1), 381(1), 383(1), 386(1), 412(1), 416(1), 455(1), 457(1), 461(1), 466-67(1), 186(2), 279(2), 286(2), 304(2), 308(2), 324(2), 328(2), 368(2), 398(2), 405(2), 410(2), 448(2), 450-51(2)*, 217, 263, 419, 456, 460-62, 464, 468, 470, 476-77, 490-92, 497, 499-500, 518, 577, 688-90, 693, 701

Institution Index

Numbers in this index refer to entry numbers rather than pages. Entry numbers in italic and followed by (1) are located in the first bibliography: *Library Services for Off-Campus and Distance Education: An Annotated Bibliography* (Ottawa, ON: Canadian Library Association, 1991). Entry numbers in italic and followed by (2) appear in the second bibliography: *Library Services for Off-Campus and Distance Education: The Second Annotated Bibliography* (Englewood, CO: Libraries Unlimited, 1996). All other entry numbers are for items in this volume.

Each entry in this index contains some reference to the corresponding institution, regardless of whether the name of the institution appears in the abstract for that work.

307

Open University, Pakistan, *217(1)*, *476(1)*
Open University, Sri Lanka, *231(1)*
Open University, Thailand. *See* Sukhothai
    Thammathirat Open University, Thailand
Open University, United Kingdom, *3(1)*, *13(1)*,
    15-16(1), *20(1)*, *33(1)*, *40-41(1)*, *65(1)*,
    69(1), *93-94(1)*, *102(1)*, *117(1)*, *122(1)*,
    124-25(1), *129(1)*, *143(1)*, *145-50(1)*,
    152-57(1), *249(1)*, *251-52(1)*, *254(1)*,
    256(1), *307(1)*, *312(1)*, *314-17(1)*, *343(1)*,
    345(1), *355(1)*, *375-76(1)*, *380(1)*, *382(1)*,
    435-36(1), *440(1)*, *483-84(1)*, *487-88(1)*,
    490-92(1), *48(2)*, *53(2)*, *67(2)*, *86(2)*,
    95(2), *147(2)*, *339(2)*, *365(2)*, *386(2)*,
    429(2), 32, 131-32, 134, 149, 165, 169,
    186, 288, 295, 423, 426, 428, 453, 587,
    643, 719, 722-23, 726
Open University of British Columbia: *See* Open
    Learning Agency, British Columbia
Open University of Hong Kong, 682-83
Open University of Hyderabad, India, *462(2)*
Open University of Pennsylvania, *355(1)*
Open University of Sri Lanka, 684
Open University of Tanzania, *338(2)*
Orange Agricultural College, New South Wales,
    259(1)
Oregon Health Sciences University, 571
Oregon State System of Higher Education, 258
Oregon State University, *240(2)*, 89, 571, 585
Osmania University, India, *380(1)*
Owensboro Community College, Kentucky,
    358(2), 762
Oxfordshire County Libraries, England, *382(1)*

Pacific Oaks College, California, *373(2)*, 163, 585
Panjab University, India, *320(1)*, *474(1)*
Park College, Missouri, *191(2)*, *373(2)*, 601
Parkland College, Illinois, 489
Parks Junior College, Mississippi, 602
Passaic County Community College, New Jersey,
    351(1)
Peking University, China, 306
Penn State. *See* Pennsylvania State University
Penn State College, Pennsylvania, *329(1)*, *532(1)*
Pennsylvania State Library, *341(1)*
Pennsylvania State University, *194(1)*, *380(1)*,
    403(1), *230(2)*, *262(2)*, *276(2)*, 158, 180,
    342, 493, 522, 585
Pennsylvania State University, Berks, 494
Pennsylvania State University, McKeesport, 487,
    494
Pepperdine University, California, 585
Perkins Library. *See* Doane College, Nebraska
Pikes Peak Community College, Colorado, 178
Pine Technical College, Minnesota, 594
Pittsburg State University, Kansas, *373(2)*
Plattsburgh State University of New York, 585,
    728
Post College, Connecticut, *394(2)*
Prescott College, Arizona, *373(2)*, 163, 585
Public Library Commission of New Jersey, *359(1)*
Pueblo Community College, Colorado, 178

Purdue University, Indiana, *363(1)*, *403-04(1)*,
    243(2), *270(2)*, *357(2)*, 89, 163, 535

Queen's University, Ontario, *160(1)*, *390-91(1)*,
    428(1), *373(2)*, *379(2)*
Queen's University of Belfast, Northern Ireland,
    430
Queensland Distance Education College of TAFE,
    448(2)
Queensland University of Technology, *259(1)*,
    381(1), 688

Radford University, Virginia, *163(2)*, *373(2)*, 585
Rainy River Community College, Minnesota, 594
Ranger Junior College, Texas, *395(1)*
Red Deer College, Alberta, *389(1)*, *373(2)*, 585
Red River Community College, Manitoba, *389(1)*,
    373(2)
Regent University, Virginia, 163, 585
Regents College, New York, 163
Regis College, Colorado. *See* Regis University
Regis University, Colorado, *342(2)*, *351(2)*,
    373(2), *498(2)*, *502(2)*, 163, 474, 582,
    585, 597, 667
Rice University, Texas, *275(2)*
Rio Salado College, Arizona, *394(1)*, *373(2)*, 163,
    585
Riverina College of Advanced Education. *See*
    Riverina-Murray Institute of Higher
    Education
Riverina-Murray Institute of Higher Education,
    New South Wales (formerly Riverina
    College of Advanced Education), *259(1)*,
    460(1), *463(1)*, *110(2)*. *See also* Charles
    Sturt University
Riverland Technical College, Minnesota, 594
Robert Gordon University, Scotland, 131, 134,
    193-97, 633, 639-41
Rochester Community College, Minnesota, *361(2)*
Rochester Institute of Technology, New York,
    403(1), *373(2)*, 163
Roger Williams University, Rhode Island, 163
Roosevelt University, Robin Campus, Illinois,
    373(2), *431(2)*, *492(2)*
Royal Holloway College, England, *486(1)*
Royal Melbourne Institute of Technology,
    Victoria, *259(1)*, *381(1)*, *422(1)*, *462(1)*,
    280
Rutgers University, New Jersey, 523
Ryerson Polytechnical Institute, Ontario, *147(2)*,
    373(2)

Sacred Heart University, Connecticut, *165(2)*,
    373(2), 585
St. Andrew's College, Manitoba, *389(1)*
St. Andrew's College, Saskatchewan, *389(1)*
St. Cloud State University, Minnesota, 594
St. Francis Xavier University, Nova Scotia,
    389(1), 585
St. John's College, New South Wales, *259(1)*
St. John's College, New York, *350(1)*
St. John's University, Minnesota, 594
Saint Joseph's College, Maine, 163

Subject Index

Numbers in this index refer to entry numbers rather than pages. Entry numbers in italic and followed by (1) are located in the first bibliography: *Library Services for Off-Campus and Distance Education: An Annotated Bibliography* (Ottawa, ON: Canadian Library Association, 1991). Entry numbers in italic and followed by (2) appear in the second bibliography: *Library Services for Off-Campus and Distance Education: The Second Annotated Bibliography* (Englewood, CO: Libraries Unlimited, 1996). All other entry numbers are for items in this volume.

AAHE. *See* American Association for Higher Education
AARNet. *See* Australian Academic Research Network
AAULC. *See* Association of Atlantic Universities Librarians Council
Academic Institution—Building Model (AIBM), 576
academic staff. *See* faculty
Access Colorado Library and Information Network (ACLIN), *342(2), 344(2)*, 178, 329
accreditation, *12(1), 83(1), 161(1), 164(1), 169(1), 175(1), 179(1), 181(1), 443(1), 507(1), 28(2), 139(2), 142(2), 148(2), 150-52(2), 154-55(2), 163(2), 165(2), 168(2), 178(2), 350(2), 397(2), 440(2), 477(2), 484(2), 489(2)*, 32, 52, 100, 102, 172, 230, 240, 271, 292, 575, 604, 736
ACLIN. *See* Access Colorado Library and Information Network
ACLIS. *See* Australian Council of Libraries and Information Services
acquisitions
  order processes, *101(1), 234-35(1), 238(1), 246(1), 90(2), 121(2), 124(2), 163(2), 184(2), 190-91(2), 196(2), 198(2), 220(2), 223(2), 377(2), 463(2)*, 177, 686
  policy statements, *226(1), 229(1), 245(1), 63(2), 91(2), 197(2)*, 231, 238
ACRL. *See* Distance Learning Section, ACRL. *See also* Association of College and Research Libraries *in the Author Index*
ADELISE. *See* Association for the Delivery of Library Services in Europe
ADENet. *See* Australian Distance Education Network
administration, *83(1), 197(1), 214(1), 216(1), 399(1), 401-2(1), 443(1), 465(1), 475(1), 484(1), 513(1), 20-21(2), 50(2), 68(2), 92(2), 97(2), 141(2), 158(2), 162(2), 168(2), 178-79(2), 183-85(2), 188-89(2), 211(2), 216(2), 243(2), 261(2), 287(2), 302(2), 360(2), 382(2), 384(2), 388-91(2), 417(2), 440(2), 451(2), 497(2), 509(2)*, 18, 34, 40, 58, 63, 65, 87, 91, 119, 132, 140, 151, 166, 174-75, 231, 236-37, 241, 248, 254, 257, 264, 274, 289, 555, 567, 595-96, 600, 604-5, 642, 644, 649, 655, 724, 743, 751, 753

structure of, *34(1), 47(1), 202(1), 211(1), 214(1), 216(1), 227(1), 484(1), 100(2), 144(2), 161(2), 176(2), 182(2), 332(2), 388(2), 490(2), 499(2)*, 51-52, 182, 232, 234-35, 247, 255, 259-63, 365, 585, 593-94, 598, 691, 695, 747.
  See also planning of library services
Adobe Capture software, 308, 353
adult learners. *See* andragogy
adult learning styles. *See* library instruction—adult learning styles
adult learning theory. *See* andragogy
agreements (formal) between libraries, *12(1), 16(1), 23(1), 161(1), 181(1), 214(1), 330(1), 350(1), 369(1), 394(1), 495(1), 504(1), 507(1), 530(1), 69(2), 72(2), 122(2), 141-44(2), 146(2), 156(2), 162(2), 167(2), 174(2), 205(2), 226(2), 293(2), 320(2), 338(2), 341-43(2), 349-53(2), 355-58(2), 360-62(2), 364(2), 366367(2), 370(2), 372(2), 382-84(2), 390(2), 465(2), 473(2), 484(2), 497-98(2), 502(2), 505(2), 507(2), 514(2)*, 34, 41, 86, 119, 141, 157, 160, 172, 174-75, 236, 244, 258, 262, 325, 481, 555, 558, 560, 563, 565, 568, 570-71, 574-76, 582, 592, 595, 597, 602, 634-635, 638, 642, 644, 649, 673, 676-683, 697, 721, 724, 734, 742, 746, 751, 763
agricultural programs, services for, 665
AIBM. *See* Academic Institution—Building Model
aims and objectives
  college and university libraries, *71(1), 171(1), 195(1), 200(1), 215(1), 219(1), 260(1), 402(1), 500(1), 504(1), 33(2), 83(2), 141(2), 144(2), 160(2), 167(2), 188(2), 360(2), 464(2), 468(2), 477(2), 517(2)*, 240, 434, 570, 637, 718
  consortium study center libraries, *372(1)*
  extra-mural libraries, *47(1)*
  package loan libraries, *52(1)*
  public libraries, *113(1), 120(1), 122(1), 141(1), 122(2), 124-25(2), 130-38(2)*, 115, 187, 191, 193-97, 216, 218, 220, 224-26, 580, 637
ALIA. *See* Australian Library and Information Association

American Association for Higher Education
(AAHE), 91
Anbar Management Intelligence Database, 298, 326
andragogy, *6(1), 71(1), 280(1), 283(1), 287(1),*
295-96(1), 300(1), 302(1), 36(2), 39(2),
52(2), 89(2), 111-12(2), 114-16(2),
118-21(2), 126-27(2), 171(2), 177(2),
207(2), 221(2), 310(2), 325(2), 344(2),
385(2), 484(2), 510(2), 62, 70, 115, 118,
142, 152, 187, 189, 193-98, 200, 204,
207, 209, 213-16, 222-23, 225, 237, 311,
363, 475, 482, 495, 507, 559, 570, 583,
586, 588-90, 623, 625, 627, 664
ANTILOPE, Belgium, 302
apartheid (South Africa), 716
Ariel software, *341(2),* 280, 302, 351, 369, 709,
712, 736-737
ARL. *See* Association of Research Libraries
armed forces libraries, *396(1),* 732. *See also*
military centers
art programs, services for, *486(1),* 377
artificial intelligence, *281(2),* 396, 408
Asian Librarians Roundtable, 12
Association for the Delivery of Library Services in
Europe (ADELISE), 557
Association of Atlantic Universities Librarians
Council (AAULC), 567
Association of College and Research Libraries
(ACRL). *See* Distance Learning Section,
ACRL. *See also entry in the Author Index*
Association of Research Libraries (ARL), *243(2),*
275(2), 593, 596, 605
Association of Theological Schools in the United
States and Canada (ATS), *142-43(2)*
AT&T, U.S.A., 733
ATM (asynchronous transfer mode), 47, 342
ATS. *See* Association of Theological Schools in
the United States and Canada
AudioPlus books, 335
audio-visual equipment, materials, and services,
86(1), 109(1), 111(1), 123(1), 154(1),
254(1), 339(1), 351(1), 372(1), 496(1),
38(2), 55(2), 59(2), 66(2), 68(2), 78(2),
101(2), 108(2), 120(2), 122(2), 125-26(2),
128(2), 133-35(2), 138(2), 142(2),
169-70(2), 183(2), 197(2), 199(2), 213(2),
223(2), 226(2), 315(2), 329(2), 338-39(2),
381(2), 417-19(2), 456(2), 465(2), 474(2),
502(2), 110, 124, 126, 201-2, 214, 226,
241, 279, 318, 427, 458, 484, 542, 563,
671, 722. *See also* multimedia materials
Australian Academic Research Network
(AARNet), *42(2), 242(2), 254(2), 266(2),*
279(2), 286(2), 290(2), 398(2), 405(2),
442(2), 447(2), 332
Australian Council of Libraries and Information
Services (ACLIS), *149(2), 186(2)*
Australian Distance Education Network
(ADENet), *290(2),* 332
Australian Library and Information Association
(ALIA), *167(1), 172(1), 184(1), 259(1),*
13(2), 40(2), 42(2), 54(2), 75(2), 156(2),
157(2), 120-21

authentication of library users, 144, 151, 231, 254,
277, 280, 302, 337, 340, 342, 346, 352,
399, 579, 711, 732, 738. *See also* security
(computer systems)
Authorware software, 511, 539

BBC television educational programming, *109(1)*
BBS. *See* bulletin board systems
BCK2SKOL (Internet course), 429
BELTEL (South African videotex system), *477(1)*
BIBDEL Project (Europe), *283-85(2), 352(2),*
355(2), 21, 101, 236, 248, 254, 260, 262,
327, 356, 359-60, 365-66, 370-71, 373,
557, 587, 724
Bible colleges. *See* theological schools
bibliographic control, 30, 327, 338, 538
bibliographic instruction. *See* library instruction
bibliographies and literature reviews, *1-3(1),*
29(1), 64(1), 124(1), 176(1), 1-3(2),
41(2), 378(2), 1-11, 39, 59, 209, 507
biology programs, services for, 458
book banks, *69(2)*
book boxes, *10-11(1), 16(1), 29(1), 35(1), 37(1),*
42-45(1), 112(1), 172(1), 255(1), 382(1),
433(1), 480-82(1), 493(1), 177(2), 387(2),
476(2), 169
bookmobiles. *See* mobile library services
borrowing privileges. *See* agreements (formal)
between libraries; circulation procedures;
interlibrary cooperation; reciprocal
borrowing
Boyer Commission on Educating Undergraduates
in the Research University, U.S.A., 485
branch campuses. *See* extended campuses
British Association for Open Learning, *112(2), 118(2)*
British Council, 303
British Library Document Supply Centre, 78, 101,
128, 298, 303
brochures. *See* publicity
BRONCO, Belgium, 302
browsing, *35(2), 246(2),* 250, 611-613, 618-619,
631, 636-637
buddy software, 385
budget and finance, *32(1), 43(1), 89(1), 91(1),*
186(1), 215(1), 273(1), 469(1), 474(1),
487(1), 500(1), 512(1), 523-24(1),
20-21(2), 42(2), 50(2), 54(2), 85-87(2),
92(2), 97(2), 105(2), 109(2), 144(2),
158-60(2), 163(2), 166-68(2), 170(2),
172(2), 175(2), 177(2), 182-85(2),
187-88(2), 196(2), 201(2), 211(2),
224-26(2), 230(2), 274(2), 283-84(2),
336(2), 366-67(2), 369(2), 374(2), 376(2),
387(2), 393(2), 397(2), 417-18(2), 428(2),
442(2), 445(2), 454(2), 490(2), 497(2),
512(2), 34, 41, 50-52, 55, 87, 97, 102,
114, 120, 124, 134, 262, 264, 281, 303,
333, 371, 373, 396, 419, 570, 599, 661,
683, 685, 697, 706, 720, 745, 759, 763
administration, *83(1), 468(1),* 231, 238, 241,
247-48, 258, 329, 352, 356, 365,
552-54, 567, 571, 575, 585, 595-96,
655, 747, 751

faculty (*cont.*)
   collaboration with librarians, *73(1), 77(1),*
       164(1), 313(1), 479(1), 22(2), 52(2),
       77(2), 100(2), 154(2), 159(2), 161(2),
       212(2), 215(2), 221(2), 305(2),
       310(2), 322(2), 414-15(2), 421(2),
       425(2), 47(2), 20, 26-27, 37, 47,
       50-51, 57-58, 61, 65, 79, 89, 108,
       113-14, 126, 133, 136, 139-41, 146,
       156, 171, 185, 230-31, 259, 281, 285,
       292, 295, 306, 312, 314, 318, 322-23,
       328, 410, 413-14, 416-20, 422, 425,
       427, 432-33, 438, 441, 457, 474, 482,
       485, 487, 489-90, 492, 493-94, 498,
       501, 503, 505-6, 512, 514, 520,
       522-23, 525, 531, 538, 540, 543,
       548-49, 551, 568, 616, 620-21, 625,
       627, 646, 652, 655, 666, 689, 707,
       709-711, 720, 723, 727-728, 731, 736,
       744, 749, 755, 757
   communication, *37(1), 57-58(1), 189(1),*
       239(1), 445(1), 463(1), 494(1), 33(2),
       77(2), 86(2), 161(2), 171(2), 183(2),
       198(2), 209(2), 211-12(2), 220-21(2),
       311(2), 321-22(2), 402(2), 431(2),
       436-37(2), 451(2), 455(2), 504(2),
       513(2), 516(2), 18, 155, 179, 228,
       231, 474, 481, 496, 666, 744, 754,
       758
   liaison with academic librarians, *70(1), 180(1),*
       408(1), 433(1), 519(1), 534(1),
       158(2), 222(2), 402(2), 428(2),
       465(2), 666, 718, 748, 756
   liaison with public librarians, *191(1), 351(1)*
   library and information needs, *204(1), 222(1),*
       236(1), 277(1), 335-36(1), 401-2(1),
       463(1), 491(1), 494(1), 506(1),
       513(1), 525(1), 527-28(1), 93(2),
       139(2), 181(2), 183(2), 194(2),
       221(2), 402(2), 428(2), 435-36(2),
       441(2), 444(2), 446(2), 451(2),
       489(2), 496(2), 509(2), 237, 336, 446,
       448, 744
   library instruction to faculty. *See* library
       instruction—faculty
   partners with librarians. *See*
       faculty—collaboration with librarians
   perspectives on library services, *1(1), 62(1),*
       76(1), 209(1), 405(1), 422(1),
       443-45(1), 448(1), 451(1), 462(1),
       507(1), 527(1), 81(2), 98(2), 103(2),
       251(2), 361(2), 402(2), 419(2),
       421(2), 435-36(2), 438(2), 440-41(2),
       517(2), 164, 186, 469, 616, 620-21,
       623, 627, 637, 643, 663, 666, 741
   professional development, *199(1), 215(2),*
       221(2), 229(2), 509(2), 518
   surveys, *57-59(1), 76(1), 204(1), 422(1),*
       443-45(1), 448(1), 451(1), 527(1),
       98(2), 181(2), 402(2), 419(2), 421(2),
       435-36(2), 440-41(2), 426, 436,
       620-21, 654, 663, 744

Fair Use Conference Subcommittee on Distance
   Learning, 274
FAQ (frequently asked questions), 386
fax services. *See* facsimile transmission
fees for library service, *259(1), 265(1), 360(1),*
       383(1), 394(1), 20(2), 42(2), 84-85(2),
       87(2), 95(2), 158(2), 164(2), 166(2),
       199(2), 209(2), 211(2), 226(2), 239(2),
       259(2), 354(2), 365(2), 378(2), 393(2),
       397(2), 399-400(2), 418(2), 425(2),
       445(2), 449(2), 465(2), 490(2), 34, 44,
       117, 119, 134, 153, 174-75, 567, 570,
       575, 586, 589, 632, 725, 736
Fielden Report, United Kingdom, 413, 417, 433,
   438
finance. *See* budget and finance
financial compensation to supporting libraries. *See*
   compensation to supporting libraries
FirstClass conferencing system, 315, 453, 719,
   726
FirstSearch service, 82, 88-90, 92-93, 95, 277,
   444, 458, 552, 562, 653
Flashlight Project, U.S.A., 28
flexible delivery. *See* flexible learning
flexible learning, *385(2),* 44, 126, 146, 166, 171,
   185, 205-6, 216, 419, 462, 470, 503, 508,
   577, 586, 588-90, 689-90, 692
flexistudy, *62(1), 485(1)*
Florida Distance Learning Library Initiative, 74,
   88, 90, 92-93, 95-96, 99, 144, 241, 247,
   277, 552-54, 562, 655
Florida Distance Learning Network. *See entry in*
   the Institution Index
focus groups, *438(2),* 229, 238, 407, 416-18, 432,
   466, 628, 638, 642, 644, 647-49, 707, 730
Follett Report, United Kingdom, 60, 165, 183,
   407, 417, 438, 587, 636-37, 718, 725
forecasting, 17, 36-37, 39, 41-44, 46-47, 49, 51,
   54, 56-57, 63, 97, 108, 167, 180, 252-53,
   284-85, 322, 328, 388, 396, 408, 422,
   458, 607, 653
forms. *See* request forms
franchised courses (United Kingdom), *146(2),*
       162(2), 352(2), 355(2), 382-84(2), 424(2),
       128, 134, 236, 248, 568, 638, 642, 644,
       647-51, 718, 724
Fretwell-Downing Company, 171
front-ends (user-system interface), *267(2),* 275,
   278, 439, 585. *See also* computer
   interfaces
Fryer Report, United Kingdom, 131
full-text electronic resources, 72, 82-83, 128, 229,
   277, 281-82, 298, 300-1, 324, 326, 345,
   351, 357, 446, 577, 660, 682-83, 703,
   711, 719, 721, 727, 737, 739, 752
funding. *See* budget and finance
future trends. *See* forecasting

GALILEO (Georgia Library Learning Online),
   737, 754
gateways, electronic. *See* electronic gateways
gender and library use, *416(1), 444(1), 410(2),*
   610, 612-13, 618-19, 623, 627

reciprocal borrowing (*cont.*)
  44, 128, 130, 144, 172, 182, 237, 241,
  243, 249, 264, 282, 297, 309, 507,
  552-54, 560, 562-63, 565, 567, 574-75,
  596, 635, 637, 655, 691, 718, 720, 729,
  734, 749, 753-754. *See also* interlibrary
  cooperation; resource sharing
REDD (Regional Document Delivery) Project,
  Australia, 688
Reference and User Services Association.
  Machine-Assisted Reference Section.
  User Access to Services Committee. *See
  entry in the Author Index*
reference collections, *32(1), 101(1), 273(1),
  372(1), 380(1), 418(1), 452(1), 70(2),
  144(2), 170(2), 186(2), 225(2), 392(2),
  441(2), 444(2), 474(2), 479(2), 516(2),*
  629, 756
reference services, *24(1), 71(1), 198(1), 215(1),
  258(1), 263(1), 267(1), 276(1), 350(1),
  363(1), 375(1), 455(1), 478(1), 484(1),
  496(1), 500(1), 510(1), 526(1), 20(2),
  25(2), 81(2), 101(2), 131(2), 136(2),
  138(2), 141-42(2), 158-59(2), 163-64(2),
  166-67(2), 187(2), 201(2), 205(2),
  207-8(2), 210-11(2), 218(2), 224(2),
  228-29(2), 243(2), 247(2), 256(2), 263(2),
  272(2), 276(2), 287(2), 301-2(2), 305(2),
  319(2), 336(2), 343(2), 349(2), 362(2),
  378(2), 422(2), 435(2), 439(2), 442(2),
  451(2), 454-57(2), 464-65(2), 467(2),
  471(2), 480(2), 484-85(2), 489-90(2),
  498(2), 502-4(2), 507(2), 514-15(2),
  517(2),* 58, 79, 83, 131, 145, 151, 157,
  160, 169, 179, 182, 228, 231, 236-37,
  241, 244, 248-51, 258, 262, 264, 282,
  302, 318, 352-53, 365, 371, 407 459, 463,
  506, 527, 555, 560, 562-63, 569-70,
  574-75, 585, 591, 594, 596-97, 603, 655,
  685, 691-92, 696, 698, 701, 724-725, 727,
  729-730, 734, 736, 743-744, 746, 753,
  759. *See also* electronic reference
  services; telephone information and
  request services
regional centers. *See* extended campuses
rehabilitation programs, services for, 364
remote access to electronic resources
  for distance learners, *22(2), 42(2), 73-74(2),
    87(2), 151(2), 165(2), 168-69(2),
    171-72(2), 200-2(2), 209(2),
    278-304(2), 327(2), 335(2), 349(2),
    374(2), 404(2), 425(2), 430-32(2),
    447(2), 458(2), 464(2), 491(2),
    494(2), 497(2), 504-5(2), 513(2),*
    14-15, 21, 35, 38-39, 43-44, 46,
    49-50, 54, 56, 72, 77-79, 82, 97, 103,
    114, 126, 134, 143-45, 147, 152,
    160-62, 171, 176, 180, 208, 213, 220,
    228, 233, 241, 245, 248-54, 258, 260,
    281, 289, 291, 303, 308, 313, 315,
    323, 325, 327, 329-30, 333-73,
    391-92, 397, 451-52, 480, 498, 543,
    552-54, 557, 559, 577, 581, 583, 587,

  599, 611, 616-18, 634, 646, 648, 655,
  657, 661, 671, 679-83, 691-93,
  709-711, 713, 715, 717-719, 721, 728,
  730-731, 736-738, 740, 747, 753-754,
  758
general works, *111(2), 227-77(2), 346-47(2),*
  28, 142, 287, 296, 331, 377, 390, 395,
  400, 404, 422, 437, 465, 472, 494,
  539, 569, 605, 633, 639-41, 660, 662,
  688
See also online catalogues—remote access
remote communications software (RCS), *237(2),
  269(2), 284-85(2), 298(2)*
remote reference services. *See* electronic reference
  services
remote teaching centers. *See* extended campuses
request forms, *51(2), 198(2), 224(2), 256(2),
  284(2), 333(2), 465(2), 490(2), 508(2),*
  247, 309, 374, 596, 622, 699, 737, 754
request systems. *See* electronic mail; facsimile
  transmission; telephone information and
  request services
research on library services for distance learning,
  4, 11, 39-40, 59, 66-67, 180, 592, 595,
  599, 637, 665, 691
research skills. *See* information literacy
reserve collections, *169(1), 200(1), 205(1), 284(1),
  322(1), 354(1), 469(1), 527(1), 142(2),
  148(2), 207(2), 360(2), 362(2), 392(2),
  464(2), 479(2), 485(2), 487(2), 498(2),
  502-3(2), 514(2),* 151, 182, 228, 237, 241,
  243, 264, 352-53, 563, 575, 585, 593,
  630, 694, 734, 742, 748, 754. *See also*
  electronic reserve materials
resource sharing, *5(1), 208(1), 229(1), 246(1),
  253(1), 337(1), 348(1), 363(1), 365(1),
  369(1), 370(1), 373(1), 40(2), 42(2),
  44(2), 57(2), 68(2), 73-75(2), 84-85(2),
  87(2), 90-91(2), 94(2), 100(2), 105(2),
  122(2), 132(2), 134(2), 162(2), 167(2),
  172(2), 174(2), 180(2), 197(2), 202(2),
  213(2), 226(2), 229(2), 233(2), 255(2),
  257(2), 266(2), 270(2), 281(2), 293(2),
  332(2), 338-39(2), 341-44(2), 346-47(2),
  350-52(2), 355-64(2), 366(2), 368-71(2),
  382-84(2), 390(2), 417(2), 442(2), 446(2),
  478(2), 487-88(2), 497(2), 502(2), 514(2),*
  55, 114, 130, 137, 148, 159, 177, 218,
  249, 280, 291-92, 312, 327, 348, 352-53,
  552-54, 556, 558, 560, 572, 574, 638,
  642, 644, 649, 676, 748, 751. *See also*
  interlibrary cooperation; interlibrary
  loans; reciprocal borrowing
Riddle Aeronautics Collection, *196(2)*
role of the library in distance learning, *6(1), 13(1),
  21(1), 56-69(1), 11(2), 13(2), 18(2),
  22(2), 41(2), 43-76(2), 231(2), 278(2),
  296(2), 425(2), 442(2), 470(2),* 11, 23-25,
  31, 40, 53, 104, 106-28, 298, 326, 459
  college and university libraries, *70-97(1), 9(2),
    25-26(2), 42(2), 45(2), 66(2),
    77-110(2), 155-57(2), 161(2), 168(2),
    172(2), 419(2), 446(2), 451(2),*

525-26(1), 70(2), 81(2), 103(2), 109(2),
141(2), 158(2), 166-67(2), 177(2), 201(2),
208(2), 211-12(2), 222(2), 224-25(2),
288-89(2), 303(2), 333(2), 368(2),
378-79(2), 392(2), 398(2), 405(2), 412(2),
442(2), 447(2), 449-50(2), 452-53(2),
457(2), 464-65(2), 478(2), 484(2), 489(2),
493(2), 498(2), 503-4(2), 513-14(2),
516(2), 34, 82, 99, 144, 160, 172, 218,
236, 244, 247-48, 250, 275, 328, 339,
350, 375, 392-93, 452, 458, 593, 604,
631, 634-37, 696, 700-701, 706, 719, 721,
724-725, 729, 742, 746, 748, 754
teletext, 337(2)
television. See educational television
Television Open Learning, Australia, 86-87(2),
95(2)
television universities, China. See TV Universities,
China
term paper consultation, 463, 475
terminology. See definitions
TESOL (Teaching English to Speakers of Other
Languages) programs, 609, 646
theological schools, 142-43(2), 311, 591, 729, 746
Third World. See developing countries,
Timbuktu Pro software, 456, 458, 461-62, 468,
497, 500
time and cost studies, 33(1), 275(1), 288(1),
487(1), 164(2), 203(2), 244(2), 449(2),
476(2), 65, 147, 231, 237, 297, 391, 714
TOPNZ. See Open Polytechnic of New Zealand in
the Institution Index
Total Quality Management (TQM), 239(2), 270,
670
TQM. See Total Quality Management
Training Agency, United Kingdom, 114-15(2),
118-21(2), 126-27(2)
training of library staff, 5(1), 19(1), 99(1),
101-3(1), 112-13(1), 116(1), 132(1),
134(1), 263(1), 304(1), 307(1), 310(1),
396(1), 59(2), 61(2), 66(2), 70(2), 73(2),
78(2), 94(2), 100(2), 111-13(2), 117(2),
120-21(2), 126-27(2), 130-31(2), 137(2),
160(2), 170(2), 186(2), 222(2), 231(2),
258(2), 263(2), 276(2), 283(2), 285(2),
341(2), 385(2), 389(2), 504(2), 513(2),
515(2), 47, 155, 187, 193-97, 201, 204-6,
214-16, 218, 221-22, 226, 229, 238,
242-43, 254, 262, 281, 302, 307, 311-12,
334, 342, 360, 362, 365, 371-72, 378,
397, 411, 416, 418-22, 428-30, 432, 434,
436, 457, 505, 524, 552, 568, 572, 581,
583, 586, 588-89, 595, 600, 605, 661-62,
670, 685, 697, 709-710, 726, 749, 760
transaction log analysis, 338, 341, 390
tutored videotape instruction, 288(1)
tutorials, web. See evaluation of library programs
and services—websites, web pages, and
Web tutorials; Web-based instruction
tutors. See faculty
TV Universities, China, 148, 672

UALC. See Utah Academic Library Consortium
unaffiliated libraries, 26, 39, 72, 555, 739. See also
agreements (formal) between libraries;
interlibrary cooperation
UnCover, 479(2), 481(2), 277, 714, 731, 734, 760
undergraduate students, library and information
needs, 7(1), 16(1), 32(1), 41(1), 97(1),
114(1), 189(1), 198(1), 203-4(1), 209(1),
287(1), 365(1), 400(1), 418(1), 421(1),
425(1), 438(1), 440(1), 444(1), 447(1),
506(1), 35(2), 50(2), 52(2), 74(2),
81-82(2), 84(2), 89-90(2), 93(2), 97(2),
139(2), 164(2), 177(2), 181(2), 183(2),
189(2), 210(2), 222(2), 310(2), 369(2),
401(2), 403(2), 406(2), 409(2), 412-13(2),
417-18(2), 420-21(2), 424(2), 426-28(2),
432(2), 436(2), 438(2), 441(2), 451(2),
467(2), 476-77(2), 489(2), 496(2), 53, 58,
61, 137, 142, 145, 153, 158, 170, 172,
186, 233, 336, 443, 467, 485, 492-93,
502, 535, 556, 609, 620-21, 624, 626,
634, 638, 642, 644, 647-49, 665, 668,
707, 721, 741, 744, 764
Uniform Resource Locator (URL), 338
Unisa. See University of South Africa in the
Institution Index
UNIverse Project, Europe, 296
University of Kentucky Interactive Television
Network, 762
University of the Highlands and Islands Project,
Scotland, 107, 131, 149
University of the West Indies Distance Teaching
Enterprise (UWIDITE), 17-18(2), 160(2),
199(2), 417-18(2), 458(2)
urban areas, 81(2), 92(2), 174(2), 363(2), 611-13,
618-19
URL. See Uniform Resource Locator
user authentication. See authentication of library
users
user education. See library instruction
user studies
Australia, 247(1), 409-24(1), 40(2), 81(2),
84(2), 87(2), 186(2), 198(2), 203(2),
219(2), 242(2), 254(2), 279(2),
286(2), 288(2), 304(2), 334(2),
346-47(2), 368(2), 371(2), 398-11(2),
4, 39, 105, 119, 139, 156, 174-75,
186, 309, 321, 345, 501, 609-27, 695
Canada, 57-59(1), 204(1), 209(1), 425-29(1),
412-16(2), 455(2), 39, 186, 628
Caribbean, 417-18(2), 39
Europe, 191
Greece, 285(2), 213, 360
Iceland, 116
India, 71(2), 380-81(2), 419(2), 39, 629
Ireland, 360
Kenya, 608
New Zealand, 430-31(1), 464-65(2), 630
Nigeria, 432(1)
Norway, 580
South Africa, 420-22(2), 468(2), 39, 713
Taiwan, R.O.C., 89(2), 423(2)